WOODWORKING

The Complete Step-by-Step Guide to
Skills • Techniques • Projects

Landauer Books

Woodworking
The Complete Step-by-Step Guide to Skills, Techniques and Projects

Published by: Landauer Corporation
3100 NW 101st Street, Suite A
Urbandale, Iowa 50322
800-557-2144
www.landauercorp.com

Tom Carpenter
Creative Director

Heather Koshiol
Managing Editor

Jennifer Weaverling
Senior Book Development Coordinator

Teresa Marrone
Book Design and Production

Mark Johanson
Editor

Dan Cary
Photo Production Coordinator

Chris Marshall
Editorial Coordinator

Steve Anderson, John English, Kam Ghaffari, Bill Hylton, Jeff Jewitt, Mark Johanson, Bruce Keiffer, Chris Marshall, Richard Steven
Writers

John Drigot, Marti Naughton, Bill Nelson
Design, Art Direction and Production

Kim Bailey, Ralph Karlen, Mark Macemon, Tad Saddoris
Photography

Tom Deveney, Robert Ginn, John Nadeau
Technical Advisors

Craig Claeys, John Drigot, Bruce Keifer, Bill Nelson
Contributing Illustrators

Tom Deveny, Bob Ginn, Jon Hegge, Rod Mechem, John Nadeau, Eric Sorensen
Project Builders

Dan Cary , Tom Deveny, John Drigot, Mark Johanson, Bruce Kieffer, Chris Marshall, Rod Mechem
Project Designers

Brad Classon, Rod Mechem, John Nadeau
Production Assistance

Special thanks to: *Terry Casey and Janice Cauley*

Library of Congress Cataloging-in-Publication Data
Woodworking : the complete step-by-step guide to skills, techniques, 41 projects.
  p. cm.
  ISBN: 1-890621-79-x
1. Woodwork.
TT185.W6575 2004
684'.08--dc22
          2004048992

ISBN 13: 978-1-890621-79-7
ISBN 10:   1-890621-79-X

PRINTED IN CHINA
10 9 8 7 6 5 4 3 2 1

Table of Contents

Chapter 1: Workshop Essentials

Chapter 2: Woodworking Tools & Skills

Chapter 3: Home Furnishings & Accessories

WELCOME TO WOODWORKING

The Complete Step-by-Step Guide to Skills, Techniques and Projects

My Uncle Darrel has been an avid wood-worker since I've known him. Whenever my family would drive down for a visit while I was growing up, the first place I wanted to go was always Darrel's workshop. In preparation for my visit, he'd set aside a few scraps and cutoff pieces for me to experiment with. At first I was only allowed to use a coping saw, a tack hammer and a few other hand tools that weren't particularly dangerous. But as I grew older and more experienced, he let me use more powerful tools and build more complex projects.

During my sophomore year of high school, I spent a weekend with Uncle Darrel helping him build a futon frame from a birch tree he'd felled on his land, then rough-cut and air-dried in his garage. I almost cried when, at the end of the weekend, he gave it to me. I slept on that futon all throughout college and I thought of it often as I developed my own woodworking skills and finally set up a shop of my own. He's not too interested in woodworking himself, but when my step-son leaves for college in a couple of years, he's looking forward to taking the futon frame with him.

Woodworking is like that. In fact, just about anyone who has taken the hobby beyond the obligatory birdhouse in junior high industrial arts class has a story like the one I always tell about the birch futon. When you craft something from wood, the process not only teaches you new skills and provides a creative outlet, it can generate an heirloom. Or at least an object that's rich with sentimental value.

Woodworking: The Complete Step-by-Step Guide to Skills, Techniques and Projects is both a teacher of skills and a source of ideas: It's about the process and the project.

In this book, you will find all of the information and project plans you need to develop a hobby that will last a lifetime. It contains great advice on setting up your own workshop and some essential background information you'll need to know about wood. It takes you through all the basic skills in the order you'll need them, including measuring, marking and layout, then using cutting and shaping tools to create solid wood joints. With clear color photos it shows you exactly how to clamp and glue your joints, then offers a complete section on sanding and finishing for professional results.

But where a lot of woodworking books only show you some skills, this new woodworking compendium gives you over 300 pages of complete project plans so you can put your skills to use. Indoor or outdoor, easy or more involved, you're sure to find projects to match your skills and needs right here. There are even a couple projects for your shop itself.

Woodworking is a never-ending journey. Whether you've been doing it for one year or fifty, there are always new skills to master and exciting projects to tackle. Let *Woodworking: The Complete Step-by-Step Guide to Skills, Techniques and Projects* be your companion every step of the way.

And while you're at it, be sure to pass the passion on to a young person who means something to you. You'll create memories—and projects—that will last a lifetime.

—Mark Johanson, Editor

WORKSHOP ESSENTIALS

The best woodworking takes place in a well-organized, safe and efficient space that is devoted to (or at least designed for) the task. Couple those factors with a detailed knowledge of the wood you'll be working with, and you're well on your way to some very rewarding times—and memorable projects—in your workshop.

That's what this *Workshop Essentials* chapter is all about. See how to set up your workshop for maximum efficiency. Make sure your layout, equipment and techniques are safe. Maintain everything in good working order. And understand the in's, out's and intricacies of all the various kinds of lumber you'll de dealing with.

Woodworking offers two rewards—the process itself, and the projects you create. These pages get you ready for the process itself.

Setting Up Shop

There's no single best way to set up your workshop. Since every handyman has unique interests, needs and resources, the trick to constructing a workshop that works for you is to learn to understand your needs and to maximize your resources. Start with your shop space—for most of us, a room in the basement or part of a garage. Draw a sketch of your shop area as it exists. Take measurements and include your main shop tools and work or storage areas. Often, just the simple exercise of sketching will reveal inefficiencies in the layout or suggest better arrangements. Be sure to include power sources, windows and doors in the drawing, as well as lights and any built-in fixtures, like shelving and wall cabinets.

Once you've drawn your existing shop, make a wish list of tools, accessories and systems you'd like to add over the next few years, including finishing booths, dust collection systems and lumber storage or drying areas. Compare that list to your current shop space. Can everything possibly fit? If not, you may want to amend your wish list, or look for ways to replace single-purpose tools with multi-purpose work areas that conserve space. For example, consider replacing your old radial-arm saw with a sliding compound miter saw, or perhaps you might replace one or two of your larger stationary tools with smaller benchtop versions. Pay attention to the space around tools as you plan, making sure to allow enough room to use each tool effectively and safely. Refer to your plan on a regular basis, and update it as your needs and circumstances change.

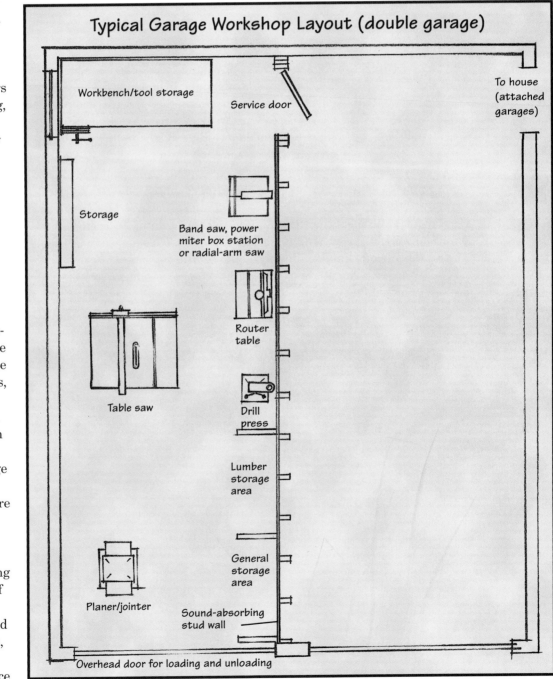

Typical Garage Workshop Layout (double garage)

Workbench/tool storage

Service door

To house (attached garages)

Storage

Band saw, power miter box station or radial-arm saw

Router table

Table saw

Drill press

Lumber storage area

General storage area

Planer/jointer

Sound-absorbing stud wall

Overhead door for loading and unloading

Choosing Your Space

Without a doubt, the best shop is a large, separate building, with plumbing and heat. It is divided up to include a storage area adjoining a large door to the outside, a central workspace, and a finishing room that's walled off from the rest of the shop and ventilated to the outdoors. Obviously, establishing and maintaining such a shop requires money and space that most of us don't have available. So look for realistic alternatives.

The two most common shop locations are the basement and the garage. Shops have been set up in spare rooms, attics, even in closed-in porches. When assessing potential shop areas, or considering upgrading or remodeling your current shop, keep the following factors in mind:

Space needs. You'll want to have enough space to maneuver full-size sheet goods and boards that are eight feet or longer. Ideally, this means a large enough area that you can feed large stock into a stationary tool with enough clearance on the infeed and the outfeed side.

Access. You'll need a convenient entry/exit point so you can carry materials into the shop and completed projects out of the shop.

Power. You should never run more than one tool at a time (except a tool and a shop vac or dust collector). Nevertheless, you'll need several accessible outlets.

Light. Adequate light is essential for doing careful, comfortable, accurate and safe work. You'll need good overall light (a combination of natural and artificial light sources is best) as well some movable task lighting.

Ventilation/climate control. To help exhaust dust and fumes,

THE BASEMENT SHOP: The basement offers many advantages as a shop location. It's accessible yet set off from the rest of the house, and the essential house systems are right there. Drawbacks tend to be limited headroom, negligible natural light, concrete floors and overall dampness/poor ventilation.

THE GARAGE SHOP: The garage, especially one attached to the house, offers the convenience of a basement shop with fewer drawbacks. Overhead doors provide excellent access, greater headroom, lower humidity and better ventilation. The main general drawback is that garages are usually home to one or more vehicles and a host of other outdoor items. A good solution is to mount your stationary tools on casters so they can be wheeled out of the way to make room for other things.

you need a source of fresh air and dust collection. Depending on where you live, year-round shop use likely will require a means of heating and/or cooling the shop as well as controlling humidity.

Isolation. Keep the inevitable intrusions of noise and dirt into the rest of the home to a minimum.

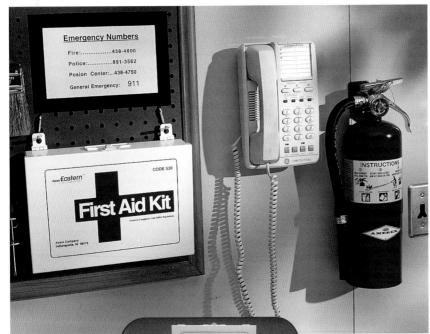

Create an emergency area

The workshop is perhaps the most accident-prone area of your home. Sharp blades, heavy objects, dangerous chemicals and flammable materials are just a few of the factors that increase the risk of accidents in the shop. While good housekeeping, respect for your tools and common sense will go a long way toward reducing the risk of accidents, you should still be prepared in the event an accident occurs. Designate part of your shop as an emergency center. Equip it with a fully stocked first aid kit, fire extinguisher and telephone with emergency numbers clearly posted.

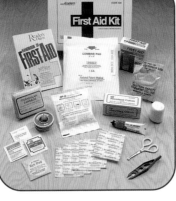

A WELL-EQUIPPED FIRST AID KIT should contain (as a minimum) plenty of gauze and bandages, antiseptic first aid ointment, latex gloves, a cold compress, rubbing alcohol swabs, a disinfectant such as iodine, and a first aid guidebook.

The ABC's of fire extinguishers

Fire extinguishers are rated by their ability to combat fires of varying causes. An extinguisher rated "A" is effective against trash, wood and paper fires. "B" will extinguish flammable liquid and grease fires. "C" can be used on electrical fires. For the workshop, choose a dry chemical extinguisher with an "ABC" rating.

PROTECT against dust and fumes. A particle mask (A) is a disposable item to be worn when doing general shop work. A dust mask (B) has replaceable filters and flexible facepiece to keep out finer particles, like sawdust and insulation fibers. A respirator (C) can be fitted with filters and cartridges to protect against fumes and very fine particles, especially when working with chemicals.

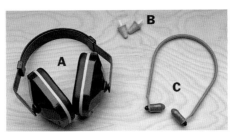

PROTECT your hearing when operating power tools or performing other loud activities. Ear muffs (A) offer the best protection, followed by expandable foam earplugs (B) and corded ear inserts (C).

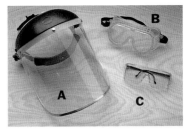

EYE PROTECTION should be worn at all times in the workshop. A face shield (A) is worn when doing very hazardous work, such as operating a lathe. Safety goggles (B) and glasses (C) should have shatterproof polycarbonate lenses.

Workshop First Aid Tips

Note: None of these treatments should be considered a substitute for medical attention. They are intended as guidelines on how to react to workshop mishaps. Whenever anyone is injured, contact a doctor as soon as possible.

Situation	Treatment
Deep gash/excessive bleeding	1) Maintain firm pressure on the wound with a clean cloth. 2) Dress with a gauze bandage. 3) If bleeding persists, and wound is a non-fracture, elevate the affected area so it is above the heart.
Deep puncture wound	1) Clean wound with soap and water. 2) Loosely cover wound with gauze bandage. 3) Apply insulated ice bag or cold compress to reduce swelling, relieve pain and impair absorption of toxins. 4) Be aware that internal bleeding may occur.
Stab wound/embedded object	1) Leave the embedded object in place. Do NOT remove it. 2) Apply a clean cloth or gauze pad to the area around the wound. 3) Prevent movement of the object by wrapping it with gauze.
Amputation	1) Maintain constant pressure with a clean cloth. 2) Carefully wrap severed item in gauze that has been moistened with either water or saline solution. 3) Place severed item in a sealed plastic bag. 4) Place this bag into a larger bag containing water and ice (never let severed part come in direct contact with ice).
Burn	1) If the burn is more severe than first-degree (skin that is red or slightly swollen) it should not be treated at home. See a doctor immediately. 2) For minor burns, immerse the affected area in cold water for five minutes. Gently apply a cold, wet cloth to areas that are unable to be immersed. Change the cloth frequently.
Electric shock	1) Quickly and safely break victim's contact with affecting current (disconnect plug or shut off breaker). 2) ALL electrical burns should be considered severe. Internal tissue may be affected more severely than the minor damage appearing on the skin. 911 should be called immediately if the electrical shock has caused any of the following: erratic heartbeat, severe jolt, abnormal tingling, unconsciousness (momentary or prolonged), muscle spasms or aches, fatigue, headaches or a visible burn.
Chemicals in eyes	1) Do not rub or irritate the affected eye. 2) Flush with warm water.

Get a grip on glove selection

Always wear the proper glove for the task at hand. Maintain a supply of good-condition gloves of the following types, and add special purpose gloves as needed.

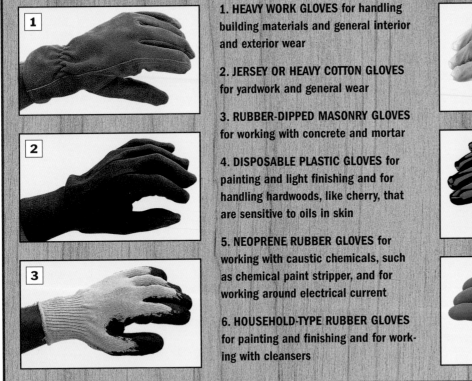

1. HEAVY WORK GLOVES for handling building materials and general interior and exterior wear

2. JERSEY OR HEAVY COTTON GLOVES for yardwork and general wear

3. RUBBER-DIPPED MASONRY GLOVES for working with concrete and mortar

4. DISPOSABLE PLASTIC GLOVES for painting and light finishing and for handling hardwoods, like cherry, that are sensitive to oils in skin

5. NEOPRENE RUBBER GLOVES for working with caustic chemicals, such as chemical paint stripper, and for working around electrical current

6. HOUSEHOLD-TYPE RUBBER GLOVES for painting and finishing and for working with cleansers

Remove-to-lock keys protect against unauthorized or unsupervised tool use

Many power tools, particularly stationary tools, come equipped with a removable lock key that is inserted into the ON/OFF switch of the tool. The tool cannot be turned on if the key is not in place. Store the lock keys in a convenient place that's out of sight from the tool.

Extension Cord Ratings

To make certain that your power tools run safely and at peak performance, use only extension cords that are rated to handle the amperage of the tool.

Cord Length	Gauge	Maximum Amps
25 ft.	18	10
25 ft.	16	13
25 ft.	14	15
50 ft.	18	5
50 ft.	16	10
50 ft.	14	15
75 ft.	18	5
75 ft.	16	10
75 ft.	14	15
100 ft.	16	5
100 ft.	12	15
125 ft.	16	5
125 ft.	12	15
150 ft.	16	5
150 ft.	12	13

Tips for dust collection & dust collection systems

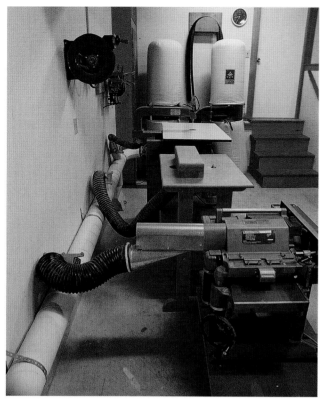

Dust from workshop activities poses many threats to safety and to producing good results. It is a fire hazard, a health hazard when breathed in, and a general irritant. It is responsible for ruining countless carefully applied finishes, and if uncontrolled it will shorten the life span of your power tools. A good dust collection system is a must in any workshop. It can be as simple as a shop vac with a dust filter used locally, but the best solution is to construct a network of hoses connected permanently to your stationary shop tools and powered by a quality dust collector.

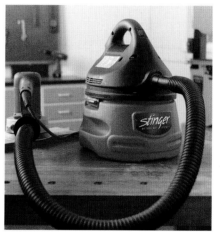

A TOOL VAC is a relatively new entry in the dust collection field. It's similar to a shop vac in size and power. Tools are connected to the power source through a receptacle mounted on the tool vac. This allows the vac to shut on and off automatically as the tool is used.

THE TWO-STAGE DUST COLLECTOR in the background of this workshop photo is connected to all of the stationary power tools in the shop with dedicated 4-in. or larger hoses mounted to the walls and positioned to be out of the way when work is taking place.

How to ground a dust collection system

Feed bare copper ground wire through hose

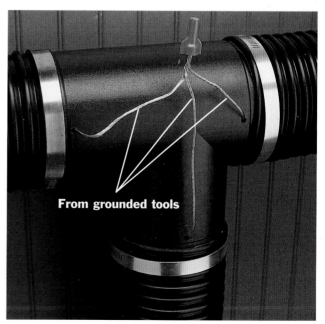

From grounded tools

1 Due to the dangers of sparking caused by static electricity, a dust collection system should be electrically grounded so the built-up electricity can escape. Attach a strand of bare copper wire to the metal cabinet of each stationary tool in the dust collection system (assumes that tools are grounded through the power supply system). Drill a small guide hole into the hose port near the tool and feed the wire into the hole.

2 Drill exit holes at hole connectors and pigtail ground wires together with a wire nut. You may need to caulk around the wire openings to maintain the vacuum seal.

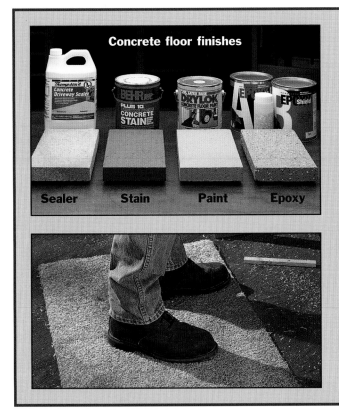

Concrete floor finishes

Sealer   Stain   Paint   Epoxy

Don't ignore the floor

If you stop and think about it, you have more direct contact with the floor of your shop than any other part. So it only makes sense to make sure your shop floor is safe, clean and comfortable. Start with the floor finish. If your shop has an unfinished concrete floor, there are several finishes you can apply to make it more attractive and easier to clean (photo, above left). *Concrete sealer* is a clear product that helps the concrete resist staining and creates a "slick" surface that's easier to sweep but isn't slippery; *concrete stain* is essentially sealer with a coloring agent for visual appeal; *concrete paint* seals and beautifies the floor, but because the product has more body it will fill small voids and cracks, eliminating areas where dirt, mildew and even insects can collect; *epoxy paint* is a two-part finish that prevents moisture seepage up through the floor, resists stains and spills, and has a very attractive appearance. Regardless of the floor type or surface treatment, sweep and clean it regularly, and provide a cushion for your feet at work areas in the form of a rubber floor mat or even old carpet scraps (photo, lower left).

Tips for keeping a tidy workshop

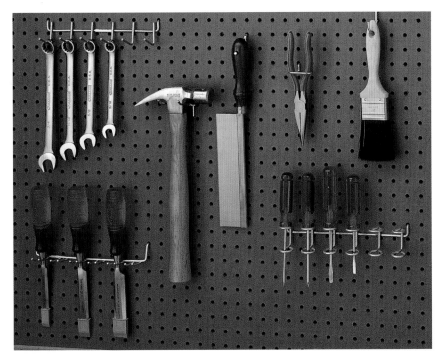

Pegboard tool hangers: A workshop standard

Perforated hardboard (pegboard) is the wallpaper of the workshop. In addition to general pegboard hooks, you can purchase whole systems of hanging devices in many sizes and configurations to effectively support and organize specific tools. Use tempered hardboard if available.

An attractive cleanup tool

Screws, washers, drill bits and other small metal parts have a way of disappearing into the nearest heap of sawdust or shavings as soon as you turn your back. Find and rescue them easily and safely with a shop magnet.

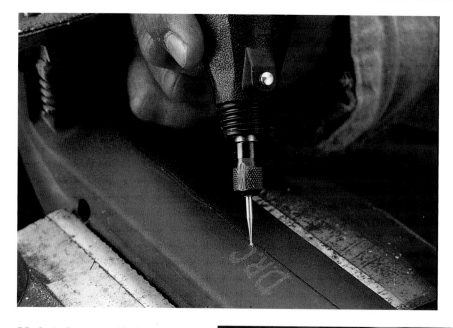

Engrave identification marks onto shop tools

Every handyman knows that borrowed tools often end up on permanent loan. Keep tabs on your shop tools by engraving your name or initials into the tool casing with a rotary tool or carving tool. In addition to reminding your friends and family members where the tool came from, identification marks may help you recover your tools in the event of a robbery.

Maintain a well-dressed grinding wheel

The bench grinder is one of the most important tools in any shop for keeping other tools up and running at peak performance levels. But it too requires occasional maintenance. Over time, the grinding wheel or wheels build up resins and other gunk that settle into the grit of the wheel, where they harden each time you use the grinder. If you notice that your wheel has a brown, burnished appearance, it's time to *dress the wheel*. This procedure can be accomplished with a dressing tool, like the one shown at right, or simply with a stick made of silicone carbide. Simply apply the dressing tool or carbide stick to the spinning grinding wheel and inspect the wheel visually until the surface is clean and fully restored.

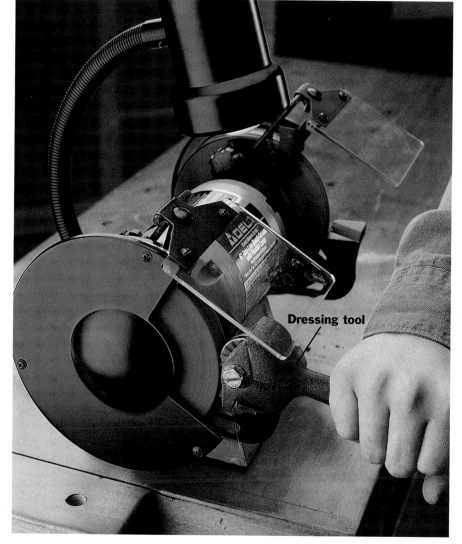

Dressing tool

Hardwoods & Softwoods: What's the Difference for Woodworking?

You've probably heard the terms "hardwood" and "softwood" when referring to the two primary categories of lumber, but what do these labels mean? From a botanist's standpoint, hardwoods come from deciduous trees — those trees like maple, cherry, oak, ash and walnut that have broad leaf shapes and reproduce with nuts, fruits or flowers. Deciduous trees have outstretched canopies of leaves. Most species shed leaves in the fall and set buds for the next spring.

Coniferous trees, or conifers, make up the softwoods. They have needle-shaped leaves and reproduce by spreading their seeds through cones instead of nuts, fruits or flowers. Pines, firs and spruces as well as redwood, cedar and cypress are all conifers. These trees keep their needles through the winter. The branch structure is generally compact, and most grow rapidly. Hardwoods, on the other hand, grow slowly. That's why softwoods are more economically viable for construction lumber and plywood than hardwood lumber.

The usual misnomer about hardwoods and softwoods is that the former is hard and the latter

Hardwood vs. softwood

HARDWOODS have broad-shaped leaves that the tree loses in the fall. Pine, a softwood, has needle-shaped leaves that it keeps through the winter. These differences in leaf types are a more accurate way to distinguish hardwoods and softwoods than differences in wood hardness.

is soft. While there's some truth here, it isn't always accurate. For instance, mahogany and walnut are hardwoods, but both are easier to cut, saw and drive fasteners into than Southern yellow pine, a dense, heavy softwood. So, it's better to think like a botanist when using "hardwood" and "softwood" terminology as a woodworker.

Choosing between hardwoods and softwoods

Hardwoods are generally preferred over softwoods for building furniture, because they often exhibit more desirable grain patterns and figure as well as color. Hardwoods with particularly tough structure, like ash or oak, also hold up better to the abrasions and abuses of life. But there's no hard-and-fast rule about hardwoods for furniture. Our forebears used whatever lumber was plentiful to them, including all types of conifers. Much of that antique softwood furniture is still in use today.

If you are planning to build outdoor projects, be sure to select lumber with natural decay resistance. Good options include white oak, mahogany, teak, cedar, redwood and cypress. Other options will decay more rapidly outside.

Color, figure & grain pattern

DRAMATIC DIFFERENCES in color, figure and grain pattern are part of what makes woodworking so compelling. Wood color is a product of of how its tannins, gums and resins react to exposure to the air. Often, wood will continue to darken and change color over time, developing a rich patina. Figure—the surface pattern on a board—can be the result of natural causes ranging from drought or freezing to prevailing winds, disease, age or insect damage. Grain display is dependent on the direction and regularity of the wood fibers relative to the center of the trunk as well as how the lumber is cut from the tree.

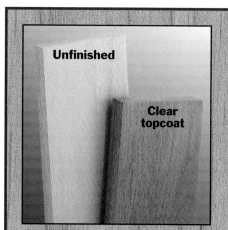

WALNUT has rich, dark tones when top-coated. Grain is relatively straight. Moderately easy to work. Moderate to expensive. Species shown is black walnut.

Choosing Wood

Choosing the best wood species for your project goes a long way toward ensuring success. Different species naturally lend themselves better to the types of machining required for a project, as well as the overall look. For example, project parts that incorporate decorative edge profiles may be easier to shape using soft wood, but ultimately harder, more straight-grained wood will stand up better over time. Cost and local availability are also important determining factors. If you're building outdoors, cedar is generally an inexpensive wood choice in the Upper Midwest, but on the West Coast redwood is typically more economical, and in the South you'll likely save money by building with cypress. When choosing wood, pay particular attention to the tone of the wood when a finish is applied. To get a good idea what the finished color will be, simply dampen a small section of a planed board with mineral spirits or rubbing alcohol.

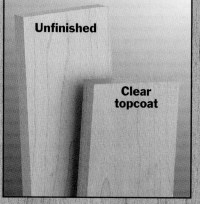

MAPLE is a light-colored hardwood with straight, tight grain. Hardness makes it durable, but somewhat difficult to work. Inexpensive to moderate. Species shown is hard maple.

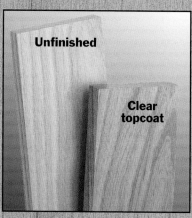

ASH is a readily available, inexpensive hardwood. Its color and grain are not distinguishing, but it can be finished to replicate more expensive hardwoods.

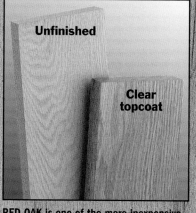

RED OAK is one of the more inexpensive and prevalent wood species in today's marketplace. Has dramatic grain figure and warm red color, Fairly easy to work.

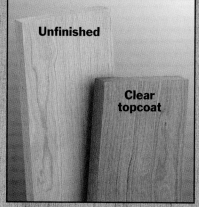

CHERRY has a deep, reddish brown color when finished (color varies greatly between heartwood and sapwood). It is hard and tends to be brittle. Occasionally splotchy when finished. Moderate to expensive. Species shown is black cherry.

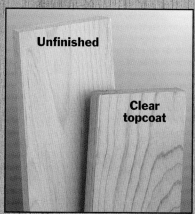

PINE is a very general species term used to refer to most coniferous softwood. It ranges from white to yellow according to species. Generally easy to work with strong grain patterns. Inexpensive to moderate. Species shown is ponderosa pine.

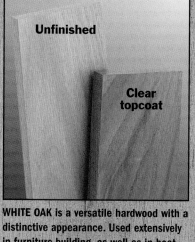

WHITE OAK is a versatile hardwood with a distinctive appearance. Used extensively in furniture-building, as well as in boat-building. It is moderate in price (quarter-sawn tends to be higher cost). Moderate workability.

Reading softwood grade stamps

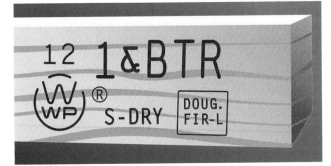

ALL CONSTRUCTION LUMBER sold in the U.S. bears an industry grading stamp such as the Western Wood Products Association (WWP) stamp shown above. Nominal softwood lumber is graded similarly, but usually the stamp doesn't show. Here's how to decipher grade stamps:

12 — Identifies the mill. This can be letters or numbers.

1&BTR — This is the grade of lumber, in this case #1 Common and better, an excellent furniture grade.

WWP — The grading association that graded the board, in this case the Western Wood Products Association.

S-DRY — The condition of seasoning at the time of surfacing, in this case dry, or seasoned lumber below 19% moisture content. If the stamp read KD-15, it would denote kiln-dried lumber with a maximum of 15% moisture content. Product stamped S-GRN stands for unseasoned (green) lumber containing more than 19% moisture content.

DOUG FIR-L — Indicates the wood species, in this case, Douglas fir.

Softwood lumber sizes

Slide your measuring tape across a 2×4 and you'll discover that it doesn't actually measure two inches by four inches. In fact, it will be $1/2$-in. shy in both directions. In its rough state, when the lumber was originally ripped into studs, this same piece was in fact a true 2×4. But after drying, it shrank a little. Then it was surfaced (planed) on all four faces, and it shrank a little more.

When you buy standard softwood lumber at your home center, surfaced and jointed on all faces and edges, the industry sells it to you in finished dimensions, but still describes it in *nominal* dimensions—the size it was before milling.

A piece of softwood lumber with a nominal 1-in. thickness is generally referred to as a board, while nominal 2-in.-thick softwood is called framing stock (as in studs, joists and rafters), or *dimension* lumber. The chart below lists nominal and dimension lumber sizes for the stock you'll find in home centers.

Softwood lumber is graded by strength and appearance as well as moisture content. For woodworking applications, the three common grades to know are Select, Finish and Common (See the chart, below left). While boards in the Common grade categories may contain some blemishes and knots, Select and Finish grades are clear or nearly clear of defects. Be aware, however, that boards within any grade may exhibit some degree of natural distortion (cupping, bowing, twisting), so it's important to examine each board carefully by sighting along its length and width before you buy.

Softwood Lumber Grades

Grade	Grading criteria
B Select and BTR	Highest quality lumber with little or no defects or blemishes. Nominal sizes may be limited.
C Select	Some small defects or blemishes permissible, but still largely clear and of high quality.
D Select	One board face usually defect-free.
Superior Finish	Highest grade finish lumber with only minor defects.
Prime Finish	High quality with some defects and blemishes.
No. 1 Common	Highest grade of knotty lumber; usually available by special-order.
No. 2 Common	Pronounced knots and larger blemishes permissible.

Nominal vs. dimension softwood lumber sizes

Nominal	Finished
1×2	$3/4 \times 1\frac{1}{2}$
1×3	$3/4 \times 2\frac{1}{2}$
1×4	$3/4 \times 3\frac{1}{2}$
1×6	$3/4 \times 5\frac{1}{2}$
1×8	$3/4 \times 7\frac{1}{4}$
1×10	$3/4 \times 9\frac{1}{4}$
1×12	$3/4 \times 11\frac{1}{4}$
Dimension lumber sizes	
2×2	$1\frac{1}{2} \times 1\frac{1}{2}$
2×3	$1\frac{1}{2} \times 2\frac{1}{2}$
2×4	$1\frac{1}{2} \times 3\frac{1}{2}$
2×6	$1\frac{1}{2} \times 5\frac{1}{2}$
2×8	$1\frac{1}{2} \times 7\frac{1}{4}$
2×10	$1\frac{1}{2} \times 9\frac{1}{4}$
2×12	$1\frac{1}{2} \times 11\frac{1}{4}$

Hardwood lumber sizes

While nominal dimensions are widely used for selling softwoods, some retailers have extended the practice to hardwood boards as well. Your local home center probably stocks a few species of hardwoods, like oak, maple and cherry. These boards generally are planed to ¾ in. thick, jointed flat on the edges and cut to standard widths and lengths. Within the lumber industry, lumber of this sort is categorized as "S4S", which stands for Surfaced Four Sides. All of this surface preparation at the mill translates to higher prices for you, but it may make the most sense to buy S4S lumber if you don't own a thickness planer or jointer to prepare board surfaces yourself.

To find specialty or thicker hardwoods, you'll need to shop at a traditional lumberyard. A good lumberyard will offer a wide selection of hardwoods in random widths and in an assortment of thicknesses and grades (See *Hardwood Lumber Grades,* below). In addition to S4S, you'll find S2S lumber (planed smooth on two faces but the edges are rough), and roughsawn boards that are simply cut from the log, dried and shipped to the lumberyard.

Because of their diverse uses, hardwoods are offered in a much larger variety of thicknesses than standard 1× and 2× softwoods. This has led to the quartering system for determining lumber thickness, which allows you to buy hardwoods in ¼-in. thickness increments from ¼ in. on up. Most yards offer popular hardwood species in three, four, five, six, eight, ten and even twelve quarter thicknesses (which read as ¾, 4/4, 5/4, 6/4, 8/4, 10/4 and 12/4 on the label at the rack). These correspond to rough (pre-planed) thicknesses of ¾ in., 1 in., 1¼ in., 1½ in., 2 in., 2½ in. and 3 in.

Roughsawn   **S2S**   **S4S**

HARDWOOD SURFACING OPTIONS:
If the extent of your hardwood needs amounts to only an occasional project, buy S4S boards at the yard. They'll come planed on both faces and jointed flat on both edges, ready for cutting into project parts. If you have access to a jointer, consider buying S2S lumber, which still has rough edges but the faces are planed smooth. The most economical hardwood comes roughsawn to the lumberyard and will require you to do all of the surface preparation yourself. Some lumberyards will plane your stock for a nominal fee, if you don't own a planer.

Calculating Board Feet

Hardwood lumber is sold at most lumberyards by the board foot, which can make calculating the amount of lumber you need a little confusing. The three boards below, for instance, all equal 2 board feet, though their physical dimensions are quite different. A board foot is actually 1/12 of a cubic foot of rough lumber, or 144 cubic inches. It is the equivalent of a piece of stock that is 12 in. wide, 12 in. long and 1 in. thick. But any combination of dimensions that multiplies to 144 is equivalent to one board foot.

To calculate the number of board feet a piece of lumber contains, its thickness times its width times its length (all in inches) then divide by 144. If one dimension is easier to calculate in feet rather than inches, divide by 12 instead.

When calculating board feet, don't forget to build some waste into the project estimate. The pros generally count on close to 30% when they're buying S2S stock, and 40% with roughsawn lumber (mostly because they can't see the defects until after planing).

1 × 6 × 48 in.

2 × 6 × 24 in.

4 × 4 × 18 in.

Hardwood Lumber Grades

Hardwood lumber is graded using a different classification system than softwoods. Grades are based on the percentage of clear face cuts that can be made around a board's defects (knots, splits, pitch pockets, and so forth). From highest grade (clearest) to lowest (most allowable defects), the grades are:

Grade	Percentage of clear cuts
FAS (Firsts & Seconds)	83⅓%
Select	83⅓%
No. 1 Common	66⅓%
No. 2A & 2B Common	50%
No. 3A Common	33⅓%
No. 3B Common	25%

Choose the lumber grade that best suits the needs of your project parts and your budget. It could be that a Common grade will provide all the knot-free lumber you need at a significant savings over FAS.

Sources for buying lumber

Depending on where you live, there may only be one or two places to buy wood or many different sources. Metropolitan areas tend to have more specialized lumber outlets in addition to the usual home center and lumberyard options. Here's a rundown of the various lumber sources to try:

Home centers: These days, there's probably a Home Depot or Lowe's store within a short driving distance of where you live. "Big box" home centers will stock a limited selection of hardwood and softwood lumber. Most of it will be surfaced and planed S4S lumber, sold either by the board or by the lineal foot. Expect to find mixed softwoods of spruce/pine/fir and possibly cedar. For hardwoods, the typical home center options are oak, poplar and occasionally cherry, maple or a lesser-known bleach-white wood called aspen.

The upside to buying lumber from a home center is convenience, but the downside is limited selection. And despite the volume of sales these stores do, lumber pricing may still be as high or even higher than a lumberyard.

Lumberyards: Here's where trim carpenters and contractors shop for framing lumber, sheet materials, moldings and other millwork products like stair treads and balusters. A general-purpose lumberyard may stock a wider range of hardwood

LARGE RETAIL LUMBER OUTLETS AND HOME CENTERS make shopping for lumber easy. Most of the lumber you'll find is fully surfaced and ready for building. Some larger home centers even stock lumber inside where it's kept warm and dry. The downside to all of this convenience is that species options are limited, especially for hardwoods and exotics.

Reclaimed lumber

In recent years there has been a lot of talk about reclaimed lumber. Most reclaimed lumber is salvaged from the beams and timbers of old buildings, and some is recovered from the chilly depths of the Great Lakes. Such lumber was culled from virgin forests a century or more ago, and it is generally very straight-grained and true. It is also extremely seasoned; only large swings in temperature or humidity seem to affect it. Reclaimed lumber is generally a great product, and numerous mills advertise on the internet. The price may be high, however, especially for premium cuts and grades.

Buying reclaimed lumber is by no means your only source for obtaining it. Before you toss an old piece of furniture or dispose of boards and trim from a big remodeling project, consider reusing the lumber for woodworking. Sometimes all it needs is to be stripped, sanded or run through a planer. Visually inspect any reclaimed lumber carefully or check it with a metal detector before passing it through a saw or router, to be sure there are no hidden metal fasteners present.

DON'T OVERLOOK "DIAMONDS IN THE ROUGH": These mahogany boards, salvaged from a discarded couch and passed through a planer, will make excellent stock for a woodworking project.

and softwood lumber, but that will depend on what its major clientele — contractors — need for their customers. Usually a lumberyard's inventory will consist of S4S lumber and roughsawn cedar for siding and fencing. Prices will be competitive with a home center but not inexpensive. One advantage to buying from a lumberyard is that you may be able to buy longer or wider lumber than a home center will carry, and the yard may stock more volume.

Specialty yards: Many metro areas have specialty yards that sell only hardwoods, veneers and special-order sheet goods. Their primary customers are commercial cabinetmakers, architectural millwork shops and professional woodworkers. Usually these yards will also sell to walk-in customers, but you'll probably have to open an account. There may also be volume minimums that apply. Be sure to ask before you start searching the racks.

Specialty yards are wonderful places to find a full selection of both native and exotic hardwoods. These yards may carry S4S lumber that's ready to use, but you're more likely to find S2S or roughsawn lumber instead. Within a given species, a specialty yard may stock several different cuts of lumber, including quartersawn and riftsawn boards as well as wood with special figure. Unlike home centers or lumberyards, specialty yards will sell their stock almost exclusively by the board foot rather than by lineal dimensions (See page 21 for more on calculating lumber by the board foot).

The salespeople at a specialty yard are used to dealing with the pros, but most will take a few minutes to offer advice about lumber options or how to buy. However, time is money to these folks, so they won't appreciate spending too much time on what will amount to a relatively minor sale. And generally, you'll have to find what you need in their warehouses on your own.

Most specialty yards understand that customers want to hand-select the boards they buy, so it's acceptable to search through the stacks. But show good etiquette when you're through by restacking boards neatly. Longer and wider boards belong at the back of the rack. Keep boards from different piles or bins sorted as the yard has them. Individual stacks may constitute specific grades and cuts that need to be kept separate from others.

Local sawmills: If you live in a rural or wooded area, there's probably a family-owned sawmill still around. Sometimes, a particularly ambitious woodworker or cabinetbuilder will have a portable sawmill to saw his or her own stock from local

Mail-order lumber

LUMBER BY MAIL: If you don't have a specialty lumberyard nearby or need a more unusual species for your project, consider ordering lumber by mail. The range of species offered is usually quite broad, and the prices are competitive. Thumb through the back of most woodworking magazines and you'll see numerous mail-order suppliers to choose from. One drawback to buying by mail is that you'll be ordering lumber sight unseen. As a safeguard, make your first order small, so you can inspect the quality. Ask about moisture levels, too, so you can use what you order right away without needing to let it dry first.

forests or storm-fallen trees. Talk with these folks and you may be able to nab an excellent price on quality, air-dried lumber. You'll also have the satisfaction of knowing the boards you use have come from nearby trees and that you are supporting local business. Volume will probably be limited, but the selection of species could be quite interesting, depending on what grows in your area. The mill may even deliver to your home for minimal cost.

Buying by mail or the internet: Look in the back of woodworking magazines and you'll find ads for specialty lumber suppliers all over the country. They can send you a catalog of their inventory, or check their web sites to buy lumber you can't find locally. Another option is to bid on lumber using eBay and other internet auction sites. But be aware that the seller usually offers no guarantees on quality — and you're buying sight unseen. Find out what shipping charges apply. They can turn a seemingly great deal into an expensive purchase.

PLYWOOD is manufactured in several thicknesses, using a variety of wood species to create the core, but 3/4-in.-thick laminated veneer-core plywood with smooth hardwood veneer faces is the type used most frequently for built-in projects.

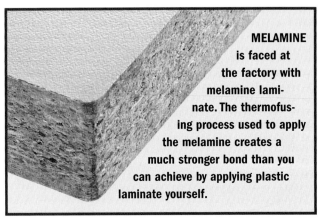

MEDIUM-DENSITY FIBERBOARD (MDF) is growing in popularity as a veneer substrate, paintable surface, and as a raw material for moldings.

PARTICLEBOARD is used almost exclusively as a substrate for plastic laminate or veneer, especially for countertops. It is inexpensive but lacks sufficient strength to be used for shelving or structural members.

MELAMINE is faced at the factory with melamine laminate. The thermofusing process used to apply the melamine creates a much stronger bond than you can achieve by applying plastic laminate yourself.

Sheet goods

The basic structural component of cabinetry is some form of sheet goods; most frequently plywood. Other commonly used sheet goods are particleboard, fiberboard, melamine panels and hardboard. These materials come in handy when you need to cover a broad project area without including seams. Sheet goods are dimensionally stable (there is no substantive wood grain to contend with) and relatively inexpensive, when compared to the price of solid lumber. You'll turn to them time and time again for different woodworking applications. Here is an overview of the options you'll find at most home centers and lumberyards:

Plywood. Plywood is fashioned from sheets of wood veneer, primarily pine and fir. By orienting the wood grain of each laminated sheet so adjacent sheets are perpendicular, the product is able to withstand greater stress than construction lumber of the same thickness. In addition, it is more dimensionally stable.

Most lumberyards stock furniture-grade plywood in several thicknesses and face veneer options (pine, red oak, birch and maple are the most common face veneers). Lumberyards can order plywood with dozens of additional veneer options.

Choosing the right plywood for your woodworking project is an important task. In addition to the various core, thickness and face veneer options, you'll also need to make a decision on the plywood grade. Basically, there are two grading systems in use today. The one most people are familiar with is administered by the APA (Engineered Wood Association, formerly the American Plywood Association). The APA grade stamps (See *Illustration*, next page) are found on sanded plywood, sheathing and structural (called performance-rated) panels. Along with grading each face of the plywood by letter (A to D) or purpose, the APA performance-rated

---

NOTICE

Particleboard and MDF usually contain urea formaldehyde resins that continue to emit low levels of formaldehyde gas for at least six months as they cure. People with high sensitivity to chemical vapors should limit the number of composite panels added to a room at one time. Always wear a particle mask or respirator as required and provide adequate dust collection and ventilation when cutting or shaping these products.

stamp lists other information such as exposure rating, maximum allowable span, type of wood used to make the plies and the identification number of the mill where the panel was manufactured. Many hardwood-veneer sanded plywood panels are graded by the Hardwood Plywood and Veneer Association (HPVA). The HPVA grading numbers are similar to those employed by APA: they refer to a face grade (from A to E) and a back grade (from 1 to 4). Thus, a sheet of plywood that has a premium face (A) and a so-so back (3) would be referred to as A-3 by HPVA (and AC by APA).

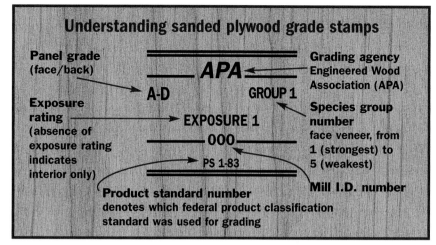

Understanding sanded plywood grade stamps

Panel grade (face/back) → A-D

Grading agency — Engineered Wood Association (APA)

Exposure rating (absence of exposure rating indicates interior only) → EXPOSURE 1

APA GROUP 1

Species group number — face veneer, from 1 (strongest) to 5 (weakest)

000

PS 1-83

Mill I.D. number

Product standard number denotes which federal product classification standard was used for grading

Every sheet of plywood is stamped with grading information. On lower-grade panels, such as exterior sheathing, the stamp can be found in multiple locations on both faces. Panels with one better-grade face are stamped only on the back, and panels with two better-grade faces are stamped on the edges.

Particleboard: Particleboard possesses several unique qualities that might make it a good choice for your next built-in project—particularly if the project includes a counter or tabletop. Particleboard is very dimensionally stable (it isn't likely to expand, contract or warp); it has a relatively smooth surface that provides a suitable substrate for laminate; it comes in a very wide range of thicknesses and panel dimensions; and it is inexpensive. But particleboard does have some drawbacks: it lacks stiffness and shear strength; it has poor screw-holding ability; it degrades when exposed to moisture; it's too coarse in the core to be shaped effectively; and it's heavy.

Medium-density fiberboard (MDF): MDF is similar to particleboard in constitution, but is denser and heavier. The smoothness and density of MDF make it a good substrate choice for veneered projects; the rougher surface of particleboard and most plywoods do not bond as cleanly with thin wood veneer. You can even laminate layers of MDF to create structural components that can be veneered or painted. MDF is also increasing in popularity as a trim molding material.

Melamine board: Melamine is fashioned with a particleboard core with one or two plastic laminate faces. Thicknesses range from $\frac{1}{4}$ to $\frac{3}{4}$ in. Stock colors at most lumber yards and building centers generally are limited to white, gray, almond and sometimes black. The panels are oversized by 1 in. (a 4 × 8 sheet is actually 49 × 97 in.) because the brittle melamine has a tendency to chip at the edges during transport. Plan to trim fresh edges.

Face grade descriptions

N	Smooth surface "natural finish" veneer. Select, all heartwood or all sapwood. Free of open defects. Allows not more than six repairs, wood only, per 4 × 8 panel, made parallel to grain and well-matched for grain and color.
A	Smooth, paintable. Not more than 18 neatly made repairs, boat, sled or router type, and parallel to grain, permitted. May be used for natural finish in less demanding applications. Synthetic repairs permitted.
B	Solid surface. Shims, circular repair plugs and tight knots to 1 in. across grain permitted. Some minor splits permitted. Synthetic repairs permitted.
C plugged	Improved C veneer with splits limited to $\frac{1}{8}$-in. width and knotholes and borer holes limited to $\frac{1}{4} \times \frac{1}{2}$ in. Admits some broken grain. Synthetic repairs permitted.
C	Tight knots to $1\frac{1}{2}$ in. Knotholes to 1 in. across grain and some $1\frac{1}{2}$ in. if total width of knots and knotholes is within specified limits. Synthetic or wood repairs. Discoloration and sanding defects that do not impair strength permitted. Limited splits allowed. Stitching permitted.
D	Knots and knotholes to $2\frac{1}{2}$ in. across grain and $\frac{1}{2}$ in. larger within specified limits. Limited splits are permitted. Stitching permitted. Limited to Interior and Exposure 1 or 2 panels.

Source: Engineered Wood Association

Plywood veneer grain patterns

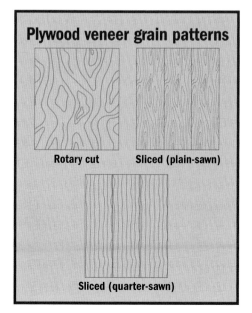

Rotary cut   Sliced (plain-sawn)

Sliced (quarter-sawn)

Common Hardwoods

A. RED OAK

Uses: Indoor furniture, trim, flooring, plywood and veneers
Sources: United States and Canada
Characteristics: Straight, wide grain pattern with larger pores. Tan to reddish pink in color. Quartersawing reveals narrow medullary rays.
Workability: Machines easily with sharp steel or carbide blades and bits. Not prone to burning when machined. Drill pilot holes first for nails or screws.
Finishing: Takes stains and clear finishes well, but pores will show through if painted unless they are filled
Price: Moderate

B. WHITE OAK

Uses: Indoor and outdoor furniture, trim, flooring, plywood and veneers
Sources: United States and Canada
Characteristics: Straight, wide grain pattern, tan with yellow to cream tints. Quartersawing reveals wide medullary rays. Naturally resistant to deterioration from UV sunlight, insects and moisture.
Workability: Machines easily with sharp steel or carbide blades and bits. Not prone to burning when machined. Drill pilot holes first for nails or screws.
Finishing: Takes stains and clear finishes like red oak, but narrower pores reduce the need for filling
Price: Moderate to expensive

C. HARD MAPLE

Uses: Indoor furniture, trim, flooring, butcher block countertops, instruments, plywoods and veneers
Sources: United States and Canada
Characteristics: Straight, wide grain with occasional bird's eye or fiddleback figure. Blonde heartwood.
Workability: Difficult to machine without carbide blades and bits. Dull blades will leave burns.
Finishing: Takes clear finishes well, but staining may produce blotches
Price: Moderate to expensive, depending on figure

D. CHERRY

Uses: Indoor furniture, cabinetry, carving, turning, plywood and veneers
Sources: United States and Canada
Characteristics: Fine grain pattern with smooth texture. Wood continues to darken as it ages and is exposed to sunlight.
Workability: Machines easily with sharp steel or carbide blades but is more prone to machine burns
Finishing: Takes stains and clear finishes well
Price: Moderate

E. WALNUT

Uses: Indoor furniture, cabinets, musical instruments, clocks, boat-building, carving
Sources: Eastern United States and Canada
Characteristics: Straight, fine grain. Moderately heavy. Color ranges from dark brown to purple or black.
Workability: Cuts and drills easily with sharp tools without burning
Finishing: Takes natural finishes beautifully
Price: Moderate

F. BIRCH

Uses: Kitchen utensils, toys, dowels, trim, plywood and veneers
Sources: United States and Canada
Characteristics: Straight grain with fine texture and tight pores.
Workability: Machines easily with sharp steel or carbide blades and bits. Good bending properties. Drill pilot holes first for nails or screws.
Finishing: Takes finishes well, but penetrating wood stains may produce blotching
Price: Inexpensive to moderate

G. HICKORY

Uses: Sporting equipment, handles for striking tools, furniture, plywood and veneers
Sources: Southeastern United States
Characteristics: Straight to wavy grained with coarse texture. Excellent shock-resistance.
Workability: Bends well, but lumber hardness will dull steel blades and bits quickly. Resists machine burning.
Finishing: Takes stains and clear finishes well
Price: Inexpensive where regionally available

H. ASPEN

Uses: A secondary wood used for drawer boxes, cleats, runners and other hidden structural furniture components. Crafts.
Sources: United States and Canada
Characteristics: Indistinguishable, tight grain pattern
Workability: Machines easily with sharp steel or carbide blades and bits.
Finishing: Better suited for painting than staining. Tight grain provides smooth, paintable surface.
Price: Inexpensive

I. WHITE ASH

Uses: Furniture, boat oars, baseball bats, handles for striking tools, pool cues, veneers
Sources: United States and Canada
Characteristics: Straight, wide grain pattern with coarse texture. Hard and dense with excellent shock-resistance.
Workability: Machines easily with sharp steel or carbide blades and bits. Drill pilot holes first for nails or screws. "Green" ash often used for steam bending.
Finishing: Takes stains and clear finishes well
Price: Inexpensive

J. POPLAR

Uses: Secondary wood for furniture and cabinetry, similar to aspen. Carving, veneers and pulp for paper.
Sources: United States
Characteristics: Fine-textured with straight, wide grain pattern. Tan to gray or green in color.
Workability: Machines easily with sharp steel or carbide blades and bits. Not prone to burning when machined. Drill pilot holes first for nails or screws.
Finishing: Better suited for painting than staining. Tight grain provides smooth, paintable surface.
Price: Inexpensive

A. WHITE PINE

Uses: Indoor furniture, plywood, veneers and trim, construction lumber
Sources: United States and Canada
Characteristics: Straight grain with even texture and tight pores
Workability: Machines easily with sharp steel or carbide blades and bits. Not prone to burning when machined. Lower resin content than other pines, so cutting edges stay cleaner longer.
Finishing: Stains may blotch without using a stain controller first. Takes clear finishes and paints well.
Price: Inexpensive

B. WESTERN RED CEDAR

Uses: Outdoor furniture, exterior millwork, interior and exterior siding
Sources: United States and Canada
Characteristics: Straight, variable grain pattern with coarse texture. Lower density and fairly light-weight. Saw- and sanding dust can be a respiratory irritant. Naturally resistant to deterioration from UV sunlight, insects and moisture.
Workability: Soft composition machines easily but end grain is prone to splintering and tear-out
Finishing: Takes stains and clear finishes well, but oils in wood can bleed through painted finishes unless primer is applied first
Price: Inexpensive to moderate where regionally available

C. AROMATIC CEDAR (TENNESSEE)

Uses: Naturally-occurring oils seem to repel moths, making this wood a common closet and chest lining. Also used for veneers and outdoor furniture.
Sources: Eastern United States and Canada
Characteristics: Straight to wavy grain pattern with fine texture. Red to tan in color with dramatic streaks of yellows and creams. Distinct aroma emitted when machined, and dust can be a respiratory irritant.
Workability: Machines similarly to western red cedar
Finishing: Takes stains and clear finishes well
Price: Inexpensive

D. REDWOOD

Uses: Outdoor furniture, decks and fences, siding
Source: West coast of United States
Characteristics: Straight, fine grain with few knots or blemishes. Relatively light weight. Reddish brown with cream-colored sapwood. Naturally resistant to deterioration from UV sunlight, insects and moisture.
Workability: Machines and sands easily
Finishing: Takes stains and clear finishes well
Price: Moderate to expensive and not widely available in all nominal dimensions

E. CYPRESS

Uses: Exterior siding and boat building. Interior and exterior trim, beams, flooring, cabinetry and paneling.
Source: Mississippi delta region of the United States
Characteristics: Straight, even grain pattern with low resin content. Naturally resistant to deterioration from UV sunlight, insects and moisture.
Workability: Machines and sands easily
Finishing: Takes stains and clear finishes well
Price: Inexpensive where regionally available

Sampling of Exotics

A. PADAUK
Uses: Indoor furniture, cabinetry, flooring, turning, veneer
Source: West Africa
Characteristics: Coarse texture, straight interlocked grain
Workability: Machines easily with sharp steel or carbide blades and bits
Finishing: Takes stains and clear finishes well
Price: Moderate to expensive

B. ZEBRAWOOD
Uses: Turning, inlay, decorative veneers, furniture and cabinetry
Source: West Africa
Characteristics: Interlocked, light and dark varigated grain pattern
Workability: Somewhat difficult to machine. Use carbide blades and bits
Finishing: Can be difficult to stain evenly
Price: Expensive

C. WENGE
Uses: Inlay, turning, decorative veneers
Source: Equatorial Africa
Characteristics: Hard, dense straight grain with coarse texture. Heavy.
Workability: Dulls steel blades and bits quickly, so carbide cutters are recommended. Drill pilot holes for screws and nails.
Finishing: Pores should be filled before finish is applied
Price: Moderate

D. HONDURAS MAHOGANY
Uses: Indoor and outdoor furniture, veneers and trim, boat-building
Sources: Central and South America
Characteristics: Straight, interlocked fine grain. Dimensionally stable.
Workability: Machines well with carbide blades and bits
Finishing: Takes stains and clear finishes well
Price: Moderate

E. PURPLEHEART
Uses: Pool cues, decorative inlay, veneers, indoor and outdoor furniture.
Sources: Central and South America
Characteristics: Straight grain with coarse texture
Workability: Gum deposits in the wood make it difficult to machine; cutting edges dull quickly
Finishing: Takes stains and clear finishes well.
Price: Moderate

F. TEAK
Uses: Boat-building, indoor and outdoor furniture, veneers, flooring
Sources: Southeast Asia, Africa, Caribbean
Characteristics: Straight grain with oily texture. Dense and hard.
Workability: High silica content will dull steel blades and bits quickly. Oily surfaces require cleaning with mineral spirits first or glue will not bond.
Finishing: Takes oil finishes well
Price: Expensive

G. ROSEWOOD
Uses: Inlays, turning, veneers, cabinetry, furniture, musical instruments
Sources: Southern India
Characteristics: Interlocked grain with medium to coarse texture
Workability: Dense structure dulls cutting edges quickly
Finishing: Takes stains and clear finishes well
Price: Expensive

WOODWORKING TOOLS & SKILLS

Good woodworkers aren't just born. Of course, there has to be some "knack" and "feel" for what is right, and we all have it to some extent. But more important is your knowledge of the tools you need, and the skills required to use them effectively.

That's what this *Woodworking Tools & Skills* chapter is all about. First, you will gain an understanding of the tools essential to successful woodworking. Then you receive detailed, step-by-step instructions that *show* you techniques and tips for using those tools safely and efficiently to make beautiful projects.

You could probably learn these techniques on your own ... through an awful lot of trial and error. But a woodworking career is too short—and your personal shop time too valuable—to spend too much time refining your skills. These pages get you ahead of the woodworking game.

Measuring, Marking & Layout

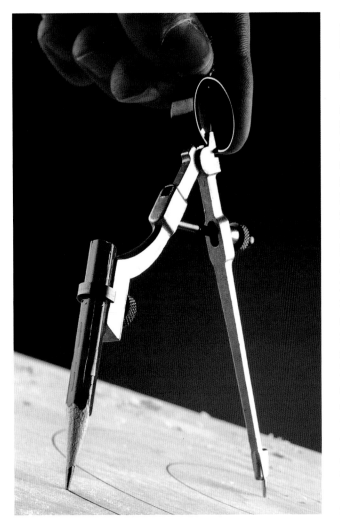

Successful workshop projects start with careful, accurate measuring, marking and layout. The most critical elements in these steps of the process are good planning, accurate measuring and using sharp marking tools that create readable lines. The level of precision needed varies according to the intricacy and complexity of your project. Rough carpentry (for example, putting up stud walls or installing floor underlayment or roof decking) requires a certain amount of care, but generally you can achieve satisfactory results using tape measures, framing squares and a lumber pencil as a marking tool. Trim carpentry (installing moldings and decorative trim) requires a higher degree of accuracy, so you'll want to involve steel rules, levels and angle gauges in the process. A good sharp pencil will usually give you marking lines of acceptable accuracy. Fine woodworking carries the highest standard of accuracy. You'll want to use marking gauges, compasses and any of a wide selection of specialty measuring tools to create well-made projects. Generally, a marking knife or a scratch awl is the marking tool of choice for fine woodworking.

Tape measure tips

To obtain accurate readings from a tape measure, start measuring at the 1-in. mark. The end hook on a tape measure often has some play in it, which can alter measurements slightly. And even a secure hook may be bent or caught against a splinter or bump. Don't forget to subtract one inch from the final reading. Steel rules are generally more accurate than tape measures, but they too can become worn or nicked—for best results, sight from the 1-in. mark on any measuring device.

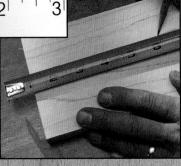

USING THE END HOOK as a starting point when taking measurements with a tape measure can be unreliable, as illustrated by the photo above.

How to scribe a parallel line

WOODWORKING: The most accurate parallel lines can be drawn with a marking gauge. Measure the distance and firmly glide the tool the length of the cut.

Rating marking tools: Four degrees of accuracy

Choosing the best marking tool for your project is a matter of weighing the amount of tolerance you're willing to accept against the readability of the lines you scribe—as well as the ease and speed with which the tool can be used. *Marking knives* create highly accurate lines because the flat blade rides flush against a straightedge and cuts through wood fibers and grain contours that can cause a pencil to waver. They're the tool of choice for most fine woodworking projects. *Scratch awls* also cut through fibers and grain, but the round shaft causes the point to be offset slightly from the straightedge. Lines scored with a scratch awl are easier to see because they're wider, which is especially helpful when marking softwoods. *Pencils* are popular marking tools for rough carpentry and some woodworking tasks. A regular pencil sharpened to a fine point will create a fairly precise, readable line. *Lumber pencils* require less frequent sharpening and create dark, highly readable lines.

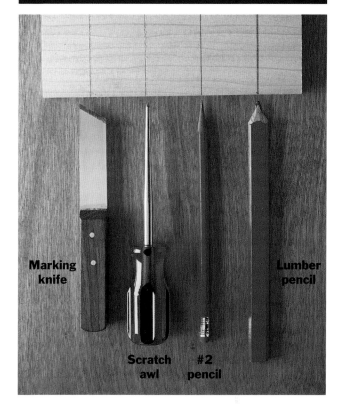

Marking knife

Lumber pencil

Scratch awl

#2 pencil

Tips for scribing & laying out

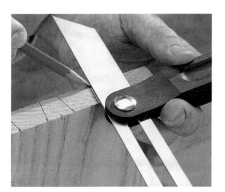

USE A WHITE PENCIL to mark dark-colored wood, like hardboard or walnut.

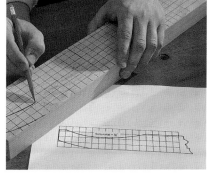

ATTACH MEDIUM-GRIT SANDPAPER to your toolbox to make a convenient and safe sharpener for lumber pencils.

USE A GREASE PENCIL to mark metal, plastic and other materials that can't be marked clearly with a pencil.

USE A SLIDING T-BEVEL to transfer angles to your workpiece.

TRANSFER GRID DRAWINGS to your workpiece by drawing a scaled grid, then re-creating the pattern using the grid as a reference.

MAKE A STURDY TEMPLATE from hardboard or another durable material when making multiple parts with the same profile.

An easy way to divide evenly

When you need to divide a board into equal sections, don't worry about performing elaborate mathematical calculations (such as dividing a 7¾-in.-wide board into four equal portions). Instead, just lay a ruler on the board and angle it until it measures a distance easily divisible by the number of cuts. Make certain one edge of the ruler is on the "0" mark. In the example to the left the ruler is angled so that the 12 in. mark touches the far edge of the board. Dividing the board into four pieces is easy: Just mark the board at inches 3, 6 and 9. Repeat the procedure farther down the board and use the marks to draw parallel cutting lines on the board.

Use a marking gauge

Mortise cuts must be extremely precise. To mark the cuts properly, use a marking gauge, available at good hardware stores. As with any marking tool, hold it firm and steady.

Build a center-marking jig

Build a simple center-marking jig with a scrap piece of 2 × 4 and doweling. The gauge can be as wide as you like. Just be certain that the dowels are an equal distance from the center pencil hole. On the reverse side of the jig, insert two dowels 1 in. from the center hole. This side will allow you to find the center on narrow pieces up to 1⅝ in. wide. When using the jig, angle it so both dowels are pressing firmly against the side of the board you are marking.

Find the center of a circle

Clamp a combination square or other straightedge to a framing square. The edge of the straightedge should be flush with the inside corner of the square where the two legs meet. Position the framing square so each leg is at a flush tangent to the workpiece, then trace the edge of the straightedge past the center of the workpiece at two or more spots. The point where the lines meet is the centerpoint.

Drawing curves & arcs

Two ways to draw shallow arcs

Creating a regular arc requires tricky calculations or an elaborate jig, right? Not necessarily. A trio of nails and a strip of wood will do the job. Tack one nail at each endpoint of the arc, and tack the third nail at the apex of the arc, spaced evenly between the endpoints. Cut a thin strip of plywood or hardboard that's at least a few inches longer than the length of the arc. Bend the strip between the nails as shown in the above, right photo. Trace along the inside edge of the strip to draw your shallow arc. A variation of this method is simply to insert the wood strip between the jaws of a pipe clamp and tighten the clamp until the strip bows to form an arc of the radius you're seeking (See photo, above left). This method is not as accurate, but it won't leave any nail holes in the workpiece.

Make a simple trammel for drawing circles

A trammel is a marking device that pivots around a centerpoint to create a circle. You can buy fancy milled steel woodworking trammels, or you can make your own with a thin strip of hardboard. Just drive a nail through one end of the strip, then measure out from the nail toward the other end an amount equal to the radius of the circle. Mark a centerpoint for drilling a pencil guide hole at that point (usually, 3⁄8 in. dia.). Tack the nail at the center of the workpiece, insert the pencil into the guide hole, then make a single revolution around the nail with the pencil to draw the circle.

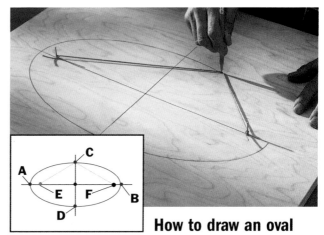

How to draw an oval

Draw perpendicular lines to mark the length and width of the oval. Measuring out from the point of intersection, mark endpoints for the length (A, B) and the width (C, D). Set a compass or trammel to draw an arc that's half as long as the length of the oval. With the point of the compass or trammel at one endpoint for the oval width (C or D), scribe hash marks on the length line (points E, F). Tack nails at points E and F. Tie a string to the nails so the amount of string between the nails is the same as the distance from A to F. Pull the string taut with a pencil tip and trace the oval.

Cutting

Cutting is a fundamental process that's critical to the success of just about any project you're likely to undertake in your workshop. It's essentially a three-part task: laying out the cutting line; setting up for the cut; and executing the cut. Setting up involves choosing the best tool and blade for the job, then adjusting the tool or position of the workpiece to ensure an accurate cut.

There are really only two ways of cutting: either you apply a tool to the workpiece (as with most portable and hand tools), or you apply the workpiece to the tool (as with table saws and other tools where the cutting instrument remains in one spot throughout the cut). When applying the tool to the workpiece, use a combination of straightedges, cutting guides and clamps to achieve accurate cuts. When applying the workpiece to the tool, you normally rely on the built-in fences and scales of the tool to guide the cut.

The basic types of cuts undertaken in workshops include: *cross-cutting* (making a straight cut across the grain of a board); *rip-cutting* (reducing the width of a board by cutting it lengthwise with the grain); *miter-cutting* (cross-cutting at an angle with the saw blade perpendicular to the workpiece) and *bevel-cutting* (making a nonperpendicular cut). In addition to these basic cuts, this section also includes information on mortising and cutting non-wood materials.

Back to the basics:
Make quick & accurate miter cuts by hand

With the recent explosion in popularity of the power miter saw, the hand miter box has become almost a forgotten tool. But for making a few quick miter cuts, you may want to revisit this handy and age-old device. A simple, inexpensive miter box with precut slots for 45° and 90° can be stored in a tool box or under your workbench, then clamped in place in no time at all. And with the precut slots, no setup time is required. To use the hand miter box, hold your workpiece firmly in place, or clamp it in place, and pull the backsaw in firm, short strokes.

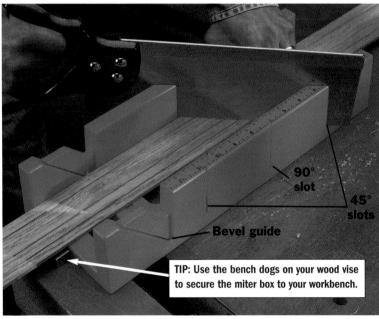

90° slot

45° slots

Bevel guide

TIP: Use the bench dogs on your wood vise to secure the miter box to your workbench.

Choosing & using handsaws

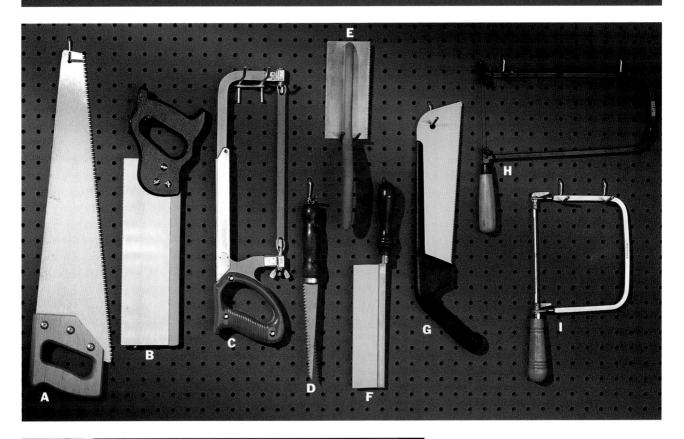

Guide keeps handsaws in line
This easy-to-build cutting guide will ensure straight, accurate cuts with a handsaw. Simply join two pieces of scrap plywood at a right angle, making sure the heads of the fasteners are recessed. Add a piece of scrap wood at the front of the jig to make a lip for holding the jig tightly against your workpiece.

Lip

Team of handsaws can handle any cut

Choosing the right tool for the job is especially important when using hand-powered tools. The collection of handsaws shown above can perform just about any cutting task you're likely to encounter in your workshop.

(A) 8- to 10-TPI cross-cut saw for general cutting of dimension lumber or sheet goods; **(B) Backsaw** for miter-cutting; **(C) Hacksaw** for cutting metal; **(D) Wallboard saw** for making cutouts in wallboard and other soft building materials; **(E) Flush-cutting saw f**or trimming wood plugs and through tenons; **(F) Dovetail saw** (saw shown is smaller version called "Gentleman's saw"; **(G) Japanese saw** (cuts on the pull stroke)for quick trim-carpentry cutting; **(H) Fret saw fo**r making delicate scrolling cuts; **(I) Coping saw** for curved cuts in trim carpentry.

Band saw & jig saw blades

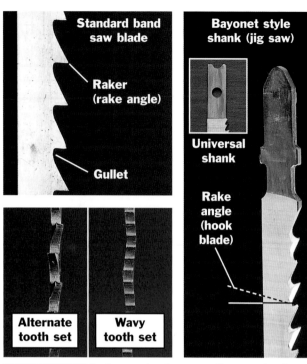

STRAIGHT BLADES for jig saws, band saws, scroll saws and recipro-cating saws vary by number of teeth per inch (tpi), the set of the teeth, the rake angle of the teeth, and the width and thickness of the blade. The type of metal used to make the blade and the presence of carbide or other hardened steel tips affect the longevity (and the price) of the blades. Blades for some tools have numerous tooth configurations: for example, band saw blades can be purchased with *standard teeth* (above), or *skip-tooth* and *hook-tooth* configurations.

Reciprocating saw blade types

RECIPROCATING SAWS are used to perform many different construction tasks. The size and shape of the blades used changes dramatically according to use. Keep a complete set of blades in your saw case.

A good set of reciprocating saw blades includes: (A) 6 in., 18 tpi blade for heavy metal; (B) 6 in., 10 tpi blade for general cutting; (C) 9 in., 6 tpi blade for fast cuts and general roughing in; (D) 12 in., 8 tpi blade for cut-ting timbers and other thick materials; (E) 6 in., 4 tpi blade for fast, rough wood-cutting; (F) 6 in., 5 tpi blade for fast, cleaner cuts; (G) 3⅝ in., 14 tpi blade for curved cuts in hard woods.

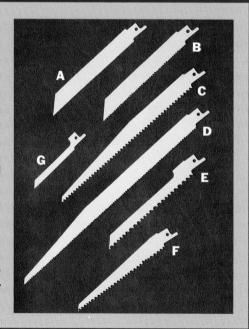

Circular saw blades

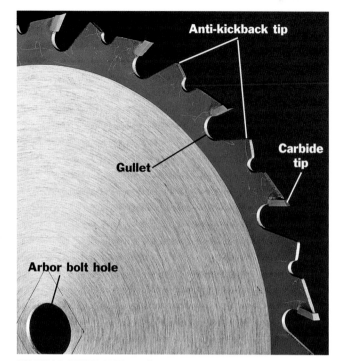

CIRCULAR SAW BLADES are fitted onto portable circular saws, table saws, radial-arm saws and power miter saws. Select blades by matching the number of teeth per inch to the task at hand—but make sure the tpi number is for the correct blade diameter (any-where from 3½ in. to 18 in. or so, with 7¼ in. the most common for portable circular saws, and 10 in. the most common for table saws, power miter saws and radial-arm saws).

COMMON CIRCULAR SAW BLADE STYLES (right) include: (A) General purpose combina-tion blade (good for ripping); (B) Thin-kerf anti-kickback blade (note expansion slots); (C) Roofer's blade (for portable circular saws); (D) Trim-cutting blade (for clean, relatively fast cross-cuts); (E) Carbide-tipped cross-cutting blade (good for power miter saws). Generally, more teeth per inch produce cleaner, slower cuts.

Saw blade selection chart

Band saw

Task	Width (in.)	Pitch	Style*	Set*
Scrollwork, joinery	1/8	14 tpi	ST	AB or R
Cutting light metal	1/8	14 tpi	ST	W
Tight curves	1/8	6 tpi	SK	AB
Smooth curves	3/16	10 tpi	ST	AB
General purpose	1/4	6-8 tpi	ST or SK	AB
Rip-cutting	1/4	4-6 tpi	H	AB or R
Gen. crosscutting	3/8	8-10 tpi	ST or SK	AB or R
Fast crosscutting	3/8	4 tpi	SK	AB
Resawing	1/2	4 tpi	H	AB

Key ST=standard, SK=skip-tooth, H=hook-tooth, AB=alternate-bevel, R=raker, W=wavy

Jig Saw

Task	Material	Length	Pitch
Fast, rough carpentry	Wood	4 in.	6 tpi
General purpose	Wood	4 in.	8 tpi
Smooth finish	Wood	4 in.	10 tpi
Extra-smooth finish	Wood	3 in.	12-14 tpi
Light metal	Metal	3 in.	12-14 tpi
Thick metal	Metal	3 in.	24 tpi

Circular Saw

Task	Type	TPI ($8\frac{1}{4}$-in./10-in. dia.)
General purpose	Combination	16-36/18-50
Trim carpentry	Cross-cut	40-64/60-80
Rough carpentry	Cross-cut	34-40/40-60
Smooth cross-cutting	Cross-cut	50-64/60-80
Rip-cutting	Ripping	16-36/18-24
Plywood and particleboard	Plywood/panel	48-64/60-80
Light metal	Metal-cutting	58-64/60-72

Scroll Saw

Task	Type	Gauge	Pitch
General cutting	Scrolling	#5	15 tpi
Cutting without tear-out	Reverse-tooth fret	#7	11.5 tpi
Fine scrollwork	Scrolling	#7	12 tpi
Very tight curves	Spiral-tooth	#2	41 tpi
Fast cuts	Fret	#9	11.5 tpi

Give your blades a bath

Saw blades that aren't performing as well as you like don't necessarily need sharpening: they may just need a quick cleaning. Special pitch/resin removing compound or ordinary oven cleaner can be used to clean blades (be sure to wear gloves).

Coping base trim for an inside corner

1 Cut one mating board square, and cut the other at a 45° bevel, using a miter saw. The beveled board should be slightly longer than the finished length.

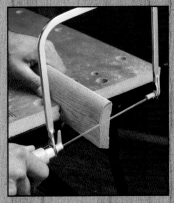

2 With the square-cut board flush in the corner, use a coping saw to trim the excess wood from the beveled end, leaving an end that's perpendicular but tapers up to follow the profile of the molding.

3 Apply the wood finish to both boards, then slip the beveled board into the corner so it overlaps the end of the square-cut board.

Make & use a straightedge

Build an 8-ft. straightedge to cut plywood and paneling with your circular saw. The straightedge shown below has a ¼-in. plywood base, and a 1 × 2 cleat (you can also use a strip of plywood) that serves as a saw guide. After assembling the straightedge, position the circular saw with the foot tight against the cleat and trim off the excess portion of the plywood base. To use the straightedge, position the trimmed edge of the plywood base flush with your cutting line and clamp the straightedge to the workpiece.

Cutting line

Good-side-down for cleaner cuts

Portable circular saws cut on the upward rotation of the blade. To avoid tearout on the better face of your workpiece, turn it good-face-down when cutting.

Two techniques for making plunge cuts

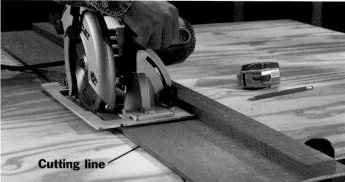

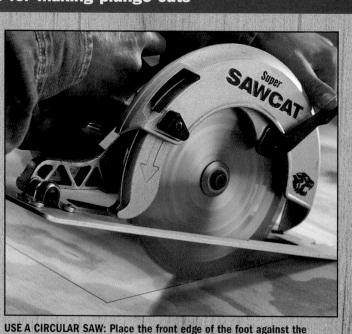

USE A JIG SAW: Tip the jig saw forward on the front edge of its foot. Align the tip of the blade with the cutting line, then turn on the saw and gently but firmly lower the blade into the cutting area. The blade will want to bounce, but by maintaining firm pressure on the front of the foot you can keep it under control until it enters the wood.

USE A CIRCULAR SAW: Place the front edge of the foot against the board, retract the blade guard and hold it in a raised position with your thumb. Turn on the saw and lower the blade into the wood, using the front of the saw foot as a fulcrum. Always wear safety goggles.

Tips for making curved cutouts

Making Curved Cuts

The easiest way to cut smooth, regular curves on large project parts is to use a cutting tool that you apply to the workpiece (as opposed to one you feed the workpiece into). Jig saws and routers are both well suited for the job. Jig saws are faster to set up and easy to use, but won't yield as smooth a cut as a router. For smaller parts, use a band saw or scroll saw.

Cutting curves with a jig saw. One of the best features of the jig saw is its ability to cut curves, particularly in sheet goods. It has no workpiece size limitations, its portability makes it handy for on-site work and such tasks as rounding corners on large tabletops. Clamp the workpiece securely and feed the saw slowly to prevent the blade from deflecting. To start internal cuts, drill an entry hole with a bit slightly larger than the width of the saw blade. Circles can be cut freehand to a line, or if you want a little more exactness you can use a shop-made or commercial circle-cutting jig that pivots about a centerpoint.

Tips for cutting curves with a jig saw

USE THE SCROLLING FEATURE. Scrolling jig saws feature a blade-angle adjustment knob at the top of the handle. By turning the knob, you change the blade direction—without turning the body of the saw.

KEEP PRESSURE DIRECTLY ABOVE THE BLADE. Whether you're using a top-handle saw, like the one above, or a barrel grip saw, hold the tool so your hand is forward and directly above the blade area. Take care not to force the saw: the blade will break or deflect from the cut line.

Minimum radius cuts for band saw blades

As a general rule, you should choose the widest band saw blade that can handle the job you're doing. But because the width of the blade limits the tightness of the curves you can cut, you should choose the widest blade that can follow your tightest cutting radius.

Blade Width	Smallest Radius Cut
1/8"	3/16"
3/16"	3/8"
1/4"	5/8"
3/8"	1 1/4"
1/2"	3"
3/4"	5"
1"	8"

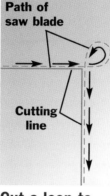

Path of saw blade

Cutting line

Cut a loop to make a square

Making square internal cuts can be a perplexing problem, but here's a simple solution: cut along one leg of the square, and keep cutting past the corner. Loop the saw blade back and cut the second leg.

Gang-cut parts for consistency and speed

When making project parts with curved lines, gang the workpieces together whenever you can. This will ensure that the cut edges are consistent. With most saws, you can tape the workpieces together with double-edged carpet tape.

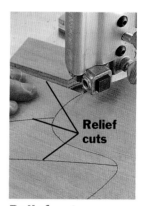

Relief cuts

Relief cuts prevent binding

When making a curved contour cut using a jig saw, band saw or scroll saw, make relief cuts from the edge of the workpiece to the cutting line, in the waste area, so waste can be removed as you cut.

Cut perfect circles with a router compass

Most handymen think of routers as primarily tools for cutting decorative profiles or perhaps an occasional dado or rabbet. But they can also be very effective tools for cutting stock to size and shape. When the right bits and techniques are used, they produce extremely clean edges that often require no sanding.

If you need to cut a square workpiece into a circular shape, a router compass is an excellent choice. Simply secure the router base to the wide end of the compass, set the adjustable center pin to the desired radius of the cut, and secure the pin at the center of the circle. For best results, make the cut in several passes of increasing depth. A single-flute straight bit or a spiral upcut bit can be used to remove large amounts of waste in the cutting area, without bogging down.

Tips for cutting with a power miter box

Stopblock speeds up repetitive cuts

When making repetitive cuts with a power miter saw (or radial-arm saw), clamp a stopblock to the saw fence at the desired length. A lag screw driven squarely into the edge of the stopblock creates a solid surface for aligning the workpiece, while keeping wood chips from building up between the block and workpiece.

Jig takes the math out of beveling molding

Cutting miter-bevels in crown molding often involves tricky math and very precise angles. To simplify the task, use this jig. Join a straight board about 3 in. high to a strip of ¼-in. plywood about 6 in. wide. These will be the "fence" and "table" of the jig. Place a piece of crown molding into the "L" formed by the fence and table, and adjust it until the beveled sides are flush against the fence and table. Mark the position on the table, remove the molding and attach a wood strip at the mark. This strip will hold the molding at the proper angle for bevel-cutting miters.

Proper setup is key to safe cutting with radial-arm saw

Over the years the radial-arm saw has earned a reputation as one of the most dangerous workshop tools. But for most cross-cutting operations, the tool can be a real workhorse that's as safe as any other tool you own. The most important aspect of cutting safely with a radial-arm saw is to secure your workpiece, while keeping your hands well clear of the saw blade. A pushstick with a birdseye cutout is a good choice for bracing smaller workpieces against the saw fence—it's particularly effective when used in conjunction with a stopblock that holds the free end of the workpiece in place. Once the workpiece is secure, start the saw and guide it through the cut with your right hand. Shut off the saw and allow the blade to stop spinning before removing the workpiece and returning the saw carriage back behind the fence.

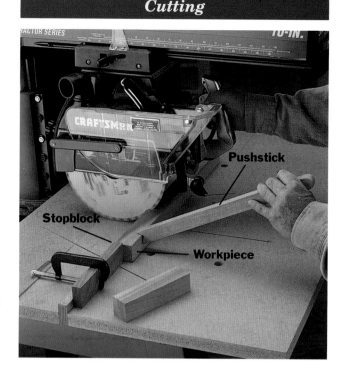

Pushstick

Stopblock

Workpiece

Resawing stock on a band saw

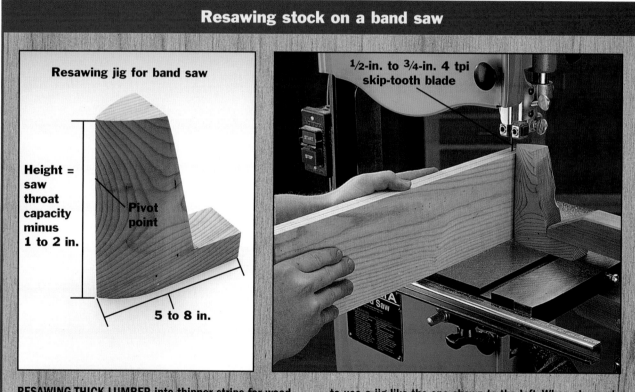

Resawing jig for band saw

Height = saw throat capacity minus 1 to 2 in.

Pivot point

5 to 8 in.

½-in. to ¾-in. 4 tpi skip-tooth blade

RESAWING THICK LUMBER into thinner strips for woodworking is a job best accomplished with a band saw. The simplest method is to attach a fence to the band saw table, parallel to the blade, and feed the stock through as you would when rip-cutting on a band saw. The downside to this method is that the saw blade tends to travel, following the grain of the wood, and resulting in an uneven cut that requires quite a bit of surface planing. One way to minimize the unevenness of the resaw cut is to use a jig like the one shown to the left. When clamped to the saw table so the pivot point is even with the cutting edge of the blade, the jig may be used as a guide to set the thickness of the cut. Because the pivot point is so narrow, you can adjust the feed direction of the board to compensate for blade travel, resulting in a more even cut. You'll still need to surface-plane the workpiece, but you'll waste less wood.

Relief block keeps cutoff pieces free and clear when cross-cutting

Use a relief block to prevent cutoff pieces from getting jammed between the fence and the blade when cross-cutting on the table saw. The relief block can simply be a piece of scrap wood clamped to the fence. Make sure the relief block is positioned behind the point where the workpiece will make first contact with the saw blade. Never stand directly behind the workpiece when feeding it into the blade.

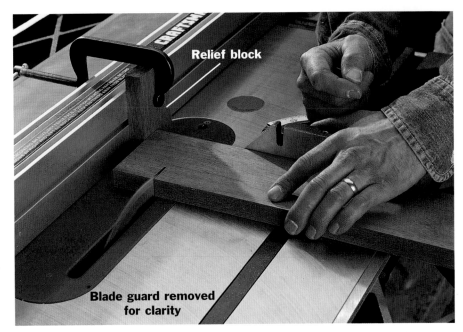

Relief block

Blade guard removed for clarity

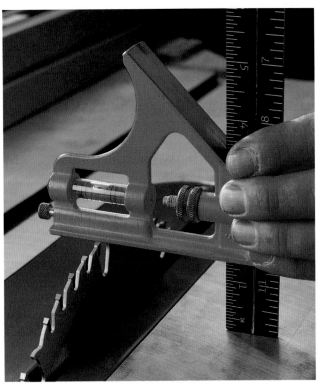

As a rule, take measurements

Don't trust the cutting scale on the table saw fence if you're making precise cuts. Instead, measure the distance from the cutting edge of the blade to the fence with a steel rule when setting up for your cut. Double-check the distance after securing the fence, and make a practice cut on scrap for added precision.

Get blade height just right

Use a combination square to set the height of a table saw blade. The bottom of the square should just be touching the tip of one of the teeth. Because tooth length is not always uniform, spin the blade by hand and make sure you're referencing off the tooth that will cut deepest (be sure to unplug the saw first).

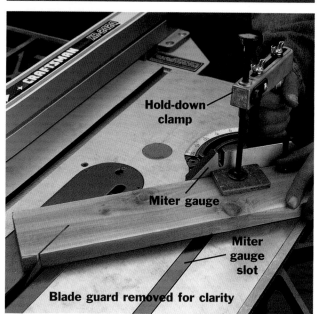

Shop vac blows cutoff pieces clear

Small cutoff pieces have a way of kicking out of the saw throat or becoming jammed around the blade. One way to keep these annoying trim pieces out of your way is simply to position your shop vac hose near the cutting area to blow clear small cutoff pieces. Be sure to leave ample clearance for the workpiece.

Add miter-gauge hold-down for quick, accurate miter cutting

Make your miter gauge more reliable by adding a hold-down clamp to keep workpieces steady during miter cutting. Hold-downs are sold at most larger tool centers or may be purchased directly from the company that manufactured your table saw.

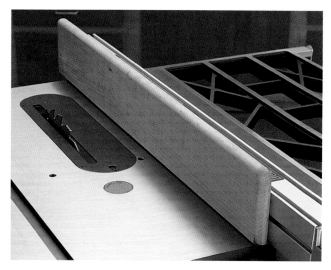

Wood fences make good sense

Adding a wooden auxiliary fence to your table saw (or just about any other tool) extends the life of both your saw fence and your saw blades by eliminating damaging metal-to-metal contact. An auxiliary fence that's taller than the saw fence also creates a good surface for clamping jigs, stopblocks and hold-downs. The fence shown here is made from hard maple and attached to the metal fence with T-bolts that fit into a slot in the saw fence so no screw heads protrude.

Reverse the miter gauge for panel cutting

Sheet goods and glued-up panels are often too wide to be fed into the blade with the saw's miter gauge. You can solve this problem by turning the gauge around so the head of the gauge is fed into the miter-gauge slot first. Attach an auxiliary fence to the miter gauge to create a more stable surface for pressing against. You can also use a miter-gauge hold-down (See photo at top of page) to keep the panel steady.

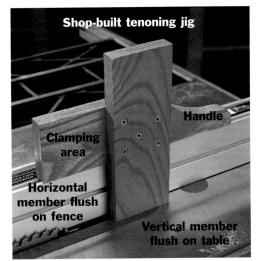

Shop-built tenoning jig

Clamping area

Handle

Horizontal member flush on fence

Vertical member flush on table

Cheek cuts

Sweet cheeks for tenons

Making the cheek cuts for tenons is clumsy and dangerous without a good tenoning jig—and the results are usually disappointing. This shop-built tenoning jig is easy to make from scrap wood and will help you produce tenons that fit on the first try. First, cut the vertical and horizontal members—the horizontal member should have a contour on the tail to create a handle, as shown above. Join the two members with wood screws, arranged so the distance from the bottom of the horizontal member to the bottom of the vertical member is equal to the height of your saw fence. Make sure the members are exactly perpendicular. To use the jig, clamp your workpiece to the jig and feed the workpiece into the blade, keeping steady pressure against the fence and the table (See photo, above right). Cut all the way through the workpiece and the jig. Always test your cuts on a scrap board before cutting your workpieces. Use your miter gauge to guide the workpiece when cutting the tenon shoulders.

Trim wedge and dowel ends with a flush-cutting saw

A flush-cutting saw with a very flexible blade is the ideal tool for trimming off the ends of tenon wedges or dowels. The saw shown above is a Japanese saw that cuts on the pull stroke.

The "poor man's mortising machine"

There are many methods you can use to cut mortises for mortise-and-tenon joinery. The best way is to purchase a special mortising machine or a mortising attachment for your drill press. But if you'd rather not spend the money on these expensive tools, the following method will produce clean mortises when done carefully. It's a little slower and takes some trial and error, but for the weekend woodworker who already owns a drill press, it's a good option.

1 Carefully lay out your mortise using a marking gauge or straightedge. Choose a drill bit the same diameter as the thickness of the mortise (3/8 in. is common), then remove the waste wood from the mortise by drilling overlapping holes using a depth stop.

2 Use a sharp chisel to clean up the sides of the mortise so they're flat and smooth. Make sure the flat face of the chisel is contacting the wood. Clean up the ends of the mortise with a chisel the same width as the thickness of the mortise.

A treat for steel tabletops

Apply rubbing or polishing compound to steel tabletops to smooth out the surface and remove rust. Then, wipe the top clean and apply a coat of car wax to seal the table and keep workpieces sliding smoothly.

Create custom throat plates

When making trim cuts or cutting small workpieces, cover the throat opening of your saw by laying a piece of thin plywood over the throat and raising the spinning saw blade. Use a piece of scrap wood to hold the plywood down.

Increase your cutting angle

To make cuts with an angle greater than the maximum tilt of your saw blade, attach a spacer to your saw fence or to the workpiece.

Spacer

Handy jig for cutting tapers

An adjustable taper jig is a handy accessory for any table saw owner. The legs of the jig can be set to cut tapers according to angle or to slope.

Taper jig

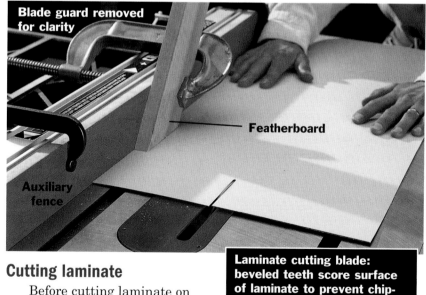

Blade guard removed for clarity

Featherboard

Auxiliary fence

Laminate cutting blade: beveled teeth score surface of laminate to prevent chip-out from cutting teeth

Cutting laminate

Before cutting laminate on your table saw, attach an auxiliary fence that's flush with the table-top so the laminate won't slide or wedge under the fence. A special laminate cutting blade (right) prevents chipping of the surface.

Cabinetmaker's chisels

Most of the wood chisels sold and owned today are bevel-edge cabinetmaker's chisels (See photo, left). Available in standard widths ranging from ¼ to 1½ in., they can handle a variety of everyday cutting tasks, including cutting mortises and paring tenons. If you're a serious woodworker who appreciates hand tools, you may want to look into a set of mortising chisels, which have thicker shanks and wider, shock-resistant handle butts. Better quality chisels are made with hardened steel that hold an edge for a long time. The main differences are in handle material, size and feel. If investing in a set of quality chisels, make sure the ones you choose feel comfortable and well balanced in your hand.

How to sharpen chisels

1 Grind off any nicks using a bench grinder with a medium-grit wheel (or a coarse-grit sharpening stone). Hold the tool on the flat portion of the tool rest, with the beveled side facing up. Hold the tip against the wheel and move it from side to side, keeping the cutting edge square. Cool the blade frequently with water to keep it from losing its temper. When all nicks are gone, turn the blade so the cutting edge is down. Adjust the tool rest so the blade touches the grinding wheel at a 25° bevel. Move the blade from side to side, keeping the blade at a 25° bevel. Continue to cool the blade regularly.

2 Place a few drops of light machine oil on a fine-grit sharpening stone. Place the back of the blade on the whetstone and draw it back and forth several times to remove any burrs.

3 Wipe the stone with a clean rag, and apply more oil. Turn the blade over, and hold it at a 25° angle so the bevel is flat against the stone. Draw the tool back and forth. Here, a bevel guide is used for a precise edge angle.

4 Put a micro-edge on the blade by lifting it slightly so just the tip touches the stone. Draw the blade lightly two or three times along the stone, until a slight burr can be felt along the back of the blade. Turn the blade over, hold it flat (as in step 2) and draw it one time along the stone to remove the burr. Done properly, this will give the chisel a razor-sharp edge.

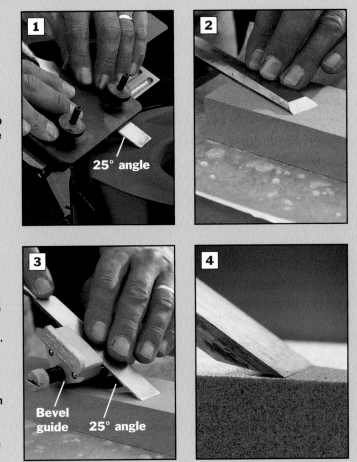

1 — 25° angle

3 — Bevel guide — 25° angle

The right way to cut hinge mortises

Installing hinges (or strike plates) is a frequently encountered task for the handyman, and as often as not we rely on the trial-and-error method—with mixed results. Here's the best way to cut a hinge mortise.

1 Remove the hinge pin (if its removable) and position the hinge leaf or strike plate on the edge of the door or on the door jamb. Tack it into place with screws, then score an outline around the plate with a utility knife. This prevents the wood from splintering past the ends of the mortise.

2 Choose a chisel that's close to the same width as the mortise. With the beveled side of the chisel facing toward the mortise, tap the butt of the chisel handle with a wood or rubber mallet. Cut into the wood to a depth equal to the thickness of the hinge leaf or strike plate. Cut along all sides of four-sided mortises.

3 With the beveled edge of the chisel tip flat against the workpiece, make a series of relief cuts in the waste wood area of the mortise. Space the cuts ⅛ to ¼ in. apart (make closer cuts in harder woods). The cuts should be equal in depth to the finished depth of the mortise.

4 Clean out the waste wood by driving the chisel against the direction of the relief cuts. To avoid digging in too deep, try to keep the beveled edge of the tip flat in the mortise. Scrape the bottom of the mortise smooth. If you need to deepen the mortise, repeat the procedure—don't simply try to make deeper scraping cuts.

Cutting options for making parts

Regardless of what project you're building, there are really only eight different kinds of cuts you'll need to master to make parts (see diagram at right). The two most common cuts are rip cuts and cross cuts. On solid wood, rip cuts follow the long dimension of a board and establish the width of a workpiece. Cross cuts set the length of a workpiece and are made across the grain direction. On plywood and other non-grain specific composite materials like particleboard, ripping and crosscutting really amount to the same thing.

There are three principal angle cuts: bevels, miters and tapers. Bevel cuts may be long-grain or cross-grain, but either way the blade is set to an angle other than square to the board face so the angle occurs through the board's thickness. Miter cuts are cross cuts that form an angle across the board face, but the blade has no bevel angle. Taper cuts follow the long-grain direction like rips cuts do, but the cut forms a gradual angle along the edge of the workpiece. The blade is set at 90°.

Other common cuts include internal cutouts or curved cuts. A few less typical cuts not shown in the diagram include edge-profile cuts, resawing cuts and cuts following a pattern. You'll see examples of these cuts in this chapter as well.

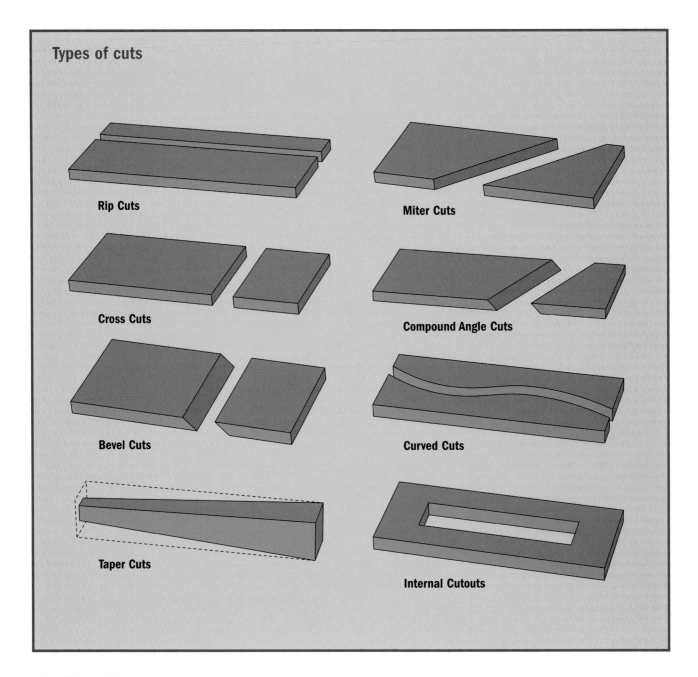

Types of cuts

Rip Cuts

Miter Cuts

Cross Cuts

Compound Angle Cuts

Bevel Cuts

Curved Cuts

Taper Cuts

Internal Cutouts

Tools for cutting parts

A CIRCULAR SAW and straightedge cutting guide can be used for cross cuts, rip cuts, bevel cuts and miter cuts.

THE VERSATILE JIG SAW (also called a saber saw) is capable of making any cut. It excels at cutting curves and making interior cutouts.

A POWER MITER SAW is perfect for making repetitive cross cuts, including mitered or beveled cuts (bevels require a compound miter saw).

A TABLE SAW is the most heavily used tool in most woodshops. It can make just about any straight cut, including bevels and miters.

A ROUTER is used to make dadoes and rabbets as well as edge profiles. With special bits and accessories it can also be used for pattern cutting, circle cutting and many other cutting tasks.

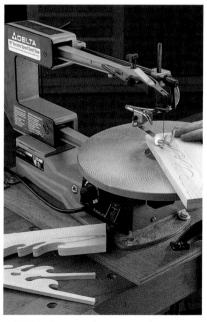

A SCROLL SAW is a favorite tool for cutting intricate curves and patterns. They are not powerful but are relatively easy to manage.

Making rip cuts

Among the tool options for making rip cuts, table saws offer excellent accuracy, repeatablilty and convenience. Good-quality table saws will have an accurate rip fence that, when adjusted parallel with the blade, make rip cutting as easy as locking the fence and pushing the board through the blade. Other power tools like circular saws and band saws can make respectable rip cuts as well, but the table saw is still the first choice for most woodworkers.

Safety first: Although rip cuts are easy to perform on a table saw, it's a dangerous operation without taking a few precautions. First, be sure the rip fence is parallel with the blade. If the fence is skewed toward the blade, it will cause the wood to bind between the blade and fence, which could lead to kickback. If the fence skews away from the blade, wood will tend to

Ripping boards to width should be done after one edge has been squared (see previous section) so a flat even surface can ride against the saw fence or be used to register your straightedge for making rip cuts with hand-held tools.

drift away from the fence during cutting and follow the blade, which leads to inaccurate cuts or possible kickback as well.

It's also critical to have the saw's guard and splitter in place.

These safety devices protect you from cuts, shield you from debris thrown off the blade and keep the wood from closing up behind the blade during the cut and binding it—another typical sce-

How to rip various materials with a table saw

LONG BOARDS: When ripping long boards, tip the back edge of the board up so it is slightly higher than the saw table. Doing this will press the leading edge of the board firmly down on the saw table. Lower the back edge of the board as the cut progresses.

SHEET GOODS: Full sheets of plywood, particleboard and other sheet goods can be ripped effectively on a table saw if you position a sturdy table on the outfeed side of the saw, at or just below the saw table surface. But many woodworkers prefer to cut the sheets down to size with a circular saw or panel-cutting saw first.

How to rip cut with a table saw

1 Start rip cuts with your left foot against the front left corner of the saw base. Feed the workpiece with your right hand, and use your left hand to keep the workpiece snug against the rip fence. Use a pushstick whenever a workpiece requires your hand to be closer than 6 in. to the blade.

2 Continue feeding the workpiece through the blade with your right hand as the end of the board approaches the front edge of the saw table. Switch to a pushstick in your right hand if necessary. Keep your left hand on the infeed side of the blade at all times.

3 When the blade cuts the board in two, push the workpiece past the blade with your right hand until it clears the blade on the outfeed side. Slide the cutoff piece away from the blade with your left hand or a pushstick to prevent it from coming in contact with the blade.

nario that invites kickback.

Safety and cutting performance always improve when you outfit your saw with a clean, sharp blade. Use a pushstick and featherboards whenever possible to keep your hands away from the cutting area (never have your hands closer than about 6 inches from the blade). Workpieces must be held securely against the saw table and rip fence throughout the cut.

Making rip cuts: Follow the three photos and captions above to learn the proper technique for making rip cuts. When you're setting up a cut, be sure to align the rip fence so the blade will cut your workpiece on the waste side of the cutting line. If you split your reference line, you'll end up with a workpiece slightly narrower than what you want, because the blade cuts a kerf that's nearly 1/8 inch wide.

Once you've got the fence locked down and the blade raised about 1/4 to 1/2 inch above the workpiece, position your body so as not to be directly behind the blade in the event the saw throws the workpiece back out of the cut. Feed the workpiece with a steady, smooth motion into the blade, anchoring it against the rip fence with one hand and pushing it through with the other hand or using a push stick.

Once the saw cuts the board in two and both pieces are past the blade, turn off the saw and wait until the blade stops before removing the cut parts. If you are making repetitive cuts, clear off the cut pieces before proceeding with the next cut.

A SINGLE PART

MULTIPLE PARTS

Pushstick

NARROW STRIPS: When rip-cutting a single narrow workpiece from a wider board, the narrow strip should be on the opposite side of the blade from the rip fence (left photo). This keeps the wider portion of the board between the blade and the rip fence to allow more room for your hand or a pushstick. To rip a series of narrow workpieces, set the distance between the blade and the rip fence to match the intended width of the workpieces you need. Use a narrow pushstick to guide the pieces along the rip fence (right photo).

Rip-cutting with a circular saw

A table saw will make rip cuts with greater precision than a circular saw, but a circular saw may be your only option if you need to make rip cuts on a job site or if it's your only power saw. For cutting large sheets goods, a circular saw is sometimes a better choice than a table saw, because it's easier to move a small saw over a large sheet than try to lift and guide an unwieldly and heavy piece of plywood over a table saw.

If all you need to make is a rough rip cut, you can guide a circular saw freehand along your cutting line. Use the notch on the front of the saw base as your guide for aligning the

THE PORTABLE CIRCULAR SAW is a handy tool for ripping sheet goods and larger stock down to a manageable width, but isn't designed to make fine woodworking cuts.

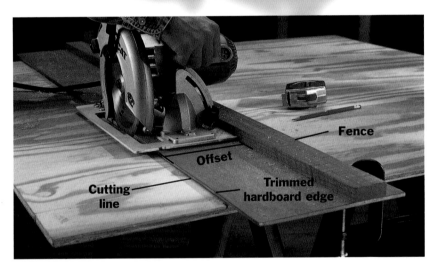

OFFSET CUTTING GUIDES: A long straightedge guide with a built-in offset can be made with two pieces of scrap from your shop. You'll need a strip of hardboard or plywood (1/4 in. works well) that's at least 12 in. wide and preferably 8 ft. long. Tack a piece of straight scrap wood (a 2 × 4 or a narrow strip of 3/4 in. plywood will work) to the hardboard so the scrap is parallel with the hardboard or aligns with one of its edges. Orient the scrap and hardboard so there is an offset that is slightly longer than the distance from the edge of the saw foot to the blade. Then, simply trim off the edge of the hardboard with the saw foot riding against the scrap "fence." Clamp the guide to your workpiece so the trimmed plywood edge aligns with your cutting line.

In the photo: Fence, Offset, Trimmed hardboard edge, Cutting line

STRAIGHTEDGE CUTTING GUIDE: With the help of a good straightedge you can use your circular saw to make rip cuts that are nearly as accurate as those made on a table saw. You can purchase a straightedge, like the extruded aluminum model shown above, or select a piece of stock (a strip of particleboard, for example) that's straight, smooth-edged and even.

ADJUSTABLE RIPPING FENCE: Most circular saws come with an adjustable ripping fence that attaches to the foot of the saw. The fence rides along the edge of the board to guide the saw so it cuts a line parallel to the board edge. These accessories are fine for rip cuts that don't demand a high level of accuracy.

blade. For better accuracy and cleaner cuts, select one of the three guide systems shown on the facing page. With one of these three options, you won't have to steer the saw to follow your line — just hold it against the guide.

A shop-made offset cutting guide is a handy accessory to make for your saw. The trimmed edge provides a blade index that you can align with your reference marks or cutting line on the workpiece. The saw follows the straightedge and the blade tracks the offset edge perfectly. Use the offset guide on workpieces like plywood where there's plenty of bearing surface to clamp to.

Another option is to clamp a straightedge (either a fabricated metal edge or a straight piece of scrap will do) to the workpiece and use it as a saw guide. You'll need to index the guide off the cutting line using the saw base as a reference so the blade follows your cutting line correctly.

For making rip cuts on particularly narrow stock, use an adjustable ripping fence. Most saws come with one of these fences that clamp to the front of the saw base and work like an outrigger. Be sure to tighten the fence securely before cutting, and keep it firmly planted against the workpiece edge as you feed the saw through the cut.

Rip-cutting with a band saw or jig saw

Both band saws and jig saws are capable of making straight rip cuts, although the cut will be smoother with a band saw than a jig saw. To make straight rip cuts with a jig saw, you can guide the saw freehand with relative accuracy, or clamp a straightedge on the workpiece and guide the saw's base against it, as you would with a circular saw. Since jig saw blades are supported only on the end where they fit into the saw's chuck, the blade will tend to drift in and out of square through the thickness of the workpiece. This tendency becomes more pronounced as workpieces get thicker. You'll get the best results by choosing a stout blade and feeding the saw slowly.

Band saw blades are held under tension both above and below the workpiece, so they tend to cut flat and true. Most band saws come with a rip fence, just like a table saw, to make rip cutting easier. You may need to set the fence slightly at an angle to the blade to account for a condition called "blade drift," in order to make accurate rip cuts against the fence.

One advantage to using either of these tools for rip cuts is that you can follow straight, curved or angled lines —or combinations of all three—in the same cut. A table saw only makes straight cuts.

RIP-CUTTING WITH A JIG SAW: While it"s possible to make straight rip cuts by feeding a jig saw freehand along a cutting line, you'll get more accurate results by guiding the saw against a straightedge. Adjust the straightedge before cutting to account for the offset created by the saw's base.

RIP-CUTTING WITH A BAND SAW: Like jig saws, a band saw can make "rip" cuts that generally follow the grain of the wood but aren't necessarily straight or parallel to the edge of the board. You can also make "true" rip cuts that are parallel to the edge using the fence that comes with most band saws. The edges of the cut won't be as smooth as a table saw cut, however.

Joinery:
Casework vs. Furnituremaking

Woodworking joinery falls into two major categories—casework and furnituremaking. Each is defined by its materials, structure and aesthetics. While there is certainly some crossover between the categories, if you're trying to determine which joints to employ for your project, making the casework/furniture distinction is a useful starting point.

Typically, sheet goods are used for casework (boxes and cabinets). Butt joints reinforced with screws, biscuits, dowels, splines or pocket screws are common, although rabbet and dado joints come in handy as well. A furnituremaker works mostly in hardwood with structures that depend on small, fitted joints, like dovetails, mortises and half-laps that need to be both strong and pleasing to the eye.

Screwed joint

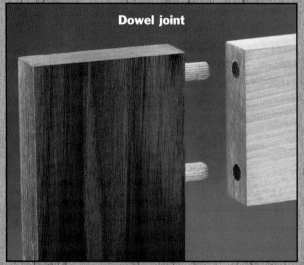
Dowel joint

Biscuit joint

Rabbet joint

Dado joint

Casework Joints

Tongue & groove joint

Mortise & tenon joint

Lap joint

Finger joint

Half-blind dovetail joint

Dovetail joint

Furnituremaking Joints

Making simple butt joints

Whenever two pieces of wood are joined together with flat surfaces, the union forms a butt joint. The usual butt joints consist of the end of one board joined to a face or edge of another board. Edge to edge butt joints are also common, especially if you're gluing up several boards to make a wide panel. Technically, joining two faces together also makes a butt joint, such as when you're creating a thick blank to use as a table leg or for turning on a lathe. With a spline or biscuit installed between the boards, you can even join the ends of two boards together, but it makes an extremely weak connection.

The strongest butt joint styles are face-to-face, face-to-edge or edge-to-edge configurations. All three combinations join long grain surfaces together. Edge grain and face grain absorb glue better than end grain, and the union of long grain surfaces means both parts of the joint will expand and contract in better harmony with one another.

Butt joints are quick and easy to make, which is their principal advantage in woodworking applications. But the downside to these joints is that without interlocking parts, they don't offer the same resistance to shearing, pulling or twisting forces as other joints do. Glue will improve joint strength, of course, but it's also important to reinforce the joint with other fasteners like screws, nails, biscuits or dowels. These fasteners form a

A BUTT JOINT can be used in just about any woodworking situation. If it will undergo stress or pressure, it's a good idea to reinforce the glued butt joint with a fastener, such as a screw.

bridge between the two parts that makes the connection significantly stronger, particularly when one member of the joint has end grain, like the photo shown above.

Another preemptive measure for ensuring good butt joint strength is to flatten the joint surfaces on a joiner or with a sharp hand plane before gluing them together. Wood glue forms bonds that are even stronger than the wood fibers it connects, but it doesn't fill gaps well, and it loses connective strength on irregular or rough surfaces.

Reinforcement options

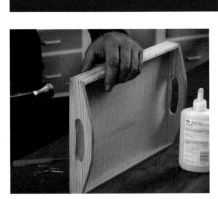

FINISH NAILS are easy fasteners to use for reinforcing butt joints. Drill a pilot hole for each nail before driving it. Set the nail head below the wood surface with a correctly-sized nail set.

DIAGONAL GLUE BLOCKS can be glued beneath a butt joint for additional support. Use them with or without additional fasteners in the joint. The blocks are attached with glue only.

WOOD SCREWS are popular fasteners for reinforcing butt joints. They should be driven into counterbored or countersunk pilot holes.

Countersinking & counterboring

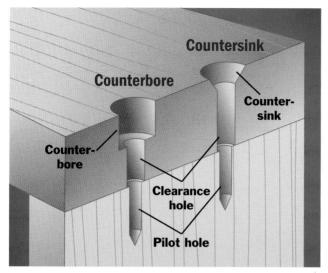

A COUNTERBORE HOLE has a cylindrical top intended to accept a wood screw plug; a countersink hole has a beveled top just deeply enough for the screw head to be driven below the wood surface, creating a small recess to be filled with wood putty.

The 2/3 rule

Follow the two-thirds rule: Screws should be driven through the thinner workpiece first, whenever possible. The lower two-thirds of the screw should end up in the lower board after the screw has been driven.

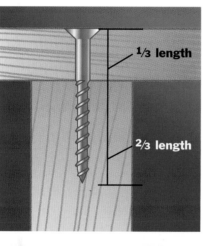

1/3 length

2/3 length

A COUNTERBORE BIT can drill a pilot hole, shank hole and counterbore hole all at the same time.

A COUNTERSINK BIT reams out the top of a pilot hole with a bevel that allows the screw head to be recessed.

Plugging a counterbore

1 Use a counterbore bit to counterbore the pilot hole for the screw (3/8 in. is the standard counterbore diameter).

2 Drive the screw, then apply glue to the end of a wood plug and insert it into the counterbore hole.

Flush-cutting saw

3 Trim the plug with a chisel, flush-cut saw or rasp, then sand the plug until it's even with the wood surface.

Reinforcing joints with biscuits

One way to reinforce butt joints is to bridge the parts with football-shaped disks made of compressed wood. The disks are called biscuits, and they fit into a pair of curved slots cut by a single-purpose tool called a biscuit joiner (see facing page). Biscuits are made in several standard sizes: #0, which is $\frac{3}{8}$ in. × $1\frac{1}{4}$ in.; #10, which is $\frac{3}{4}$ in. × $2\frac{1}{8}$ in.; and #20, which is 1 in. × $2\frac{3}{8}$ in.). A few manufacturers also make "micro" biscuits for use in making picture frames or small face frames for cabinetry. A special joiner installs this size biscuit.

When biscuits come into contact with wet glue, the moisture expands them into the slots, tightening the joint. There are several benefits to employing biscuits in butt joints. First, the biscuit helps keep the joint parts aligned so they're easier to clamp. Second, the biscuit adds mechanical strength to the joint by turning a glue-only union into an interlocking connection. Biscuits also add more surface area to the joint than just the narrow workpiece edges. The larger the surface area, the more room there is for glue, which improves its adhesive strength.

FOOTBALL-SHAPED BISCUITS are a good way to improve the alignment and strength of ordinary butt joints when screws or nails aren't feasible. The tool used for cutting a pair of curved slots in the joint parts is called a biscuit joiner. When the slots are cut, the biscuit fits midway between the two joint parts forming a wooden "bridge". It turns an adhesive-only union into a mechanical one.

How to edge-glue a panel with biscuits

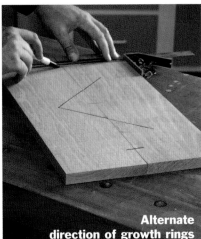

Alternate direction of growth rings

1 Arrange the jointed boards together to get the most pleasing match of the different grain patterns. This can take some trial and error. Tip: alternate the direction of the growth rings at the ends of the boards. This helps keep the panel from cupping. Once you've got all the boards arranged to your satisfaction, draw a "V" across all joints in the panel. Use the legs of the "V" to maintain your alignment as you glue-up the panel.

2 Once the boards are laid out and marked, place them in position and mark the biscuit locations. Use a square to mark all mating edges to ensure that the slots align. Biscuits should be spaced about 8 to 10 in. apart, with a biscuit about 2 in. in from each end. After marking biscuit locations, cut the slots by aligning your marks with the permanent mark on the biscuit joiner.

3 Apply glue to one edge of each board to be joined, then squeeze glue into the slots. Commercial glue applicators that reach into the slots are available, or you can simply squeeze the glue in with a regular glue bottle and spread the glue with a popsicle stick. Add the biscuits to the slots on one board. If edge-gluing more than one board at a time, apply the glue and insert the biscuits in every board. Now you're ready to clamp the assembly.

How a biscuit joiner works

Standard biscuit sizes
(shown actual size)

A BISCUIT JOINER consists of a small circular saw blade (about 4 in. dia.) mounted at a right angle to the motor shaft at the front of the tool. The blade is enclosed in a spring-loaded housing; plunging the tool into the workpiece exposes a portion of the blade, which cuts a semicircular slot in each of the mating wood pieces. Into each pair of slots, you glue a flat, football-shaped biscuit. The biscuit swells as the glue hardens, creating a tight, secure joint.

Reference marks on the tool face and an adjustable fence enable you to accurately locate the biscuit slots in mating surfaces.

Most biscuit joiners have a three-position depth of cut adjustment that enables you to cut slots to the correct depth and length for standard-size biscuits. After cutting matching slots in the pieces to be joined, you glue the slightly undersized biscuits into the slots.

How to reinforce a right-angle butt joint with biscuits

1 Lay out the position of the two mating parts using a square (note whether you're marking the top or bottom of the workpiece). Set the mating workpiece in position against the mark. Draw a perpendicular reference line on both workpieces at each biscuit location. With the workpieces clamped together and secured to your worksurface, align biscuit joiner with the reference lines and cut the slots in one workpiece.

2 With the workpieces still clamped together, cut matching slots in the other workpiece, using the reference lines to align the biscuit joiner.

3 With all the slots cut, you're ready for assembly. Apply glue in the biscuit slots and on the mating surfaces. Insert all the biscuits into the slots in one workpiece, then slip the mating workpiece into position so the parts butt together cleanly. Clamp the parts together, check for square and adjust the clamps as necessary to square up the joints.

Reinforcing joints with dowels

Ancient Egyptians were the first woodworkers to use primitive dowels for strengthening joints, and we've used them ever since. Dowels provide the same three advantages as biscuits: They aid in joint alignment, form an interlocking connection and add some degree of glue surface area. If you

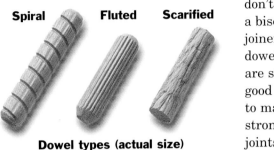

Spiral   **Fluted**   **Scarified**

Dowel types (actual size)

don't own a biscuit joiner, dowels are still a good way to make stronger joints, and

A PAIR OF DOWELS installed across a butt joint turn an otherwise weak connection between long grain and end grain into a durable, long-lasting joint. Aside from strength, dowels aid in aligning the joint parts and disappear when the joint is clamped together.

How to make a dowel joint with a doweling jig

1 To lay out the dowel joints, butt the two mating parts together, making sure the mating surfaces are flush. Mark the dowel hole locations by drawing a single line across the joint for each dowel. For best results, use at least two evenly spaced dowels at each joint.

Depth stop

2 Slip the doweling jig over each mating edge. Align the mark on the jig corresponding to the diameter of the dowel hole with each location line you drew on the workpiece. Drill a dowel hole the same diameter as the dowel at each mark— use a depth stop to keep the holes of uniform depth (masking tape will suffice if you don't have a depth stop collar).

3 After drilling all the holes, apply a dab of glue into each hole. Also apply glue to the mating wood surfaces. Slide the dowels into the holes to make the joint.

4 Create all the joints, then clamp the assembly together with pipe clamps or bar clamps. Be sure to use a clamp pad between the wood and the clamp jaws so the jaws don't mar the wood. Do not overtighten the clamps.

they're relatively easy to install.

The tricky part to building dowel joints is getting the dowel holes drilled straight and in perfect alignment on both sides of the joint. If the holes are at all crooked or misaligned, the joint won't fit together properly.

For best results, buy an adjustable doweling jig like the one shown at right. It will allow you to drill parallel, straight holes in a range of stock thicknesses. For situations when you can't clamp the doweling jig to each half of the joint, drill holes into one member, then insert metal dowel points into the dowel holes (see below right). They'll mark the exact locations for drilling the other holes.

Drilling guides for dowel joints

A DOWELING JIG functions as a drilling guide for boring straight, parallel dowel holes. The steel center of the jig is milled with holes of various drill bit diameters, and you align the centers of the dowel holes using index marks on the side of the jig. The jig fits over the workpiece and clamps in place for quick and easy drilling operations.

Through dowels

Through-dowel joints are those with the end of the dowel left exposed. In this setup, it passes through one member of the joint and sometimes both. Through dowels are a good way to build butt joints without metal fasteners. You can also use dowels to pin mortise and tenon joints together (see page 78). The way to install the dowels is to cut them ¼ to ½ in. longer than necesssary and sand one end to a slight taper. Squeeze a small amount of glue into the dowel hole so it dribbles down the side, and smear an even coating on the dowel. Use a wooden mallet to gently tap the tapered end into the hole until the dowel seats at the bottom. Be careful not to split or crush it when driving it in. Then saw it flush and sand smooth.

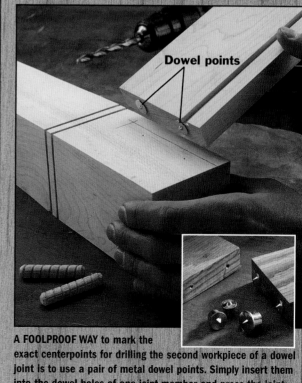

Dowel points

A FOOLPROOF WAY to mark the exact centerpoints for drilling the second workpiece of a dowel joint is to use a pair of metal dowel points. Simply insert them into the dowel holes of one joint member and press the joint together. Sharp spurs mark the second joint part precisely.

Dado and rabbet joints

Joints with dadoes and rabbets form strong, interlocking connections. They're commonly used for building bookshelves, drawers and other casework. Dadoes are square grooves cut across the grain of a workpiece, usually about 1/3 to halfway through the workpiece thickness. A dado can be cut with either a router and straight bit or using a table saw with a dado blade set. When a dado follows the grain direction instead of crossing it, the cut technically is called a groove or plough, although long-grain grooves are often called dadoes as well.

A rabbet is a stepped cut that follows the edge or end of a workpiece, forming an offset tongue. Depending on the joint style, this tongue sometimes fits completely over the end of its mating part (top left photo, next page) or into a dado (top right photo, next page). Rabbets can be cut with a router guided against a straightedge using a straight bit bit or freehand with a piloted rabbeting bit. You can also cut rabbets on a router table with a straight bit and adjustable fence.

Dado joints: Dado joints are good choices when you want to install shelving into a cabinet. Fitting the entire end of a shelf into a dado in the cabinet wall provides excellent resistance to the shearing

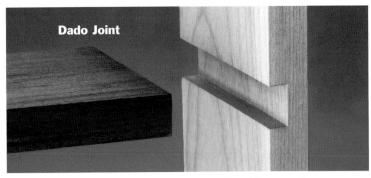

Dado Joint

DADO & RABBET JOINTS interlock to add strength and increase glue surface. There are many variations of the joint, including the dado joint, (above) the rabbet joint (next page, top left) and the combination dado/rabbet joint (next page, top right).

forces that take effect when the shelf is loaded with books or other weight. Here, even if the glue fails to hold, the shelf usually won't give way. Cut the dado width carefully so the mating workpiece slips in snugly for a seamless fit.

Rabbet joints: Conventional, overlapping rabbet joints are stronger options for building a box or drawer than simple butt joints, and the rabbet tongue adds more surface area for glue. Drive nails or screws through the tongue to lock these joints.

Dado/rabbet joints: A hybrid of both dado joints and rabbet joints, here the rabbet tongue fits into a dado cut about halfway through the thick-

How to make dado/rabbet joints

CUT THE DADOES FIRST at the joint locations, using a straight router bit or a table saw and dado-blade set. Measure the dadoes and use the measurements as a guide for cutting rabbets with lips that fit exactly into the dadoes (in the photo above, a guide block is clamped to the router base and the rabbet cut is made with a straight bit). Make sure the rabbeted ends will not extend more than halfway into the dadoed board.

TEST-FIT THE JOINT and adjust the thickness of the rabbet ledge by trimming, if needed. Apply glue to both surfaces, then assemble and clamp the joint.

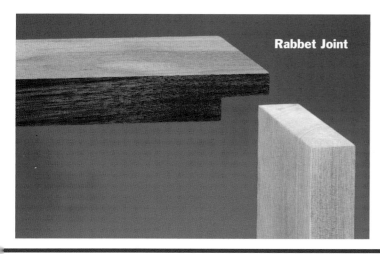

Rabbet Joint

Dado/Rabbet Joint

ness of the mating joint part. Dado/rabbet joints are another option for installing shelving in a case or cabinet. The shear strength isn't as great as a dado joint, but it's typically more than enough to bear substantial load.

Dado/rabbet joints are good options if you don't own a dado blade set for your table saw. For typical 1x stock, just use a 3/8-in. straight bit in your router to cut the dado. Make the rabbet using whatever tooling method you prefer. If you cut the rabbet carefully, the tongue will conceal the dado perfectly when the joint is assembled.

Options for cutting dadoes with a router

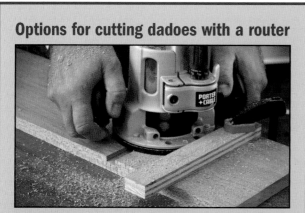

STRAIGHT BIT AND CUTTING GUIDE. A router guide is needed to make a dado or plough with a straight router bit. The simplest guide is a plain, straight board clamped to the workpiece the correct distance from the cutting line.

ROUTER EDGE GUIDE. For rough work, sliding attachments that fit onto the router base may be used as a guide. Select a bit with a diameter equal to the desired width of the dado. Make the cut in multiple passes of increasing depth, moving the router left to right.

Options for cutting rabbets with a router

USE A PILOTED RABBET BIT to cut rabbets on the insides of frames or on the outer edges of any workpieces. Make several passes of increasing depth with the router, then square the rabbet corners with a chisel. When profiling an outside edge, clamp scrap blocks at the ends of the workpiece.

USE A ROUTER TABLE fitted with a wide straight bit to cut rabbets into a board edge. Create a partial recess for the bit by opening the fence on your router table. Use a featherboard to hold the workpiece securely against the fence. Set the bit height to the rabbet depth and adjust the fences to the width of the cut.

Router table fence

Featherboard

Anatomy of a stacked dado blade set

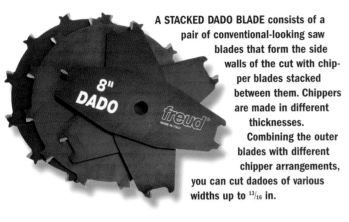

A STACKED DADO BLADE consists of a pair of conventional-looking saw blades that form the side walls of the cut with chipper blades stacked between them. Chippers are made in different thicknesses.

Combining the outer blades with different chipper arrangements, you can cut dadoes of various widths up to $^{13}/_{16}$ in.

A WIDE OPENING THROATPLATE is a necessity when using a stacked dado blade set to provide safe blade clearance. Most table saw manufacturers offer these throatplates as accessories, or you can make a wooden one and cut the dado opening.

USING A DADO SET FOR JOINERY is different than cutting with a conventional saw blade, because the dado doesn't cut all the way through the workpiece. Instead, it works more like a router bit, cutting a channel with both a specific width and height. Make test cuts on scrap first to ensure that you've got the correct dado dimensions you need. When making dado cuts, feed workpieces slowly. The saw must work harder to cut a dado, and you'll feel greater resistance when pushing through the cut. Hold workpieces firmly against the saw table and rip fence. For even better safety, install featherboards and hold-downs (see above, right).

Options for cutting rabbets on a table saw

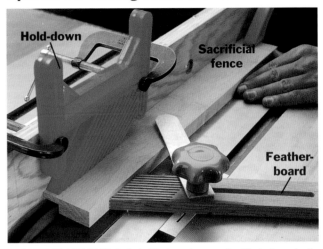

RABBETS IN ONE PASS. A dado blade set can cut rabbets in a single pass safely, provided the depth of cut isn't greater than about $^{1}/_{2}$ in. Set up the dado blade wider than you need, and install a sacrificial fence to your rip fence. Raise the blade into the wooden fence to create a relief area, then adjust the fence and blade height until the amount of blade exposure matches the rabbet dimensions you need. Use featherboards and hold-downs to secure the workpiece.

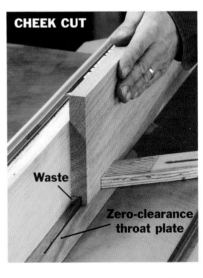

RABBETS IN TWO PASSES. You can also make rabbets with a standard saw blade, but it takes two set-ups and passes to cut the joint. For rabbets that follow the edge of a workpiece, make the cheek cut by setting the rip fence so the blade will cut on the waste side of the cheek. It's a good idea to install a zero-clearance throatplate in the saw before making the second cut. Once the cheek cut has been made, reset the rip fence so you can lay the workpiece flat for cutting the shoulder. Adjust the blade height, if necessary. Orient the cut so the thin stick of waste material can fall away from the blade when it's cut free. Don't trap this stick between the rip fence and blade, or it could catch on the blade and cause kickback. On narrow workpieces, use a push block to keep your hands clear.

TONGUE-AND-GROOVE JOINTS are easy to build and create a sturdy mechanical connection between two workpieces. The tongue provides more surface area for glue than a flat edge would, and the centered groove hides it when the joint is assembled. Generally, these joints are proportioned so the tongue thickness is one-third the thickness of the grooved workpiece. For joining common 1x materials, make the tongue 1/2 in. long.

Tongue-&-Groove Joints

If you've ever installed hardwood flooring, you know that the floorboards are connected by a network of tongue-and-groove joints. These joints combine a centered tongue on one workpiece that fits into a matching groove on the other workpiece, forming a strong mechanical union. In woodworking applications, tongue-and-groove joints are commonly used to make dry-fitted back panels for early American or country-styled cabinets. They're an excellent choice for making plywood shelving with a solid-wood edge. You can even use them for connecting the rails and stiles on frame-and-panel cabinet doors. Make these versatile joints with a table saw and dado blade or with a router and straight bits.

How to make a tongue-and-groove joint

1 Use a table saw outfitted with a dado blade or a router table and straight bit to cut the groove first. One way to ensure the groove is centered is to flip the workpiece end-for-end after cutting and make a second pass. It will adjust for any misalignment.

2 To cut the tongue, reset the saw so the dado blade is partially buried in a sacrificial fence. Or set up your router table similarly with the bit partially concealed by the fence. Set up the blade to cut one side of the tongue.

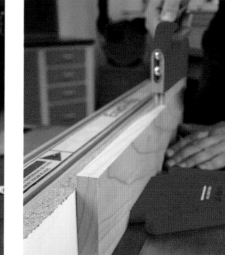

3 Flip the workpiece and remove the waste on the other side of the tongue without changing the saw or router table set-up. If the tongue is too thick, move the fence slightly away from the blade and make two more passes.

4 Spread wood glue over the tongue and into the groove, then fit the joint together. The tongue should seat fully in the groove.

Cutting dovetail joints by hand

The hand-cut dovetail joint is perhaps the most famous, and intimidating, woodworking joint. As with any other woodworking skill, mastering them is mostly a matter of practice. But with these joints, visualization also helps. For many first-timers, the biggest hurdle to get past is simply studying the way dovetail joints fit together until they make sense.

Dovetail joints require a fair amount of planning and a good layout drawing. As you lay out the joint, keep a few basic principles in mind: The dovetail joint has two parts: the pin and the tail—always begin making dovetails by cutting the pins first. For joint strength and integrity, the joint should begin and end with a half-pin. The angle of the pin should not be steeper than 80° (a 1:6 ratio of slope to pin depth). The pin-and-tail spacing doesn't need to be exact: the tails can be up to three times as wide as the pins. In fact, the pin and tail sizes can even vary within a joint, which creates an interesting look that's unique to hand-cut dovetails.

DOVETAIL JOINT

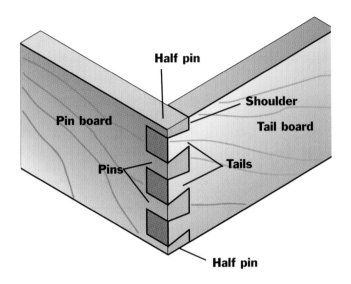

How to make hand-cut dovetail joints

1 Draw the dovetail pin angle and use it to set the angle on a sliding T-bevel that you can use to mark the pins on the ends of the pin boards. Make a scale drawing of a dovetail pin and use it to set a sliding T-bevel for marking the layout lines for the pins. A standard angle is 80°, which equals a 1:6 ratio of slope to pin depth.

2 After edge-gluing and cutting the workpieces to size, begin work by laying out the pins. Use the drawing labeled "Pin/tail layout" to lay out the pins on the end of the board with a pencil and the adjustable square.

OPTION: Use a flanged dovetail layout jig to mark the dovetail pins. These inexpensive little devices can be found in most woodworking stores and catalogs. They're easy to use and yield consistent results. The only real drawback to these jigs is that they're not adjustable, and dovetails aren't a one-size-fits-all joint.

3 Next, mark the pin length with a marking gauge. This line lets you know how deep to cut, so scribe it well.

4 Finally, transfer the lines drawn on the end of the board to both faces of the board with a try square or combination square. These lines are your guides to make sure your cuts are straight.

5 Use a tenon saw, also called a dovetail saw, to cut the shoulders of the pins. Split the lines with the saw, favoring the waste side. Cut down to the scribed lines, but do not cut below the lines or the kerf cut will show when the joint is assembled.

Continued next page

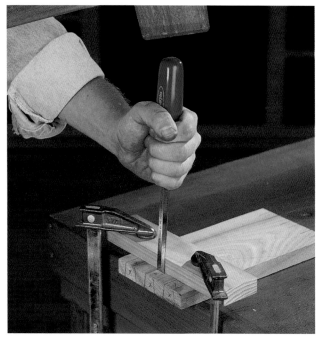

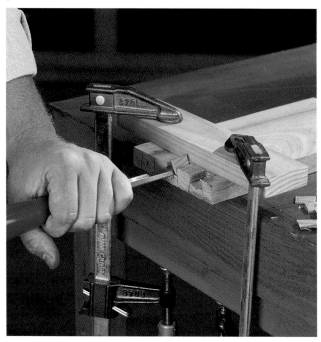

6 Score along the scribed baseline with a chisel to prevent tearout when you remove the waste around the pins. To ensure a straight scored line, clamp a block of wood next to the scribed line and use it as a chisel guide.

7 Carefully drive the chisel into the end-grain of the waste area between the pins so the waste wood will break off cleanly at the chisel cut along the baseline.

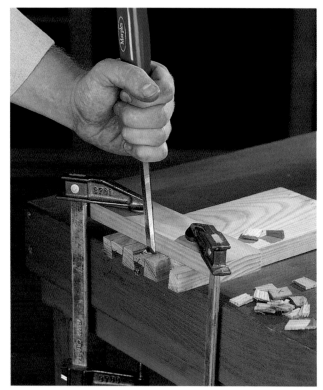

8 Remove waste in half the area, then flip the board over and continue removing waste from the other side. The beveled face of the chisel should face toward the ends of the dovetails, with the flat face contacting the guide board. When all the waste is removed, clean up the cuts carefully with a smoothing file.

9 Once the pins are cut, lay out the tails by laying the pin board on the face of the tail board and marking the pin profiles. Use a sharp pencil so the marks are true. Also use a marking gauge to scribe a line on the face of the board, establishing the bottom line for the tails. Make sure the pin board and tail board are flush at the edges before making any marks.

10 Draw straight cutting lines across the end of the tail board, using a combination square or try square. The cutting lines should align with the outline marks transcribed from the pin board.

11 Clamp the board in a vise and use a dovetail saw to make the cuts down to the scribed line. Remove the waste from between the tails with a sharp chisel, the same way you removed the waste from the pin boards. Make the shoulders of the tail board by sawing along the base line to the first tail on each end.

12 Prepare for glue-up by cutting wood cauls the width of the assembly and lining the cauls with masking tape. Apply glue to the pins and the inside edges of the tails, then assemble the joints. The joint should be tight enough that it must be tapped together with a mallet. Use a block of wood between the mallet and the workpiece to keep from damaging the joints or the workpiece. Offset the cauls from the dovetail joints and clamp them (offsetting allows the joint to close if it's cut slightly deep, so the ends of the pins protruding beyond the outer surfaces of the tailboard don't interfere with the clamp). Sand or file any long pins flush with the tail board where they can be sanded or filed down.

Cutting finger joints with a jig

Finger joints (sometimes called *box joints*) typically are made on a table saw with a dado-blade set and a jig—an auxiliary board screwed or clamped to the miter gauge. When joining parts of equal thickness, a finger joint is a good choice because it's strong and effective. Like a dovetail, the finger joint is visible after it's assembled—a plus if you like to show off your handiwork (and what woodworker doesn't?). Unlike dovetail pins, finger joint pins are straight, so it's an easier joint to make than a dovetail, although it's not as strong.

To make accurate box joints, first rip-cut and cross-cut the parts to size. Cut some test slots in waste pieces with the dado blade set and check the fit of an actual workpiece in the slot. The workpiece should fit snugly without having to pound it in.

FINGER JOINT

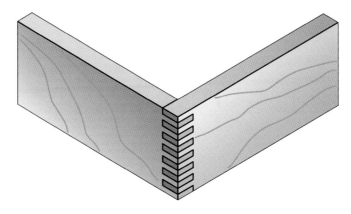

ALSO KNOWN AS BOX JOINTS, finger joints are a good choice for joining two workpieces that are the same thickness. The mating boards in the joint are identical, except that the notches are offset the thickness of one notch on one of the boards. A table saw with a jig can be used for cutting finger joints. You can also use a router (you can buy specialty finger-joint shapers) or a radial arm saw with the blade spinning on a horizontal plane.

How to make a finger joint on the table saw

1 Install a dado-blade set and throat plate in your table saw. Set the cutting width of the dado-set to equal the thickness of the finger pins to be cut. Raise the blade set to cut the full depth of the pins. Clamp an auxiliary fence board to your table saw miter gauge. The board should be about 6 in. wide and at least 18 in. long. Make a pass of the auxiliary fence over the blade, then cut a strip of hardwood to use as a pin to fit in the slot, and glue it into the fence slot.

2 Reset the auxiliary fence by moving it a distance equal to the thickness of one pin to the outside edge of the blade set. Reclamp or screw the fence to the miter gauge.

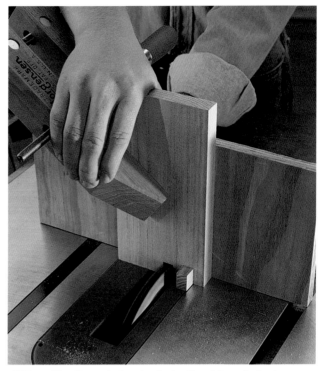

3 With the pin spacer inserted in the fence slot and the fence in position, butt the first workpiece against the strip and make the first pass. You can hold the workpiece in place by hand or clamp it to make the cut. After the workpiece and fence clear the blade, shut off the saw and back the workpiece off.

4 Reposition the workpiece by placing the slot you just cut over the pin space, then make the next cut. Continue in this manner until all the joints in that board are cut. Flip the board end-for-end and cut the fingers on the other end of the board the same way.

5 To cut the joints in the mating boards, fit the last notch you cut in the first piece over the pin, then butt the mating piece against the first piece, creating a one-notch offset. Make the first pass on the mating piece. Now remove the first piece, butt the notch in the mating piece against the pin and make the second pass. Continue until all the joints are cut in one end, then flip the board end-for-end and repeat.

6 When all the joints are cut, the pieces are ready for assembly. Glue the joints and clamp them together with wood cauls offset from the joints to allow the joints to close.

Tenon

Mortise

THE MORTISE-AND-TENON is one of the simplest and strongest wood joints. It's comprised of a narrow tenon carved in the end of one mating workpiece, which fits into a mortise hole in the other mating workpiece. The joint can simply be glued, or you can reinforce it with dowels or wedges.

MORTISE-AND-TENON JOINT

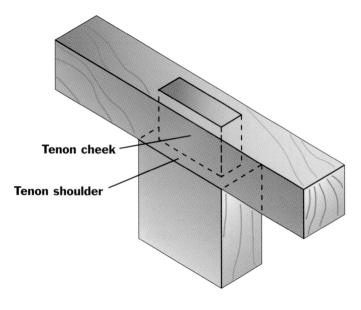

Tenon cheek

Tenon shoulder

Making mortise-and-tenon joints

The mortise-and-tenon joint is one of the strongest joint types for one simple reason: the fastener (the tenon) is actually part of the workpiece. In addition to their great strength, mortise-and-tenon joints are exceptionally versatile. Because you cut the parts of the joint yourself, you can give them just about any size or configuration you want. You can also reinforce them in any of a number of ways (if you want to reinforce them). Throughout this book, you'll find many variations of the basic mortise-and-tenon joint.

Cutting mortises

When making a mortise-and-tenon joint, it's best to begin by cutting the mortises first (after the workpieces are cut to size). In general, it's much easier to cut the tenon portion to fit the mortise— the range of thicknesses for cutting mortises is limited by the thickness of the workpiece and the diameters of the drill bits or router bits in your shop.

The most common method for cutting mortises is to use a drill or drill press to remove most of the waste in the mortise, then square the edges with a wood chisel. For shallow mortises, however, you can also use a router and straight bit (a plunge router is the better choice for this cut). If you expect to do a lot of mortising, look into buying a mortising attachment for your drill press. These attachments feature bit-type cutters housed in a sharpened sleeve that actually performs a chiseling action as you lower the spinning bit into the workpiece.

In general, you don't want to cut a mortise that's more than half the thickness of the workpiece. There should be at least 3/8 in. of wood between the edges of the mortise and the edge of the workpiece (except for mortises that begin at the top or bottom of a workpiece).

The best way to get consistent mortises is to perform each step in the operation on all workpieces before changing the tool set-up. And as with most joinery operations, make a test piece and check accuracy and dimensions before cutting actual workpieces.

How to cut a mortise by drilling and chiseling

1 In your drill press, install a brad-point bit or Forstner bit with a diameter equal to the planned thickness of the mortise. Set the depth stop on the drill press to equal the depth of the mortise. Align the bit with the layout lines at one end of the mortise. To keep the bit aligned throughout, clamp a fence to the drill press table behind the workpiece. Bore one hole at a time. Once a hole is bored, move the workpiece so the next hole will be next to, or slightly overlapping, the first hole. Continue drilling until you reach the other end of the outline. Clamp the workpiece to the drill press table before drilling each hole.

2 Use sharp wood chisels to remove the remaining waste wood and clean the mortise walls. To avoid splitting the wood, start with a narrow chisel, equal to the width of the mortise, and square one end of the mortise. Keep the flat face of the chisel against the mortise wall as you work. Then use a wider chisel to clean out the length of the mortise. Let the chisel enter the mortise at an angle to help you control the cut, paring away the waste as you work. Finish the cut by chiseling straight up and down to clean the walls all the way to the mortise floor, or bottom. For square tenons, square off the ends of the mortises with a chisel. Some woodworkers prefer to round-over the ends of the tenons to fit the mortises.

How to cut mortises with a plunge router

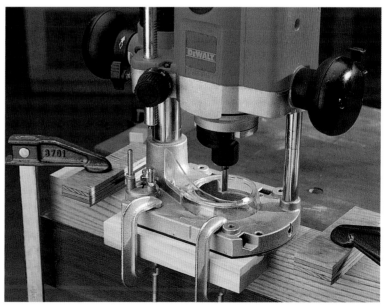

1 Lay out an outline for the mortise on the workpiece using a pencil and combination square. If you need to make mulitple mortises the same width and in alignment, use a marking gauge.

2 In your plunge router, install a straight bit with a diameter equal to the width of the mortise. Clamp a stop block guide to the router base so the bit aligns with the mortise outline. Set the cutting depth to the depth of the mortise. With the workpiece secured, plunge the bit into the wood and make the mortise cut.

Cutting tenons with a tenoning jig

The safest way to cut tenons on a table saw is with a tenoning jig. Variations on the jig abound. Some slide along the top of the saw fence or straddle it while others have a bar that fits into the miter slot. But the guiding principle should be the same for any jig: a safe tenoning jig should support the workpiece on one face and from behind, and act as a cradle to keep the workpiece secure as it passes through the saw blade. In addition, the jig should provide a means to clamp the workpiece so it resists the tendency to ride up over the blade or wander away from the fence. Clamping becomes more crucial the longer a tenon gets because more stock is being removed in a single pass, creating greater resistance on the blade.

The jig we show here can be made from two pieces of scrap stock screwed together at a right angle. It rides on top of the saw fence, which allows you to keep your hands at a safe distance from the blade and also provides additional vertical support for tall workpieces such as table aprons or face frame stiles. A contoured handle is cut at the rear of the jig for better gripping.

How to cut tenons with a tenoning jig

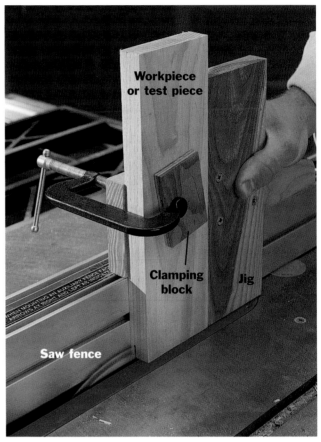

Workpiece or test piece

Clamping block

Jig

Saw fence

1 Make the cheek cuts first (parallel to the wood grain). Clamp the workpiece to the jig so it's snug against the face of the vertical support and the front edge of the horizontal support, resting flat on the saw table. Set the saw fence so the distance to the opposite face of the blade equals the amount of waste being removed, and raise the blade to equal the depth of the tenon. Rest the jig on the fence and feed the workpiece through the blade to make the cut. Flip the workpiece, reclamp, and make the cheek cut on the other face (for centered tenons). Always make cuts on a test piece first, and check the dimensions for accuracy.

This shop-made tenoning jig rides on the saw fence, giving support to workpieces set on-end as they pass through the blade. The vertical member extends down to the saw table and serves to square the workpiece to the blade and to support it from the rear. It's very important that the distance from the bottom of the horizontal member to the bottom of the vertical member be exactly the same as the height of your table saw fence.

Tenoning jig (for use with table saw)

Clamping area

Five wood screws in a cross pattern can be withdrawn to adjust the jig to fit a taller or shorter fence

Distance equals height of saw fence

Overall Size: 12 in. × 12 in.

Vertical member

Base rides on saw table

Handle

Horizontal member

Bottom of horizontal member rides on saw fence

2 For notched tenons that don't run the full width of the workpiece, make additional cheek cuts on the short edges of the workpiece. Clamp the workpiece at a right angle to the jig, with the edge flat against the horizontal member and the face of the workpiece pressed against the front edge of the vertical member. Reset the saw fence if the amount of waste being removed is different than with the first cheek cuts. Make sure that everything is held securely in place, and guide the jig and workpiece through the blade. Flip and reclamp the workpiece to cut the other short cheek.

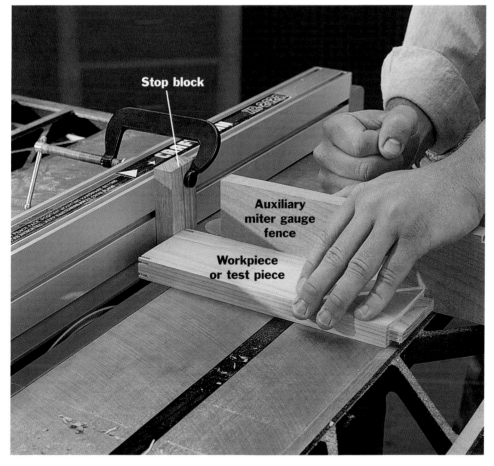

Stop block

Auxiliary miter gauge fence

Workpiece or test piece

3 Make the shoulder cuts (across the grain of the workpiece) using a miter gauge as a guide. For stability, we attached an auxiliary wood fence to the miter gauge. Also clamp a stop block to the table saw fence for use as an alignment guide and to keep the workpiece from binding against the fence and allows the waste to fall away freely rather than getting trapped between the fence. Adjust the fence so the workpiece, when butted against the block, can slide forward on the miter gauge and meet the blade at the base of the tenon cheek. Raise the blade above the table high enough to cut the shoulders without scoring the tenon. Cut the shoulders on each face, then reset the blade height if necessary, and cut shoulders on the ends of the tenon.

Pinning mortise-and-tenon joints

Mortise-and-tenon joints are inherently strong, but for a little extra reinforcement they can be pinned with through dowels. A pinned mortise-and-tenon joint is ideal for high-stress joints, like those found where vertical and horizontal furniture members are joined.

There are two basic methods for constructing a pinned (sometimes called *pegged*) mortise-and-tenon joint. One is to bore a hole through the tenon and another through the mortise before the joint is assembled. If you offset these holes slightly, the joint will be drawn together tightly when the dowel is driven through it. A more common method is simply to drill a dowel hole through the joint after it is glued and assembled, as shown here. This type of pinning doesn't contribute greatly to the strength of the joint, but it does provide a valuable back-up in the event that the glue joint fails.

The exposed ends of dowels provide a nice decorative detail, especially when they're oriented so the grain runs in the opposite direction of the board the dowel is set into.

How to make pinned mortise-and-tenon joints

1 Cut the mortises and tenons, then glue and clamp the joint. Let the glue set up, then lay out the location of the pins with a pencil and combination square. Use at least two evenly spaced pins for each joint, making sure the guide holes are at least ⅜ in. from the edges of the boards.

Pinned mortise and tenon joint illustration

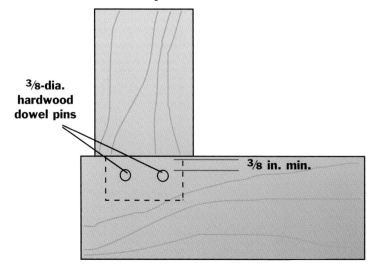

⅜-dia. hardwood dowel pins

⅜ in. min.

2 Punch a small starter hole at the centerpoint of each pin hole. If your project is a manageable size, use your drill press to drill the holes, as we did in the photo above. Using a brad-point bit will ensure that the hole starts precisely in the centerpoint. Drill the holes all the way through the tenon and into the other side of the mortise. Use a bit stop if your plan calls for stopped pins. If you're creating through-pin joints, drill all the way through the joint and into a piece of scrap.

3 Cut the pins from hardwood dowels, normally of the same species as the workpieces. Tip: For a decorative touch, use dowels made of wood with a naturally contrasting wood tone (for example, maple pins driven into walnut workpieces). Taper the lead tip of the dowel slightly so it will enter the hole more easily. Squeeze a little glue into each hole, then tap the dowel pins home with a wood mallet. Stop tapping when the dowel seats at the bottom of the hole.

4 Trim the dowels flush with the leg surface—here we use a flexible, fine-tooth Japanese-style saw. Depending upon the amount of dowel you need to remove, you may be able to smooth the ends flush with a file instead of sawing them off.

5 Finally, remove any excess glue with a scraper and sand the surface smooth with sandpaper and a wooden sanding block.

Lap Joints and Their Variations

Lap joints are the simplest kinds of frame joints and a good choice for quick, strong connections where it's acceptable for the wood joints to show. Lap joints consist of a an offset tongue on one workpiece that fits into a wide dado notch or over another offset tongue on the other workpiece. The joint members are usually cut so the parts fit together flush when assembled, but this isn't always the case. When the workpiece thicknesses aren't the same, only one pair of workpiece faces will be flush.

Choose lap joints for building strong table and bench frameworks where legs meet stringers and aprons. The joints are interlocking and provide large, long-grain surface areas for gluing. For even more strength, lock the joints with pegs or fasteners.

Types of lap joints. Lap joints take many forms, as shown at left. Corner half-laps combine two matching rabbets arranged at 90°. T half-laps marry an end rabbet on one workpiece with a dado notch on the other workpiece. Cross lap joints form an intersection where two wide dadoes lock together at 90°. You can also make angled cross laps where workpieces meet at non-square angles.

Cutting lap joints. Lap joints can be cut with a table saw and either a standard blade or a dado blade set. The standard blade makes quick work of cutting the wide offset tongue in two passes (See next page, top). Mill the notched portion of the joint with a dado blade in several side-by-side passes.

You can also use a handheld router and wide straight bit for cutting lap joints. Guide the cuts by running the router against a clamped stopblock or two to limit the cutting area. Make several passes of increasing depth to remove the waste.

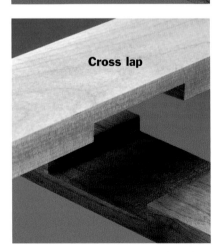

Corner half lap

"T" half lap

Cross lap

LAP JOINTS are, in essence, extra-wide rabbet and dado joints. They're used primarily in furnituremaking and frame-making, where the extra gluing surface in the sturdy interlocking joints greatly increases the strength of any project.

Common uses for lap joints

CHAIRS AND BENCHES. Lap joints are often used to join the arms and/or spreaders of a chair base to the legs. The fitted nature of the joint provides good resistance to downward and racking stresses.

FRAMES. Flush-fit lap joints are a good choice for picture frames when it's acceptable that the joint parts show. Use them to highlight these connections.

How to cut tongues (rabbets) with a table saw

Relief block

1 Cut the tongue portion of the lap joint on your table saw, using a tenoning jig to support and guide the workpiece. Set up the saw as if you're cutting a deep rabbet, and begin by making the cheek cuts.

2 Cut the shoulders of the tongues on a table saw, using the miter gauge to feed each workpiece past the blade. Clamp a relief block to the fence and measure out from its position to the blade to set up the cut. Never make this cut without a relief block and directly against the rip fence. It could cause kickback.

Options for cutting notches (dadoes)

Sacrificial wood fence

Stop blocks

USE A DADO BLADE. A dado blade set installed in your table saw is the fastest tool for cutting notches in stock to create lap joints. Set the dado blade to its maximum cutting width and set the cutting height to equal the depth of the notch. Attach a sacrificial wood fence to the miter gauge for your table saw. Hold or clamp the workpiece securely against the fence so the area to be notched is clear of the miter gauge. Cut through the stock and the fence in several passes.

USE A ROUTER. Mount a straight bit in your router and set the cutting depth to equal the depth of the notch. Clamp stop block guides to the workpiece at each end of the notch. The guides should be positioned so their distance from the end cutting lines is the same as the router setback (the distance from the bit to the edge of the base). Remove the waste wood with the router, working between the stop blocks (the middle area of the notch is routed freehand).

Drilling

Drilling precise and uniform holes is an overlooked art form in most workshops. But the fact is, it doesn't take much longer to set up drilling guides that will help make your drilling projects virtually foolproof. Choosing the right tool and the right style of bit is also very important to drilling success. The basic selection of drill types includes:

• **Hand drills** (brace-and-bit, egg-beater style and others). These tools are becoming less common with the advent of the cordless power drill, but they're still nice to have around for drilling a few quick holes on-site (and the battery never runs down).

• **Corded portable drills**. These too have lost prominence to the cordless, but every shop should still be equipped with one of these workhorses. With few exceptions, they can still create more torque than cordless drills, and they're very reliable for large projects, like screwing down decking.

• **Cordless drills**. How did we ever get along without these tools? Technology continues to evolve, but generally a 12-volt model with an exchangeable battery pack will perform just about any workshop drilling task.

• **Drill press**. For power and precision, a drill press is unbeatable. For most tasks, a benchtop model will do the job. But if you do a lot of woodworking or metalworking, look for a floor-standing model with easily adjustable speed and a larger throat capacity.

A backer board prevents tearout

Regardless of the type of drill and bit you're using, bits will cause splintering and tearout when they exit a board. To prevent this from happening, simply slip a backer board beneath the workpiece before drilling. Any piece of wood scrap can be used as a backer board. For a more permanent backer board, many woodworkers attach pieces of scrap wood to their drill press table with screws driven up through the guide holes in the table. In addition to preventing tearout, a wood auxiliary table on your drill press helps prevent damage that can occur to drill bits if they're inadvertently driven into the metal table.

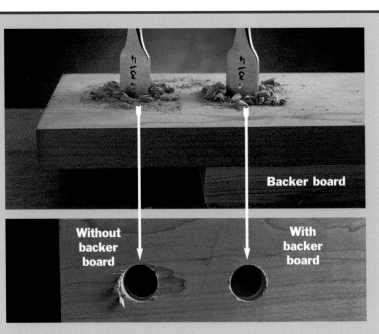

Backer board

Without backer board

With backer board

Drill press speeds

Material	Hole dia.	Speed (rpm)
Plastic	$\frac{1}{16}$ in.	6000-6500
	$\frac{1}{4}$ in.	3000-3500
	$\frac{1}{2}$ in.	500-1000
Soft metal	$\frac{1}{16}$ in.	6000-6500
	$\frac{1}{4}$ in.	4500-5000
	$\frac{1}{2}$ in.	1500-250
Steel	$\frac{1}{16}$ in.	5000-6500
	$\frac{1}{4}$ in.	1500-2000
	$\frac{1}{2}$ in.	500-1000
Wood	0-$\frac{1}{2}$ in.	3000-4000
	$\frac{1}{2}$-1 in.	2000-3000
	1+ in.	700-2000

Note: Multispur bits should be used at very low speed (250 to 700 rpm)

Portable drill types

Hand-held power drills are made in two basic handle styles: the *T-handle* and the *pistol grip*. If you use your drill for extended periods of time, the T-handle is probably a better choice because it's more balanced and won't cause fatigue as soon. The T-handle also is easier to control for precision drilling. Pistol-grip drills are preferred by people who work with harder materials because the design allows you to apply more downward pressure directly over the bit—but never press too hard.

Pistol grip

T-handle

Drill bit diameters

Bit type	Range of dia.
Twist	$\frac{1}{64}$ to 1 in.
Spade	$\frac{1}{4}$ to $1\frac{1}{2}$ in.
Brad-point	$\frac{1}{8}$ to $\frac{5}{8}$ in.
Masonry ($\frac{3}{8}$-in. drill)	$\frac{1}{8}$ to 1 in.
Masonry ($\frac{1}{2}$-in. drill)	$\frac{1}{8}$ to $1\frac{1}{2}$ in.
Forstner	$\frac{1}{4}$ to $2\frac{1}{8}$ in.

Secure a sphere

Drilling holes into a wood sphere is easy with this home-made holder. Drill holes slightly smaller than the diameter of the sphere into the centers of two small pieces of scrap wood. Sandwich the sphere between the holes and secure with a woodscrew clamp.

Steady a cylinder

A block of wood with a V-groove will hold dowels and other cylinders steady during drilling. Simply set the blade on your table saw to 45° and cut 1-in.-deep grooves from opposite ends, forming a "V" in the center of the board. Adjust the width and depth of the "V" according to the diameter of the cylinder.

Drill perfect pilots on the fly

Take the guesswork out of drilling pilot holes for finish nails by chucking one of the nails into your drill and using it as a drill bit.

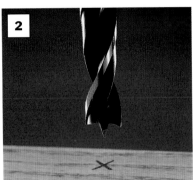

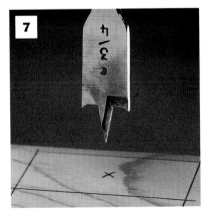

1. Twist bit will bore through angle iron, flat iron or sheet metal and can be used for rough drilling in wood and other materials. Twist bits are available in a wider range of diameters than any other bit type.

2. Brad-point bit looks like a twist bit, but has a center spur and side spurs to keep it from wandering. These bits can make clean cuts in wood and softer materials (but not metal).

3. Auger bit will bore deep, straight holes into timber or thick softwood. The threaded bit point helps keep the bit cutting true while the spiral cutting head carries wood shavings to the surface. Best used with hand-powered brace-and-bit or a power right-angle drill.

4. Counterboring bit creates a pilot hole and countersink hole to accommodate a screwhead and wood plug. Some bits are fully adjustable as to their depth. Common sizes are for #5, 6, 8, 10, 12, or 14 wood screws and 1/4-, 3/8- (most common) or 1/2-in. wood plugs.

5. Forstner bit will cut very clean holes with flat bottoms. It is especially useful in fine woodworking or when drilling into hardwoods. The bit will produce holes in any grain direction. Sold individually, or in sets. Use with a drill press only.

6. Countersink bit will ream out an existing hole so a screw can be driven flush, or slightly recessed, into the wood surface.

7. Spade bit is useful for boring through wood where precision is not critical. It is the bit of choice when boring wiring holes through studs or removing wood before chiseling (as when cutting a mortise).

8. Vix bit is designed to drill perfectly centered screw pilot holes through guide holes in hardware plates.

Helpful drilling guides

Portable drill guide

This drilling accessory gives a portable power drill the precision of a drill press. You can use it to drill perfectly straight holes on the job site, and many models are scaled to drill at precise angles.

Guide for shelf pin holes

A strip of perforated hardboard (pegboard) makes a handy guide for drilling evenly spaced shelf pin holes in shelf standards. Typically, holes are spaced about 1 in. apart and are drilled with a ¼-in. bit.

Drill press table stopblocks

Straight lengths of scrap wood can be clamped to your drill press table to make stopblocks for drilling uniform holes in multiple workpieces.

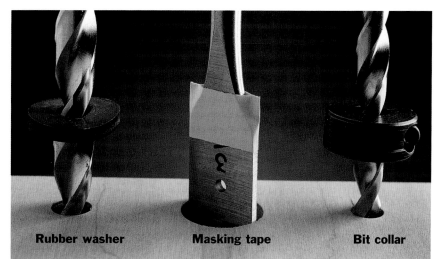

Rubber washer   Masking tape   Bit collar

Do-it-yourself depth stops for portable drills

Drilling depth can be set with a gauge on your drill press, but what about with a portable drill? To take the guesswork out of drilling holes to an exact depth, mark the drill bit at the appropriate depth with a rubber washer or masking tape. You can also use special drill bit collars that are sold at most building centers and hardware stores.

Drilling template

Plot out hole spacing on a paper or hardboard template for woodworking projects. The template will help you drill identical hole patterns on matching workpieces.

Shaping

Shaping is a fairly broad category when it comes to workshop skills. In one sense or another, just about anything you do to a workpiece with a tool alters its shape. But this chapter concerns shaping exercises that don't necessarily change the size of the workpiece, but rather alter its appearance or, in some cases, prepare it to be joined with another workpiece. Routing, planing, filing and shaving or paring are the activities normally done for this purpose.

Shaping is the area of woodworking where hand tools are still used most prevalently. Hand planes, files, drawknives, spokeshaves and other hand-powered tools offer a level of precision and control that's hard to find with power tools. But for their part, power tools (particularly the router) are much faster and, for some types of shaping tasks, more accurate. Making grooves, rabbets, dovetails and other joinery cuts is a perfect chore for the router, provided you use the correct router bit. Shaping complex edge profiles, like ogees and coves, is much easier to do with a router bit than with any hand tool.

Whether you're using hand or power tools, the key to good results when shaping wood is not to try to remove too much material at one time. Make a habit of making several precise, controlled passes with the tool whenever possible. This will yield cleaner, more accurate results, and you're less likely to ruin your workpiece: it's tough to put wood back on once you cut it off.

Invest in a router table

A router is one of the most versatile power tools ever created, but mounted in a router table its usefulness and accuracy become even greater. Commercial models are available, but many handymen prefer to build their own. You can purchase kits for making the mounting plate, fence and even the table surface. The router table shown to the right is made using an inexpensive bathroom vanity as a cabinet, with a piece of post-form countertop for the tabletop. If you plan to use your router table frequently, it's a good idea to buy a dedicated router for it. Look for a fixed-base model with a 1/2-in. collet. A soft start feature will make the router table safer and easier to manage.

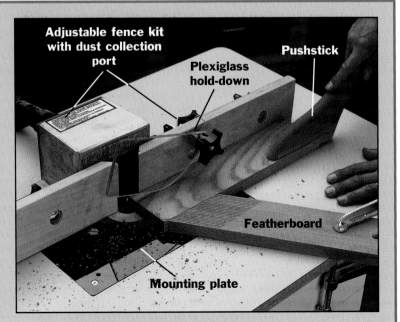

Adjustable fence kit with dust collection port

Plexiglass hold-down

Pushstick

Featherboard

Mounting plate

Jointer plane

Block plane

Jack plane

THREE COMMON HAND PLANES for workshop use are the block plane, jack plane and jointer plane. Block planes are very handy general purpose tools. They can be used to plane with the grain, but they have shallow blade angles and flat soles so they can also plane end grain effectively. Their small size makes them easy to manage and convenient to store in your tool box. Jack planes are medium-sized planes with a slight curve in the sole. Their main purpose is to reduce board thickness by surface planing (see photo above). Jointer planes (also called try planes) have long soles that can ride a board edge smoothly. Their main use is to smooth board edges, especially in preparation for edge gluing.

Thickness planing with a hand plane

If you don't own a power planer and need to reduce the thickness of a board slightly, a jack plane is the tool you'll want to use. The fastest way to remove stock is by roughing with the plane: scraping the plane diagonally to the direction of the grain. To remove smaller amounts of material, and to smooth out after roughing, use a smoothing motion: orient the blade so the blade is diagonal to the wood grain, but follow the grain direction as you push the tool across your workpiece.

Sharpening plane irons

Plane blades (called irons) are sharpened in much the same way as wood chisels, typically at an angle of 25°. To maintain a steady angle on the irons, you can purchase a honing guide through most woodworking catalogs.

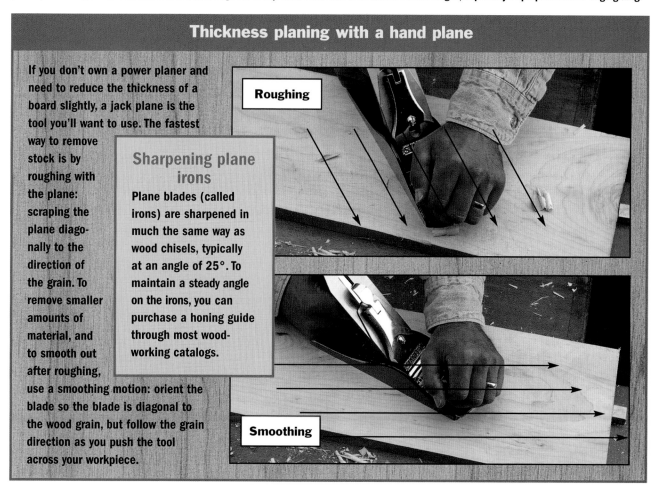

Roughing

Smoothing

Follow the grain as you plane

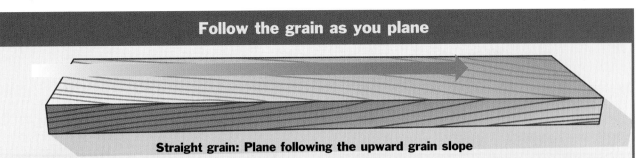

Straight grain: Plane following the upward grain slope

For best results when planing, pay attention to the direction of the wood grain, keeping in mind that the grain is a three-dimensional feature of the wood. In addition to running longitudinally along a board, it also has a general up or down slope on most boards. Inspect the edge of the board to see which direction the grain is running (illustra-tion above) and plane the board to follow the wood grain upward. On some face-sawn boards, the wood grain is wavy or cupped from the side view. On such boards, you'll need to switch planing direction as you work along the board, always planing toward a crest in the wood grain.

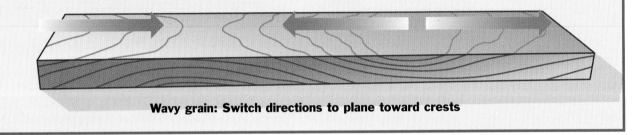

Wavy grain: Switch directions to plane toward crests

Mini-plane cuts clean grooves for inlays

A special hand plane, called an *inlay plane*, can be used to cut shallow grooves into wood for recessing decorative veneer inlay bands. Clamp a straightedge to the workpiece as a guide.

Overlooked shop tool has multitude of uses

Remove bulges, dips and bumps from contoured cuts by filing them away with a flat or half-round, single cut file. A file or rasp also makes quick work of cutting a roundover or easing a sharp edge.

Traditional shaping tools have a place in any shop

Drawknife works quickly and cleanly

Once used primarily to strip bark from felled trees, the drawknife can resurface a piece of rough or damaged wood stock as fast as any belt sander, but without the dust and noise. They're also a good choice for chamfering sharp edges on woodworking projects. When left unsanded, the surface marks created by the drawknife can add rough-hewn charm to your project.

Spokeshave makes easy roundovers

You don't need to be a wheelwright to make good use of this time-honored tool. The spokeshave can round over just about any furniture leg or table edge. And may woodworkers enjoy using the spokeshave to make chair spindles and other round parts. Spokeshaves are made in several different sizes with concave blades of varying radii.

Yet another use for the versatile drill/driver

For enlarging holes or reshaping internal cutouts, try installing a rasp bit into your drill/driver. Most tool catalogs and hardware stores carry a nice selection of rasp bits that vary by size and shape. You can also use the rasp bits to strike off bumps and imperfections from contoured cuts.

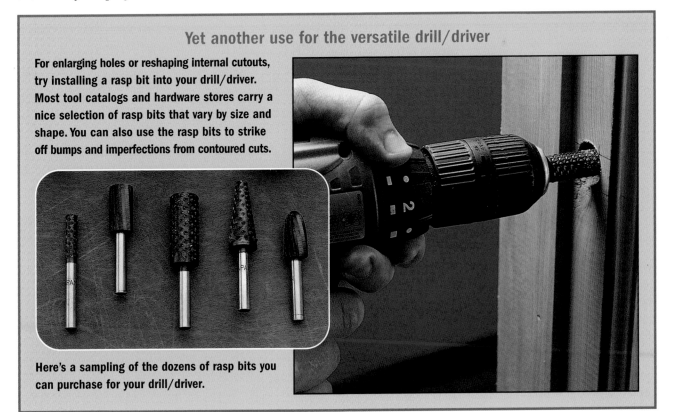

Here's a sampling of the dozens of rasp bits you can purchase for your drill/driver.

Plunge router

Router feed direction

Non-slip router pad

Use a guide when grooving

Guides for making groove cuts can be as simple as a straight piece of scrap wood clamped to the workpiece. You can also use an extruded steel straightedge (See photo, right), or an edge guide that connects to the base.

Find router base setback

To figure out how far from the cutting line to secure your guide, measure the router "setback." Secure a straight-edge to scrap and make a practice cut, following the guide. Measure from the closer shoulder of the cut to the guide.

A primer on router usage

It's not unusual for beginning do-it-yourselfers and woodworkers to be a little intimidated by routers. They're loud, aggressive shaping tools and they sometimes seem to have a mind of their own when it comes to following a guide or the edge of a board. But by keeping a few basic points in mind, and with some practice, these extremely versatile tools will amaze you with the variety and quality of work they can produce.

Setup is a very important aspect of correct router usage. Make sure the bit is well secured in the collet and set to an appropriate cutting height. The workpiece must be secured, either with clamps or bench dogs or with a non-slip router pad like the one shown at left. If using a piloted edge-forming bit, you won't need a straightedge or guide for the router base to follow, although you secure scrap pieces the same thickness as the workpiece at each if you're only routing one side (this prevents the router from following the corner and cutting into the adjacent sides). With non-piloted groove-forming bits, you'll need to use a straightedge or router guide to keep the tool cutting on line (See photo, left).

Whether you're using a fixed-base router or a plunge router, the bit should be spinning at full speed before you apply it to the workpiece. Wearing hearing and eye protection, engage the bit into the workpiece and draw it toward yourself, keeping your body out of the line of the tool as best you can. To be effective, the bit should cut against the rotation of the bit. In most cases, this means you should feed the router counterclockwise. Maintain an even cutting pace, and don't set the router down until the bit has stopped spinning. Always practice your cut on scrap wood before cutting the workpiece.

Router bits

Router bits fit into two general categories: *edge-forming bits* and *groove-forming bits*. Edge-forming bits are used to cut decorative profiles on the edges of boards; they are equipped with integral pilots that guide the bit along the edge of the material being cut. Some more inexpensive bits have fixed pilots that are an extension of the bit shank, but most today have ball-bearing pilots that allow the cutter to spin but won't burn the edge of the board as fixed pilots can. Groove-forming bits cut channels of various profiles into the material. Except when carving freehand, they require a cutting guide. Most basic bits are made with either a $1/4$-in. or $1/2$-in.-dia. shank. Bits with a larger cutting radius can only be used with a router that accepts a $1/2$-in. shank. Unless otherwise noted, the sizes listed below refer to cutting radius.

ROUNDOVER BIT. Piloted bit eliminates sharp edges. Available sizes: $1/16$, $1/8$, $3/16$, $1/4$, $3/8$, $1/2$ in.; $1/2$ in. shank only: $5/8$, $3/4$, $7/8$, 1, $1 1/8$, $1 1/4$ in.

CORE BOX BIT. Grooving bit for fluting, veining and carving. Available sizes: $1/4$, $3/8$, $1/2$, $5/8$, $3/4$ in.; $1/2$ in. shank only: $7/8$, $15/16$, 1 in.

FLUSH-TRIMMING BITS. Piloted edge-trimming bits for trimming laminates and pattern routing; 2 or 3 flutes. Available sizes: $1/4$, $3/8$, $1/2$ in.; $1/2$ in. shank only: $3/4$, 1*, $1 1/8$* in.*top-mounted bearing typical

ROMAN OGEE BIT. Cut decorative edge profiles and manufacture trim moldings. Available sizes: $5/32$, $1/4$ in.

DOVETAIL BIT. Used to cut dovetail joints, generally with a dovetail jig. Angles of flutes vary between 7 and 14°. Available sizes: $1/4$, $5/16$, $3/8$, $1/2$, $5/8$, $11/16$, $3/4$ in.; $1/2$ in. shank only: $13/16$, 1 in.

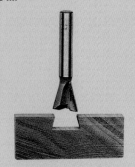

CHAMFER BITS. Piloted bit eliminates sharp edges, making smooth, clean angle cut. Vast majority are 45° angle (both $1/4$ in. and $1/2$ in. shank). Can find bits with 15, $22 1/2$ and 30° cutting angles as well.

PILOTED RABBETING BIT. Cut rabbets, tongue-and-grooves and shiplap joints without need for straightedge or other guide. Available sizes (by depth of cut): $1/4$, $3/8$, $1/2$ in.; $1/2$ in. shank only: $3/4$ in. Can also purchase rabbeting bit with interchangeable bearings varying rabbet depth.

VEINING (V-GROOVE) BIT. Used for carving, lettering and cutting decorative V-shaped veins. Most are 90° cutting angle, but 45° and 60° bits can be found. Available sizes: $1/4$, $3/8$, $1/2$, $5/8$, $3/4$ in.; $1/2$ in. shank only: $15/16$, 1, $1 1/4$, $1 1/2$, 2 in.

STRAIGHT BIT. Cleans up edges, cuts grooves, can be used for mortising and carving. Most have 2 flutes. Available sizes: $1/4$, $5/16$, $3/8$, $7/16$, $1/2$, $9/16$, $5/8$, $3/4$, $7/8$, 1 in.; $1/2$ in. shank only: $1 3/8$, $1 1/4$, 2 in.

Save money and increase trim options by cutting your own trim molding with a router

Anyone who's done much trim carpentry knows that milled trim moldings can be very expensive, especially if they're made of hardwood. It can also be very difficult to find the size, profile and wood species you're looking for from stock millwork. One good solution to this dilemma is to cut your own trim moldings. Simply choose an edge-forming bit with the profile you like and rout the shape into a piece of stock. You can rout the shape freehand, using a piloted bit, but make sure the stock is wide enough to provide a stable bearing surface for the router base. If you own a router table, use it to make the profile cuts. After the profile is cut, rip-cut the profiled board to the desired trim width on your table saw. If you need more molding, rout the profile into the cut edge of the stock then rip-cut again.

Any edge-forming bit (and some groove-forming bits) will cut a suitable edge. But as you experiment with cutting your own moldings, look into new bit options with more sophisticated profiles, like the double Roman ogee bit shown here. If you're using a router that can accept a ½-in. shank, you'll find a wide selection of interesting bits in just about any woodworking catalog. You can also use two or more bits in combination to form complex and interesting edge treatments.

Double Roman ogee bit

Use a roundover bit to remove sharp edges or renew a beat-up edge

The piloted roundover bit is a quick and reliable tool for easing sharp edges on just about any piece of furniture or trim. In most cases, the best time to roundover the edge is after the furniture is assembled, as with the picnic table that's receiving the roundover treatment in the photo to the right. A roundover bit doesn't have to be used on new furniture projects only. It's also a great device for giving a shot of new life to an older piece of furniture that has damaged, dented or even rotted edges. A bit with a 3/8- or 1/4-in. cutting radius is a good general purpose choice.

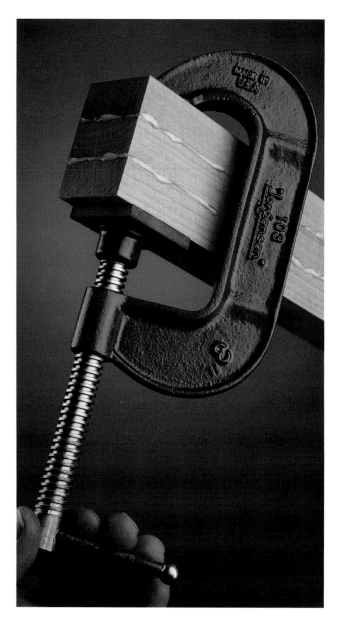

Clamping, Gluing & Fastening

No matter how carefully you cut project parts and no matter how painstakingly you form the joints, without good clamping, gluing and fastening techniques your project likely will fail.

Clamping serves two fundamental purposes in woodworking: first, it draws parts together tightly and ensures that joints that should be square are square; and second, it holds parts together until the glue that will hold them together permanently sets. For non-woodworking shop projects, clamping is also very important. Among its more common jobs are holding workpieces together while fasteners are driven; securing jigs for cutting and drilling; and holding small workpieces so they stay steady while you work on them.

Successful gluing is a matter of choosing the best adhesive for the job, making sure the mating surfaces are properly prepared, and applying the correct amount of glue. From bonding retaining wall blocks together with construction adhesive to applying cabinet veneer, gluing is a skill every handyman should possess.

Fastening is an easy project step to rush through. By the time you're ready to fasten, the last thing you want to do is spend additional time fussing with pilot holes, counterbores and screw patterns. But take the time—there's no more discouraging shop experience than to see a project fail because you neglected to drill a pilot hole and the wood split.

Choosing adhesives

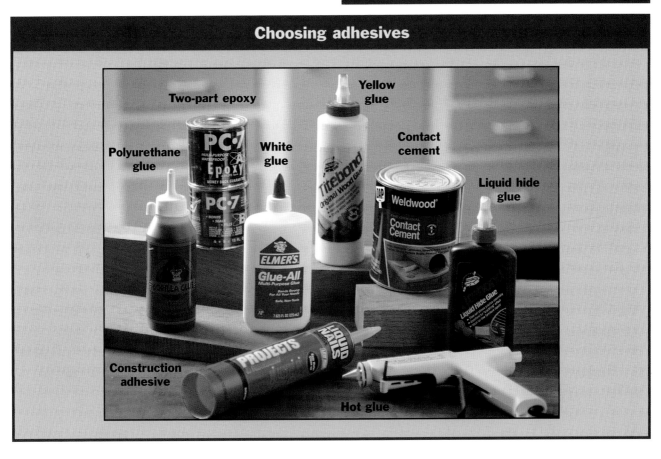

Two-part epoxy

Yellow glue

Polyurethane glue

White glue

Contact cement

Liquid hide glue

Construction adhesive

Hot glue

Selecting the right adhesive for your bonding task

WHITE GLUE: Used on wood, paper or cloth. Interior use only. Dries in several hours and has a moderately strong bond. Poor resistance to water and heat. Emits no harmful odors. Cleans up with soap and water.

YELLOW GLUE: Used on wood, paper or cloth. Interior use only. Dries faster than white glue and has a slightly stronger bond. Moderate resistance to water and heat. Emits no harmful odors. Cleans up with soap and water.

LIQUID HIDE GLUE: Ideal for fine wood furniture or musical instruments. Interior use only. Sets slowly. Has good bond and is resistant to solvents and wood finishes. An eye irritant. Will clean up with soap and water.

POLYURETHANE GLUE: Used to bond a variety of materials including wood, metal and ceramics. Sets quickly and produces a strong bond. Waterproof. Warning: this glue can cause immediate and residual lung damage. This product should only be used with excellent ventilation. Asthmatics and people with chronic lung conditions should not use this product. Cleans up with acetone or mineral spirits.

CONSTRUCTION ADHESIVE: Used on framing lumber, flooring and roof sheathing, plywood and paneling, wallboard, masonry. Dries within 24 hours and has a very good bond.

Cleans up with mineral spirits.

CONTACT CEMENT: Joins laminates, veneers, cloth, paper, leather, and other materials. Sets instantly and dries in under an hour. Produces a bond that is not suitable for structural applications. Very flammable and an irritant to eyes, skin and lungs (non-flammable contact cement is also available). Cleans up with soap and water.

HOT GLUE: Joins wood, plastics, glass and other materials. Sets within 60 seconds. Strength is generally low, but depends on type of glue stick. Good resistance to moisture, fair to heat. Heat will loosen bond.

TWO-PART EPOXY: Joins wood, metal, masonry, glass, fiberglass and other materials. Provides the strongest bond of any adhesive. Bond has excellent resistance to moisture and heat. Drying time varies. Warning: fumes are very toxic and flammable. Cleanup sometimes possible with acetone.

INSTANT (CYANOACRYLATE) GLUE: Bonds smooth surfaces such as glass, ceramics, plastics and metal. Has excellent strength, but little flexibility. Dries in just a few seconds. Has excellent resistance to moisture and heat. Warning: toxic and flammable, and the glue can bond skin instantly.

Glue applicators

A GLUE ROLLER is used to apply an extremely even coating of glue on large, broad surfaces, such as when applying veneer. Once the hopper is loaded with glue, it will dispense glue over the roller at an even rate when the surface is rolled.

A SPECIAL GLUE TOOL FOR BISCUITS can be slipped into a biscuit slot to deliver glue with no spillage or mess.

A GLUE BRUSH will deliver just the right amount of glue to tight working spots. These disposable brushes more than make up for their low cost in savings on the clean-up side.

A DISPOSABLE FOAM paint brush is a perfect tool for spreading even layers of contact adhesive on smaller project parts. For larger parts, like countertops, use a low-nap paint roller sleeve.

Helpful hints for glue cleanup

Straw scoops wet glue from tight corners

Removing excess glue from corners and edges can be tricky. Often, the best tool for the job is a common plastic drinking straw. The straw can be bent into corners and the sharp edge does a good job of lifting glue. Remember to let the glue set partially before removing it. Otherwise, the excess glue will smear.

Old chisel scrapes away filmed-over glue

Use an old wood chisel to scrape glue squeeze-out from edge-glued joints, or from any flat surface. Keep the beveled edge of the chisel down to avoid marring the wood. Make certain the chisel edge is free of nicks. Wait for the glue to set partially (it should have a light film on the surface) before scraping.

Clamping tips

Ready-made clamp pads

Hardboard clamp pads

Wood tabs

Felt tabs

Quick & easy pipe clamp supports

Pipe clamps can be awkward to use when laid flat on a workbench. To remedy the problem, drill a series of 1½-in.-diameter holes down the center of a 4-ft.-long 2 × 4, then rip-cut the board in half. The resulting semicircular cutouts will cradle the pipes, increasing their stability and improving access to the cranks.

Attach pads for hands-free clamping

Eliminate the hassle of trying to slip loose clamping pads between the jaws of your clamps and your workpiece by attaching pads directly to your clamps or clamp jaws. Hot-glue tabs of wood or felt to C-clamp jaws. Slip ready-made clamp pads on the heads of your bar clamps, or make your own bar-clamp pads by drilling 1-in.-dia. holes in pieces of scrap hardboard.

"Wedge-gluing" panels

Applying clamp pressure to the edges of a glue-up panel ensures strong, tight joints, but it does little to prevent the panel from buckling. In fact, the side pressure from the clamps can even contribute to buckling problems. To help keep your glue-up panel from looking like corrugated metal, try this simple technique. Alternate the bar clamps on opposite faces of the panel (this is easier to do if you use clamp supports, like those shown on the previous page). Then, cut several hardwood wedges. Drive the wedges between the clamping bars and the panel (don't get too aggressive here). Visually inspect the panel to make sure the pressure is even and it's not buckling. If necessary, adjust the pressure of the wedges.

Wood cauls

Clamping aids come through when duty cauls

Because most clamp jaws are less than 2 in. wide, tightening the clamps directs the clamping pressure to only a small section of the workpiece. As a result, joints (and entire woodworking projects) can be pulled out of square. A good solution to this effect is to use wood cauls when gluing up your projects.

Wood cauls are simply strips of wood that are slipped between clamps and the workpiece to distribute the clamping pressure evenly. Woodworkers have been using them for centuries to help create strong, square joints. You can use any hardwood, or even strips of plywood, to make your own wood cauls. Be sure to have plenty on hand before beginning the glue-up.

Clamping & gluing techniques

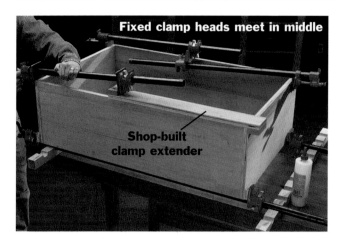

Two simple tricks for stretching pipe clamps

For those occasions when you get caught short during glue-up, here are two clever ways to get more reach out of your pipe clamps. If you have two clamps that are both too short, arrange the fixed heads so they meet in the middle: the clamping pressure will hold them together. Or, you can build a clamp extender like the one above from scrap wood.

One way to get around this clamping problem

Clamps aren't designed to work well with round workpieces, such as the tabletop shown above. One way to get even clamping pressure on round workpieces is shown above. Trace the arc of the workpiece onto the edges of two sturdy boards, then cut out the arc with a jig saw to make your clamping aids.

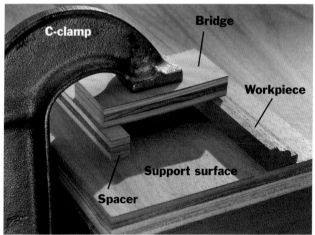

A foolproof system for clamping frames

Build this frame clamp with a few pieces of scrap wood and a woodscrew clamp. It will apply equal pressure on all four corners of a frame. Cut four equal-length wood strips and drill center holes at 1- to 2-in. increments. Cut two shorter strips and drill a hole near each end. Fabricate four L-shaped corner braces out of scrap wood (or an old frame) and drill a hole in the corner of each. Form the strips into two V-shaped assemblies with wing nuts, as shown above. Attach the corner braces, set the frame inside the corners, then use a woodscrew to draw the "V" together.

Wooden bridge extends C-clamp capacity

C-clamps are useful for many tasks, but their relatively shallow throats limit their range. Extend the reach of the clamp by fashioning a clamping bridge with two pieces of scrap wood. One piece (the *spacer*) should be the same thickness as the workpiece being pressed down. The second scrap (the *bridge*) needs to be long enough to span over the spacer and the workpiece. Set the spacer between the workpiece and the edge of the support surface, then lay the bridge across the spacer and over the workpiece. Clamping down on the bridge creates clamping pressure on the workpiece.

Gallery of Clamps

The corner clamp

A corner clamp holds mitered corners firmly in alignment. When fastening frames, glue and clamp opposite corners and let them dry before gluing the remaining two corners.

The C-clamp

This classic clamp has nearly unlimited applications in the workshop. Keep a wide assortment of sizes on hand, including a few deep throat C-clamps. No clamp type works better for laminating, as above.

The strap clamp

Reinforced webbing is wrapped around irregular shapes and tightened with a ratcheting cinch. Perfect for gluing up round tabletops and casework, as well as repairing table legs, lamp bases, and other hard-to-clamp objects. Also called band clamps or web clamps.

The pipe clamp

Another indispensable weapon in the clamp arsenal, the pipe clamp is the workhorse of wood glue-ups. The clamp heads are purchased separately from the pipes. Typically, ¾- or ½-in. black pipe is used (diameter depends on hole size in clamp heads). One clamp head is fixed in rough position, then the adjustable head is tightened with a hand screw.

The woodscrew

Also called *handscrew clamps* or *Jorgenson's* (after their primary manufacturer), these all-wood clamps have excellent gripping power, wide throat capacity and the wood jaws won't dent or mar most types of wood. Jaw lengths range in size from 4 to 16 in.

The 3-way clamp

The right angle screw in the spine of the clamp is used to apply downward pressure on the edge of a workpiece after the jaws at the top and bottom of the throat are tightened. Perfect for attaching edge trim to sheet goods or for repairing moldings.

The quick clamp

This trigger-activated bar clamp head lets you tighten the clamp with only one hand. They're great for holding workpieces in rough position for fastening. The bars are sold with the clamps. They range from 6 to 50 in. in length.

Use a magnetic guide for one-handed screw driving

Most woodworkers know that a magnetized drill bit will help hold a screw in place. But a magnetic screw guide will go one better. This simple device will hold a screw firmly to the bit as the metal sleeve guides the screw straight and true when downward pressure is exerted on the driver. With this handy tool you can drive screws straight and without stripping using only one hand, allowing you to hold the workpiece with your free hand.

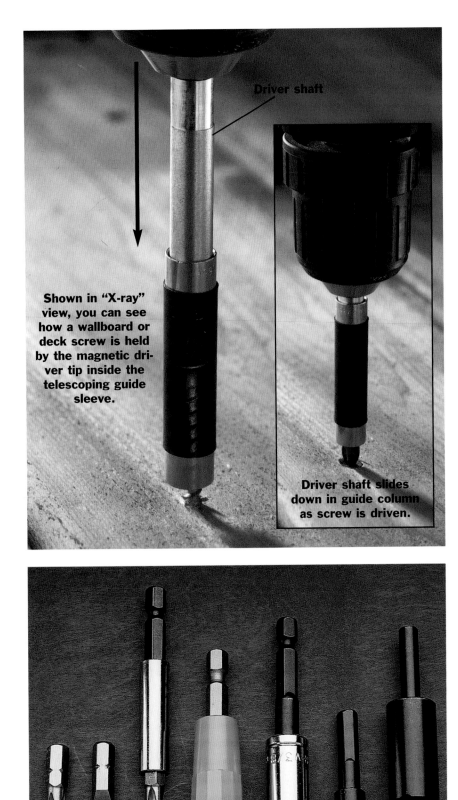

Driver shaft

Shown in "X-ray" view, you can see how a wallboard or deck screw is held by the magnetic driver tip inside the telescoping guide sleeve.

Driver shaft slides down in guide column as screw is driven.

Tip: Wax your screw threads

Keep a block of beeswax in your shop to lubricate the threads of screws. The wax greatly reduces friction, which makes for less work and fewer stripped screw heads. You can use hand soap for a similar purpose, but it's more likely to discolor the wood.

Drill driver bits

These bits and accessories for drill/drivers (left) will handle just about any fasteners. They are: (A) phillips-head driver; (B) slotted-head driver; (C) magnetic tip holder; (D) hooded slotted-head driver; (E) socket driver; (F) hex driver; (G) finish nail spinner.

A   B   C   D   E   F   G

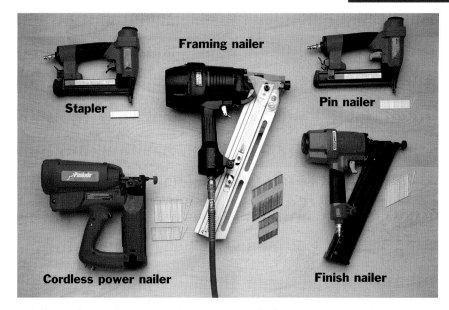

Framing nailer

Stapler

Pin nailer

Cordless power nailer

Finish nailer

Adding air tools can take your workshop to a new level

Compressed-air-powered fasteners can dramatically decrease the amount of time you spend on a project. Many tools will fire fasteners as fast as you can pull the trigger. Most air nailers require a ½ to 1 hp compressor with tank capacity of at least 3 gallons of air. Smaller air nailers and staplers usually run on 2 to 5 cubic feet per minute (cfm) or air volume at a pressure of 70 to 90 pounds per square inch (psi). Larger framing nailers can require as much as 9 cfm and 100 to 120 psi. If you already own a compressor, check to make sure it's able to drive new air tools before purchasing them. When working with air-powered fasteners, it is essential to wear approved safety goggles and ear protection. Familiarize yourself with the operation of the tool before beginning work. A device that can send a nail deep into a 2 × 4 can do a great deal of harm to the human body. Note: Recently, a similar tool to air nailers, the cordless power nailer, has become available for home use or for rental (See description below).

Pneumatic staplers: Air-powered staplers can drive crown-style staples from ¼ to ½ in. wide, and up to 2 in. long. Smaller staplers are useful for installing carpeting, roofing felt, floor underlayment and insulation. Larger capacity staplers can attach fence boards, strip flooring and even roof decking (check with your local building codes first).

Framing nailers: The "big boy" of air-powered fasteners, these powerful, high-capacity tools will drive nails up to 3½ in. long for all types of frame construction. The magazine can hold upwards of 100 nails.

Pin nailers: Drive brads up to 1¼ in. long. Used to attach trim, carpet strips and moldings. This lightweight tool allows you to nail one-handed, a real help when aligning trim molding pieces.

Finish nailer: Drives finish nails from ¾ to 2 in. long. Useful for installing siding, flooring, door and window casing and most types of finish carpentry.

Cordless power nailer: Relies on battery power and disposable fuel cells to power-drive nails. Also called *impulse nailers*. Require special fasteners, generally 16 gauge, from 1½ to 3¼ in. long, depending on the model. Each fuel cell will drive from 1200 to 2500 nails, depending on length, and a single battery charge will drive up to 4000 nails.

5-gallon bucket with dividers keeps hardware organized

If you do any amount of taping wallboard seams, your shop or garage is likely cluttered with the leftover 5-gallon buckets used to package premixed joint compound. They seem so useful, it's hard for most of us to throw them away. Here's one good way to put these leftover buckets to use: make them into hardware/fastener organizers. Use a jig saw with an edge guide to trim off the bottom 3 in. or so of several buckets, then cut pieces of scrap plywood so they're 2½ in. wide and the same length as the inside diameter of the bucket. Fasten the strips to the buckets by driving wallboard screws up through the bucket bottom. To divide the bucket bottom into quadrants, simply add shorter scrap strips. Because the buckets are wider at the top than the bottom, several bucket bottoms can be stacked inside one bucket, creating a totable hardware store.

Sanding & Finishing

After spending hours, days or even months of labor on a workshop project, don't let an incorrectly or hastily applied finish spoil all your hard work. Take the time to prepare the wood for the finish by sanding thoroughly with a sequence of finer-grit sandpapers. Make sure all screw plugs are securely in their counterbores and flush with the wood surface. Don't let the project sit for more than 48 hours between final sanding and finish application so that it has time to attract dust. Then, choose the finishing products that best meet your needs: both in terms of protection and appearance. And once the finish is applied, patch up any dents, nail holes or small cracks with tinted wood putty.

Choosing the best finishing products can be very daunting. There are dozens upon dozens of paints, stains, dyes, varnishes, penetrating oils, lacquers and countless other finishing products on the shelves of most building centers. Deciding which to use is a matter of learning a little bit about the products. Don't rely too much on the claims you'll see on the labels—look for basic information on the composition of the product and see how it fits into finish selection charts. But with today's labeling practices it's sometimes difficult to determine exactly what kind of product you're examining even after reading the label top to bottom. In such cases, don't be shy about asking the store clerk for information. And whenever you decide to try a product you've never used before, always test it out first on some scrap.

Highlight surface flaws

Sanding marks, small scratches and dents and other minor surface flaws can be very difficult to detect—until you apply your wood finish, when they show up with glaring clarity. To spot these surface imperfections before applying your finish, use a desk lamp or other low lamp source (a 60-watt bulb is about right). Set the lamp next to the surface so the light hits it at a low angle. From the opposite side of the workpiece, view the surface. Even slight scratches and flaws will be highlighted by the shadows created by the light. Mark flawed areas with a light pencil mark, sand them away, then check again.

Sanding strategies

Prolong life of sandpaper and sanding belts

Sandpaper, sanding pads and sanding belts will gum up quickly when sanding, losing most of their tooth. But don't throw them away. Belts, pads and papers can be cleaned with a sanding stick (shown above) or just about any clean, uncolored rubber (an old tennis shoe sole, for example). With power sanders, simply turn on the tool and apply the sanding stick to the paper until the residue disappears.

Turn a band saw into a band sander

Stationary belt and disc sanders are powerful tools that remove a lot of material quickly. This characteristic is great for many sanding tasks, but if you're doing more delicate work more power isn't what you're looking for. The band saw can provide a solution for delicate sanding projects. Simply replace the band saw blade with an abrasive band to create a sanding tool that lets you remove very small amounts of wood.

Keep belt sanders on track

To impart a smooth, crisp edge on a board, use a belt sander. To prevent the sander from rocking and causing roundovers along the edge, sandwich the workpiece between two pieces of scrap wood, making sure all three edges are flush. Clamp the "sandwich" into the vise in your workbench.

Smooth rough cuts with a cabinet scraper

A lot of experienced woodworkers view sanding as a last resort. It's messy, noisy, time-consuming and it creates sanding marks. A cabinet scraper is a better tool for smoothing out rough cuts. It works equally well on curved surfaces, as above, or on broad, flat surfaces.

Emery cloth for metal and plastics

40-grit aluminum oxide

100-grit aluminum oxide

220-grit aluminum oxide

400-grit wet/dry

Sandpaper Grit Chart

Grit Number	Description	Use
12	Very Coarse	Very rough work requiring high speed, heavy
16		machinery. Used for unplaned woods, uneven wood
20		floors and rough-cut lumber.
24		
30	Coarse	Rough carpentry.
36		
40		
50		
60	Medium	General carpentry.
80		
100		
120	Fine	Preparation of hardwoods and final smoothing of
150		softwoods.
180		
220	Very Fine	Final and between-coat sanding. Used to remove
240		sanding marks left by coarser grits.
280		
320	Extra Fine	Sanding between finish coats and wet sanding
360		paints and varnishes.
400		
500	Super Fine	Sanding metal, plastics, ceramics and wet sanding.
600		

Slick trick for a rough customer

Sandpaper is difficult to tear in a straight line, and cutting it with scissors or a utility knife will dull blades very quickly. Build yourself a sandpaper cutter by attaching a hacksaw blade to a piece of scrap wood, with the sharp edge of the blade facing toward the edge of the board. Attach a strip of wood parallel to the blade. Position the strip so it's the same distance from the cutting edge of the blade as the most common dimension you'll need to fit your pad sander. Slip a piece of sandpaper underneath the blade and up against the strip. Pull upward against the blade for a neat cut.

Keep sandpaper scraps on file

An expanding, accordion-style file holder makes a great storage center for sandpaper scraps. Assign a grit number to each storage compartment and file your sandpaper sheets in the appropriate compartment so they'll be easy to find when needed.

PORTABLE POWER SANDERS

3 × 24 belt sander

Random-orbit sander

Detail sander

Finishing sander (1/4 sheet)

HAND SANDERS & SANDING BLOCKS

Commercial sanding block

Sanding sponges

"Tear-drop" sanding blocks

A sander for any sanding task

Assemble a team of sanders for your woodworking and carpentry projects. The most versatile sander is the *random-orbit sander*. The irregular sanding action of this tool keeps sanding marks to a minimum, and is suitable for both rough sanding and fine finish sanding. *Belt sanders* can remove a lot of material in a hurry, making them useful for resurfacing as well as smoothing very rough stock. A *detail sander* has a small, triangular pad that can get into those hard-to-reach spots. A 1/4 or 1/3 *sheet finishing sander* does a fine job preparing surfaces for a finish, and is cheaper than a random-orbit sander.

A sampling of sanders and sanding blocks

Fabricated sanding blocks have soft pads and are designed to be easy and comfortable to grip. *"Tear-drop" sanding blocks* are made to fit the most common molding profiles. *Sanding sponges* can remove surprising amounts of material quickly and will conform to irregular surfaces.

1 Cut a 4- to 6-in. strip of the molding or trim you need to sand. Tack a small piece of scrap wood to each end of the molding strip to create "forms." Fill or cover the molding with auto body filler, smoothing the filler so it's level with the tops of the forms. Let the filler dry according to the manufacturer's recommendations.

2 Remove the molded auto body filler and hot-glue a block of wood to the flat face to give the sanding block greater rigidity and durability. Wrap a piece of sandpaper around the shaped face and start sanding. Note: This technique also works with convex sanding profiles.

Sanding tips

Sanding wallboard

Use a wallboard sanding block fitted with metal sanding mesh to smooth out dried wallboard compound on taped wallboard seams. The sanding mesh removes compound smoothly, without creating fine dust.

Try detail sanders

New power sanders are hitting the market all the time. Many of the more recent innovations are in the detail sander area. These compact tools have triangular sanding pads that let them fit into areas that otherwise could only be hand-sanded.

Build a drum sander dust-collection box

Drum sander attachments for the drill press are terrific for smoothing curves and sanding interior cutouts, but they can make quite a mess. Keep sanding dust in check by building a dust collection box that's clamped to your drill press table. Make a cutout in the side of the box for a vacuum hose port, and another cutout on the top for the sanding drums to fit into. The top of the box also comes in handy as a sanding table.

Cabinet scrapers

Flex blade to bow toward the direction of the scraping motion

TO USE A CABINET SCRAPER, hold the ends and press in with your thumbs to cause a slight flex. Hold the scraper at a fairly steep angle and push it away from yourself, applying downward pressure as you push (you can also flex the scraper inward and draw it toward yourself).

The cabinet scraper isn't just a tool for cabinetmakers. This simple metal blade can do away with almost all of the need for sanding in woodworking shops. As long as the cutting burr is sharp, the cabinet scraper will shave off paper-thin wisps of wood, leaving behind a glass-smooth surface that has no sanding marks. If you've never used a cabinet scraper, it's well worth investing a few dollars to try out this valuable tool. You may never go back to sanding again.

How to make sharp burrs on cabinet scraper edges

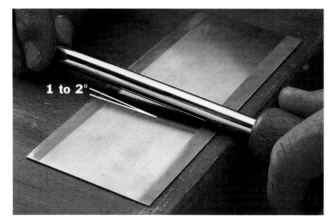

1 File down any traces of the old burrs on all edges of the cabinet scraper, using a fine single-cut metal file. Don't get too aggressive with the file—it doesn't take much power to remove a fine burr.

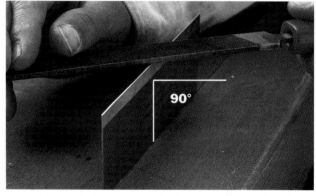

2 With the cabinet scraper held firmly in a vertical position, file the edges flat at an exact 90° angle, using the metal file. Take care not to overwork the edge.

3 With the scraper lying flat on a worksurface, rub across the edges of the scraper with a burnishing tool held at a very slight angle. If you don't have a burnishing tool, any piece of round hardened steel (like the top of a chisel shank) will do. The edge of the scraper should be set back just slightly from the edge of the worksurface to prevent you from burnishing at an angle that's too steep.

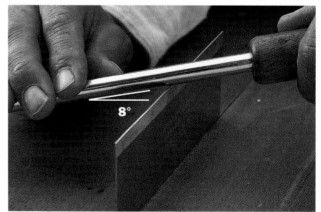

4 Scrape across the edge of the scraper with the burnishing tool, holding the tool at an angle of about 8°. This will create a slight burr that accomplishes the cutting action of the scraper. Create burrs on all four edges of the scraper, flipping the tool as each edge becomes dull.

SCREW HOLE COUNTERBORES can be plugged with matching wood plugs or with contrasting plugs that give the project decorative flair, as above.

Screw Counterbore Sizes

Gauge	Head bore	Shank bore	Pilot hole
2	11/64	3/32	1/16
3	13/64	7/64	1/16
4	15/64	7/64	5/64
5	1/4	1/8	5/64
6	9/32	9/64	3/32
7	5/16	5/32	7/64
8	11/32	5/32	7/64
9	23/64	11/64	1/8
10	25/64	3/16	1/8
12	7/16	7/32	9/64
14	1/2	1/4	5/32

How to counterbore and plug for wood screws

1 Drill a counterbored pilot hole using a counterboring bit or by drilling a pilot hole, then counterboring for the screw shank and the screw head, according to the dimensions in the chart above.

2 After the screw is driven, apply wood glue to the end of a screw plug. Set the plug into the counterbore hole with a wood mallet. For contrast, the grain in the plug should be perpendicular to the workpiece grain. For concealment, align the patterns.

3 After the glue has dried, trim the plug flush with the wood surface using a flush-cutting saw (See photo, above left). Take care not to mar the surrounding wood surface. Sand the plug smooth.

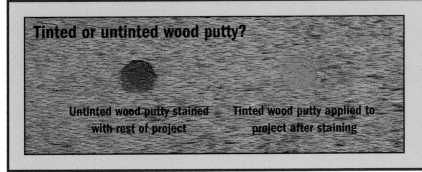

Tinted or untinted wood putty?

Untinted wood putty stained with rest of project

Tinted wood putty applied to project after staining

Debate over the best method to conceal nail and screw heads with wood putty has raged for generations. We've had the best success filling holes with putty tinted to match the finished color of the surrounding wood, rather than applying untinted putty and staining it at the same time as the rest of the project.

Steel Wool Types and Uses

Type	Description	Suggested uses
#3	Coarse	Remove old paint and varnish
#2	Med. coarse	Clean rough metal, concrete or brick. Clean garden tools, remove paint from molding
#1	Medium	Clean resilient floors, copper pipe and fittings
#0	Med. fine	Clean grills, pots, pans. Remove rust from metal tools (use oil)
#00	Fine	Buff painted finish. Clean screens and frames. Remove old finish from antiques
#000	Very fine	Polish aluminum, copper, brass and zinc. Remove minor burns from wood and leather
#0000	Super fine	Buff woodwork, shellac and varnish. Smooth clear finishes. Clean delicate tools

STEEL WOOL AND ABRASIVE PADS (synthetic steel wool) have many uses in the shop, from general cleanup to buffing to stripping old finishes.

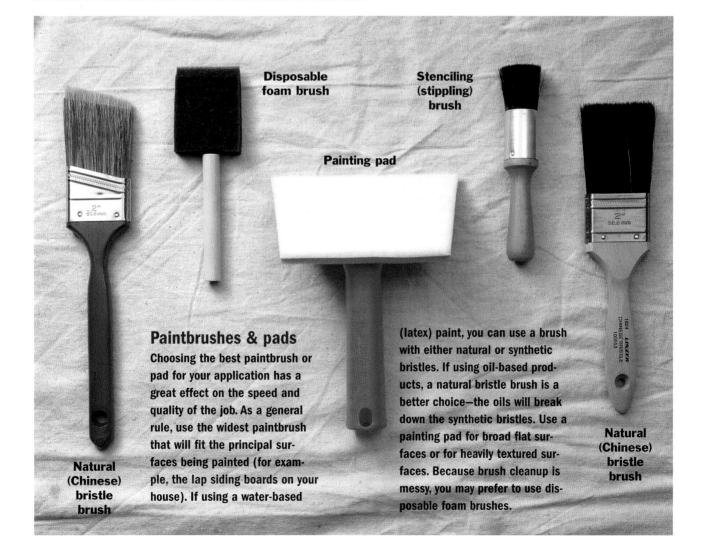

Disposable foam brush

Stenciling (stippling) brush

Painting pad

Natural (Chinese) bristle brush

Natural (Chinese) bristle brush

Paintbrushes & pads

Choosing the best paintbrush or pad for your application has a great effect on the speed and quality of the job. As a general rule, use the widest paintbrush that will fit the principal surfaces being painted (for example, the lap siding boards on your house). If using a water-based (latex) paint, you can use a brush with either natural or synthetic bristles. If using oil-based products, a natural bristle brush is a better choice—the oils will break down the synthetic bristles. Use a painting pad for broad flat surfaces or for heavily textured surfaces. Because brush cleanup is messy, you may prefer to use disposable foam brushes.

Wood Coloring Agents

Type	Strengths	Weaknesses	Recommended for:
Liquid stain	Can be built up to control color. Both conditions and seals the wood. Spray-on application can speed up and simplify application process.	Difficult cleanup. Application can be messy Slow curing time allows dust to settle in the finish. May show brush marks	Previously stained wood. Touching up wood finish.
Gel stain	Neat and easy to apply, with no running. Even drying. Color can be deepened with layering. Buffing will result in a hard surface.	High cost, difficult clean-up and limited color selection. Requires buffing between coats. Does not penetrate wood. Vulnerable to streaking.	Woodwork with vertical surfaces. Furniture with spindles and other rounded parts.
Aniline dyes	Color can be lightened or changed with a solvent long after initial application. Wide range of colors available. Greater control of tone.	Granular dyes must first be mixed with a solvent. Do not penetrate or bond well with pores of open-grain woods like oak or ash, requiring application of wood filler in spots.	Touch-up and repairs. Coloring or tinting a topcoat made of a similar solvent.

Do-it-yourself tack cloths

Make your own tack cloths for wood finishing by dampening cheesecloth with equal amounts of boiled linseed oil and varnish. Store them in a covered jar.

Sand lightly between coats of finish

After each coat of finish dries, sand it lightly with 400- to 600-grit sandpaper to knock down bubbles and surface defects. Wipe with a tack cloth when done.

Store finishing materials in a metal cabinet

Finishing materials and other potentially flammable or dangerous chemicals should be stored in a sturdy, lockable metal cabinet. Used office furnishing stores are an excellent source for this kind of cabinet.

Topcoat Types and Characteristics

Type	Uses	Characteristics
Oil-based polyurethane	High-use furniture and outdoor projects.	A durable, hard finish that resists water and alcohol.
Water-based polyurethane	Floors, interior woodwork (especially eating surfaces and toys).	Dries fast and cleans up easily resisting water and alcohol. Nontoxic and nonflammable.
Lacquer	Low-use furniture.	Medium durability in a rich-looking finish that is easily buffed to a luster.
Paste wax	Floors, antiques and fine furniture.	Provides a natural appearance that is easily renewed, but wears away quickly and must be re-applied with some regularity.
Shellac	Initial sealer coat and repairing blemishes in other finishes.	Highly resistant to humidity. Nontoxic and long lasting.
Tung oil	Uneven surfaces (e.g. chairs with spindles) and wood with highly figured grain.	A durable, moisture-resistant and nondarkening finish. It gives a low-luster, natural appearance while being easily applied or renewed.
Danish oil	Low-use furniture and antique restoration.	A durable, easily repaired finish that gives a warm, natural-looking tone with higher sheen than tung oil.
Linseed oil	Antique restoration.	Provides a low-luster, hand-rubbed look, but lacks durability and longevity.

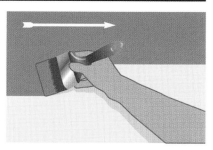

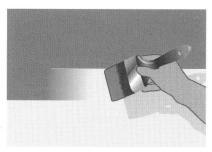

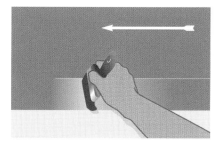

Feather paint for a smooth finish

Painting large, broad surfaces with a brush can produce streaking and brush strokes that remain visible after the paint has dried. Using the proper feathering technique is the best way to ensure that painted surfaces are smooth and even. Start by applying a fully loaded brush (paint should be 1/3 to 1/2 way up the bristles) across the surface from left to right—always begin at the top of the project area. As soon as the paint coverage begins to thin out, lift the brush slowly. Then, reload the brush and apply paint from right to left, in line with the previous stroke. Slowly lift the brush as you approach the endpoint of the previous stroke. Partially load the brush with paint and sweep it back and forth in the area between the two strokes to blend them together.

Water-based vs. oil-based finishing products

Wood coloring agents and topcoating products are available in both water-based and oil-based varieties. Each has its own advantages and drawbacks.

1960s' clean-air legislation prompted manufacturers to produce water-based finishes, and recent health concerns have bolstered their popularity. They are nontoxic and nonflammable. They also have weaker odors than oil-based varieties and can be cleaned up with soap and water. However, the transparent nature of water-based products produces a flatter finish than the oil-based versions, which tend to carry a more vivid sheen. It is easier to achieve an even application when finishing with oil-based products than with water-based.

Another characteristic of oil-based products is their enhanced workability, due to their slower drying times and weaker penetration of the wood. Water-based versions are absorbed deeper into the wood, drying quickly and producing an extremely hard finish. They also have a tendency to raise the wood grain.

Although technology for creating non-petroleum-based finishing materials is advancing quickly, the majority of tradespeople still prefer the oil-based products. But when deciding between the two finish types, be sure to consider the available ventilation and whether or not there are youngsters present. If ventilation is poor or kids may be in the area, water-based products may be a better idea.

How to revitalize hardened paintbrushes

Bristles hardened with shellac

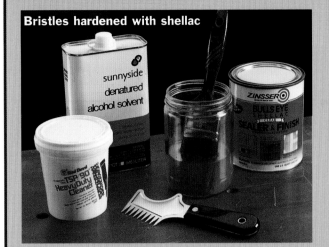

Bristles hardened with other finishing products

Most of us have a few old crusty paintbrushes that have been lying around the basement for months or even years. Whether they were cleaned improperly or not cleaned at all, we can't bring ourselves to admit that they're ruined. Well, they may not be. Try one of these tricks for softening bristles and giving new life to old hardened brushes. If the brush was used to apply shellac, simply soak it in alcohol overnight, then rinse and wash in a trisodium phosphate (tsp) solution. Use a brush comb to help clean and condition the bristles. For brushes that are crusted with other materials, try soaking them in paint and varnish stripper to dissolve the gunk, then rinse with tsp and comb. If you know the exact type of solvent used for the product that has dried, try soaking the brush in that product (for example, lacquer thinner) before opting to use stripper.

A one-two punch for cleaning oily hands

You should always wear rubber gloves when working with finishing materials, but just in case some product does get on your hands, here's an effective trick for cleaning it off. Wash your hands in ordinary vegetable oil to dissolve the oily mess. Then, rinse your hands with grease-dissolving dish detergent and warm water. You'll be amazed at the effectiveness of this one-two punch.

Suspend discarded oily rags in water

There is perhaps no greater fire hazard in the workshop than oily rags. Left crumpled in a corner or, worse yet, in a pile, rags containing petroleum distillate are highly flammable, and have been known to spontaneously combust. Don't take any chances. When you're through with an oily rag, drop it into a bucket of water until it can be properly disposed of at a hazardous waste collection site.

Storing hazardous finishing materials

All oil-based products, most solvents and paint removers, and even some water-based products fall into the hazardous waste classification. Leftovers should be handled and stored with care until they can be disposed of properly at a hazardous waste disposal site. Here are a few tips to note:

· Store in a cool, dark location, away from direct sunlight and heat sources.

· Do not set metal cans on damp concrete floors.

· Leave the product in the original container so you know exactly what it is and how to handle it.

· Do not store products in old food or beverage containers.

· Dispose of all products in a timely fashion. Most local waste manage-ment centers operate hazardous waste collection programs.

Evaporate unused paint before disposing of cans

Containers for water-based paints and finishes that are not considered hazardous wastes (See Tip, left) can be disposed of in your normal trash collection if they are completely empty and dry. Before disposal, set open cans in a well-ventilated area and allow the old product to evaporate until only a dry residue remains.

Using chemical strippers

Get the facts on chemical strippers before making your choice

Chemical strippers are very controversial these days. Most of the traditional strippers contain dangerous solvents that can cause health issues if proper protection isn't taken. Methylene chloride, acetone, tuolene and xylene are some of the active ingredients in chemical strippers that are considered dangerous. Because of these hazards, "safer" paint and varnish strippers have been introduced. Some have organic active ingredients that are less caustic, others simply evaporate more slowly, reducing the exposure. Many people who have tried these newer strippers have found them to be less effective than the older types (although frequently the problem is a failure to follow the directions properly). The best advice is to try a few different products, taking care to follow the manufacturer's directions, and decide which one you prefer. Perhaps even better advice is to avoid using chemical strippers altogether. A good sharp scraper will remove most finishes quickly and safely.

Save those planer shavings

The messiest part of using chemical strippers is scraping off and disposing of the goo and residue that's created by the stripping process. To make this step a little neater, scatter shavings from your power planer (sawdust is ineffective) onto the stripper after it has done its job, and allow the chemicals to soak into the shavings. Then, simply wipe up the shavings and dispose of them properly.

HOME FURNISHINGS & ACCESSORIES

Woodworking is about both the process and the project. In this book, you've heard that before. Now that we've thoroughly covered the process—your shop is all set up, you've mastered essential skills or improved those you already had—let's get into the items you can create.

That's what this *Home Furnishings & Accessories* chapter is all about. Here are 43 complete projects that walk you step-by-step, from start to finish, through each creation. You'll find all the details you need right here—"vital statistics," tool lists, shopping list, cutting list, and step-by-step, how-to-create-it photographs.

Woodworking does offer two rewards—the process, and the project. These pages give you the project ideas and instructions you need for guaranteed success.

Plant Stand

Both practical and attractive, this unique plant stand will brighten up any corner of your house. The ceramic tile top is mounted on a removable tray for easy cleaning or replacement. We used inexpensive Philippine mahogany to build the base, but you can use just about any wood you choose.

Vital Statistics: Plant Stand

TYPE: Plant stand

OVERALL SIZE: 15⅞W by 28H by 15⅞D

MATERIAL: Mahogany

JOINERY: Dowel joints

CONSTRUCTION DETAILS:

· Tile top is mounted to a removable tray so the tile can be cleaned or replaced if it breaks or becomes worn

· Top rails keep objects from sliding off tiled surface

· Decorative chamfers on tops of solid mahogany legs

· Lower shelf functions as a stretcher between legs

FINISHING OPTIONS: Clear coat with tung oil varnish. Paste filler for wood grain is a good option for mahogany. Match wood tones to tile color.

Building time

PREPARING STOCK
1-2 hours

LAYOUT
2-4 hours

CUTTING PARTS
2-4 hours

ASSEMBLY
2-4 hours

FINISHING
1-2 hours

TOTAL: 8-16 hours

Tools you'll use

· Table saw

· Jointer

· Planer

· Router table with piloted chamfering bit

· Tape measure

· 24-in. or longer bar or pipe clamps (6)

· C-clamps

· Spring clamps

· Combination square

· Doweling jig

· Drill/driver

· Back saw or dovetail saw

· Portable drill guide

· Power sander

Shopping list

☐ (2) 1½ × 1½ in. × 6 ft. mahogany (Philippine or Honduras—Philippine is shown here)

☐ (1) ¾ × 8 in. × 8 ft. mahogany

☐ ½-in.-plywood scrap for tray bottom (birch plywood is shown here)

☐ (1) 12 × 12-in. ceramic floor tile (or smaller tiles to create a 12 × 12-in. sheet)

☐ Tile adhesive, grout and penetrating sealer

☐ (1) ⅜-in.-dia.; (1) ¼-in.-dia. wood dowel for shelf pins

☐ #6 × 1, 1¼-in. wood screws

☐ Wood glue

☐ Finishing materials

Plant Stand

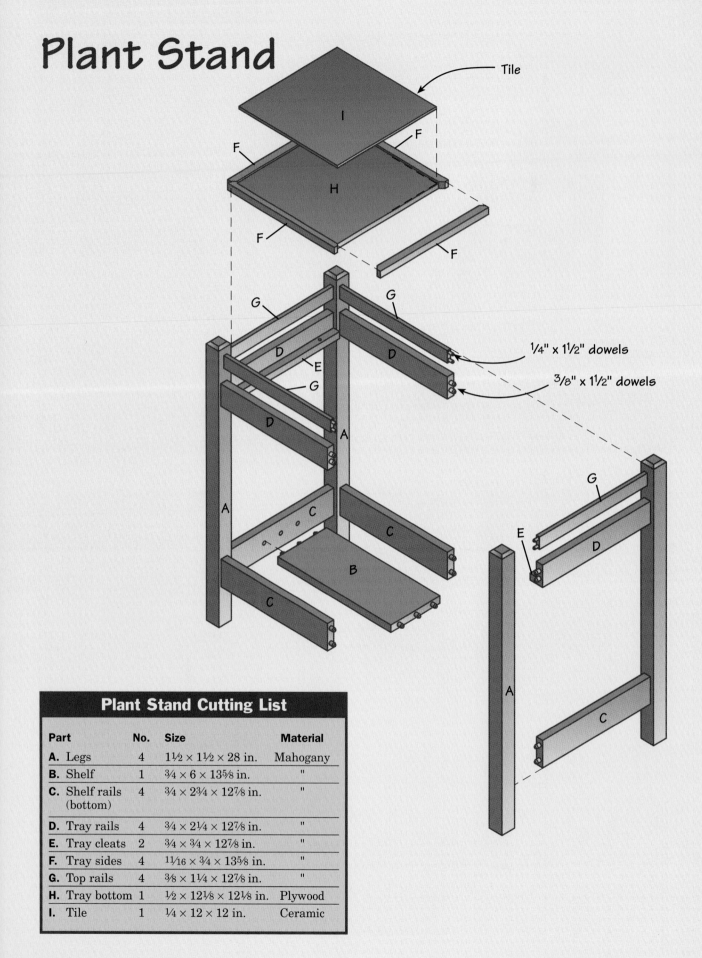

Tile

F

F

F

F

I

H

G

G

D

D

E

G

D

A

A

C

C

C

B

C

¼" x 1½" dowels

⅜" x 1½" dowels

G

E

D

A

C

Plant Stand Cutting List

Part	No.	Size	Material
A. Legs	4	1½ × 1½ × 28 in.	Mahogany
B. Shelf	1	¾ × 6 × 13⅝ in.	"
C. Shelf rails (bottom)	4	¾ × 2¾ × 12⅞ in.	"
D. Tray rails	4	¾ × 2¼ × 12⅞ in.	"
E. Tray cleats	2	¾ × ¾ × 12⅞ in.	"
F. Tray sides	4	11/16 × ¾ × 13⅝ in.	"
G. Top rails	4	⅜ × 1¼ × 12⅞ in.	"
H. Tray bottom	1	½ × 12⅛ × 12⅛ in.	Plywood
I. Tile	1	¼ × 12 × 12 in.	Ceramic

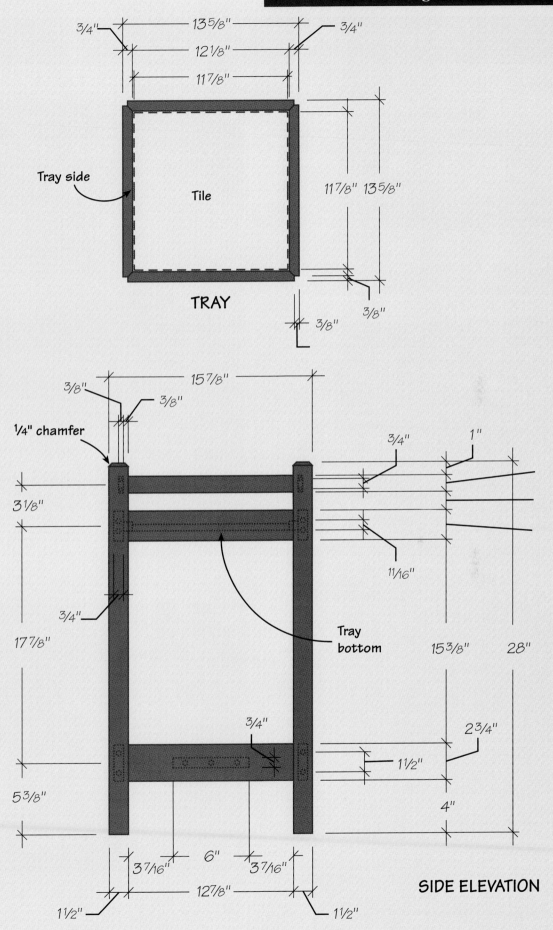

TRAY

SIDE ELEVATION

Plant Stand: Step-by-step

MAKE UP THE PARTS

1 Joint, plane and rip-cut stock to 1½ × 1½ in. square. Cross-cut the four legs to 28 in. long.

2 Chamfer the tops of the legs. We used a router table with a chamfering bit, but you could also use a stationary disc sander with a table, or even a small block plane. Set up your tool to cut a ¼-in. chamfer. If using a router table, position a fence with a bit relief cutout so its face is flush with the pilot bearing of the bit. To prevent tearout of the grain on the trailing edge of the cuts, back up each leg with a block of scrap wood as you feed the workpiece over the bit. We used a square pushboard to feed the workpieces and to provide a surface for keeping the backup block tight against the workpiece (**See Photo A**). Chamfer all four edges of each leg top.

3 From ¾-in. stock, rip-cut and cross-cut the four tray rails, the two bottom shelf rails, and the bottom shelf to size, using the dimensions given in the *Cutting list* on page 120. Then cut the four top rails to size from ⅜-in. stock (either resaw or plane thicker stock to ⅜ in. thick). All 10 rails can be cross-cut together at the same setting (12⅞ in. long). A power miter saw is a good tool for these crosscuts.

ASSEMBLE THE PLANT STAND

4 Lay out and drill all of the dowel holes to join the rails to the legs. There are two dowels per joint. Refer to the *Illustration* on page 120 for placement. A doweling jig like the one shown in *Photo B* will greatly simplify this work. The dowel joints for the tray rails and the bottom shelf rails are centered on the legs. They require ⅜-in. holes for 1½-in.-long dowels, but the dowel holes are only drilled ½ in. deep into the legs. The ¼-in.-dia. dowel holes in the legs for the top rails are off-center. If you place a ⅜-in.-thick spacer on the inside of the leg before clamping the doweling jig to the workpiece, this will shift the centerpoints of the jig holes the correct amount off-center (**See Photo B**).

5 Drill the ⅜-in. dowel holes for attaching the bottom shelf to the bottom shelf rails. Use the same doweling jig to drill the holes into the ends of the shelf (three in each end). To bore the holes in

PHOTO A: Chamfer the top edges of each leg. A backup block of scrap wood prevents tearout on the trailing edge of the cut, while a pushboard keeps it tight against the workpiece and permits a uniform, safe pass over the cutter and against the fence. Use a wood fence with a bit relief cutout.

PHOTO B: Drill dowel holes in the legs for the top rails. Since these joints are not centered on the legs, use a ⅜-in.-thick spacer to offset the doweling jig the proper amount.

the shelf rails, use a portable drill with a drill guide or a drill press with a brad-point bit **(See Photo C).** Drill only ½ in. deep into the rails.

6 Assemble two sides of the plant stand separately. Glue, dowel and clamp the parts together. For each side assembly, attach one bottom shelf rail, one tray rail, and one top rail between two legs **(See Photo D).** Measure the diagonals from corner to corner to check for square, and adust the clamp pressure as needed until the diagonals are equal.

7 Glue the dowels into the joints and clamp up the two side assemblies and remaining rails to complete the plant stand framework. Be sure to glue and clamp the bottom shelf in place at the same time. This serves as a stretcher to tie the lower legs together, as well as a shelf **(See Photo E).**

8 Rip-cut a ¾ × ¾-in. strip to make the tray cleats, and cross-cut to 12⅞ in. long. Due to the delicateness of parts this small size, the most effective tool to use is a sharp back saw in a miter box.

9 Drill countersunk screw holes for attaching the cleats to the inside faces of two opposing tray rails. Also drill two countersunk screw holes up through the bottom of each cleat for attaching the tray.

10 Apply glue to the tray cleats and use a spring clamp to hold them to the inside faces of tray rails on two opposite sides of the plant stand. The bottom edges of the cleats should show the countersunk ends of the screw holes and should be flush with the bottom edges of the tray rails. Drive #6 × 1¼-in. wood screws through the countersunk screw holes to attach the cleats to the tray rails **(See Photo F).**

ASSEMBLE THE TRAY

11 Cut the ½-in. plywood tray bottom to 12⅛ × 12⅛ in. We used birch plywood sanded on both sides.

12 Make up four tray sides from ¾-in.-thick stock. Rip them to ¾ in. wide. This will limit the depth of the tray recess so the top surface of the tile will be slightly above the tray sides. Leave the strips over-size in length.

13 Miter-cut the ends of the tray sides so they wrap around the tray bottom with their miters fitting together tightly. This can be done on a table saw with a miter gauge or on a chop saw.

PHOTO C: Drill dowel holes in the bottom shelf rails. We used a portable drill mounted in a portable drill guide equipped with a depth stop. Use a brad-point bit.

PHOTO D: Using dowel joints, glue and clamp up the legs and cross supports on a flat surface. Waxed paper protects your worksurface from glue spillage.

14 Glue and clamp the tray sides to the tray bottom. Apply glue to the miters and to the edges of the plywood. Use scrapwood cauls to distribute the clamping pressure and to protect the wood from the clamps **(See Photo G).** Glue-up the tray on a flat surface, making sure the bottom of the tray bottom and the tray sides are flush.

15 After the glue has dried, remove the clamps. Use a combination square to mark out ⅜ × ⅜-in. notches in the mitered corners of the assembled tray to fit around the inside corners of the legs.

PHOTO E: Glue up the frame base for the plant stand. Slip wood cauls between the heads of the bar or pipe clamps and the plant stand. Position the cauls so they distribute the clamping pressure evenly across multiple joints, if possible.

PHOTO F: Attach the tray cleats to the inside faces of the tray rails, using glue and #6 × 1¼-in. wood screws. The bottoms of the cleats should be flush with the bottom edges of the tray sides and should feature countersunk screw holes for attaching the tray bottom.

PHOTO G: Glue and clamp the tray sides to the tray bottom, aligning the mitered corners. No additional reinforcement is required.

PHOTO H: Cut ⅜ × ⅜-in. notches in the outside corners of the tray to allow it to fit around the inside corners of the legs. Use a small, fine-tooth saw like the dovetail saw shown above. Make sure to keep the tray plumb as you cut.

Use a back saw or dovetail saw to cut out the notches, cutting carefully along the waste sides of the lines **(See Photo H).**

APPLY FINISHING TOUCHES

16 Finish-sand the plant stand and the top surfaces of the tray sides. Ease all exposed sharp edges with sandpaper (but only ease the top, inner edges of the tray sides).

17 Apply the wood finish. We used Danish oil. For a fine finish, apply grain filler to the wood first—mahogany responds well to filler.

18 After the finish is thoroughly dry, tape off the top surfaces of the tray sides to protect the wood.

19 Lay a base of tile adhesive on the tray bottom and set the tile or tiles.

20 Seal the tile and any grout lines with penetrating sealer **(See Photo I).**

21 When the sealer is dry, remove the tape from the wood. Set the finished tray in place on the cleats, and screw it to the cleats from below with #6 × 1-in. flathead wood screws **(See Photo J).**

PHOTO I: Seal unglazed tile and grout joints with penetrating sealer. Use a disposable foam brush to apply the sealer. Because a plant stand is likely to be exposed to a considerable amount of moisture, sealer is important to protect the plant stand top and to help inhibit mildew and other forms of discoloration that can affect the grout.

PHOTO J: Lay the plant stand on its side and attach the finished tray by driving #6 × 1-in. screws up through the countersunk screw holes in the bottoms of the tray cleats.

Library Bookends

These sturdy white-oak bookends will support reading
materials of all sizes—including oversized books. To help
keep the bookends stationary, you can drill holes in the bases
and fill them with metal ballast. A layer of walnut, sandwiched
between the vertical oak frames, adds a sophisticated touch.

Vital Statistics: Library Bookends

TYPE: Bookends

OVERALL SIZE: 8½W by 11¾H by 8L

MATERIAL: White oak, walnut

JOINERY: Butt joints reinforced with glue and screws

CONSTRUCTION DETAILS:

· Holes in the bases are filled with ballast and hidden by base caps

· All exposed edges are rounded over with the router

· Cutout edges on frames receive routed chamfers

FINISH: Satin polyurethane varnish

Building time

PREPARING STOCK
1 hour

LAYOUT
1 hour

CUTTING PARTS
2-3 hours

ASSEMBLY
3-4 hours

FINISHING
1 hour

TOTAL: 8-10 hours

Tools you'll use

· Table saw

· Scroll saw

· Drill/driver

· Router with ¼-in. roundover bit, 45° piloted chamfering bit

· Drill press with 1¼-in. Forstner bit

· Jointer (optional)

· Planer

· Files

· Clamps

Shopping list

☐ (1) ¾ × 10 in. × 6 ft. white oak

☐ (1) ¾ × 6 in. × 8 ft. white oak

☐ (1) ¾ × 8 in. × 2 ft. walnut

☐ #8 flathead wood screws (1½-, 2-in.)

☐ Ballast (steel shot, sinkers, small nails, bolts, etc.)

☐ Wood glue

☐ Finishing materials

Library Bookends

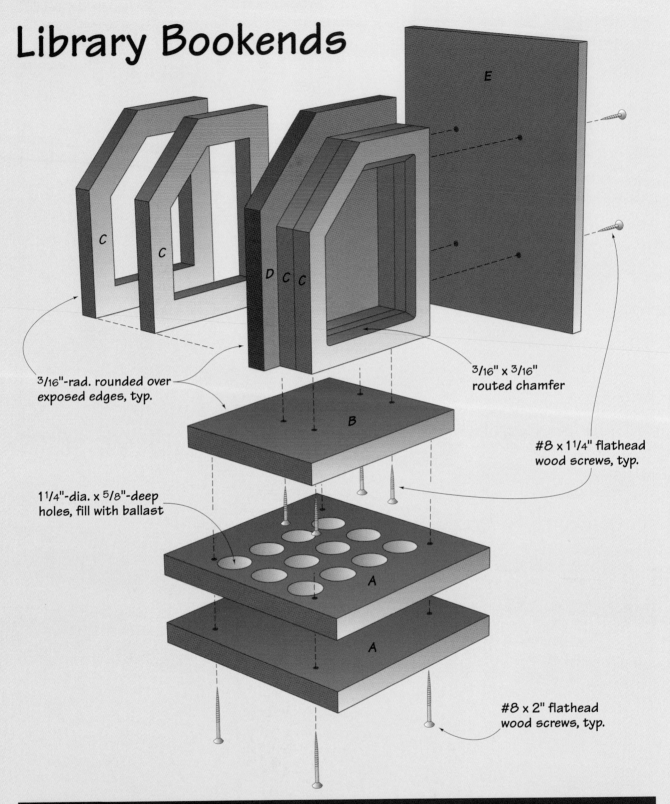

3/16"-rad. rounded over exposed edges, typ.

3/16" x 3/16" routed chamfer

1 1/4"-dia. x 5/8"-deep holes, fill with ballast

#8 x 1 1/4" flathead wood screws, typ.

#8 x 2" flathead wood screws, typ.

Library Bookends Cutting List

Part	No.	Size	Material
A. Bases	4	3/4 × 8 1/2 × 8 in.	White oak
B. Base caps	2	3/4 × 6 × 7 1/4 in.	"
C. Frames	8	3/4 × 6 × 7 1/8 in.	"

Part	No.	Size	Material
D. Dividers	2	3/4 × 6 3/4 × 8 in.	Walnut
E. Front plates	2	1/2 × 8 × 10 1/4 in.	White oak

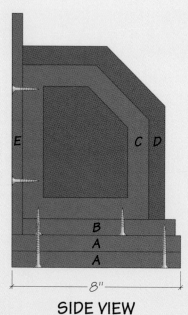

SIDE VIEW

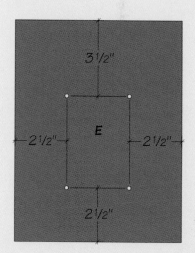

FRONT VIEW

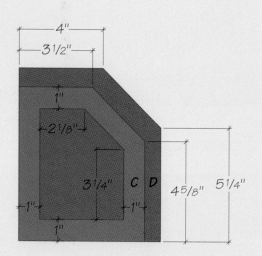

FRAMES & DIVIDER

FRONT PLATE

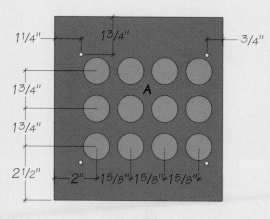

BASES

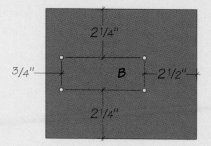

BASE CAP

START WITH THE BASES

1 Laminate the bases together: First, rip and crosscut the four base pieces to size, according to the *Cutting List* dimensions on page 128. Glue pairs of base pieces together to form two 1½-in.-thick bases.

2 Round over the top edges of each base assembly: Ease one end and two edges around the top face of each base assembly with a router and ¼-in. roundover bit.

3 Bore the ballast holes in the bases (optional). Lay out the locations of the ballast holes on the bases, following the *Bases* drawing on page 129. Drill the 12 holes in each base with a 1¼-in. Forstner bit on the drill press **(See Photo A).**

ASSEMBLE THE FRAMES & DIVIDERS

4 Cut the eight frame pieces to size and shape: First, crosscut eight 7⅛-in.-long blanks from your 6-in.-wide white oak board. Lay out the frame shape (See the *Frames & Divider* drawing, page 129) onto one of the blanks, and cut out the frame piece. Remove the center cutout area by drilling relief holes at each of the cutout corners large enough for a scroll saw blade, then trim out the waste piece on the scroll saw. Clean up the cut edges with a file and sandpaper. Use this frame piece as a pattern for tracing the shape on the other seven workpieces. Cut them all to shape **(See Photo B).**

5 Join the frames together and ease the edges: Glue and clamp pairs of frames together to form four frame assemblies. Be sure the edges and ends of the parts are flush. When the glue dries, rout around the cutout area on one face of each frame assembly with a piloted 45° chamfer bit set to a depth of ³⁄₁₆ in. Then ease the top end and angled and back edges of this chamfered face with a router and ¼-in. roundover bit.

6 Make the dividers: Rip and cross-cut blanks for the walnut dividers. Transfer the shape of the divider onto one of the blanks, following the *Frames & Divider* drawing on page 129. Cut the divider to

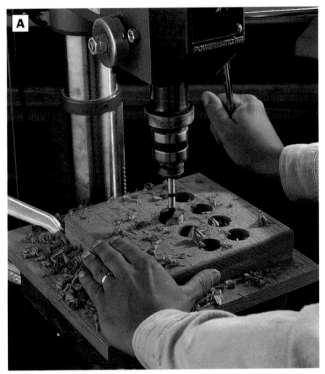

PHOTO A: *(Optional)* Drill three rows of 1¼-in.-dia. holes into the top face of both bases with a Forstner bit in the drill press. These holes will be filled with ballast and concealed by the base caps.

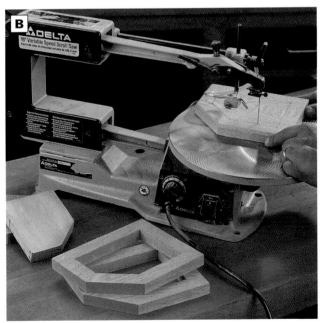

PHOTO B: Lay out and cut one frame to shape on the scroll saw, then use this first frame piece as a pattern for tracing the shapes of the other seven frames. To remove the center cutout from each frame, drill relief holes at each corner of the cutout so you can turn the workpiece on the scroll saw as you cut.

shape, trace its profile onto the second walnut blank and cut out the other divider. Rout the top ends and angled and back edges with the ¼-in. roundover bit.

❼ Glue up the frames and dividers: Spread glue over the inside faces of two frame assemblies and sandwich them around a divider. Clamp up the parts, making sure the flat, square edges of the three parts are flush. Then flatten the flush edges and ends of both frame/divider assemblies on a jointer **(See Photo C).** You could also use a stationary sander.

MAKE THE BASE CAPS & FRONT PLATES

❽ Cut the two base caps to size, then round over one end and two edges of the top face of each cap with a router and ¼-in. roundover bit.

❾ Make the front plates. Surface-plane an 8-in.-wide, 20⅝-in. oak blank down to ⅝ in. thick. Cross-cut the blank in half to form the two front plates, and sand the parts smooth.

ASSEMBLE THE BOOKENDS

❿ Fasten the base caps to the frame/dividers. Glue and screw a base cap to each frame/divider, so the flat end (without the roundover) of the base cap is flush with the long, flat edge of the frame/divider. Drive four countersunk 1¼-in. wood screws up through the base caps to attach them to the frame/dividers. See the *Base Cap* drawing, page 129, for screw placement.

⓫ Install the bases. First, fill the ballast holes with weight (steel shot, sinkers, brads or short screws will all do the trick). Then glue and screw the bases to the base caps with four countersunk 2-in. flathead wood screws **(See Photo D).** Note that the flat end of each base cap assembly is set back ⅝ in. from the flat end (without the roundover) of the bases to leave room for installing the front plate.

⓬ Fasten the front plates to the bookends with four countersunk 1¼-in. flathead wood screws and glue **(See Photo E).**

FINISHING TOUCHES

⓭ Break any remaining sharp edges with sandpaper and clean up residual glue squeeze-out. Apply three coats of clear polyurethane varnish.

PHOTO C: Flatten the long edges and bottom ends of the frame/divider assemblies on the jointer or sander. The purpose here is to produce flat, even surfaces to attach to the base caps and front plates.

PHOTO D: Attach the bases to the frame/base cap subassemblies with glue and countersunk 2-in. wood screws. Clamp and fasten the parts together carefully to keep from spilling the ballast.

PHOTO E: Position the front plates on top of the bases, clamp them in place and attach them to the frame/divider assemblies with glue and four 1¼-in. flathead wood screws.

Oak Cabinets

Store your best table linens and display your favorite china, glassware or curios in this handsome, efficient pair of stacked oak cabinets. Constructed as two separate units, the upper and lower cabinets are attached together to form a hutch-style storage unit that's at home in a dining room, kitchen or even a living room.

Vital Statistics: Oak Cabinets

TYPE: Storage and display cabinet

OVERALL SIZE: 36W by 75H by 16D

MATERIAL: Red oak, oak plywood and glass

JOINERY: Rabbet joints, double-rabbet joints, dowel joints

CONSTRUCTION DETAILS:

· Upper cabinet fitted with glass doors in oak frame

· Lower cabinet has two $8 \times 14 \times 31$-in. drawers

· Oak trim is profiled with ogee router bit

· Sturdy base structure

· Decorative crown molding frame on upper cabinet

· Visible carcase panels made from solid oak

FINISHING OPTIONS: Stain with clear topcoat

Building time

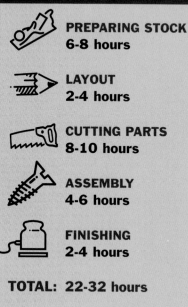

PREPARING STOCK
6-8 hours

LAYOUT
2-4 hours

CUTTING PARTS
8-10 hours

ASSEMBLY
4-6 hours

FINISHING
2-4 hours

TOTAL: 22-32 hours

Tools you'll use

· Table saw

· Jointer

· Power miter saw

· Jig saw or hand saw

· Router and router table with straight, rabbet and ogee bits

· Drill/driver

· Tape measure and metal rule

· Combination square

· 36-in. or longer bar or pipe clamps (8)

· C-clamps

· Hammer or tack hammer

· Screwdriver

· Wood chisels

· Doweling jig

· Nailset

· Pegboard drilling guide

Shopping list

☐ (1) $1/2 \times 4 \times 8$ birch plywood

☐ (1) $1/4 \times 4 \times 4$ birch plywood

☐ (1) $3/4 \times 4 \times 4$ oak plywood

☐ (1) $1/4 \times 4 \times 8$ oak plywood

☐ (13) $4/4 \times 6$ in. $\times 8$ ft. oak

☐ (5) $4/4 \times 4$ in. $\times 8$ ft. oak

☐ (1) $3/4 \times 3^7/16$ in. $\times 6$ ft. oak crown molding

☐ (2) $1/8 \times 11^{15}/16 \times 19^7/8$ tempered glass

☐ (2) $1/8 \times 11^{15}/16 \times 21^3/8$ tempered glass

☐ Hardware: (6) $2^1/2$-in. brass butt hinges; (2) pairs 14-in. drawer slides; (6) $3^1/4$-in. pulls; (4) door catches; (4) foot levelers

☐ Fasteners: 1-in. wire brads, 4d finish nails, $3/8$-in. dowel pins, #8 $\times 1^1/4$-in. screws

☐ Wood glue

☐ Finishing materials

Base Cutting List

Part		No.	Size	Material
A.	Foot Blocks	4	$1\frac{1}{2} \times 1\frac{1}{2} \times 4\frac{1}{4}$ in.	Poplar
B.	Bottom	1	$\frac{1}{2} \times 15\frac{1}{4} \times 34\frac{1}{2}$ in.	Birch plywood
C.	Base side	2	$\frac{3}{4} \times 5\frac{1}{2} \times 16$ in.	Red oak
D.	Base front	1	$\frac{3}{4} \times 5\frac{1}{2} \times 36$ in.	"

Lower Cabinet Cutting List

Part		No.	Size	Material
E.	Sides	2	$\frac{3}{4} \times 15\frac{1}{4} \times 18\frac{3}{8}$ in.	Red oak
F.	Top	1	$\frac{3}{4} \times 15\frac{1}{4} \times 34\frac{1}{2}$ in.	"
G.	Bottom	1	$\frac{3}{4} \times 15\frac{1}{4} \times 34\frac{1}{2}$ in.	Oak plywood
H.	Back panel	1	$\frac{1}{4} \times 33\frac{5}{8} \times 18\frac{1}{4}$ in.	"
I.	Trim	3	$\frac{3}{4} \times \frac{3}{4} \times$ Cut to fit	Red oak

Upper Cabinet Cutting List

Part		No.	Size	Material
J.	Sides	2	$\frac{3}{4} \times 10\frac{3}{4} \times 49$ in.	Red oak
K.	Top/bottom	2	$\frac{3}{4} \times 11\frac{9}{16} \times 32$ in.	"
L.	Adj. shelves	2	$\frac{3}{4} \times 9\frac{11}{16} \times 30\frac{1}{4}$ in.	Oak plywood
M.	Back panel	1	$\frac{1}{4} \times 31\frac{1}{8} \times 48\frac{1}{8}$ in.	"
N.	Stiles	4	$\frac{3}{4} \times 2\frac{1}{4} \times 47\frac{3}{8}$ in.	Red oak
O.	Rails (top)	2	$\frac{3}{4} \times 2\frac{1}{8} \times 11\frac{7}{16}$ in.	"
P.	Rails (mid)	2	$\frac{3}{4} \times 2\frac{1}{4} \times 11\frac{7}{16}$ in.	"
Q.	Rails (btm)	2	$\frac{3}{4} \times 2\frac{3}{4} \times 11\frac{7}{16}$ in.	"
R.	Retainer	8	$\frac{1}{4} \times \frac{3}{8} \times$ Cut to fit	"
S.	Light (upper)	2	$\frac{1}{8} \times 11\frac{15}{16} \times 19\frac{7}{8}$ in.	Glass
T.	Light (lower)	2	$\frac{1}{8} \times 11\frac{15}{16} \times 21\frac{3}{8}$ in.	"
U.	Crown	3	$\frac{3}{4} \times 3\frac{7}{16} \times$ Cut to fit	Red oak
V.	Trim	5	$\frac{3}{4} \times \frac{3}{4} \times$ Cut to fit	"

Drawer Cutting List

Part		No.	Size	Material
W.	Sides	4	$\frac{1}{2} \times 8 \times 14$ in.	Plywood
X.	Front/back	4	$\frac{1}{2} \times 8 \times 31\frac{1}{2}$ in.	"
Y.	Bottom	2	$\frac{1}{4} \times 13\frac{1}{2} \times 31\frac{1}{2}$ in.	"
Z.	Drawer front	2	$\frac{3}{4} \times 8\frac{3}{4} \times 34\frac{1}{2}$ in.	Red oak

Oak Cabinets

U (typ)

Magnetic catches

$2\frac{1}{2}$" butt hinges

O

N (typ)

Glass

$3\frac{1}{4}$" pull

V (typ)

I (typ)

$\frac{1}{4} \times \frac{1}{2}$" slots

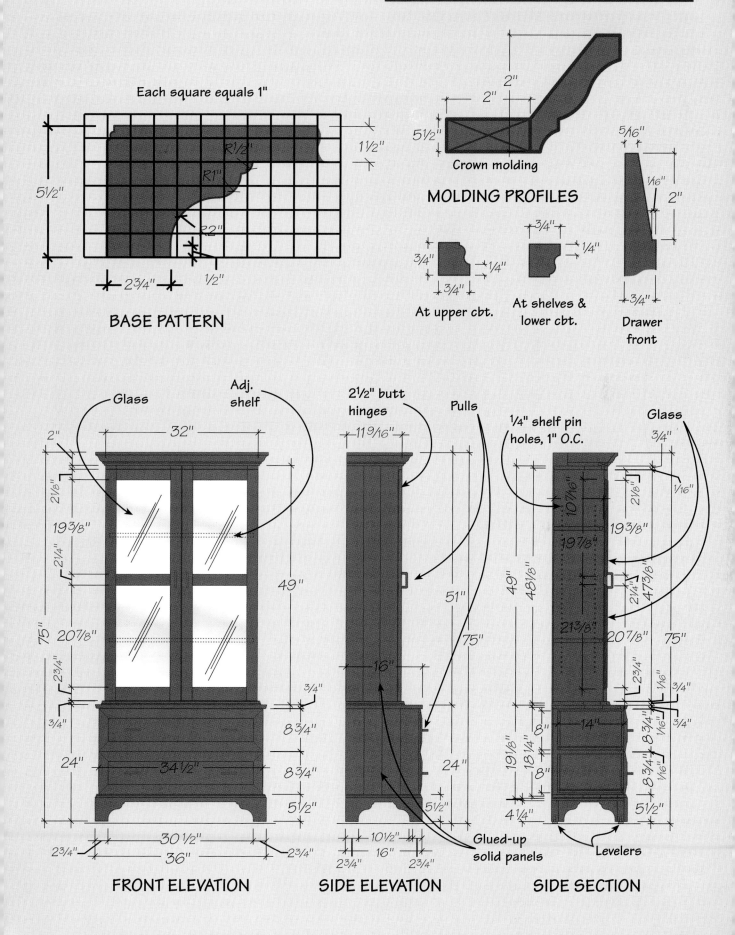

Each square equals 1"

R1½"

R1"

R2"

5½"

1½"

2¾"   ½"

BASE PATTERN

2"
2"
5½"

Crown molding

MOLDING PROFILES

¾"   ¼"
¾"
At upper cbt.

¾"
¼"
At shelves & lower cbt.

5⁄16"
1⁄16"
2"
¾"
Drawer front

Glass   Adj. shelf

2½" butt hinges   Pulls

¼" shelf pin holes, 1" O.C.   Glass

2"
2⅛"
19⅜"
2¼"
20⅞"
75"
2¾"
3¼"
24"
32"
49"
¾"
8¾"
34½"
8¾"
5½"
30½"
36"
2¾"   2¾"

11⁹⁄16"
51"
75"
16"
3¼"
24"
5½"
10½"
16"
2¾"   2¾"

10⁷⁄16"
19⅞"
49"
48⅛"
21⅜"
20⅞"
2¾"
14"
8"
19⅛"
18¼"
8"
8¾"   8¾"
4¼"
5½"

2⅛"
19⅜"
2¼"
47⅜"
75"
1⁄16"   ¾"
¾"
1⁄16"
1⁄16"
¾"

FRONT ELEVATION   **SIDE ELEVATION**   **SIDE SECTION**

Glued-up solid panels   Levelers

Oak Cabinets: Step-by-step

BUILD THE CABINET CARCASES
The upper and lower cabinets in this project are built using the same basic principles and techniques used to make kitchen cabinets and other forms of casework. Except for the back panels and the bottom panel of the lower cabinet (which is hidden by drawers and thus made of plywood), all the panels used to make the carcases are made from glued-up strips of red oak.

❶ Create edge-glued panels for the sides, top and bottom of the upper cabinet, and the sides and top of the lower cabinet. We used 4/4 × 4-in. red oak to make the panels. Plane the individual boards down to slightly more than ¾ in. thick before jointing, ripping to width and square, and gluing them up. *NOTE: If you have a surface planer with more than a 15-in. width capacity, you can plane down all the panels after the glue-up.* We used biscuits for alignment and to reinforce the glue joints. If you're gluing up long panels and then cross-cutting the individual parts to length, plan the biscuit layout so the biscuits don't cross the cutting lines.

❷ Rip-cut, cross-cut and plane the panels to finished size for the carcase parts. Also cut a bottom panel for the lower cabinet from ¾-in. plywood. Cut ¾-in. × ⅜-in.-deep rabbets in the top and bottom edges of the side panels for the upper cabinet. Cut ⅜-in. × ⅜-in.-deep rabbets in the top and bottom edges of the side panels for the lower cabinet, as

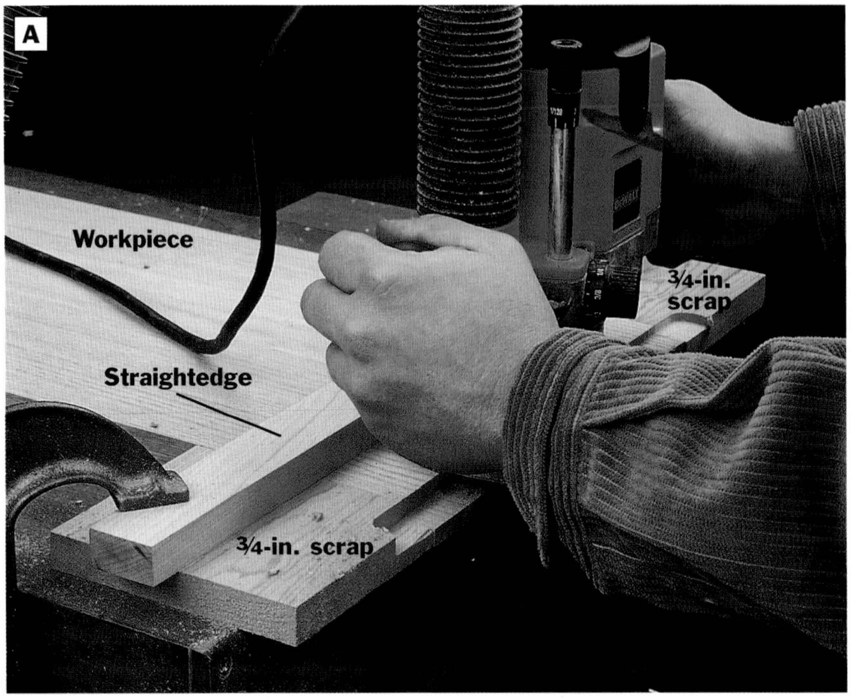

PHOTO A: Cut ¾ × ⅜-in.-deep rabbets in the top and bottom of the side panels for the upper cabinet, and cut ⅜ × ⅜-in.-deep rabbets in the top and bottom of the side panels for the lower cabinet. Also cut ⅜ × ⅜-in.-deep rabbets in the ends of the top and bottom panels for the lower cabinet. Use a router and straight bit to make the cuts. Clamp pieces of ¾-in.-thick scrap on each side of the workpiece, and clamp a straightedge cutting guide for the router to follow.

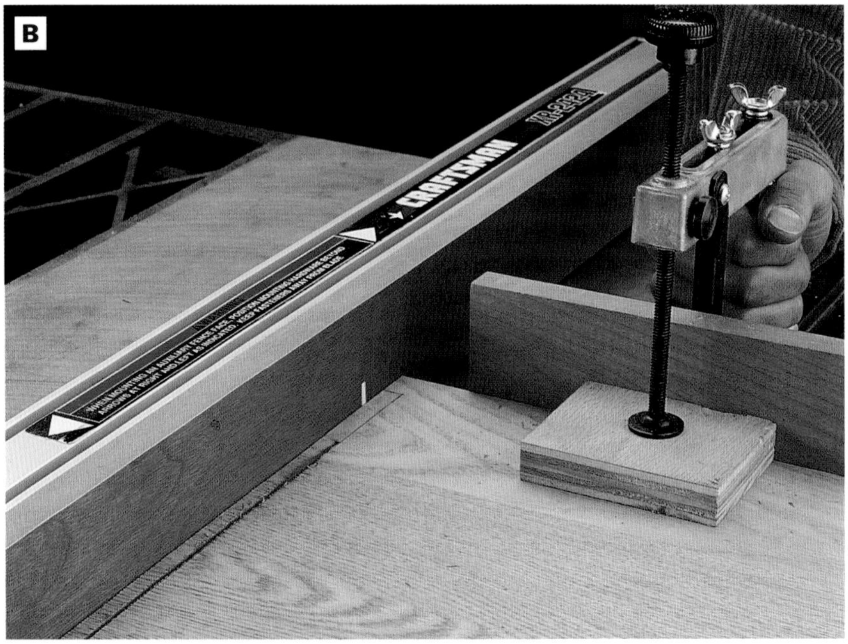

PHOTO B: Cut notches in the ends of the upper cabinet's top and bottom panels. Stop the cuts before the blade cuts past the end line of the cuts, and finish the cuts with a hand saw or jig saw. The notches create a ⅜ × ¾-in. tab that fits over the front edge the side panel on the upper cabinet, creating a recess below for the cabinet door frames.

PHOTO C: Drill shelf pin holes in the sides of the upper cabinet, using pegboard as a template. Orient the guide the same way on facing sides to ensure that the holes are aligned.

PHOTO D: Cut ¼ × ¼-in. rabbets into the back edges of the side, top and bottom panels to create recesses for the back panels. We used a router with a piloted rabbet bit.

Piloted rabbet bits

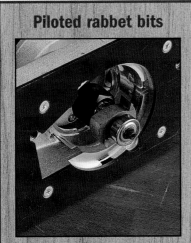

Piloted router bits have a bearing or a fixed spindle that follows the edge of a board as you cut, allowing the cutters to engage the wood and maintain a uniform depth of cut without the need for a straightedge guide. Piloted rabbet bits, like the one shown above, are generally available in sizes that will cut rabbets ranging from ¼ in. to ¾ in. deep.

well as in the ends of the top and bottom panels. The carcase joints in the lower cabinet are double-rabbet joints, and the upper carcase uses single-rabbet joints. We used a router with a ¾-in. straight bit to cut the rabbets **(See Photo A).**

❸ The top and bottom panels in the upper cabinet extend past the front edges of the side panels by ¾ in. to create a recess for the flush-mounted cabinet doors (which are attached with hinges to the front edges of the side panels). The front edges of the top and bottom panels should overlay the edges of the side panels. For this reason, cut a ⅜-in.-wide notch that starts at the back of the top and bottom panel, on each end, and stops ¾ in. from each front edge. Draw an outline of the waste material being removed at each end of the top and bottom panels, then set

up your table saw and cut most of the way from the back to the front. Stop the cut short of the end line and finish it with a hand saw or jig saw. Cut into the end of each panel to remove the waste, leaving a ⅜-in.-wide tab at each front end **(See Photo B).**

❹ Drill two rows of holes for adjustable shelf pins in each side of the upper carcase. We used a piece of perforated hardboard (pegboard) for a drilling template **(See Photo C).** Our plan called for shelf pins made from ¼-in. doweling, so we drilled ¼-in.-dia. × ⅜-in.-deep holes. We spaced the holes 1 in. apart on-center to allow for maximum adjustability. But if you do a little planning up front, you can eliminate most of the holes (and their "knock-down" look) by planning your shelf height and drilling only one or two holes for each shelf pin. Use a portable drill guide with a

PHOTO E: Assemble the carcases for the upper and lower cabinets. Use pairs of bar or pipe clamps and wood cauls to draw the panels together. Positioning the back panel in the back panel recess serves as a helpful reference for squaring the carcase.

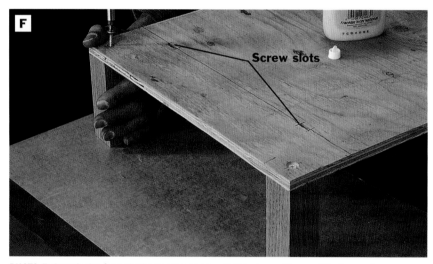

Screw slots

PHOTO F: Attach the foot blocks to the corners of the plywood base with glue and screws. Note the screw slots cut into the platform for attaching the base to the lower cabinet carcase.

PHOTO G: Cut the pattern shapes in the base trim pieces. We used a jig saw. Wait until you've cut the miters before making the contour cuts so you can be sure each cutout shape is centered and the correct distance from the ends of the trim piece.

depth stop to ensure the holes are perpendicular and the same depth.

5 Cut $\frac{1}{4} \times \frac{1}{4}$-in. rabbets in the back edges of the sides, top and bottom of each cabinet. This will create $\frac{1}{4}$-in.-deep recesses for the back panels when the carcases are assembled. Use a router with a $\frac{1}{4}$-in.-dia. piloted rabbet bit to make the cuts (**See Photo D**). Since the rabbets can run the full lengths of the parts, a table saw with a dado-blade set also could be used.

6 Cut the back panel to size for each cabinet from $\frac{1}{4}$-in. plywood.

7 Finish-sand the carcase parts. Glue and clamp together the carcases for the upper (**See Photo E**) and lower cabinets. Set the back panel in the recess at the back of each cabinet (without glue) to help square them up. Also check for squareness by measuring across the diagonals. Adjust the clamps as necessary. Use wood cauls to distribute the clamping pressure evenly. After the glue has cured, remove the clamps, then tack the back panels into the recesses with 1-in. wire nails.

BUILD THE BASE STRUCTURE
Unlike kitchen cabinets that are attached permanently, movable cupboards, cabinets and hutches require some type of sturdy base structure for support. For our oak cabinets, we decided to build a simple plywood platform supported by four square legs. The structure is trimmed with profiled red oak. And because wood movement is an issue with solid-wood cabinets like those shown here, we cut screw slots in the platform so the screws used to

PHOTO H: The trim pieces wrap around the base structure, adding decoration and "feet" to the cabinets. Use 4d finish nails and glue to attach the mitered trim pieces. Drill pilot holes for the nails (you can remove the head from a finish nail and chuck it into your drill if you don't have a drill bit small enough for the job). Set nails with a nailset.

PHOTO I: Attach the base to the underside of the lower cabinet with screws and washers. The screw slots in the platform allow the screws to move as the wood moves.

attach the lower cabinet to the base structure can move with the wood.

8 Cut a piece of ½-in. construction-grade plywood the same dimensions as the plywood bottom panel for the lower cabinet (if all you have on hand is ¾-in. plywood, you may use that instead, but be sure to subtract ¼-in. from the height of the foot blocks that attach to the platform). Cut four ¼-in.-wide × 1-in.-long screw slots, running front-to-back, about 4 in. in from each corner of the bottom platform board.

9 Cut four hardwood foot blocks, 1½-in.-square × 4½-in.-long. Apply glue, then drive a countersunk wood screw through the platform and down into each foot block (**See Photo F**).

10 The trim boards for the base feature an ogee profile, cut with a router, along the top edges and decorative cutouts on the bottom to create "feet" for the base. They are mitered together at the front corners. To make the trim pieces, rip-cut to 5½ in. wide a ¾-in.-thick strip of red oak that's at least 72 in. long.

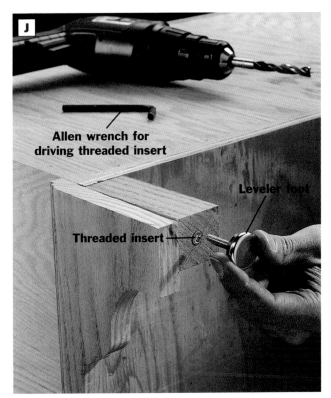

Allen wrench for driving threaded insert

Leveler foot

Threaded insert

PHOTO J: Leveler feet are attached to the foot blocks to protect the floor and to allow you to adjust the height of the cabinet to conform to unevenness in the floor.

PHOTO K: The sides, front and back for each drawer can be cut from a single 8-ft.-long strip of ½-in. plywood. By cutting the groove for the drawer bottom before cross-cutting the parts, you can ensure that the groove will line up on all four parts.

PHOTO L: The glued double-rabbet joints used to construct the drawer boxes are strong enough that no additional reinforcement is needed. Do not use glue or fasteners to secure the drawer bottom, which is inserted into the inside grooves prior to drawer assembly.

⓫ On a router table, rout an ogee profile along the top edge of the workpiece, using a ¾-in. ogee bit.

⓬ Cut the three base trim pieces to length, mitering the ends to form the front joints and making square cuts on the back ends of the side pieces. Make the mitered cuts on a table saw, using a miter gauge, or with a miter box (hand or power).

⓭ Enlarge the *Base pattern* from page 135 to size and transfer it to the front of each trim piece, starting 2¾ in. from each end (reverse the pattern for the right side of each cutout). Cut out the shapes along the waste sides of the lines with a jig saw or scroll saw (**See Photo G**). Sand or file the edges smooth.

⓮ Attach the trim to the base. Apply glue to the front and side edges of the plywood, the outside

faces of the foot blocks, and the mitered corners of the trim. Use 4d finish nails to fasten the trim to the foot blocks and the edges of the plywood. Set the nails below the surface of the wood with a nailset (**See Photo H**). Make sure the bottom edges of the trim are flush with the bottoms of the foot blocks (the tops of the trim pieces should extend ¾ in. past the top of the plywood platform).

ATTACH THE LOWER CABINET TO THE BASE

⓯ Turn the lower cabinet carcase upside down and screw the base structure to the carcase bottom through the centers of the slotted holes, using #8 × 1¼-in. wood screws with washers (**See Photo I**). Drill pilot holes into the bottom of the lower cabinet.

⓰ Install foot leveler hardware into the bottom of each foot

block. First, find the centerpoints in the bottoms of the foot blocks by using a miter square or a straightedge to draw diagonal lines connecting the corners. Drill guide holes for the threaded inserts, according to the manufacturer's specifications. Then insert the threaded inserts and thread the leveler feet into the inserts (**See Photo J**).

MAKE & HANG THE DRAWERS

The lower cabinet is fitted with two large drawers for convenient storage. If it better meets your needs, you could replace the drawers with shelves and cabinet doors, as in the upper cabinet. To save on materials cost, we made the drawers out of plywood, then attached a solid-oak drawer front to each drawer.

⓱ Rip-cut two 8-in.-wide strips from an 8-ft.-long sheet of ½-in. plywood to make the drawer

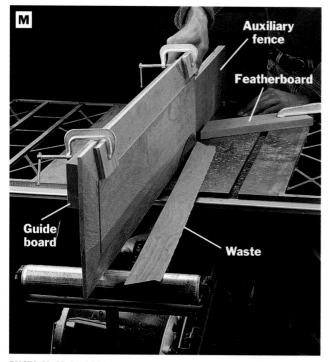

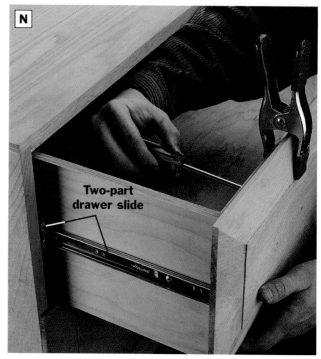

PHOTO M: Make 10° bevel cuts on all four sides of each drawer front face to create raised panels. Install a tall auxiliary fence and clamp a guide board onto the back of the panel high enough so it will ride on top of the auxiliary fence as you feed the workpiece into the blade.

PHOTO N: Attach the drawer fronts to the drawers with screws driven through the front, inside face of the drawer box and into the back face of the raised-panel drawer front. Hang the drawer boxes first so the drawer fronts will be perfectly positioned.

sides, front and back (one strip is enough material to make all four parts for each drawer). Cut a ¼ × ¼-in. dado in one face of each strip, ½ in. up from the bottom edge. This will be the groove to hold the drawer bottom. The dado can be cut on a table saw or a router table.

⓭ Cross-cut the drawer sides, fronts and backs to length **(See Photo K).**

⓮ On the ends of each of the drawer sides, cut ¼ × ¼-in. rabbets on the inside faces for double-rabbet joints.

⓴ Cut the drawer bottoms to size from ¼-in. plywood or hardboard.

㉑ Glue and clamp the drawer boxes together, with the bottoms captured in (but not glued into) their grooves **(See Photo L).**

㉒ Hang the drawer boxes inside the lower cabinet. Use two full-extension, 14-in. metal drawer slides for each drawer. Follow the hardware manufacturer's instructions for positioning the slides, and be sure to allow for the 8¾ × 34½-in. drawer fronts that will be attached to the drawer boxes.

㉓ Cut the drawer faces to size. You'll need to glue up two strips of oak if you don't have any stock that's wider than 8 in.

㉔ Cut a raised panel bevel into each drawer front on the table saw. Tilt the saw blade to 10°, and set the cutting height to 2 in. Set the rip fence ⁵⁄₁₆ in. away from the blade (the tilt of the blade should be facing away from the rip fence). Make a bevel cut along all four edges of each drawer front. Using a featherboard and a tall auxiliary fence,

make a test cut into ¾-in. scrap: The top of the bevel cut should form a square ledge about ¹⁄₁₆ in. wide (roughly the thickness of the saw blade), as shown in the *Drawer front* diagram on page 135. Adjust the blade tilt or cutting height as needed until the profile of the cut is correct. Cut all four edges of each drawer front to create a raised center panel **(See Photo M).**

㉕ Attach the drawer fronts to the drawer boxes. First, hang the drawer boxes in the lower cabinet. Then, position the drawer fronts against the drawers and adjust them until they are centered on the drawer openings and there is a gap of about ¹⁄₁₆ to ⅛ in. between the drawer fronts. Clamp the drawer fronts to the drawer boxes. Attach the drawer fronts by driving four #6 × 1-in. roundhead screws, with washers, through the inside faces of the drawer

PHOTO O: After the molding profile has been routed into the edge of a wide, ¾-in.-thick oak board, rip-cut a ¾-in.-wide strip of the molding on the table saw. Repeat the process to make up as much molding as you'll need (about 13 lineal feet for the project as shown). This process is easier and safer than ripping the molding to width first and trying to feed narrow strips across a large cutter on the router table.

PHOTO P: Make dowel joints at all the rail/stile joints on each cabinet door, then glue the joints and assemble the door frames. Position a bar or pipe clamp beneath each rail location and use clamp pads to protect the wood.

boxes and into the backs of the drawer fronts (**See Photo N**).

ATTACH THE CABINET TRIM

The bottom of the upper cabinet, the top of the lower cabinet and the front edges of the upper cabinet shelves are trimmed with ¾ × ¾-in. molding strips. We cut our own trim using a ¾-in. ogee bit, but you could purchase pre-milled molding with a similar profile if you don't have a router table.

26 Plane oak stock to a thickness of ¾ in. and square one edge on your jointer. Prepare enough stock to cut eight trim pieces of the following lengths: (2) 12 in.; (2) 18 in.; (4) 34 in.

27 Mount a ¾-in. ogee bit into your router table and cut an ogee profile along the jointed edge of each piece of oak stock. On your table saw, rip-cut a ¾-in.-wide strip from the profiled edges of the stock (**See Photo O**). Repeat this to make up as much trim as you need.

28 Miter-cut the molding to length to fit around the bottom edge of the upper cabinet and the top edge of the lower cabinet. Note that the molding on the upper cabinet is installed with the profile facing up, but on the lower cabinet and the upper cabinet shelves the profile faces down. Cut the adjustable shelves to size (if you haven't already). Attach the molding with glue and 1¼-in. wire nails. *NOTE: To allow for wood movement, attach molding to the short sides of the top of the bottom cabinet with nails only—no glue.* Set the nailheads. Make sure the trim pieces are flush with the the top surface of the cabinet part to which they're being attached.

MAKE THE UPPER CABINET DOORS

We built glass doors for the upper cabinet to allow the cabinet to be used for display purposes. The doors consist of oak face frames and ⅛-in. tempered glass panels.

29 Cut the door rails and stiles to size from ¾-in.-thick oak.

30 The rails are joined to the stiles with butt joints reinforced by dowels. Arrange the rails and stiles for each door and mark the locations of the rails onto the stiles according to the *Front elevation* drawing on page 135. Lay out and drill holes for dowel joints, using a doweling jig.

31 Assemble the door frames with glue and clamps **(See Photo P).** Check the diagonal measurements and adjust the clamps as needed to bring the frames into square.

32 Rabbet the inside back edges of the door frames to accept the glass panels **(See Photo Q).** Use a ¼-in. piloted rabbet bit to cut ¼-in.-wide × ½-in.-deep rabbets all around both openings in each door. Scribe the corners of the rabbet recesses with a straight-edge and utility knife, and chisel out the corners until they're square.

33 Lay out and cut mortises for 2½-in. butt hinges on each door. We used three brass butt hinges per door. The hinges are spaced 2 in. up from the bottom and 2 in. down from the top. The middle hinge is centered between the top and bottom hinges. Trace around a hinge leaf on the door stiles to make cutting lines for the mortises. Before chiseling out the mortises, score along the edge of the cutting lines to keep the wood from splintering. Use a

PHOTO Q: Rout a ¼ × ⅜-in.-deep rabbet recess around the perimeter of each opening in the upper cabinet doors. Use a ¼-in. piloted rabbet bit (See page 137) to make the cuts. Square off the rounded corners left by the router bit, using a sharp chisel. To keep the wood from tearing, score along the chisel lines with a sharp knife before squaring the corners.

PHOTO R: Chisel mortises for the hinges into the inside faces of the outer door stiles and into the front edges of the cabinet sides. Use one of the leaves from the 2½-in. butt hinges as a template for tracing the cutting lines for the mortises.

PHOTO S: Miter-cut the ends of the front crown molding strip and the front end of each side strip at 45° to make the crown molding assembly that is attached to the top of the upper cabinet. We used a simple crown molding miter jig to set up the cuts on our power miter saw.

PHOTO T: Attach the crown frame to the top of the cabinet with screws and washers. The screw slots in the tops of the scrapwood backer frame allow for cross-grain expansion and contraction of the solid wood top.

sharp wood chisel (the same width as the mortise, if possible) to cut out each mortise to a depth equal to the thickness of the hinge leaf **(See Photo R).**

㉞ Position each cabinet door in the door opening, making sure the outside edge of each door is flush with the edge of the cabinet. Mark the locations of the hinge mortises on the cabinet, then remove the doors. Lay out and cut hinge mortises at the correct locations in the front edge of each cabinet side. Do not hang the cabinet doors yet.

ATTACH THE CROWN MOLDING

We framed the top of the upper cabinet with crown molding for a nice decorative touch. Although it's possible to make crown molding yourself, using a shaper or molding cutters in the table saw, we purchased pre-milled, 3⁷⁄₁₆-in. red oak crown molding. If you've never tried to make miter joints with crown molding before, you may want to pick up some inexpensive pine or mahogany molding to practice your cutting skills before you cut into the oak stock. To simplify the process, we built a frame the same dimensions as the top of the cabinet, using scrap wood (we used 1 × 2-in. pine). Then, we attached the crown molding to the frame and mounted the assembly to the top of the cabinet. The main advantage to this method is that you can build the scrap frame so the corners are precisely square (no matter how careful you've been with the cabinet assembly, it's likely that the carcase is slightly out of square by this point, which will throw off the miter angles for the crown molding).

㉟ Mitered joints on crown molding require tricky compound angles. We built a simple jig for our power miter saw and used it to accurately cut the corners of the molding **(See Photo S).** To build the jig, cut a wide board (10 in. or so) and a narrow board (2 in. or so) to about 1 ft. in length, and butt-join them together into an "L" shape. Be very careful that the narrow board (the fence of the jig) is perpendicular to the wider board. Set a piece of the crown molding into the jig so one of the flared edges on the back side of the molding is flush against the fence of the jig, and the other flared edge is flush against the surface of the wider board. Slide a narrow strip of scrap up to the leading edge of the crown molding as it rests on the wide jig board. Be careful not to dislodge the crown molding. Mark the position of the narrow strip, then fasten it to the wide jig board with screws. To make a 45°

miter cut, simply set your crown molding into the jig as shown, swivel your miter saw to 45° and make the cut. Be sure to use the inside dimensions of the crown molding when measuring.

36 Attach the crown molding to the scrapwood frame with glue and 4d finish nails driven into pilot holes. Drive a finish nail into each miter joint to lock the joint together. Set all the nails below the surface with a nailset.

37 Drill screw slots in the molding frame to attach it to the cabinet top the same way the base is attached to the lower cabinet. Attach the crown molding assembly to the top of the cabinet, using #8 × 1¼-in. wood screws with washers **(See Photo T).**

APPLY FINISHING TOUCHES

38 Rip-cut scraps of your red oak stock into ¼ × ⅜-in. strips to make the glass retainer strips (you'll need about 22 lineal ft.).

39 Fill all nail holes with stainable wood putty, then finish-sand all wood parts to 180-grit, easing any sharp edges as you work. Wipe the surfaces clean with a tack cloth, then apply your finish (we used medium walnut stain and tung oil).

40 Set the glass panels into the recesses in the cabinet doors, then attach the retainer strips on the inside of each recess, using 1-in. wire nails, to hold the panels in place **(See Photo U).** Install the door hinges, pulls and catches. Screw the lower cabinet to the upper cabinet **(See Photo V).**

PHOTO U: Set the glass panels in place in the doors and secure them with ¼ × ⅜-in. oak retainer strips. Use 1-in. wire brads driven into pilot holes to fasten the strips to the inside edges of the rabbet grooves in the door frames.

PHOTO V: Screw the upper and lower cabinets together. Lay the cabinets down so their backs are flush. Center the upper cabinet on the lower cabinet, side to side, and hold them tightly together. Drill countersink holes for the screws (a tapered countersink hole will allow the screws to draw the parts together tightly).

Butcher-block Wine Bar

Combine storage for wine bottles and wine glasses with a handy surface for serving your wine and hors d'oeuvres in one sleek project. The durable butcher-block top can be used as a cutting board for slicing cheese or fruit. The bar fits neatly against the wall and blends with just about any decorating scheme.

Vital Statistics: Butcher-block Wine Bar

TYPE: Wine rack with bar top

OVERALL SIZE: 30W by 15D by 35H

MATERIAL: Red alder

JOINERY: Edge-glued joints, butt joints reinforced with screws

CONSTRUCTION DETAILS:

· Butcher block-style top

· Three racks hold up to 15 wine bottles with a slight downward tilt

· Beveled stemware holders provide hanging storage for glasses

· Screw heads concealed with wood buttons

FINISHING OPTIONS: As shown, three coats of tung oil were applied to the entire project. If you plan to use the bar top as a cutting board, finish it separately with a non-toxic finish, such as salad bowl oil or special butcher block oil.

Building time

PREPARING STOCK
3-4 hours

LAYOUT
2-4 hours

CUTTING PARTS
2-3 hours

ASSEMBLY
1-2 hours

FINISHING
1-2 hours

TOTAL: 9-15 hours

Tools you'll use

· Planer

· Jointer

· Table saw

· Biscuit joiner

· Band saw

· Drill/driver

· Router with 1/4-in. roundover bit

· Drill press

· 4-in. hole saw

· 1 1/2-in. Forstner bit

· Bar or pipe clamps

Shopping list

☐ (2) 6/4 × 6 in. × 8 ft. red alder

☐ (2) 3/4 × 6 in. × 8 ft. red alder

☐ #8 flathead wood screws (1 1/2-, 2 1/2-, 3 1/2-in.)

☐ 3/8-in.-dia. wood buttons

☐ Wood glue

☐ Finishing materials

Butcher-block Wine Bar

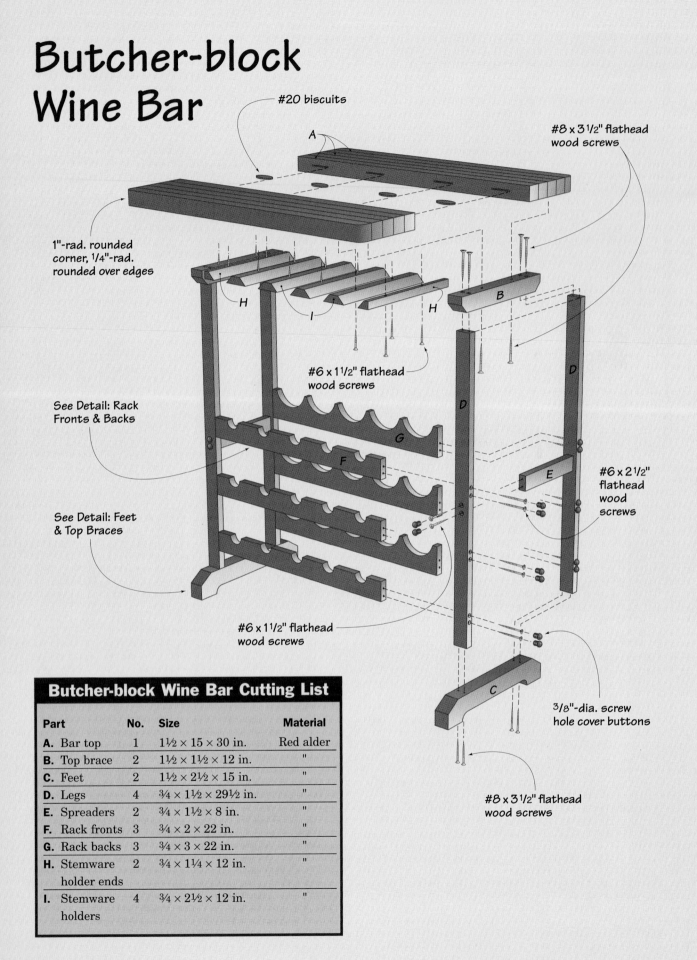

#20 biscuits

#8 x 3½" flathead wood screws

1"-rad. rounded corner, ¼"-rad. rounded over edges

A

H

I

H

B

See Detail: Rack Fronts & Backs

#6 x 1½" flathead wood screws

G

F

D

E

D

D

#6 x 2½" flathead wood screws

See Detail: Feet & Top Braces

#6 x 1½" flathead wood screws

C

3/8"-dia. screw hole cover buttons

#8 x 3½" flathead wood screws

Butcher-block Wine Bar Cutting List

Part	No.	Size	Material
A. Bar top	1	1½ × 15 × 30 in.	Red alder
B. Top brace	2	1½ × 1½ × 12 in.	"
C. Feet	2	1½ × 2½ × 15 in.	"
D. Legs	4	¾ × 1½ × 29½ in.	"
E. Spreaders	2	¾ × 1½ × 8 in.	"
F. Rack fronts	3	¾ × 2 × 22 in.	"
G. Rack backs	3	¾ × 3 × 22 in.	"
H. Stemware holder ends	2	¾ × 1¼ × 12 in.	"
I. Stemware holders	4	¾ × 2½ × 12 in.	"

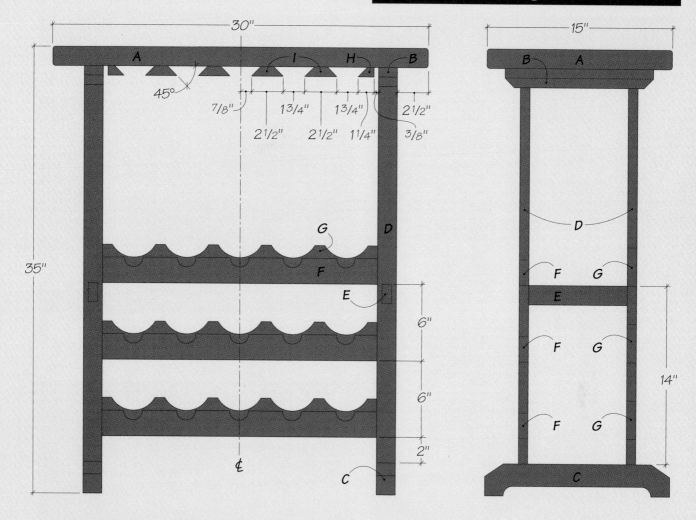

FRONT VIEW

SIDE VIEW

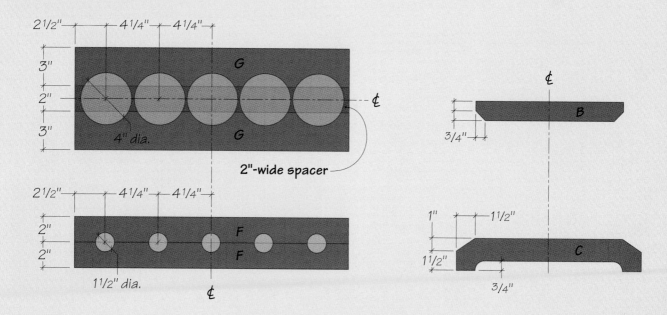

DETAIL: RACK FRONTS & BACKS

DETAIL: FEET & TOP BRACES

MAKE THE BAR TOP

The 1½-in.-thick bar top is built using butcher-block construction techniques. While a standard butcher-block surface (normally maple) is made with chunks of wood glued together with their edge-grain facing up, the bar top shown here consists of long wood strips (we used red alder) glued together with their face-grain edges up. In this way, it resembles a workbench—actually, the whole construction of this project is very much like a workbench.

❶ We used unplaned, 6/4 red alder to make the butcher block top (so in reality, the top was slightly thinner than 1½ in. after we jointed and planed the boards). If you would like a full 1½-in.-thick top, you'll need to buy 8/4 stock and plane it to 15/8 in. thick. Joint and plane the stock for the top so all sides are flat and square. Cross-cut it into ten 31-in.-long strips, and rip the strips to 1½ in. wide.

❷ Spread glue evenly on the mating faces (not the edges) of the strips and glue the sections together. We assembled the top in two groups of five strips to make the glue-up a little more manageable and reduce the risk of warpage **(See Photo A).** Creating two narrower sections also allowed us to use a 12-in. surface planer to smooth out the top. NOTE: *Cutting biscuit joints between the strips will help keep them aligned during glue-up, but it isn't necessary from a structural standpoint.*

❸ Wipe off glue squeeze-out with a wet rag (or, some people prefer to wait until it hardens, then scrape it off). Feed the two sections of blocks through the planer to smooth both faces of each, and plane them down to uniform thickness. OPTION: *Cut biscuit slots into each bar-top section to aid in alignment. Then, glue and clamp the two halves together.*

❹ When the glue is dry, remove the clamps and level off the joints with a sharp cabinet scraper **(See Photo B).** Don't just focus on one area though, or it will become dished out. Scrape the entire surface of the bar top. Scraping with a cabinet scraper can remove material more quickly and neatly than sandpaper, and you'll end up with a smoother surface.

PHOTO A: Edge-glue the bar top sections together in two five-strip sections. You can use biscuit joints to help in the alignment if you want. Alternate clamps top and bottom to ensure even clamping pressure.

PHOTO B: After edge-gluing the two sections together, use a sharp cabinet scraper to smooth out the seams between strips.

Roundover bit

PHOTO C: Roundover the edges on the top and bottom of the bar top. We used a router with a ¼-in. piloted roundover bit (See inset photo). A high-friction router pad holds the top steady.

5 Cross-cut the bar top to 30 in. Check the width, and trim to 15 in. if it's too large. Use a compass or a circle template to draw 1-in.-radius roundovers at the corners. Cut the roundovers with a band saw or a jig saw, and sand smooth. Ease all edges with a router and a ¼-in. roundover bit **(See Photo C)**. We held the bar in place during routing on a high-friction router pad, to keep from having to clamp it to the workbench.

MAKE THE BASE

6 Cut the workpieces for the top braces and feet to size (as shown in the *Cutting List,* page 148). Lay out the angled corner cuts on each part, using the *Feet & Top Braces* drawings on page 149 as guides. Also lay out the curved cutouts on the feet. Cut the parts to shape on a band saw **(See Photo D)**.

7 The wine racks that are connected between the legs are made from opposing wood strips with cutouts for the wine bottle base on one side and the neck on the other side. As shown, we installed three sets of rack pairs that hold five standard wine bottles each. If you're looking for a little more storage capacity, you can eliminate the stemware holders on the underside of the bar top, and add another rack pair 6 in. above the upper rack shown in the plan. To make the semicircular cutouts for the neck, we found it was easiest to cut circular shapes into wider boards, then rip them in half. Start by cutting two boards to 4 × 22 in. for the fronts. Draw a centerline down the length of each board, then use the detail drawings on page 149 as guides for laying out centerpoints for the holes. Cut 1½-in.-dia. holes at the centerpoints in the front board, using a Forstner bit, a spade bit or a 1½-in.-dia. hole saw in the drill press.

8 Cut three boards to 3 × 22 in. for the back members of the racks. Cut a 2-in.-wide spacer from ¾-in.-thick scrap wood and clamp it between two of the boards. Mark a centerline on the scrap board, then lay out centerpoints for 4-in.-dia. holes along the centerline, according to the drawing on page 149. Cut the holes with a 4-in. hole saw **(See Photo E)**. Cut another spacer, clamp it to the third back rack board, and lay out and cut holes.

9 Rip boards for the front rack in half along the centerline to create the racks with the bottleneck cutouts **(See Photo F)**.

PHOTO D: Cut out the profiles for the feet and top braces on a band saw or with a jig saw. Use relief cuts and starter holes to make tight curves and keep waste out of the way of the saw blade.

PHOTO E: Drill 4-in.-dia. holes at the centerpoints on a 2-in.-wide spacer to make the semicircular cutouts for the bottle bases on the rack backs.

Blade guard removed for clarity

PHOTO F: Rip-cut the rack fronts in half to yield the finished parts with arched cutouts. The extra rack piece can be installed above the upper rack, along with a rack back, if you choose to eliminate the stemware hangers.

PHOTO G: Lay out reference lines on the edges of the legs to mark where the rack fronts and backs should be attached. For speed and accuracy, gang the legs together and mark them all at the same time.

PHOTO H: After attaching the rack members, attach the feet and the top braces so the legs are 8 in. apart on the ends of the base.

⓾ Cut the four legs to size. Lay out the locations of the front and back racks on the inside edges of the legs, following the spacing shown on the *Front View,* page 149. You can mark all four legs at once by clamping them together, with the ends flush **(See Photo G).**

⓫ Finish-sand the racks, the feet, top braces and legs with 180-grit sandpaper.

⓬ Attach the racks to the legs with glue and two #8 × 2½-in. flathead wood screws. Drill counterbored screw holes for ⅜-in.-dia. wood buttons.

⓭ Attach the feet to the bottoms of the leg pairs with glue and #8 × 3½-in. flathead wood screws, driven through countersunk pilot holes in the undersides of the feet **(See Photo H).** The feet should be arranged so the insides of the legs are 8 in. apart. Attach the top braces to the legs the same way you attached the feet.

⓮ To keep the base from bowing (especially when loaded with wine bottles), we attached a spreader at each end of the assembly. The spreaders should be centered on the width of the legs, and the top edges should be level with the lower edges of the upper racks. Cut the spreaders to size, sand them, and attach them with glue and #8 × 1½-in. wood screws driven through counterbored pilot holes **(See Photo I).**

INSTALL STEMWARE HOLDERS
⓯ We attached beveled wood strips on the underside of the bar top to function as stemware holders. To make the stemware

PHOTO I: Glue and screw the spreaders between the front and back legs. The tops of the spreaders should be level with the lower edges of the upper racks. All visible screw holes on the legs should be counterbored to accept wood buttons.

PHOTO J: Bevel-rip six strips of ¾-in.-thick stock at 45° and cross-cut the strips in 12-in. lengths to make the stemware holders and holder ends. The holders should be beveled on both edges, and 2½ in. wide on the wider face. The stemware holder ends should be beveled on one edge and be 1¼ in. wide.

holders, bevel-rip strips of ¾-in.-thick stock so they're 2½ in. wide, with 45° bevels on each edge **(See Photo J).** Cross-cut six pieces to 12 in. long. Rip two of the pieces to 1¼ in. wide to make the two end pieces.

16 Attach the stemware hangers to the underside of the bar top according to the spacing shown on *Front View,* page 149. The ends of each piece should be 1½ in. from the edges of the the bar top. Attach the stemware holders with #8 × 1½-in. wood screws driven through countersunk pilot holes in the holders, and into the underside of the bar top.

17 Center the bar top on the top braces and attach it with #8 × 3½-in. wood screws driven through the top braces and into the bar top **(See Photo K).** Do not use glue to attach the bar top.

FINISHING TOUCHES

18 Inspect the project and sand any surfaces that still need it. Ease all sharp edges with sandpaper. Apply a dab of wood glue to the wood plugs and tap them into the countersunk holes in the legs **(See Photo L).**

19 Apply the finish. We used three coats of tung oil. NOTE: *If you plan to use the bar top as a cutting board, finish it separately using linseed oil, salad bowl oil or butcher-block oil.*

PHOTO K: After the stemware holders are attached to the underside, screw the bar top to the top braces. Don't use glue to attach the top.

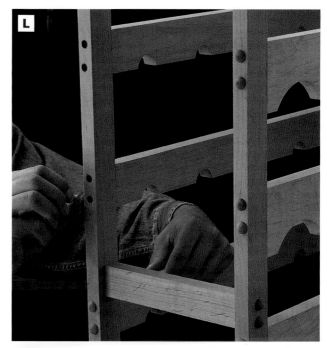

PHOTO L: Glue ⅜-in.-dia. wood buttons into the screw counterbores on the legs. The mushroom-cap-style wood buttons are used for decorative effect. If you prefer, you can use standard wood plugs and trim them flush with the surrounding wood.

Night Stand

Tuck remote controls and reading materials away neatly in this compact night stand project. Our simple design makes use of a variety of building materials including solid maple, maple and birch plywoods and melamine-covered particleboard. Most noticeable however, is the curly maple veneer that spruces up the tabletop and drawer face to create decorative flair. Although it's designed to be used as a night stand, this project could suit a variety of other purposes, such as an end table or telephone table.

Vital Statistics: Night Stand

TYPE: Night stand

OVERALL SIZE: 18D by 20W by 26H

MATERIAL: Solid maple, maple (or birch) plywood, melamine plywood

JOINERY: Butt joints reinforced with biscuits, nails or screws; dado and miter joints

CONSTRUCTION DETAILS:

· Tabletop and drawer face are covered with maple veneer and edge-banding

· Curved sides, front edges and top

· Drawer outfitted with full-extension metal drawer slides that allow complete access to drawer contents

· Cabinet has a finished back so it can stand in the middle of a room

FINISHING OPTIONS: Three coats of polyurethane varnish, Danish oil or tung oil

Building time

PREPARING STOCK
2-3 hours

LAYOUT
2-3 hours

CUTTING PARTS
1-2 hours

ASSEMBLY
4-5 hours

FINISHING
1-2 hours

TOTAL: 10-15 hours

Tools you'll use

· Jointer

· Planer

· Jig saw or band saw

· Oscillating spindle sander or drum sander on the drill press

· Table saw

· Router with 1/4-in. straight bit, 1/2-in. flush-trimming bit, 1/2-in. roundover bit

· Biscuit joiner

· Power miter saw

· Drill/driver

· Hand plane

· Bar or pipe clamps, C-clamps, wood screw clamps, spring clamps

Shopping list

☐ (1) 3/4 in. × 2 ft. × 2 ft. melamine particleboard (melamine on one side)

☐ (1) 3/4 in. × 2 ft. × 4 ft. maple plywood

☐ (1) 1/2 in. × 2 ft. × 2 ft. birch plywood

☐ (1) 1/4 in. × 2 ft. × 2 ft. birch plywood

☐ (1) 1/32 in. × 2 ft. × 2 ft. maple veneer

☐ (3) 4/4 × 4 in. × 8 ft. maple

☐ #8 flathead wood screws (1-, 1 1/4-in.); 1-in. brads

☐ Wood glue

☐ #20 biscuits

☐ (2) 12-in. full-extension drawer slides

☐ (1) 1 × 1-in. wood knob

☐ Finishing materials

Night Stand

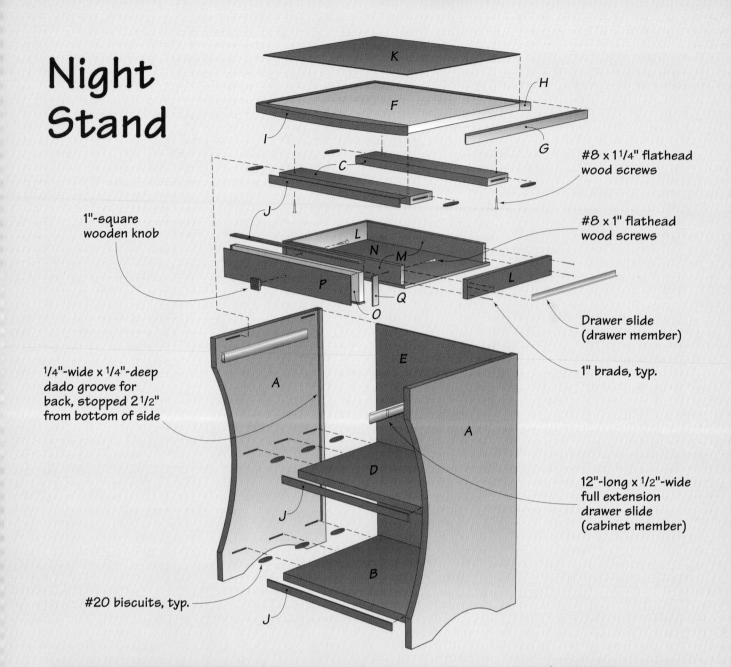

1"-square wooden knob

1/4"-wide x 1/4"-deep dado groove for back, stopped 2 1/2" from bottom of side

#20 biscuits, typ.

#8 x 1 1/4" flathead wood screws

#8 x 1" flathead wood screws

Drawer slide (drawer member)

1" brads, typ.

12"-long x 1/2"-wide full extension drawer slide (cabinet member)

Night Stand Cutting List

Part	No.	Size	Material
A. Sides	2	3/4 × 15 1/2 × 25 1/4 in.	Maple
B. Bottom	1	3/4 × 15 1/8 × 17 in.	Maple plywood
C. Top supports	2	3/4 × 3 × 17 in.	"
D. Shelf	1	3/4 × 11 7/8 × 17 in.	"
E. Back	1	1/4 × 17 1/2 × 22 1/2 in.	"
F. Top core	1	3/4 × 15 5/8 × 18 1/2 in.	Melamine
G. Top edging (sides)	2	13/16 × 3/4 × 17 1/8 in.	Maple
H. Top edging (back)	1	13/16 × 3/4 × 20 in.	"
I. Top edging (front)	1	13/16 × 15/8 × 20 in.	"
J. Edging	6	1/8 × 7/8 × 17 1/4 in.	"

Part	No.	Size	Material
K. Top veneer	1	1/32 × 8 1/2 × 19 1/2 in.	Maple
L. Drawer sides	2	1/2 × 1 3/4 × 12 in.	Birch plywood
M. Drawer front, back	2	1/2 × 1 3/4 × 15 in.	"
N. Drawer bottom	1	1/4 × 12 × 16 in.	"
O. Drawer face core	1	3/4 × 2 3/4 × 16 5/8 in.	Melamine
P. Drawer face veneer	1	1/32 × 3 × 17 in.	Maple
Q. Drawer face edging (ends)	2	1/8 × 13/16 × 3 in.	Maple

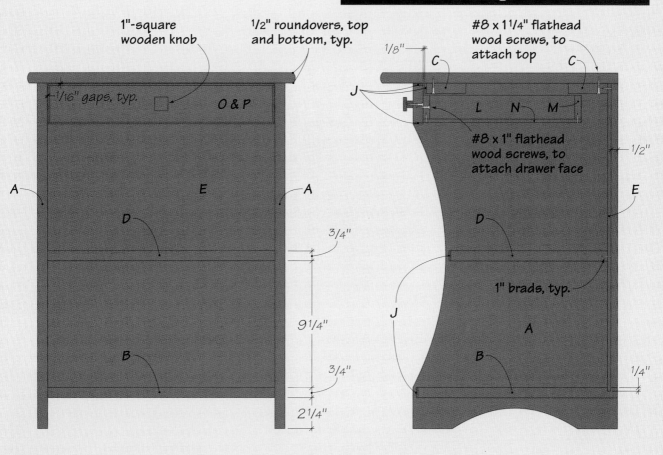

1"-square
wooden knob

1/2" roundovers, top
and bottom, typ.

1/16" gaps, typ.

O & P

A

E

D

A

B

3/4"

9 1/4"

3/4"

2 1/4"

FRONT VIEW

1/8"

C

#8 x 1 1/4" flathead
wood screws, to
attach top

C

J

L N M

#8 x 1" flathead
wood screws, to
attach drawer face

1/2"

D

E

1" brads, typ.

J

A

B

1/4"

SIDE SECTION VIEW

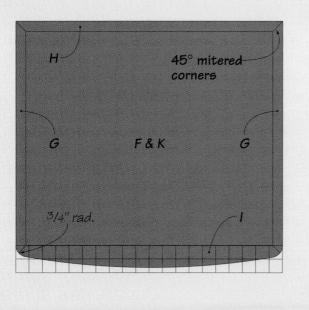

H

45° mitered
corners

G

F & K

G

3/4" rad.

I

Grid squares are 1" x 1"

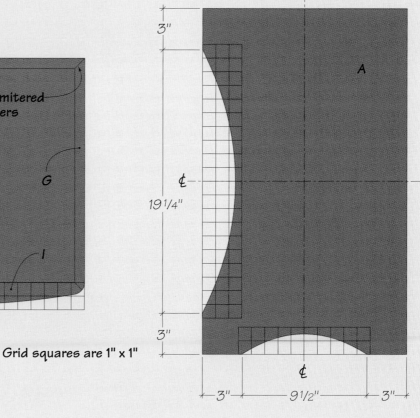

3"

A

¢

19 1/4"

3"

¢

3"   9 1/2"   3"

MAKE THE SIDES

1 Edge-glue panels to make the sides. First, surface-plane the 4/4 maple stock you plan to use for the side panels to ¾ in. thick and joint the edges. Since the side panels are 15½ in. wide, we used four 4-in.-wide boards per side panel. Cross-cut the boards to 26 in. long. Glue up each side panel with bar or pipe clamps, alternating the clamps above and below the panels to distribute clamping pressure evenly. After the glue dries, scrape and sand the panels smooth, then cut them to final size.

2 Lay out the curved shapes on the front and bottom edges of one side, using the grid drawings on page 157 as guides. Make the cutouts with a jig saw or band saw, then use the side as a template to trace cutting lines onto the other side **(See Photo A)**.

3 Clamp the two sides together and gang-sand them to the layout lines, using an oscillating spindle sander **(See Photo B)**. *TIP: If you don't have access to a spindle sander, you can still make identical curves in the sides. Sand one side panel smooth with a drum sander or by hand sanding. Then, clamp the two sides together and use a flush-trimming bit in your router to duplicate the curves of the sanded side onto the other unsanded side.*

4 Rout a ¼-in.-wide by ¼-in.-deep dado for the back panel along the inside face of each side panel. Locate the dado ½ in. in from the back edge of each side, and stop the groove 2½ in. from the bottom. Use a router with a ¼-in. straight bit, and clamp a straightedge to the side panel to guide the router as you make the cuts **(See Photo C)**. Make a mark on the straightedge or clamp on a stopblock to ensure the dado stops at the 2½-in. point.

ASSEMBLE THE CARCASE

5 Cut the bottom, top supports and shelf to size from maple plywood.

6 Resaw strips of ⅛-in.-thick edging from 4/4 maple stock that's at least 17¼ in. long. Before resawing, joint one edge of the maple stock, then plane the top and bottom faces until it's ⅞ in.

PHOTO A: Lay out curves on the sides, and cut them out with a jig saw or a band saw.

PHOTO B: To smooth the profiles on the sides (and to make them identical), we clamped the sides together and gang-sanded them on an oscillating spindle sander.

Dado stop mark

Straight bit

PHOTO C: Rout ¼ × ¼-in. dadoes along the inside faces of the sides, ½ in. in from the back edges, using a ¼-in. straight bit (See inset photo). Stop the cuts 2½ in. from the bottom edges of the sides.

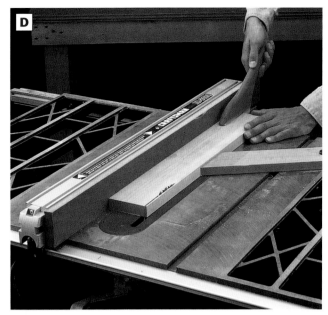

PHOTO D: Resaw ⅛-in.-thick edging strips from ¼ maple stock, using a table saw or band saw. Joint the cut edge of the board flat before you rip each edging strip.

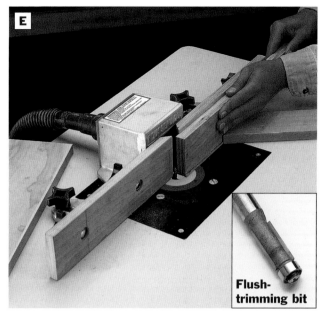

Flush-trimming bit

PHOTO E: Trim the ⅛-in.-thick edging flush with the plywood on the shelf, bottom, and front top support using a piloted flush-trimming bit (See inset photo). Secure the workpieces with a featherboard.

thick. Resaw six strips of edging, jointing the cut edge of the board after you rip each strip of edging **(See Photo D).** This will give you enough edging for the front edge of the front top support, drawer face top and bottom, the front edge of the shelf, and the front and back edges of the bottom.

❼ Glue edging strips to the front and back edges of the bottom, the front edge of the shelf, and the front edge of a top support. Spread glue along the jointed face of the edging and the mating plywood edge. Use four bar or pipe clamps to clamp the edging on the panel, spacing the clamps evenly along the length of the glue joint. Insert long wood cauls between the jaws of the clamps and the edging to distribute clamping pressure evenly. As you tighten the clamps, you'll need to readjust the edging, if it shifts, to make sure it overhangs evenly all around.

❽ Trim the top and bottom of the edging strips flush with the faces of the panels **(See Photo E).** Do the trimming on a router table using a ½-in.-dia. flush-trimming bit. Set the router table fence flush with the bearing on the bit to make the trim cuts, and clamp a featherboard to the table to keep the workpieces held tightly against the fence. Trim the edging flush with the ends of each workpiece using a fine-toothed back saw.

❾ Rout a ¼ × ¼-in. dado across the top face of the

bottom panel for the back. Position the dado ½ in. in from the back edge of the bottom panel, and cut the groove with a router and a ¼-in. straight bit.

❿ Lay out and cut #20 biscuit joints in all the parts to join the top stretchers, shelf and bottom to the side panels. Use one biscuit in the end of each top support and three biscuits per end for the bottom and shelf joints. Center the biscuits on the thickness of the supports, shelf and bottom, and use a straightedge to guide the biscuit joiner when cutting slots in the side panels **(See Photo F).** *NOTE: Locate the joints for the back top support so the back edge of the support is flush with the front edge of the back-panel dadoes in the side panels.*

⓫ Cut the back panel to size from ¼-in.-thick plywood. Finish-sand both faces, as well as the rest of the parts.

⓬ Assemble the carcase. Spread glue along the edges of the top supports, shelf and bottom and into the biscuit slots. Spread glue into the biscuit slots in the side panels. Clamp the carcase parts together, making sure the parts are properly aligned **(See Photo G).**

⓭ Before the glue sets in the carcase assembly, slide the back panel (without glue) into the dadoes in the side panels and bottom. If the dadoes are

PHOTO F: Cut biscuit slots in the sides and in the ends of the bottom, top stretchers, and shelf for assembling the carcase. Clamp a plywood straightedge to the side panels to help align the base of the biscuit joiner when cutting biscuit slots in the side panels.

PHOTO G: After gluing and clamping the carcase together, slide the back into the side panel and bottom grooves. Loosen the clamps a bit and adjust the carcase as necessary to square it up so the top edge of the back is flush with the top edge of the rear top stretcher. Then re-tighten the clamps and nail the back to the rear top support with three or four 1-in. brads. No glue should be used with the back panel.

exactly ¼ in. deep and the back panel is cut squarely, you should be able to slide the back in from the top and square the cabinet up by flushing the top edge of the back with the top edge of the rear top support. Make any adjustments necessary to square the carcase by adjusting the clamps. Attach the back to the top back stretcher with three or four evenly-spaced 1-in. brads. Set the brads below the surface with a nailset and fill the holes with wood putty.

APPLY THE TABLETOP VENEER

When you apply veneer to any wood surface, the opposite surface must be veneered also, to keep the panel from warping. On the tabletop and drawer face in this project, we're using particleboard covered on one side with melamine. We'll apply the veneer to the unfinished side of the particleboard, so the melamine will be opposite the veneer.

🄒 Cut the tabletop to size from melamine stock.

🄓 Select the veneer sheets you'll use for the tabletop. We used curly maple veneer for extra visual interest. Chances are you won't find a single 16-in.-wide sheet, so you'll need to join two narrower pieces of veneer together as we show here. If you have two consecutively-cut sheets from a flitch (a pile of veneers stacked in the order they were sliced from the log), the grain on one piece will mirror the grain pattern on the other piece. Arrange the two pieces so that the grain matches along the joint between the veneer sheets (called book-matching). If you have one long sheet of veneer, cut two 20-in. sections with similar grain pattern and lay them side-by-side in different configurations to determine which arrangement looks most pleasing.

🄔 Cut the adjoining edges of the veneer sheets. Each veneer sheet needs to have a straight and square edge so the seam between the sheets will be as tight and unnoticeable as possible. Here are two methods for trimming the veneer joint:

Method 1: With the sheets lying side-by-side, flip one sheet over on top of the other, as if you're closing a book. Align the edges and clamp them between two sheets of plywood or particleboard, leaving the edges that will join together protruding slightly. Lay a jointing plane or jack plane on its side, with the sole of the plane against the edges of the plywood. Run the plane along the veneer edges, trimming them until they are jointed straight and even. *TIP: Be cautious on the first couple of passes. If the veneer grain starts tearing out, try planing from the other direction. If the edge is grossly uneven, unclamp the plywood and back off the veneer overhang so only a little protrudes. Then reclamp and plane the veneer edge in two stages to avoid cracking the loose, flapping sheets.*

Method 2: Clamp the veneer sheets between smooth-edged sheet goods (like medium-density fiberboard or high-quality hardwood plywood). Set a router with a flush-cutting bit on the stack and run the pilot bearing along the lower board's edge to joint the edges of the veneers.

⑰ Unclamp the setup and lay the veneers side-by-side with the jointed edges together and the grain and figure matched up to your satisfaction. On the top face of the veneer, place a short strip of low-adhesion masking tape across the joint at each end and another strip in the middle. If you stretch the tape slightly as you lay it down, it'll pull the joint tight. Then, run a long strip of tape down the length of the joint **(See Photo H).** A second option for securing the veneer together is to use veneer tape (See *Tip,* below).

⑱ Glue the maple veneer to the tabletop panel. Apply regular wood glue to the particleboard side of the tabletop core panel (Do not apply glue to the veneer, or it'll immediately curl up into a roll). We used a glue bottle with dispenser rollers, but a foam paint roller or even a finely-notched trowel would also work to spread the glue. Completely cover the panel surface with a thin, even coating of glue **(See Photo I).**

PHOTO H: Tape the jointed edges of the veneer together. Use short strips of tape to hold the joint tight. Then lay a strip down the entire length of the seam.

PHOTO I: Apply an even, light coat of glue to the unfinished particleboard face of the melamine board. Because the glue sets up quickly, have the veneer and your veneer press close at hand.

PHOTO J: Clamp the veneer to the glued-up panel in a homemade caul-and-particleboard plate veneer press. Allow a few minutes for the glue to squeeze out, then check to see if the clamps need tightening again. Let the glue dry for at least four hours before you remove the veneered panel from the press.

Using veneer tape

Water-moistened veneer tape, available from most woodworking and veneer suppliers, is easier to remove than masking tape after it's been clamped under pressure—just wet it again and it peels right off with a cabinet scraper. Use a few strips of masking tape to hold the veneer together while you place strips of veneer tape across the seam. Then remove the masking tape and lay a strip of veneer tape along the length of the joint.

PHOTO K: Trim overhanging veneer with a router and a flush-trimming bit so the edges are flush with the tabletop.

PHOTO L: Glue and clamp the edging to the tabletop, using #20 biscuits to keep the parts aligned. Match up the miters. *Note: The long miters on the wider front edging will protrude past the sides.*

⑲ Position and clamp the veneer in place. Lay the veneer on top of the core panel with the tape facing up and immediately clamp the veneer to the core between two pieces of plywood or particleboard. The sheet goods will act as a veneer press, applying even pressure over the whole veneer surface. Use wood cauls across the setup to distribute clamping pressure **(See Photo J)**. *TIP: Since glue dries quickly, it pays to have the press ready and everything close at at hand before you spread the glue. It's also a good idea to slip a sheet of waxed paper between the veneer and the top plate of the veneer press; glue squeeze-out will occur through the wood grain of the veneer, which can bond the veneer to the top plate.* Leave the veneered panel in the press for at least four hours if using yellow or white glue—overnight is best.

⑳ Trim the veneer flush with the edges of the tabletop core panel. First remove the veneered tabletop from the press and use a router with a flush-cutting bit to trim off the overhanging veneer on all the tabletop edges **(See Photo K)**.

APPLY THE TABLETOP EDGING

㉑ Cut the tabletop edging to size from solid-maple stock. Cut 45° miters on the ends of the four edging pieces with a power miter saw or a table saw and miter gauge.

㉒ Lay out and cut biscuit joints for #20 biscuits, to help align the edging with the top surface of the tabletop. Apply glue to the edging and miters, and into the biscuit slots. Clamp the edging to the tabletop with bar or pipe clamps **(See Photo L)**. Clean up squeeze-out with a wet rag.

㉓ Transfer the grid drawing for the tabletop front edge profile (page 157) to the tabletop panel and use it as a guide for laying out the front edge profile. Cut along the curved layout line with a jig saw or band saw, and sand the sawn edges smooth. Then, use a router with a ½-in.-radius roundover bit to round-over the top and bottom edges of all edging strips (See *Front* and *Side Section Views,* page 157). Finish-sand the curved edges and the top face just enough to level the surface and smooth the grain, being careful not to sand through the veneer.

MAKE & INSTALL THE DRAWER

㉔ Cut the drawer sides, front and back to size from ½-in. plywood. Assemble the drawer parts with glue and 1-in. brads so the drawer front and back butt against the drawer sides at the corner joints. Cut the plywood drawer bottom to size. Sand all drawer surfaces smooth, then use glue and 1-in. brads to attach the drawer bottom to the drawer. Use the drawer bottom to square the drawer box before you fasten the bottom in place.

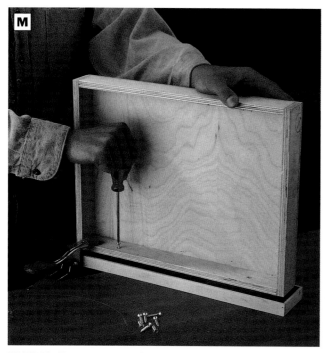

PHOTO M: Clamp the drawer face in position on the drawer front. Drill countersunk pilot holes and drive two 1-in. flathead wood screws to join the parts.

PHOTO N: Install the full-extension metal drawer slides and hang the drawer in the cabinet carcase. Be sure there is an even overhang between the drawer face and the cabinet carcase.

㉕ Cut the drawer face core an inch or so larger than the final dimensions given in the *Cutting List.* Select a sheet of veneer for the drawer face and cut it oversize as well. Glue the drawer face veneer to the drawer face core on the particleboard side, using a smaller veneer press and the veneer gluing methods you used for the tabletop.

㉖ Cut the drawer face to finished size. Rip-cut and cross-cut ⅛-in.-thick edging pieces for the drawer face ends. Glue and clamp the end edging in place. When the glue dries, remove the clamps and trim the edging flush with the drawer face edges. Glue and clamp the top and bottom edging pieces you cut earlier to the drawer face, and trim the edging flush when the glue dries.

㉗ Finish-sand the drawer face. Tack it into place on the drawer box **(See Photo M).** Allow even overhangs at the ends of the drawer face. The top of the drawer face should sit ¹⁄₁₆ in. below the tops of the carcase side panels and the bottom edge of the drawer face, minus the edging, should be flush with the bottom of the drawer box.

㉘ Hang the drawer at the top of the night stand opening, following the manufacturer's instructions for attaching the metal drawer slides **(See Photo N).** We used two 12-in. full-extension drawer slides.

FINISHING TOUCHES

㉙ Finish-sand any remaining rough spots and ease all sharp edges. Remove the drawer hardware.

㉚ Apply the finish of your choice to all parts. We used three coats of clear polyurethane varnish to enhance the natural color of the maple.

㉛ Reinstall the drawer slides and fasten the wooden drawer knob in place. Center the knob on the drawer face and attach it, screwing through the drawer front.

㉜ Attach the tabletop. Position the tabletop on the carcase so that the back is even with the carcase back panel and the sides and front overhang evenly. Attach the tabletop to the carcase with #8 × 1¼-in. flathead screws, screwing up through countersunk pilot holes in the top supports and into the tabletop.

Wall-hung Coatrack

Hang coats in style on this Arts-and-Crafts-inspired wall-mounted coatrack. The flat top even provides a place for gloves or keys. We built this rack from red oak, but you could use quartersawn white oak to make the project even more authentically Arts-and-Crafts.

Wall-hung Coatrack

Vital Statistics

TYPE: Coatrack

OVERALL SIZE: 32L by 10¾H by 8D

MATERIAL: Red oak

JOINERY: Butt joints reinforced with glue and screws

CONSTRUCTION DETAILS:
- Decorative end profiles duplicated using a full-size pattern
- Screwheads concealed with ⅜-in.-dia. oak plugs

FINISH: Stain and varnish

BUILDING TIME: 3-4 hours

Shopping List

- ☐ (1) 1 × 10 in. × 6 ft. red oak
- ☐ (1) 1 × 6 in. × 6 ft. red oak
- ☐ (4) Coat hooks
- ☐ #8 × 1½-in. flathead wood screws
- ☐ ⅜-in.-dia. oak wood plugs
- ☐ #8 × 2-in. brass screws, finish washers, wall anchors (if necessary)
- ☐ Wood glue
- ☐ Finishing materials

Wall-hung Coatrack: Step-by-step

LAY OUT THE PARTS

❶ Cross-cut a 32-in. board from the oak 1 × 10, and rip the board to 8 in. wide to form the coatrack top.

❷ Make the coatrack ends: Cross-cut a 21-in. board from the oak 1 × 10 then rip it to 7 in. wide. Cross-cut this workpiece to make the coatrack end pieces.

❸ Cross-cut a 28½-in. workpiece from the oak 1 × 6, and rip the board to 5 in. wide, forming the coatrack back.

❹ Draw the back profile: Make a mark 14¼ in. along one edge of the back workpiece to locate the widest point of the back profile. Refer to the *Back Layout* drawing, page 166, to draw the two tapering lines from this point out to the ends of the back panel.

PHOTO A: Lay out the tapered profile on the back panel with a straightedge, and use a full-size paper or cardboard template as a guide for drawing the curved end profiles.

Wall-hung Coatrack

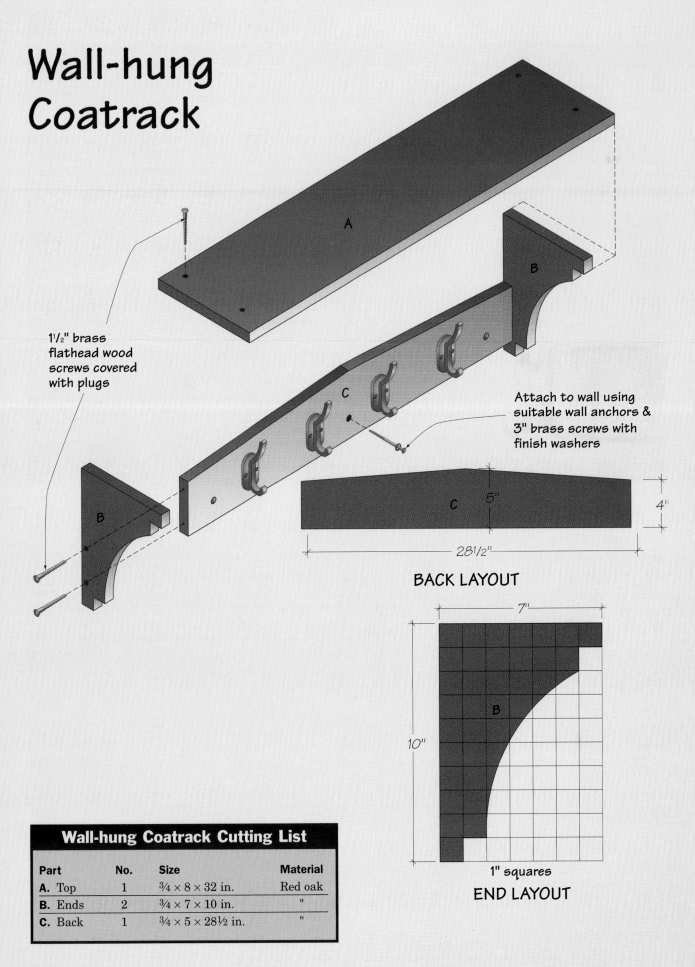

1½" brass flathead wood screws covered with plugs

Attach to wall using suitable wall anchors & 3" brass screws with finish washers

5"

4"

28½"

BACK LAYOUT

7"

10"

B

1" squares

END LAYOUT

Wall-hung Coatrack Cutting List			
Part	**No.**	**Size**	**Material**
A. Top	1	$\frac{3}{4} \times 8 \times 32$ in.	Red oak
B. Ends	2	$\frac{3}{4} \times 7 \times 10$ in.	"
C. Back	1	$\frac{3}{4} \times 5 \times 28\frac{1}{2}$ in.	"

PHOTO B: Fasten the coatrack ends to the back with glue and flathead wood screws driven into counterbored pilot holes. Clamp the parts together first to hold them securely while you install the screws.

5 Enlarge the *End Layout* grid drawing, page 166, to form a full-size paper or cardboard pattern of the coatrack end profile. Cut out the pattern and use it as a template for drawing profiles on both coatrack end workpieces **(See Photo A).**

CUT OUT THE PARTS

6 Cut the back profile using a jig saw or circular saw. Make these straight cuts with your saw guided against a straightedge.

7 Cut the coatrack ends to shape: Clamp each end to your worksurface, providing sufficient clear space beneath the workpiece for the saw blade. Install a narrow, fine-toothed blade in your jig saw and cut out the end profiles. TIP: *If your jig saw has various settings for adjusting blade orbit, set the saw for no orbiting action to minimize tearout while you cut.*

ASSEMBLE THE COATRACK

8 Fasten the coatrack ends to the back: Arrange the parts so the back will be flush with the long edges of the ends and inset 1 in. up from the bottoms of the ends. The profiled edge of the back should face up. Drill two counterbored pilot holes through each coatrack end and into the ends of the back panel for screws using a bit that bores a ⅜-in.-dia. counterbore. Spread glue on the ends of the back panel, set the ends and back together and attach the parts with 1½-in. brass flathead wood screws **(See Photo B).**

9 Install the top. First, clamp the coatrack assembly in a bench vise to hold it securely while you attach the top. Set the top in place on the coatrack ends so the back edges of the parts are flush and a 1-in. overhang is provided around the ends and front. Mark the top to indicate centerlines of the end pieces for locating pairs of attachment screws. NOTE: *Be sure to position the front screws far enough in on the end pieces so the screws won't pierce the notched cutouts.* Drill pilot holes with ⅜-in.-dia. counterbores through the top and into each coatrack end at the screw locations. Spread glue on the top edges of the ends. Fasten the top to

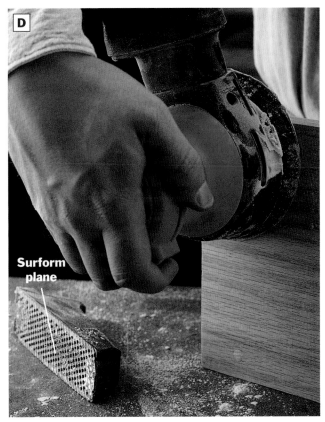

PHOTO C: Once you've attached the coatrack parts, cover the screwheads with face-grain red oak plugs held in place with glue. Tap each plug into its counterbore with a wooden mallet.

PHOTO D: Shave the plugs so they're nearly flush with the surrounding wood surface using a Surform plane or a wood rasp. Sand away the remaining waste with coarse sandpaper.

PHOTO E: Brush or wipe on a coat of wood stain with a foam brush or clean rag, then wipe off the excess stain before it dries. Wear disposable gloves to protect your hands. Topcoat the project with varnish.

the ends with #8 × 1½-in. brass flathead wood screws.

INSTALL WOOD PLUGS

10 Squeeze a drop of glue into each screwhead counterbore, and tap in oak wood plugs with a wooden mallet to conceal the screws (**See Photo C**).

11 Use a Surform plane or wood rasp and file to trim the wood plugs down until they are nearly flush with the surrounding wood surface. Sand the plugs flush with 80-grit sandpaper (**See Photo D**).

FINISHING TOUCHES

12 Sand all project surfaces with 150-, then 220-grit sandpaper until smooth. Hand-sand the coatrack end profiles as well to remove any saw marks.

Beeswax

PHOTO F: Lay out and attach four coat hooks to the coatrack back. Drill pilot holes for the screws, especially if the screws are made of brass. Space the hooks about 6 in. apart. TIP: *Coat the screw threads with beeswax to make them easier to drive into the oak.*

13 Brush or wipe on several coats of wood stain, and wipe off the excess stain before it dries **(See Photo E).** Protect the project with two coats of varnish.

14 Lay out and install the coat hooks: Arrange the four hooks so they're spaced about 6 in. apart and centered vertically on the coatrack back. Drill pilot holes for the attachment screws, and fasten the hooks using the screws provided with the hooks **(See Photo F).**

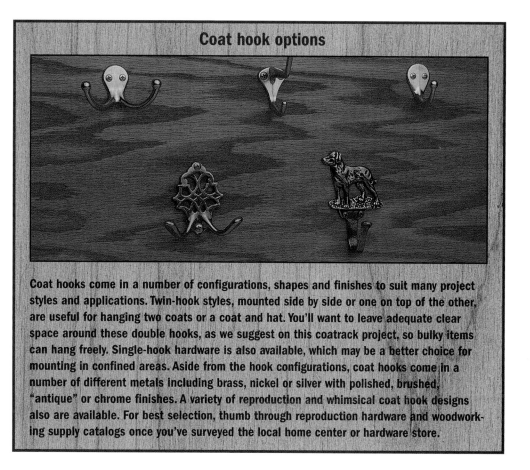

Coat hook options

Coat hooks come in a number of configurations, shapes and finishes to suit many project styles and applications. Twin-hook styles, mounted side by side or one on top of the other, are useful for hanging two coats or a coat and hat. You'll want to leave adequate clear space around these double hooks, as we suggest on this coatrack project, so bulky items can hang freely. Single-hook hardware is also available, which may be a better choice for mounting in confined areas. Aside from the hook configurations, coat hooks come in a number of different metals including brass, nickel or silver with polished, brushed, "antique" or chrome finishes. A variety of reproduction and whimsical coat hook designs also are available. For best selection, thumb through reproduction hardware and woodworking supply catalogs once you've surveyed the local home center or hardware store.

Colonial Step Stool

Take a step back in time by building this practical step stool. Based on a traditional Colonial bench design, this solid and sturdy companion for the kitchen or bathroom is made almost exclusively with hand tools and traditional woodworking techniques. The keyed tenons on the single spreader, the simple scallops and gentle splay of the legs, and the solid hardwood construction are the elements that give the stool a sense of character and history. For added effect, we distressed the wood surfaces to lend an antique flavor to this faithful reproduction.

Vital Statistics: Colonial Step Stool

TYPE: Step stool

OVERALL SIZE: 18W by 12H by 10D

MATERIAL: Ash

JOINERY: Dowel joints, keyed mortise-and-tenons (pinned)

CONSTRUCTION DETAILS:

· Legs and top are made from 10-in.-wide boards (solid or edge-glued)

· All parts are cut and shaped with hand tools, including a coping saw (leg contours) and a draw knife (spreader)

· Legs splay inward at 10° angle

· Keys at ends of spreader are pinned with dowels

· Wood surfaces are distressed

FINISHING OPTIONS: For an antique look, use a medium to dark wood stain, followed by a low-gloss (satin) topcoat. As shown, the stool is finished with maple stain and three coats of satin tung oil.

Building time

PREPARING STOCK
2 hours

LAYOUT
1-2 hours

CUTTING PARTS
1-2 hours

ASSEMBLY
1-2 hours

FINISHING
1-2 hours

TOTAL: 6-10 hours

Tools you'll use

· **Cross-cut saw**

· **Ripping saw**

· **Back saw or tenon saw**

· **Coping saw**

· **Drill**

· **No. 5 jack plane**

· **Block plane**

· **Draw knife**

· **Wood mallet**

· **Strap clamp**

· **Combination square**

· **Wood chisels**

· **Woodscrews or C-clamps**

· **Drill guide**

· **Heavy chain (optional)**

Shopping list

☐ (3) $3/4 \times 4$ in. $\times 6$ ft. ash boards

☐ (1) $1^1/2 \times 1^1/2 \times$ at least 24 in. ash board

☐ (8) $3/8$-in.-dia. wood dowel (hardwood)

☐ (2) $1/8$-in.-dia. wood dowel (hardwood)

☐ Finishing materials

Colonial Step Stool

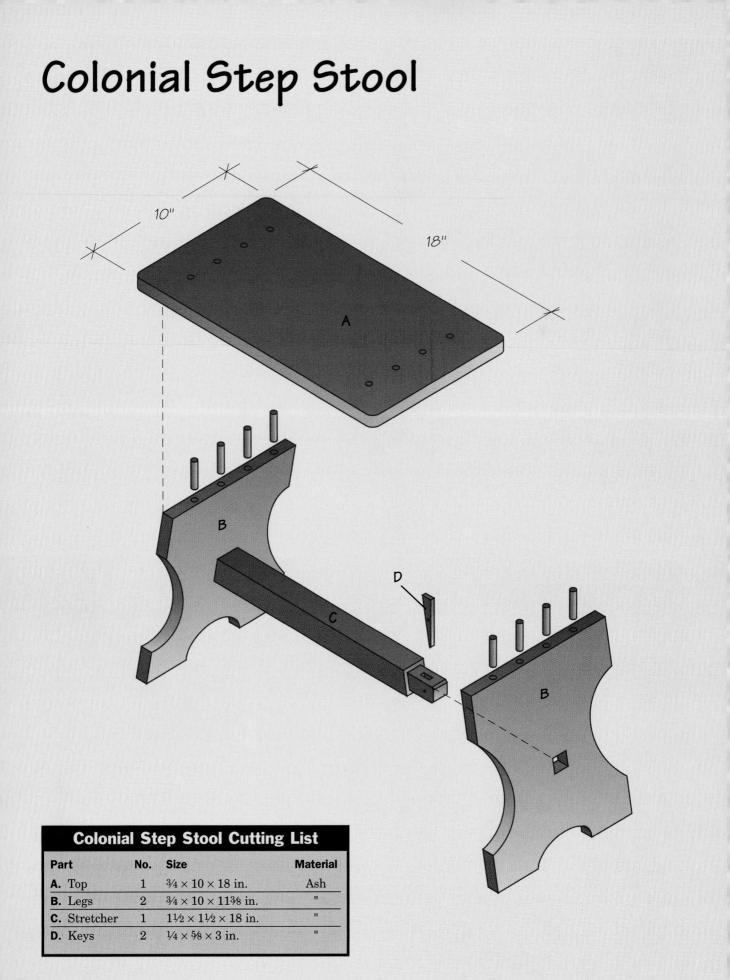

10"

18"

A

B

C

D

B

Colonial Step Stool Cutting List

Part	No.	Size	Material
A. Top	1	¾ × 10 × 18 in.	Ash
B. Legs	2	¾ × 10 × 11⅜ in.	"
C. Stretcher	1	1½ × 1½ × 18 in.	"
D. Keys	2	¼ × ⅝ × 3 in.	"

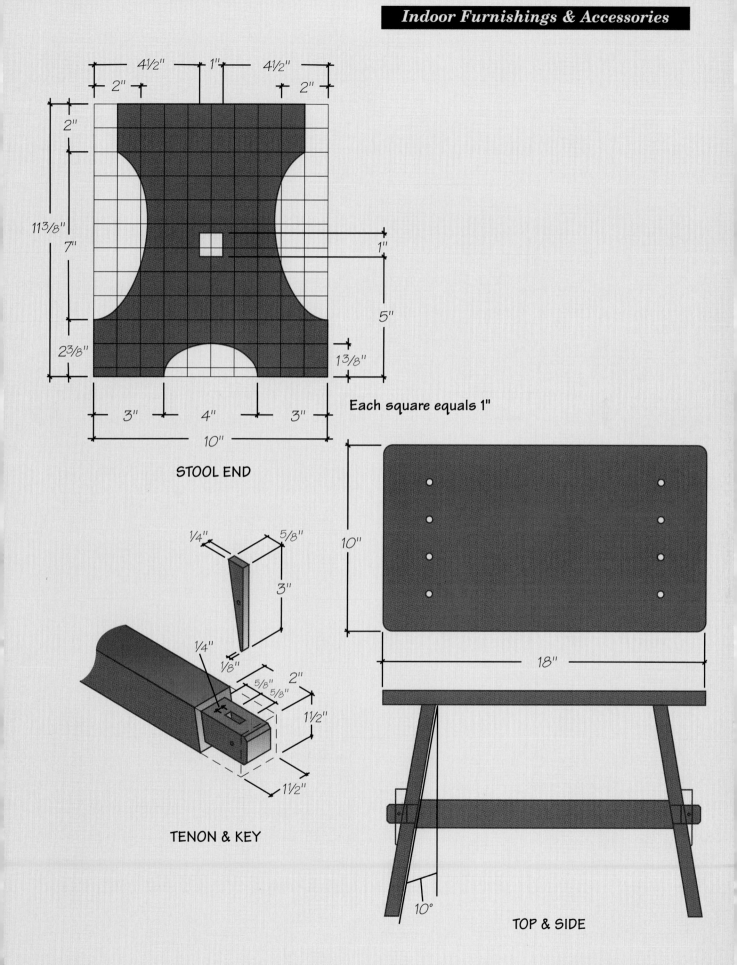

4½" 1" 4½"

2" 2"

2"

11³⁄₈"
7"

1"

5"

2³⁄₈" 1³⁄₈"

3" 4" 3"

10"

Each square equals 1"

STOOL END

¼" 5⁄₈"

3"

¼"

1⁄₈"

5⁄₈" 2"
5⁄₈"

1½"

1½"

TENON & KEY

10"

18"

10°

TOP & SIDE

MAKE THE LEGS & TOP

In Colonial times, it was not difficult to find lumber wide enough to build furniture with 10-in.-wide or larger parts without the need for edge-gluing stock to width. But today, it's likely that you'll need to glue up boards to make the top and legs for this step stool.

❶ Select enough lumber to make the blanks for the top and legs (if you use boards at least 42 in. long, you can cut all three parts from one glued-up panel). Plane the boards to thickness, then joint one edge of each board using a power jointer or a jointing plane. Rip-cut the boards to width, then joint the sawn edge of each board. Edge-glue the boards to make your panel, using dowels or biscuits to align the boards and reinforce the glue joints. After the glue cures, smooth out the seams, as needed, using a plane, power planer, cabinet scraper or sander **(See Photo A).**

❷ Cross-cut all three parts to length (we used a hand saw in keeping with our "traditional" approach to building this project). Round over the corners of the top with a hand file or block plane. Ease the sharp edges all around.

❸ Set a sliding T-bevel gauge to 10° and mark the angle on the sides of both ends of the legs. Square the lines across the faces. Using these lines as guides, bevel the top and bottom of each leg at 10°—we used a hand plane **(See Photo B).**

PHOTO A: Secure the board you'll use to make the tops and legs to your workbench, then plane the surface with a No. 5 jack plane to level the edge-glued joints. A power planer can also be used for this task. Plane in diagonal strokes with the grain.

Backup board

PHOTO B: Plane parallel 10° bevels in the top and bottom edge of each leg with a block plane. A backup board the same thickness as the workpiece will keep the side grain of the wood from splitting off at the end of the planing stroke.

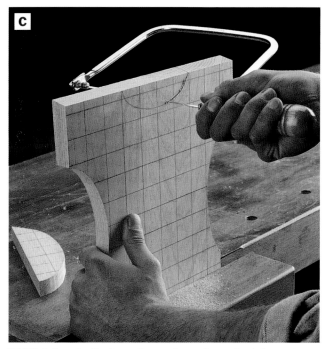

PHOTO C: Transfer the leg pattern onto one leg and cut the contours with a coping saw. File the cuts smooth, then use the leg as a template to trace the pattern onto the other leg.

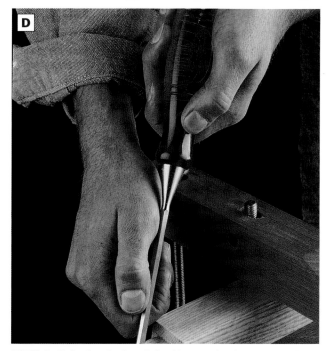

PHOTO D: Make the cheek and shoulder cuts for the tenons at the ends of the spreader with a sharp back saw. Make sure the shoulder cuts follow the 10° angle of the leg bevels.

❹ Draw a grid pattern on one of the legs and transfer the shape from the *Grid pattern* shown on page 173 onto the workpiece. Cut the contours with a coping saw, cutting carefully along the waste side of the lines **(See Photo C).** Smooth out the contours with a file or rasp, then trace the contours onto the other leg. Cut the second leg, then ease all the sharp edges of both legs (except the top edges).

❺ Cut a 1-in. square mortise in each leg for the stretcher. Draw outlines, then drill an entry hole and make the cutout with a coping saw. The bottom of each mortise should be 5 in. up from the bottom of the leg. The top and bottom of each mortise should be parallel to the top and bottom of each leg end (this means they will be angled at 10°, rather than square, to the faces). Smooth the cuts and square the corners with a file.

MAKE THE STRETCHER

❻ Cut the stretcher to length (18 in.) from a piece of 1½× 1½-in. ash. With a bevel gauge, mark 10° shoulder cuts on the front and back faces. Start the shoulder cut at the maximum distance of 2 in. in from each end, and angle it back from there, as shown in the *Tenon & key diagram* on page 173. Square the lines across the top and bottom faces. Set a marking or cutting gauge to ¼ in. and outline the tenon on the ends of the stretcher.

PHOTO E: Use a sharp chisel to square off the mortises in the tops of the spreader tenons. Use a drill to remove most of the waste. These tapered mortises will accept the keys used to pin the mortise-and-tenon joints that secure the spreader and the legs.

PHOTO F: Shape the edges of the spreader with chamfers to give it a more rustic appearance. We used a draw knife, but you could also use a spokeshave or a hand plane for a hand-hewn look.

PHOTO G: Use a strap clamp to draw the top tight against the tops of the legs while the glue dries. Double-check your reference lines to make sure the top is centered properly.

Continue the lines back to the shoulders on the top and bottom faces only.

7 Make the angled shoulder cuts ¼ in. deep with a back saw, with the stretcher clamped horizontally in a vise. Then clamp it vertically and cut straight down

PHOTO H: Drill 10° dowel holes through the top and into the centers of the legs. We used a drilling guide to set the drilling angle and the 1½-in. drilling depth.

along the waste sides of the cheek lines to the shoulders. The waste pieces will fall off.

8 With the marking gauge, mark the ¼-in. cutting lines for the tops and bottoms of the tenons along the faces of the cheeks you've just cut. Make shoulder cuts and cheek cuts **(See Photo D).** Clean up the surfaces and corners with a file. Test the fit in the mortises and adjust as necessary.

9 Cut mortises for the keys in the ends of the stretcher. The mortises should be ¼ in. wide and centered along the thickness of the tenons. Make them ⅝ in. long at the top, but taper the inside end of each mortise so it's parallel with the shoulder. Mark the top and bottom of each mortise by drawing lines around the tenon with a square and bevel gauge. Remove waste with a drill, then square the edges with a chisel **(See Photo E).**

10 Clamp the stretcher firmly and chamfer the edges with a draw knife or a hand plane **(See Photo F).** Make several light passes rather than trying to do the chamfer in one cut.

ASSEMBLE THE STOOL
11 Cut two keys 3 in. long, ⅝ in. wide, and ¼ in. thick. Trim the keys so they taper from ⅝ in. at the top to ⅛ in. at the bottom. Round-over the square corner at the wide end of each key.

12 Dry-assemble the legs and stretcher, tapping the keys gently into place. Set the assembly on a flat surface and make sure it is square and level. Adjust the joints as needed. Don't glue it together yet. Set the top onto the assembly and center it so there is an equal overhang at both ends, and at the front and back. Mark the position of the legs on the underside of the top.

13 Apply glue to the tops of the

PHOTO I: Drive ⅜× 2-in. dowels into the dowel holes to reinforce the joints between the top and the legs. Apply glue to the ends of the dowels before inserting. Trim the exposed dowel ends flush with the top.

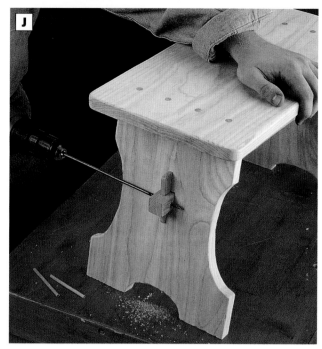

PHOTO J: Use an extended bit to drill ⅛-in.-dia. holes through the spreader tenons and each key, then pin the tenons into the mortises with ⅛-in.-dia. dowels.

PHOTO K (OPTION): For an antiqued appearance, distress the wood surfaces with a chain or ring of car keys before applying the finish.

legs, put the top in position, and clamp it down to the legs with a strap clamp **(See Photo G).**

⓮ After the glue cures, remove the strap clamp and mark two lines across the top, centered along the tops of the legs. Mark four evenly spaced drilling points along each line, then drill 10° guide holes for dowels at each drilling point, using a ⅜-in.-dia. bit set to drill 1½ in. deep **(See Photo H).** The dowel holes should stay centered in the legs.

⓯ Cut eight ⅜-in. hardwood dowels to a length of 2 in., then apply glue and drive them into the dowel holes with a wood mallet **(See Photo I).** Trim the ends of the dowels with a flush-cutting saw and sand or plane them flush with the surface of the top.

⓰ Drill a ⅛-in.-dia. guide hole through each tenon key for a ⅛-in. dowel pin. Center the holes on the keys. This will be easiest to do with an extended drill bit **(See Photo J).** Drive ⅛-in. hardwood dowels through the guide holes to pin the keys in place. Trim the ends of the pins with a flush-cutting saw.

APPLY FINISHING TOUCHES
⓱ Finish-sand all surfaces with 150-, then 180-grit sandpaper. For an antiqued appearance, we decided to distress the stool before applying the finish. There are many ways to accomplish this. We elected to rake a piece of heavy chain across the top and the outside faces of the legs **(See Photo K).** For a finish, we used maple stain with a tung oil topcoat.

Personalize that special family photo when you mount it in a photo frame you've built yourself. The frame oval is milled from a single piece of red oak, so there's no complicated joinery or exacting miter work involved. Though this frame project is designed for standard 4 × 6-in. photo prints, you can enlarge or reduce the template dimensions to make photo frames of any size.

Oval Picture Frame

Vital Statistics: Oval Picture Frame

TYPE: Picture frame

OVERALL SIZE: 5W by 1D by 7L

MATERIAL: Red oak, glass

JOINERY: None

CONSTRUCTION DETAILS:

· Oval is made from one piece of oak

· Inside front edge of frame is chamfered

· Inside back edge of the frame is rabbeted to house the glass and back panel

· Stand is joined to the frame with a brass hinge

FINISH: Satin polyurethane varnish

Building time

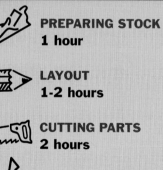

PREPARING STOCK
1 hour

LAYOUT
1-2 hours

CUTTING PARTS
2 hours

ASSEMBLY
1 hour

FINISHING
1 hour

TOTAL: 6-7 hours

Tools you'll use

· Scroll saw or jig saw

· Table saw

· Drill/driver

· Router with 45° piloted chamfer bit, $\frac{1}{4}$-in. piloted rabbeting bit

· Drum sander

· Needle-nose pliers

· File

Shopping list

☐ (1) $\frac{3}{4} \times 6$ in. × 1 ft. red oak

☐ (1) $\frac{1}{4} \times 4$ in. × 1 ft. red oak

☐ (1) $\frac{1}{4} \times 1$ ft. × 1 ft. hardboard (for templates)

☐ (1) $1\frac{1}{4}$-in. brass butt hinge

☐ (2) #4 × $\frac{1}{2}$-in. brass flathead bolts, nuts

☐ (2) #4 × $\frac{1}{4}$-in. brass flathead wood screws

☐ (4) Brass turn buttons

☐ (1) $\frac{1}{8} \times 4 \times 6$-in. glass

☐ Finishing materials

Oval Picture Frame

#4 x 1/2" brass flathead bolts attach hinge to stand (D)

1" x 1 1/4" brass hinge

#4 x 1/4" brass flathead screws attach hinge to back (C)

3/4"-long brass turn buttons with screws, 4 total

1/4" x 3/8" routed rabbet

1/4" x 1/4" routed chamfer

A

B

C

D

Oval Picture Frame Cutting List

Part	No.	Size	Material
A. Frame	1	3/4 × 5 × 7 in.	Red oak
B. Glass	1	1/8 × 4 × 6 in.	Non-reflective
C. Back	1	1/4 × 4 × 6 in.	"
D. Stand	1	1/4 × 3 × 5 7/8 in.	"

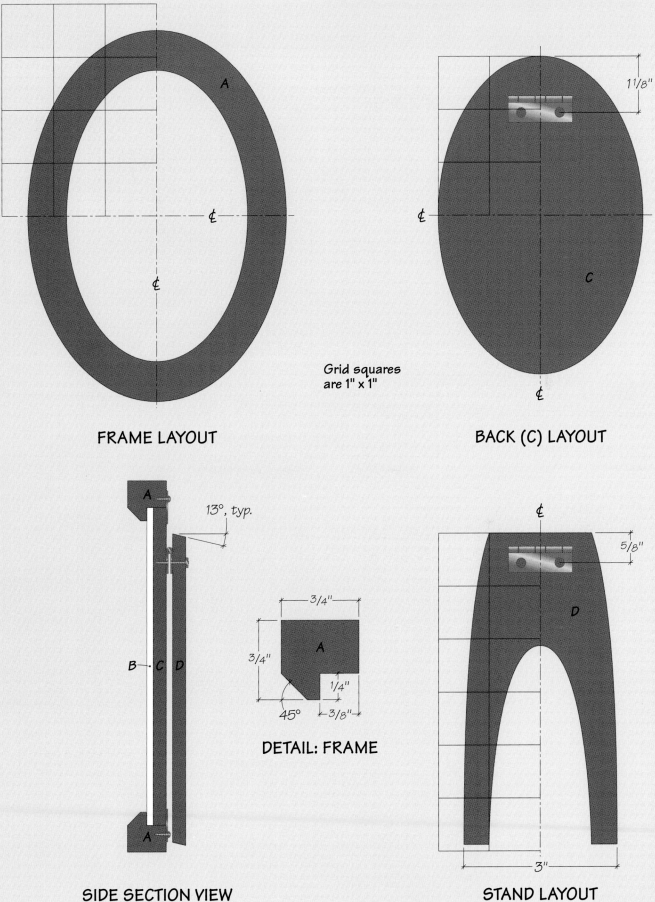

FRAME LAYOUT

BACK (C) LAYOUT

Grid squares
are 1" x 1"

1¹/₈"

SIDE SECTION VIEW

13°, typ.

DETAIL: FRAME

3/4"

3/4"

1/4"

45°

3/8"

STAND LAYOUT

5/8"

3"

MAKE TEMPLATES FOR THE FRAME & STAND

If you plan to build a number of these frames, we suggest you make a hardboard template for the frame and stand. Sturdy templates will make quick work of drawing the frame parts to size again and again.

❶ Transfer full-size copies of the frame and stand layout patterns shown on page 181 to your hardboard. We enlarged the patterns on a photocopier, cut them out and used spray adhesive to stick the patterns to the hardboard. Scroll-saw the templates to rough size, cutting just outside your layout lines. Smooth the edges of the patterns on a drum sander, if you have one.

MAKE THE FRAME, STAND & BACK

❷ Cut the frame to shape. First cross-cut a 7-in.-long blank for the frame from your ¾-in. oak stock. Use the hardboard template for the frame to trace the part onto your oak blank, then cut out the frame on the scroll saw or with a jig saw **(See Photo A).** Sand the cut edges smooth on the drum sander.

❸ Chamfer the inside edges of the frame: Install a piloted 45° chamfer bit in your router, set the bit for a ¼-in.-deep cut, and rout a decorative chamfer around the inside edge of the frame **(See Photo B).** If you want to mill a decorative profile on the outside of the frame as well, this is the time to do it. Guide the router counterclockwise around the workpiece.

❹ Cut a rabbet into the back of the frame for the glass and back panel. You'll make this cut in two passes. For the first pass, install a ¼-in. piloted rabbeting bit in your router and cut a ¼-in.-deep rabbet around the inside edge of the frame back (See *Detail: Frame* drawing, page 181). Then reset the bit depth to ⅜ in. and make a second pass around the frame to finish up the rabbet.

❺ Cut the stand to shape. Cross-cut a 5⅞-in.-long blank of ¼-in.-thick oak for the stand. On the table saw, bevel the top and bottom edges of the blank at 13° **(See Photo C).** See the *Side Section View*

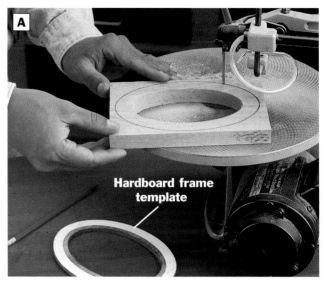

PHOTO A: Draw the frame shape onto ¾-in. oak stock, then cut out the frame on the scroll saw. We made a hardboard template to trace this shape and to keep on hand for making more frames. Drill a starter hole for the blade in order to cut out the center of the frame.

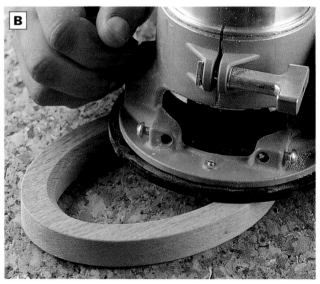

PHOTO B: Mill the 45° chamfer on the inside edge of the frame with the router held free-hand. Use a non-slip pad beneath the workpiece while you rout. Then turn the frame over, switch to a ¼-in. piloted rabbeting bit and rout the back rabbet around the inside edge.

drawing, page 181, to determine the orientation of these bevel cuts. Your goal here is to trim just enough material off the ends of the blank to form the bevels. Then use the hardboard pattern to trace the shape of the stand on your blank and cut it out on the scroll saw. Smooth the cut edges on the drum sander.

PHOTO C: Tilt the table saw blade to 13° and bevel-cut the top and bottom ends of the stand blank. Hold the workpiece against the miter gauge to make these cuts.

PHOTO D: Four brass turn buttons hold the glass, photo and back in the frame. Install the hardware so the turn buttons are spaced evenly around the frame. Drill pilot holes for the tiny turn button screws.

❻ Make the back panel. Lay out the back on a piece of ¼-in. oak, using the *Back Layout* grid pattern on page 181 as a guide for drawing the shape. Cut out the back, and sand the edges until the back panel fits easily into the rabbet on the frame.

FINISHING TOUCHES

❼ Smooth the entire project with 220-grit sandpaper. Apply several coats of clear satin polyurethane, sanding lightly between each with 320-grit paper or #0000 steel wool. Since the frame parts are small, we sprayed the varnish from an aerosol can rather than brushing on the finish.

❽ Install the glass, back and turn buttons. Drill pilot holes for the tiny turn button screws (**See Photo D**).

❾ Attach the hinge to the frame and stand with screws, bolts and nuts. Since the hinge is small and the space confined, install it as follows: Mark the hinge position on the frame back and on the stand as shown in the *Back Layout* drawing, page 181. Mount the hinge to the frame back first with ¼-in. flathead wood screws driven into pilot holes. Slip two #4 × ½-in. bolts through holes in the hinge leaf that will be attached to the stand, so the heads of the bolts face the frame. Drill holes through the stand for the hinge bolts. Then slide the bolts through the holes in the stand and attach with nuts

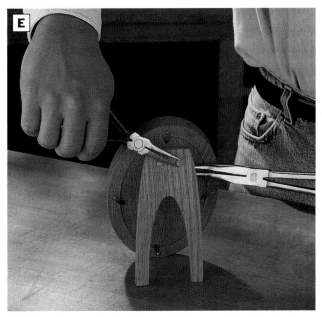

PHOTO E: After locating the hinge position, mount the hinge to the frame back with #4 × ¼-in. brass flathead wood screws. Fasten the hinge to the stand with bolts and nuts. Arrange the bolts so you can thread the nuts on from the back of the stand. Tighten the nuts and bolts with a pair of needle-nose pliers.

(**See Photo E**). Tighten the nuts with needle-nose pliers. File the bolt ends flush with the nuts.

❿ Mount your photo. Remove the frame back and use it as a template for tracing a cutting line onto your photo. Trim the photo to shape, slip it into place and reinstall the frame back.

Display Cabinet

Show off a variety of collectibles or family treasures in less space than it takes to store a vacuum cleaner with this display cabinet. Made of rich mahogany and accented with cabriole-style legs, decorative fluting, glass shelves and a mirrored back, this cabinet has enough sophisticated features to charm even the most discriminating of guests. It's sure to become a focal point of room decor.

Vital Statistics: Display Cabinet

TYPE: Display cabinet

OVERALL SIZE: 18W by 15½D by 60H

MATERIAL: Mahogany and birch plywood

JOINERY: Dowel, biscuit, butt, miter joints

CONSTRUCTION DETAILS:

· Fluted front stiles and profiled top edge add a sophisticated touch

· Shaped legs and a separate base give cabinet an elegant, traditional look

· Mirrored back, adjustable glass shelves, and glass panels

· Glass panels held in place with wood stops

FINISHING OPTIONS: Wood stain and clear topcoat

Building time

PREPARING STOCK
3-4 hours

LAYOUT
4-6 hours

CUTTING PARTS
3-5 hours

ASSEMBLY
6-8 hours

FINISHING
2-3 hours

TOTAL: 18-26 hours

Tools you'll use

· Jointer

· Planer

· Table saw

· Power miter saw

· Band saw

· Hot glue gun

· Drill/driver

· Doweling jig

· Right-angle drill guide

· Bar or pipe clamps

· Spring or C-clamps

· Plunge router with ¼-in. core box bit, ⅜-in. piloted rabbet bit, Roman ogee bit

· Biscuit joiner

Shopping list

☐ (4) ¾ × 6 in. × 8 ft. mahogany

☐ (1) ¾ in. × 1 ft. × 2 ft. birch plywood

☐ (1) ¼ in. × 2 ft. × 4 ft. birch plywood

☐ (1) ¼-in.-thick mirrored glass

☐ (1) ¼-in.-thick glass for shelves

☐ (1) ⅛-in.-thick glass for light panels

☐ ⅜-in.-dia. dowel

☐ #20 biscuits

☐ 1¼-in. flathead wood screws; ¾-in. brads

☐ (3) 3-in. brass ball-tip hinges; brass doorknob

☐ Shelf pins, bullet catch

☐ Glue, finishing materials

Display Cabinet

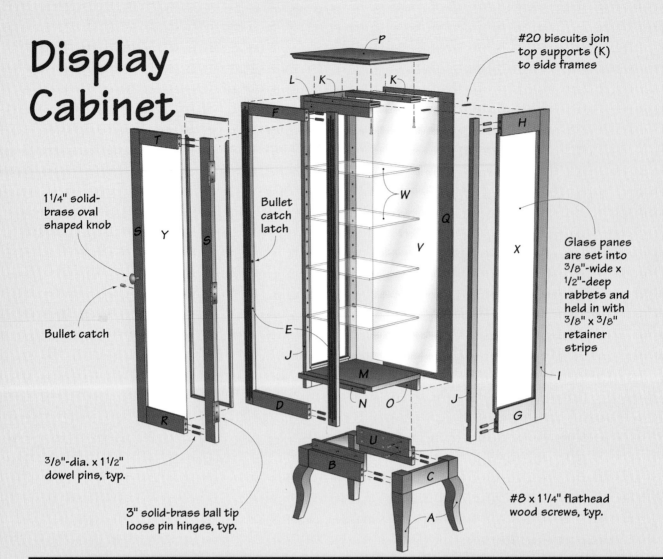

1¼" solid-brass oval shaped knob

Bullet catch

Bullet catch latch

#20 biscuits join top supports (K) to side frames

Glass panes are set into ³/₈"-wide x ¹/₂"-deep rabbets and held in with ³/₈" x ³/₈" retainer strips

³/₈"-dia. x 1¹/₂" dowel pins, typ.

3" solid-brass ball tip loose pin hinges, typ.

#8 x 1¹/₄" flathead wood screws, typ.

Display Cabinet Cutting List

Part	No.	Size	Material	Part	No.	Size	Material
A. Legs	4	3 × 3 × 12 in.	Mahogany	L. Door stop	1	¾ × 1½ × 14½ in.	Mahogany
B. Base rails (front)	2	¾ × 3 × 12 in.	"	M. Bottom	1	¾ × 11¾ × 15 in.	Birch plywood
C. Base rails (side)	2	¾ × 3 × 9 in.	"	N. Bottom front edge	1	¼ × ¾ × 15 in.	Mahogany
D. Face frame lower rail	1	¾ × 2¼ × 12½ in.	"	O. Bottom back support	1	¾ × 2 × 14½ in.	"
E. Face frame stiles	2	¾ × 1¾ × 47¼ in.	"	P. Top	1	¾ × 14 × 17½ in.	"
F. Face frame upper rail	1	¾ × 1¾ × 12½ in.	"	Q. Back	1	¼ × 15¼ × 47¼ in.	Birch plywood
G. Side frame lower rails	2	¾ × 3½ × 9 in.	"	R. Door rail (lower)	1	¾ × 2½ × 8⅜ in.	Mahogany
H. Side frame upper rails	2	¾ × 3 × 9 in.	"	S. Door stiles	2	¾ × 2 × 43⅛ in.	"
I. Side frame back stiles	2	¾ × 2¼ × 47¼ in.	"	T. Door rail (upper)	1	¾ × 2 × 8½ in.	"
J. Side frame front stiles	2	¾ × 1¼ × 47¼ in.	"	U. Base cleats	2	¾ × 3 × 12 in.	"
K. Top supports	2	¾ × 2½ × 14½ in.	"	V. Mirror	1	¼ × 14⁷/₁₆ × 44⅞ in.	Mirrored glass
				W. Shelves	4	¼ × 11⅞ × 14¼ in.	Glass
				X. Side panes	2	⅛ × 9⅝ × 41⅜ in.	"
				Y. Door pane	1	⅛ × 9⅛ × 39⅜ in.	"

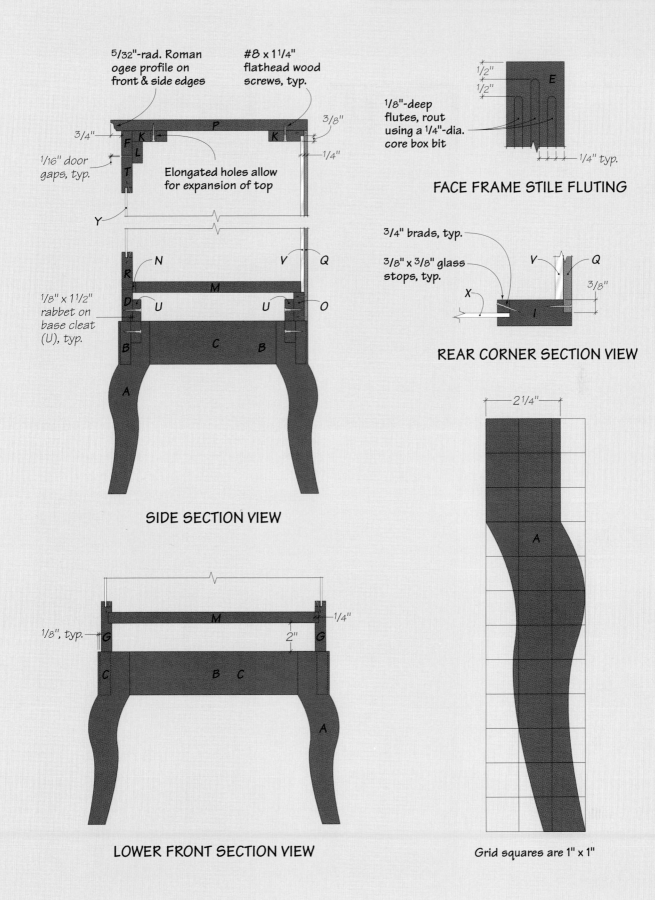

5/32"-rad. Roman ogee profile on front & side edges

#8 x 1 1/4" flathead wood screws, typ.

3/4"

3/8"

3/4"

1/16" door gaps, typ.

1/4"

Elongated holes allow for expansion of top

F K L T

P

K

Y

1/8" x 1 1/2" rabbet on base cleat (U), typ.

R N

V Q

D U

M

U O

B C B

A

SIDE SECTION VIEW

1/8"-deep flutes, rout using a 1/4"-dia. core box bit

1/2"
1/2"

E

1/4" typ.

FACE FRAME STILE FLUTING

3/4" brads, typ.

3/8" x 3/8" glass stops, typ.

V Q

X

I

3/8"

REAR CORNER SECTION VIEW

1/8", typ.

M

1/4"

2"

G

G

C

B C

A

LOWER FRONT SECTION VIEW

2 1/4"

A

Grid squares are 1" x 1"

ASSEMBLE THE BASE

1 Laminate strips of mahogany to create a face-glued blank that's at least 3½ in. square and 50 in. long. After the glue cures, run one edge through your jointer until it's flat and smooth. Then, rip-cut the workpiece to 3⅛ in. square, making sure the jointed edge rides against your table saw fence. Cross-cut four 12-in.-long blanks for the legs.

2 Draw the leg profile on a scrap piece of hardboard to create a leg template, using the grid drawing on page 187 as a guide. Cut out the template and smooth the edges with sandpaper. Trace the template shape onto two adjacent faces of each leg blank, butting the inside squared edge of the template against the corners of the wood **(See Photo A).**

3 Cut out the profile of the legs on the band saw. This will need to be done in two stages. First cut along the outlines on one face of each blank **(See Photo B).** Try to cut each curved line in one smooth pass (this will be easier to do with a narrower band saw blade; we used a ¼-in.-wide blade). Reattach the waste pieces with several dabs of hot glue so the blank resumes its original shape **(See Photo C).**

4 Cut along the outlines of the adjacent edges **(See Photo D).** After these cuts are made, pop off the hot-glued waste pieces with a stiff putty knife and sand the sawn edges smooth. Cut and sand the profiles in all four leg blanks.

PHOTO A: Create a leg template from scrap hardboard. Trace the leg shape onto one face of each leg blank, holding it flush against the inside top corner of the wood. Then trace the leg profile onto the adjacent side of the blank.

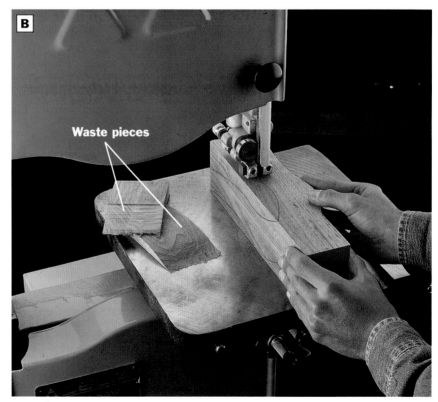

Waste pieces

PHOTO B: To cut the legs to shape, start by cutting out the profile on one face of each leg blank on the band saw. Save the waste pieces, and try to cut them out in single sections.

5 Cut the front and side base rails to size. The rails will attach to the legs with dowels. To prepare these dowel joints, first lay out and drill two ⅜-in.-dia. × ¾-in.-deep dowel holes in the ends of each rail using a doweling jig. Center the holes on the thickness of each rail and space them ¾ in. in from each edge.

6 Lay out and drill pairs of ⅜-in.-dia. × ¾-in.-deep dowel holes in the top edges of each leg to correspond with the holes you drilled in the rails. Drill these holes into the two adjacent edges of the legs that will face into the center of the base assembly. Position the holes so the rails will set ¼ in. back from the front surfaces of the legs when the base is assembled.

7 Finish-sand the base rails and the legs, and ease all sharp edges. Then, glue 1½-in.-long dowels into the dowel holes, spread glue on the ends of the rails and clamp up the base assembly with bar or pipe clamps **(See Photo E)**.

8 Cut the base cleats to size, then rip-cut a ⅛-in.-deep by 1½-in.-wide rabbet along one face of each cleat on the table saw. The rabbet will create a ⅛-in. reveal between the cabinet and the base rails. Run the cleats on-edge through the blade, using an auxiliary fence attached to your table saw fence to support the workpieces and a featherboard and pushstick to guide them.

9 Attach the cleats to the inside faces of the front and back rails with three #8 × 1¼-in. flathead wood screws per cleat **(See Photo F)**. Position the cleats so the rabbets face out from the

PHOTO C: Use a few dabs of hot glue to reattach the waste pieces to the leg blanks in their original positions.

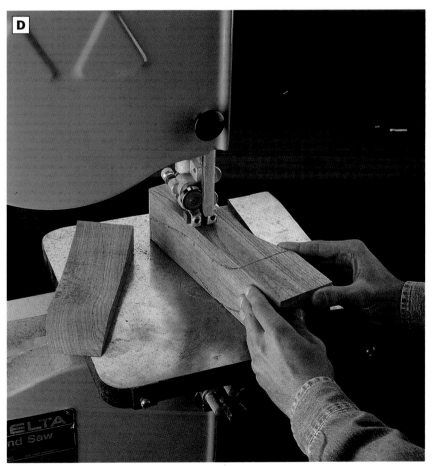

PHOTO D: Cut the profile on the adjacent side of each blank just as you did with the first side. The reattached waste pieces lend you flat surfaces for easier, accurate cuts.

PHOTO E: Glue the dowel joints, insert the dowels and assemble the base. Clamp across the sides with bar or pipe clamps. Measure across the corners of the assembly and square it up.

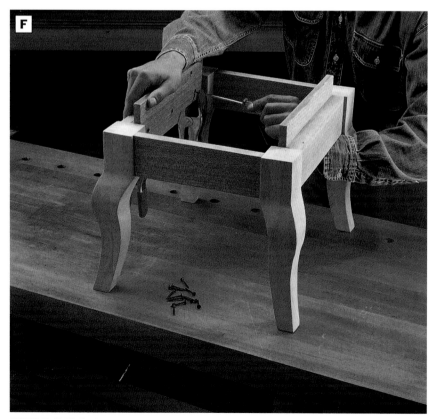

PHOTO F: Hold the base cleats in position with spring clamps so each cleat's rabbet shoulder is flush with the top of the adjoining front or back rail. Drill pilot holes and drive #8 × 1¼-in. flathead wood screws to attach the parts.

base assembly, and the ⅛-in. rabbet shoulders are flush with the tops of the rails.

BUILD THE FACE FRAME, SIDE FRAMES & DOOR

⑩ Cut the face frame stiles and rails to size.

⑪ Rout three ⅛-in.-deep flutes in each of the face frame stiles using a ¼-in. core box bit in a plunge router (**See Photo G**). We cut the flutes by first building a jig from ¾-in.-thick plywood to hold a stile in place. On top of this plywood layer, we attached a second plywood frame to the first to serve as an edge guide for the router base when cutting the two outside flutes. By screwing a ½-in.-wide strip to one long inside edge of the frame, the jig then shifts the router into position to cut the center flute. We added short blocking to the ends of the jig frame to serve as references for starting and stoping the flute cuts (See *Face Frame Stile Fluting*, page 187, for spacing the flutes). Experiment with this jig on scrap wood before you cut the actual workpieces.

⑫ Smooth the ends of the stile flutes and sand out any burns. *TIP: To sand out burns in the flutes, cut a pencil about 3 in. long and round-over the eraser with sandpaper. Wrap a small piece of 180-grit adhesive-backed sandpaper over the eraser and mount the pencil shaft in a drill. Operate the drill at low speed while you work the sandpaper tip into the flute ends* (**See Photo H**).

⑬ Lay out three 3-in.-long hinge mortises in one edge of one face frame stile. Cut the hinge mortises. We used a router and straight bit and a jig built from scrap plywood. The jig straddles the edge of the stile and captures the base of the router to guide it in cutting each mortise. Clamp a stile on-edge in a bench vise, clamp the jig on the stile, over the mortise layout lines, and cut the mortises **(See Photo I).** You could also cut these mortises with a sharp chisel.

14 Lay out and drill holes for dowel joints in the ends of the face frame rails. Drill two holes per joint. The ⅜-in.-dia. dowel holes should be ¾ in. deep and centered on the thickness of the rails. Space the holes on the rail ends, ½ in. from both edges.

15 Lay out and drill ¾-in.-deep dowel holes in the face frame stiles that will align with the holes you drilled in the rails.

16 Cut the rails and stiles for the side frames and door to size. Drill dowel-joint holes in the side frame rails and the door rails as you did for the face frame, but use the following spacing for the holes: side frame lower rails— ½ in. and 1½ in. from the bottom edge; side frame upper rails— 1 in. from both edges; door frame lower rail—¾ in. from both edges; door frame upper rail— ¾ in. and 1½ in. from the bottom edge. Drill dowel holes in the side frame stiles and door stiles that align with pairs of holes in the corresponding rails.

17 Assemble the face frame, side frames and door. Apply glue and insert 1½-in.-long dowels in the face frame, side frame and door dowel joints. Also spread glue along the rail ends, then clamp up the assembly **(See Photo J).** Check the frames for square by

Base

Spacer block

Top frame

Core box bit

PHOTO G: Rout three flutes into the face frame stiles using a ⅜-in. core box bit (See inset photo) in a plunge router. Guide the router against a shop-made jig, which consists of two parts: a base that holds a stile captive and a top frame that serves as an edge guide for the router and establishes the proper position of the two outside flutes. A spacer block attached to the top frame offsets the router to cut the center flute.

PHOTO H: Use a homemade flute sander to remove any burn marks and smooth the ends of the flutes. Wrap adhesive-backed sandpaper around the eraser of a pencil section chucked in your drill, and run the drill at low speed.

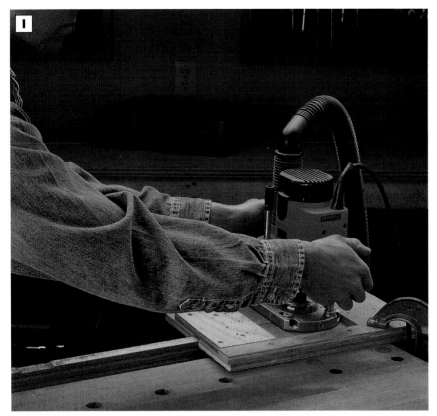

PHOTO I: To rout the hinge mortises, clamp a face frame stile on-edge in your bench vise. Clamp a shop-made hinge-mortising jig to the bench so it straddles the stile edge. Run the router around the inside of the jig frame to cut the hinge mortise.

PHOTO J: Glue the dowel joints and clamp together the rails and stiles for the face frame, side frames and door.

measuring the diagonals; the frames are square when the diagonal measurements are equal.

PREPARE SIDE FRAMES & DOOR FOR CARCASE ASSEMBLY

⓲ Cut ⅜-in.-wide by ¼-in.-deep rabbets in the back edges of the side panels to accept the back panel as shown in the *Rear Corner Section View* drawing on page 187. We used a dado-blade set in the table saw to cut the rabbets. Attach a scrap plywood auxiliary fence attached to the saw's fence to keep the dado blade from cutting the metal saw fence.

⓳ Rout ¼-in.-deep, ¾-in.-wide dadoes for the bottom panel into the side frames. Space the dadoes 2 in. up from the bottoms of the frames. The dadoes can be cut on the table saw with a dado-blade set or with a straight bit in a router. If you use a router, guide the router with a straightedge.

⓴ Cut ⅜-in.-wide by ½-in.-deep rabbets in the side frames and door for the glass. We used a ⅜-in. piloted rabbet bit to cut around the inside edges of the side frames and the door frame. Cut the rabbets in several passes of increasing depth, to keep from burning the wood or damaging the router bit (**See Photo K**). Square the corners of the rabbets with a sharp chisel.

㉑ Lay out and drill holes for the adjustable shelf pins along the inside faces of the side frame stiles. Use a piece of perforated hardboard as a drilling guide, clamping it in the same position on both side frames when you drill so the shelf pin holes on the side frames will align with one another when the cabinet carcase is assembled. Circle the desired hole spacing on the hardboard to keep your drilling pattern uniform, and use a right-angle drilling guide to keep the shelf pin holes perpendicular to the side frames (**See Photo L**).

CUT THE GLASS RETAINER STRIPS

㉒ Cut stock to ⅜ × ⅜ in. to make the retainer strips that hold the glass panes into the frames. Cross-cut the stops to length to fit into the rail and stile rabbets, then miter the ends of each strip at 45°, using a power miter saw or table saw and miter gauge. Label each stop on the back side and mark the same symbol on the corresponding rabbet surface as you fit each one, so it will be easy to sort the stops into their correct locations when you install the glass.

㉓ Drill ¹⁄₁₆-in.-dia. pilot holes in the glass retainer strips for nails. When you install the retainer strips, the brads used to attach them will slide easily into the pilot holes. You'll just need to tap or push the brads home into the door frame, which minimizes the risk of breaking the glass. *TIP: If you don't have a ¹⁄₁₆-in.-dia. drill bit, just nip off the head of one of the brads you plan to use to install the glass, chuck the brad in your drill, and drill your pilot holes.*

PREPARE THE BOTTOM PANEL & TOP SUPPORTS

㉔ Cut the bottom plywood panel to size. Resaw a piece of mahogany to ¼ in. thick to make the bottom front edge. Glue and clamp the bottom front edge piece to the front edge of the bottom panel to conceal the plywood edges. Use full-length wood cauls to distribute clamping pressure

Piloted rabbet bit

PHOTO K: Use a ⅜-in. piloted rabbet bit (See inset photo) to cut rabbets on the insides of both side frames and the door frame. The rabbets create recesses for the glass panels. Make several passes of increasing depth with the router, until you reach the final depth (½ in). Then square the rabbet corners with a chisel.

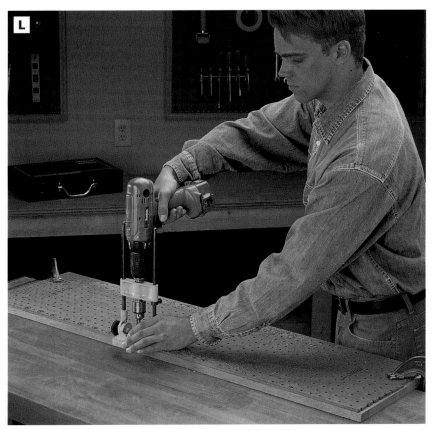

PHOTO L: Drill shelf pin holes in the side frame stiles using a piece of perforated hardboard as a template and a drill guide to ensure perpendicular holes.

PHOTO M: Clamp up the cabinet frame temporarily and mark the biscuit locations on the top supports and side panels. Disassemble the cabinet and cut slots for #20 biscuits.

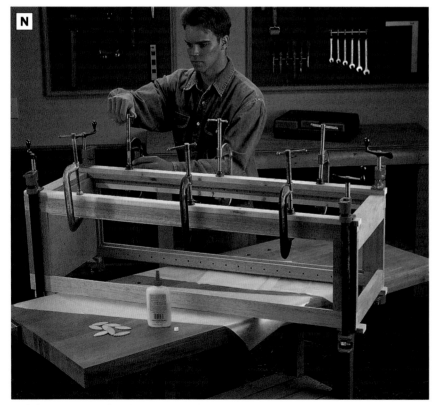

PHOTO N: Attach the face frame to the cabinet assembly with glue and biscuits, and clamp it up with a combination of C-clamps and pipe or bar clamps. Use full-length clamping cauls above and below the cabinet to distribute the clamping pressure evenly over the whole joint and to protect the cabinet parts from damage.

evenly along the length of the edging. Allow the glue to dry.

25 Cut the top supports to size. The top supports align and reinforce the side frames and provide a surface to fasten the top panel in place. Cut a ¼-in.-wide, ⅜-in.-deep rabbet along the back edge of the rear top support. We used a dado-blade set in the table saw to make the cut. The rabbet provides a recess and fastening surface for the back panel and matches the rabbets you cut in the back edges of the side frames.

26 Temporarily clamp the carcase framework together, with the top supports in position between the side frames and the bottom panel in the side frame dadoes. Align the rabbet in the back edge of the rear top support with the rabbets in the side frames for the back panel. Mark locations for biscuit joints to attach the top supports to the side frames (**See Photo M**), then disassemble the carcase parts and cut #20 biscuit slots in the top supports and the side frames with a biscuit joiner. You can use dowel joints instead of biscuits if you prefer.

ASSEMBLE THE CARCASE
27 Finish-sand the side frames, top supports and the bottom panel. Glue and clamp the side frames, top supports, and bottom panel together using biscuits or dowels in the top support joints. Allow the glue to dry and remove the clamps.

28 Cut the door stop and bottom back supports to size. Set the door stop into position beneath the front top support and mark the joint between the parts for two #20 biscuits or dowels. Cut the slots or dowel holes, install the biscuits or dowels and glue the door stop to the carcase frame.

29 Position the bottom back support so it aligns with the back edge of the bottom panel. Attach the bottom back support to the carcase with glue and biscuits or dowels.

30 Lay out and cut #20 biscuit slots or dowel holes to attach the face frame to the front of the carcase. Clamp the face frame to the cabinet when you mark the joints to be sure the face frame remains aligned with the side frames and top supports.

31 Attach the face frame to the cabinet body. Spread glue into the biscuit slots and along the front edges of the carcase framework, then clamp the face frame to the carcase **(See Photo N).** Use long wood cauls between the clamp jaws and the face frame to distribute clamping pressure evenly.

32 Set the cabinet body on the base and drill countersunk pilot holes for screws to attach the parts. Drill three holes through the front base cleat and into the back of the bottom face frame rail. Drill three holes through the back base cleat and into the bottom back support. Temporarily attach the carcase to the base with six #8 × 1¼-in. flathead wood screws.

HANG THE DOOR

33 Lay out and cut hinge mortises along the outside edge of the right door stile as you did on the face frame stile in Step 13. *NOTE: Be sure the door is oriented properly when you mark the hinge mortises; the wider*

PHOTO O: Cut hinge mortises into the edge of the face frame stile and attach the door to the cabinet with hinges and screws. Drill pilot holes for the screws to keep them from splitting the wood. Support the door from beneath as you attach the hinges.

Roman ogee bit

PHOTO P: Clamp the top panel to the workbench and use a Roman ogee bit to rout a profile around the side and front edges. Insert scrap plywood between the benchtop and the top panel to give clearance for the bit's pilot bearing.

PHOTO Q: Set the glass into the recess in the door, and nail the mitered retainer strips in place. We drilled pilot holes in the strips first to make driving the nails easier. A brad driver (shown here) allows you to push the nails into place rather than swing a hammer close to the glass.

door rail should be at the bottom of the cabinet. Once the mortises are cut, install the door on the carcase with hinges, drilling pilot holes for the hinge screws **(See Photo O).**

34 Check the fit of the door in the face frame opening and trim the door with a hand plane, if necessary, so there is an even ¹⁄₁₆-in. gap all around the door. Plane a slight chamfer around the front edge of the door frame, which will create a shadow line when the door is closed.

35 Lay out and drill holes in the edges of the door stile and face frame to mount the bullet catch and its latch opposite each other, but don't mount the hardware yet. Then remove the hinges from

the door and cabinet body to prepare the wood parts for finishing.

ATTACH THE TOP & BACK

36 Edge-joint and glue up solid mahogany stock to make a panel for the cabinet top. The panel should be about an inch oversize in length and width. When the glue dries, remove the excess glue with a cabinet scraper and cut the top to its final dimensions, as given in the *Cutting List,* page 186.

37 Install a piloted Roman ogee bit in your router. Clamp the top securely to your workbench and rout the ogee profile on the side and front edges of the top panel only, taking care not to let the ball-bearing pilot roll the bit around the back edge of the top

(See Photo P). Sand the routed edges smooth by hand and remove any burn marks left by the router. Then finish-sand the rest of the cabinet top with 150-, then 180-grit sandpaper.

38 Position the top on the cabinet body. Adjust it so the back, flat edge of the top is flush with the back edge of the rear side frame stiles, overhanging the cabinet sides and front evenly. Clamp the top temporarily in position and drill countersunk pilot holes for #8 × 1¼-in. flat-head wood screws up through the top supports and into the top. *NOTE: To allow the top panel to expand and contract, we made slotted screw holes in the top supports. To make slotted holes, drill pairs of holes side-by-side and connect them with a chisel.* Fasten the top to the cabinet with screws driven through the slotted holes. Check the fit, then remove the top for finishing.

39 Rip-cut and cross-cut the back plywood panel to size from ¼-in.-thick plywood. Set the mirror and back panel into place on the back of the cabinet body and check the fit of the parts. Then detach the cabinet from the base to prepare the parts for finishing.

APPLY THE FINISH

40 Finish-sand all surfaces, and check carefully for any glue left on the wood, which will repel your stain finish.

41 Apply the wood stain of your choice to all inside and outside surfaces of the display cabinet parts, including the rabbets for the glass and mirror. We used mahogany stain. Top-coat the parts with three coats of polyurethane varnish, tung oil or Danish oil.

ASSEMBLE THE CABINET

42 Reattach the top to the cabinet carcase with screws, driven up through the top supports.

43 Install the glass in the door frame. Place the door frame on a padded worksurface with the rabbeted side facing up. Set the glass into the rabbets and insert the retainer strips around the glass. Attach the strips carefully using a small tack hammer or a brad pusher to drive the ¾-in. brads **(See Photo Q).**

44 Install the glass in the cabinet side frames. Position the cabinet so the side frame you are working on is facing down. Set the glass in place and attach the retainer strips with brads.

45 Install the mirror and back panel. Set the cabinet down on its front face with padding under it to protect the front edge of the top from damage. Clean the mirror and lay it into position on the back of the cabinet. Place the plywood back panel on top of it in the side-panel rabbets, and nail or screw the plywood into place, being careful not to damage the mirror.

46 Attach the base to the cabinet. Lay the cabinet on its back and place scrap 2 × 4 blocking under the cabinet to raise it off the worksurface. Slide the base into position and screw it to the bottom of the cabinet through the base cleats **(See Photo R).**

47 Mount the doorknob and bullet catch on the left door stile. Reinstall the hinges and hang the door on the face frame, making sure it opens and closes

PHOTO R: Attach the base to the cabinet with screws driven through the pilot holes. Set blocks beneath the cabinet to allow clearance for the base.

correctly. Install the door latch in the face frame and adjust the action of the catch and latch. *TIP: You can make minor adjustments to the door's position in its frame by shimming behind a hinge with a piece of thick or thin paper or a matchbook cover, or by paring a hinge mortise a bit deeper with a small paring chisel.* Apply small adhesive-backed felt dots to the inside left corners of the door frame to cushion it when it closes.

48 Insert the shelf pins in their holes in the side frames. Determine the spacing you need between the shelves by measuring the objects you want to display on each shelf. Don't crowd the height; allow a little extra headroom above the objects to permit easy removal.

49 Clean the glass shelves and set them on the pins inside the cabinet (you'll need to tilt the shelves to the side to get them in). We used ¼-in.-thick tempered glass for the shelves instead of wood to enhance the mirrored effects inside the cabinet. Glass this thick can be quite expensive, but it's plenty strong and a good choice for small sections of shelving. Be sure to give the glass shop exact cutting dimensions when you buy it, and have them bevel and polish the razor-sharp edges.

Shaker-style Keepsake Box

Shaker craftsmen created marvelous steam-bent oval boxes to store and organize such personal items as sewing kits, button collections and correspondence. Try your hand at steam-bending when you build our rendition of a Shaker-style box. Bending the ash parts of the box and lid is easier than it looks, thanks to an inexpensive steaming jig you can build yourself.

Vital Statistics: Shaker-style Keepsake Box

TYPE: Oval box with lid

OVERALL SIZE: Lid: 1⅛H by 4⅞W by 7⅛L
Box: 2⅜H by 4⅜W by 6⅞L

MATERIAL: Air-dried ash

JOINERY: Butt and rabbet joints

CONSTRUCTION DETAILS:

· Lid and box sides are bent from single pieces of ash

· Fingers on the lid and box sides are glued and finished with decorative brass pins

· Ash parts are made pliable by steaming in a plywood, shop-built steamer jig

· Sides of lid fit into a rabbet cut around the oval box top

FINISH: Wipe-on Danish oil

Building time

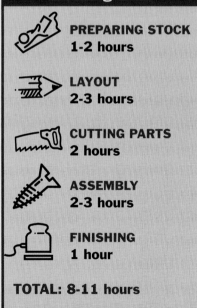

PREPARING STOCK
1-2 hours

LAYOUT
2-3 hours

CUTTING PARTS
2 hours

ASSEMBLY
2-3 hours

FINISHING
1 hour

TOTAL: 8-11 hours

Tools you'll use

· Table saw

· Band saw or scroll saw

· Clamps

· Drill/driver

· 2-in.-dia. hole saw

· Stationary belt sander

· Shop-built steamer jig (See page 202 for construction details)

· Large cooking pot and heat source (hotplate or stove)

Shopping list

☐ (1) ⅛ × 6 in. × 2 ft. air-dried (green) ash

☐ (1) ½ × 6 in. × 2 ft. ash

☐ (1) ¾ in. × 4 ft. × 8 ft. exterior plywood

☐ (1) 2-in.-dia. × 2 ft. heat-resistant hose

☐ #8 × 1½-in. galvanized deck screws

☐ (3) ⅜-in.-long brass pins

☐ Moisture-resistant and regular wood glue

☐ Finishing materials

Shaker-style Keepsake Box

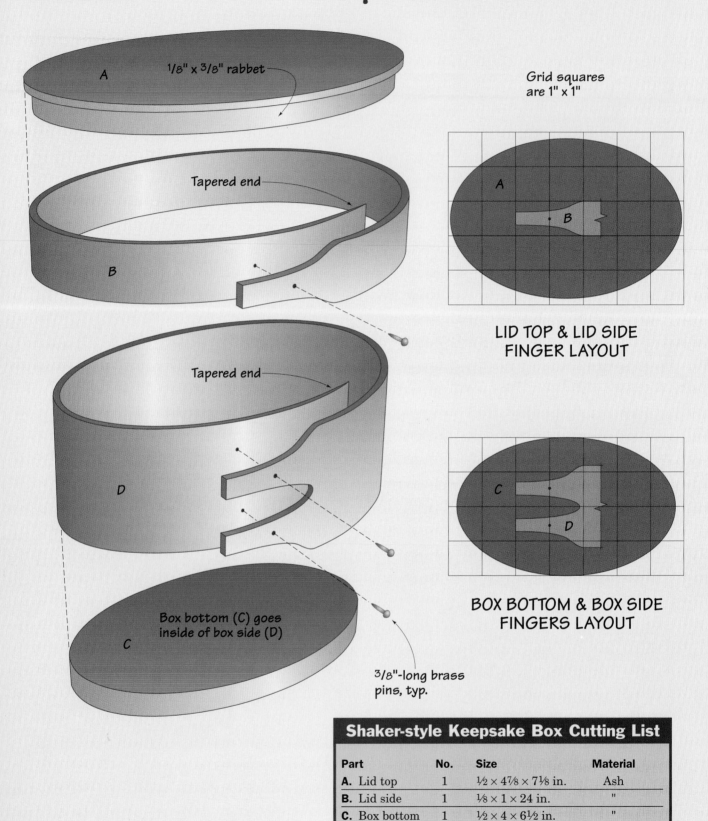

1/8" x 3/8" rabbet

A

Grid squares
are 1" x 1"

A

B

Tapered end

B

**LID TOP & LID SIDE
FINGER LAYOUT**

Tapered end

D

C

D

Box bottom (C) goes
inside of box side (D)

C

3/8"-long brass
pins, typ.

**BOX BOTTOM & BOX SIDE
FINGERS LAYOUT**

Shaker-style Keepsake Box Cutting List			
Part	**No.**	**Size**	**Material**
A. Lid top	1	$\frac{1}{2} \times 4\frac{7}{8} \times 7\frac{1}{8}$ in.	Ash
B. Lid side	1	$\frac{1}{8} \times 1 \times 24$ in.	"
C. Box bottom	1	$\frac{1}{2} \times 4 \times 6\frac{1}{2}$ in.	"
D. Box side	1	$\frac{1}{8} \times 2\frac{3}{8} \times 24$ in.	"

Shaker-style Keepsake Box: Step-by-step

MAKE THE LID & BOX SIDES

Some hardwoods are easier to bend than others. Ash is a good choice, as well as oak and cherry. Whatever species you choose, be sure it has been air-dried (often called "green") rather than kiln-dried. Kiln-drying destroys the elasticity of wood fibers and makes the wood prone to breaking when it bends. There's no way to tell, visually, if the stock has been air-dried, so ask your lumber supplier before you buy.

❶ Make the lid and box sides: Rip and cross-cut the lid and box sides to size. You'll probably then need to resaw these workpieces on a band saw to reach the ⅛-in. thickness of the parts.
CAUTION: *If you need to resaw these parts, do your resawing first on a wider piece of ash, then rip and cross-cut the parts to size. This way, you'll keep your fingers a safer distance from the blade during resawing.* Sand one end of each workpiece starting about 2 in. in and tapering to the end **(See Photo A).** This taper will be necessary to compensate for the double thickness that results when the box sides overlap during assembly. Finally, use the *Finger Layout* drawings on page 200 to lay out and cut the fingers on the other ends of these parts. Sand the side pieces smooth.

BUILD A BENDING FORM

Once the thin ash parts are steamed, they must be clamped to an oval form immediately in order to form and retain their shape as they dry and cool. We built the plywood bending form shown in Photo B, right, which sandwiches the ash between an inner oval, made of four pieces of exterior plywood laminated together and screwed to a board, and two outer presses, also made of four plywood laminations. A pair of bar clamps squeeze the outer presses against the inner oval, holding the ash in shape.

❷ Build the bending form: Face-glue four 1 × 1-ft. pieces of exterior plywood to form a 3-in.-thick blank. Lay out an oval in the center of the blank that matches the size of the box bottom (See *Box Bottom* drawing, page 200). Draw a line across the blank from edge to edge that splits the oval in

PHOTO A: The side pieces of both the lid and the box get tapered on one end to minimize the thickness of the overlap after they are bent to shape. Begin the taper about 2 in. in from one end of each part. A stationary belt sander works well for sanding these tapers.

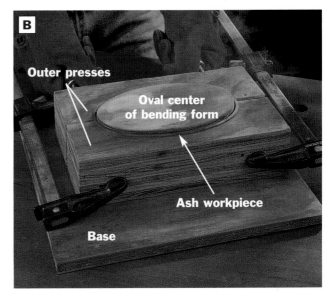

PHOTO B: Steam the ash workpiece until pliable, then remove it quickly from the steamer box and wrap it around the oval center of the bending form. Set the outer presses in place around the ash and clamp the presses together. Tighten the clamps so the ash conforms as closely as possible to the oval center of the bending form. Wear gloves when working with steamed wood—it will be extremely hot.

half, lengthwise. On the band saw, cut along your centerlines up to the oval, then cut out the oval shape. The result is a thick oval as well as two waste pieces that become the two outer presses. Trim off another ¼ in. of plywood along the curved edges of the outer presses to provide clearance for the bending stock. Belt-sand any irregularities on the cut edges of these three parts.

Shop-built steamer jig

The steamer jig you'll need for this project is simply a long, narrow box made of exterior plywood with a 2-in.-dia. heat-resistant hose attached to one end and a hinged door on the other. A pot of boiling water supplies steam to the box through the hose, and the hose attaches to a plywood lid that covers the pot. As steam builds inside the jig, it surrounds the thin Shaker-box parts and softens them until they are pliable.

How to build the steamer jig

The proportions of the steamer box aren't critical, so long as there is space inside the box for the steam to make contact with the ash workpieces on all sides. We built our box from ¾-in. exterior-grade plywood and sized it 6 in. wide, 6 in. tall and 3 ft. long. Cut the top, bottom, sides, hose end and door to size. Cut four sticks for the steamer box legs and a round plywood lid to fit over the pot you'll use to boil water. Protect all surfaces that will face into the steamer box with a coat of exterior primer and paint. Use a hole saw to bore a 2-in.-dia. hole through the hose end of the box as well as the pot lid for the hose.

Attach the box sides and hose end to the box top and bottom pieces with moisture-resistant wood glue and 1½-in. galvanized deck screws. Install the door on the other end of the box with a galvanized hinge, and screw a knob to the door. Drill a ½-in.-dia. hole through the box bottom near the door for a drain tube. Then screw the legs to the steamer box.

Fasten the hose to the box end and to the pot lid. Car radiator hose works well for the tubing, but any 2-in.-dia. heat-resistant hose will do the trick. We used short lengths of threaded pipe attached to metal fittings to fasten the hose to the box end and pot lid. The hose ends friction-fit over the metal pipes. However you choose to fasten the hose, be sure the connections form a tight fit around the pot lid and steamer box holes.

Cut a handful of dowels or thin scrap sticks to 4-in. lengths; these will be used as spacers inside the steamer to keep the ash parts elevated off the box bottom so they'll steam evenly.

Pot lid

Construct the steamer jig from exterior-grade plywood, moisture-resistant wood glue and galvanized deck screws. Install a hinged door on one end of the steamer box, and drill a 2-in.-dia. hole in the other box end and the plywood pot lid for installing a length of heat-resistant or automotive radiator hose. Attach the hose to the steamer box and pot lid. We used metal fittings and threaded pipe for making these hose connections.

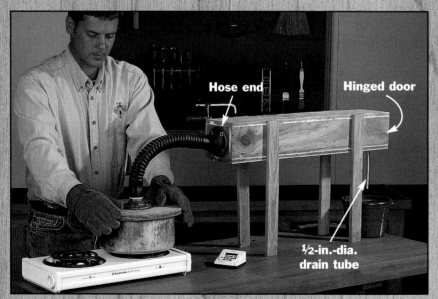

Hose end

Hinged door

½-in.-dia. drain tube

Attach a drain tube through a hole in the bottom of the jig near the door to let excess steam and condensed water vapor escape into a pail. Elevate your steamer on legs until it is higher than the pot to minimize bending the hose. This way, steam can rise and pass more easily into the box.

PHOTO C: Use a piloted rabbeting bit in the router table to mill the rabbet around the edges of the lid top. Hold the workpiece securely against the router table and bit with a foam-soled pushpad. Feed the workpiece around the bit clockwise to cut the rabbet.

PHOTO D: Glue the side pieces to the box top and bottom. Hold the bentwood parts in position while the glue dries with strap, spring and C-clamps. Mask off the area around the fingers to protect these spots from glue squeeze-out.

Fasten the laminated oval to the center of a 2 × 2-ft. plywood base.

STEAM & BEND THE LID & BOX SIDES

❸ Set up your steaming jig (See *Steamer Jig,* previous page) and steam the lid and box side pieces. Plan to steam one workpiece at a time. Insert spacers beneath the ash part in the steamer box so the steam penetrates the workpiece from all sides. Insert the part and steam it for about 15 minutes until it is pliable. When the time is up, remove the workpiece and immediately wrap it around the oval center of the bending form, set the two outer presses in place and tighten the clamps (**See Photo B).** The ash will begin to cool and lose its flexibility almost instantly, so work quickly. Leave the workpiece clamped in the jig for two days so it dries thoroughly.

ASSEMBLE THE LID & BOTTOM

❹ Make the box top and bottom ovals: Lay out and cut the box top and bottom to size, according to the grid drawings on page 200. The lid sides fit into a ⅛-in.-deep, ⅜-in.-wide rabbet in the edge of the box top. Cut the rabbet with a piloted rabbeting bit in the router table (**See Photo C).** Sand these parts.

❺ Glue and clamp the bent ash parts to the box top and bottom. First, dry-fit the lid and box parts together with clamps, and mark the locations where the fingers overlap the sides. Release the clamps, and apply masking tape along the outsides of the finger outlines. Then glue and clamp the bent

PHOTO E: Drill pilot holes through the fingers on the lid and box sides, then tap the decorative brass pins into the pilot holes and against an anvil to flatten and bend over the pin tips inside the box.

wood parts to the box top and bottom ovals (**See Photo D).** When the glue stops squeezing out, remove the tape.

❻ Install the decorative brass pins: Drill a pilot hole through the fingers on the lid and box sides about 1 in. from the ends of the fingers. Tap the pins through the pilot holes and flatten them against an anvil inside the box (**See Photo E).**

❼ Finish the box by wiping on several coats of Danish oil. For a decorative touch, we covered the bottom of the box with a piece of felt.

Jewelry Box

Add this jewelry box to your list of must-build projects for gift giving, and surprise a special person in your life. Our compact maple jewelry box features walnut accents to highlight the beauty of contrasting wood tones and features a removeable tray with compartments to store many precious trinkets and jewelry. The raised-panel lid and tapered feet and handle give the design a clean, contemporary look.

Vital Statistics: Jewelry Box

TYPE: Jewelry box

OVERALL SIZE: 12W by 7H by 8D

MATERIAL: Maple

JOINERY: Miter, dado, rabbet joints

CONSTRUCTION DETAILS:

· Corner grain matches all around box sides

· Raised-panel lid

· Tray rests on the top edges of tray supports. When lid is opened, tray protrudes above box and can be lifted out

· Divided tray compartment

· Walnut feet and handle details

FINISHING OPTIONS: A clear finish, like Danish oil or varnish, is recommended to bring out depth of the maple wood grain, particularly if curly maple stock is used

Building time

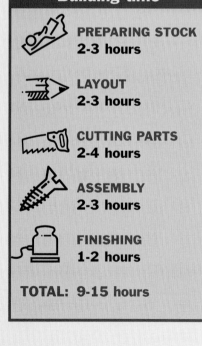

PREPARING STOCK
2-3 hours

LAYOUT
2-3 hours

CUTTING PARTS
2-4 hours

ASSEMBLY
2-3 hours

FINISHING
1-2 hours

TOTAL: 9-15 hours

Tools you'll use

· Jointer

· Planer

· Router table with auxiliary fence and featherboard

· Raised-panel router bit

· Band saw

· Table saw

· Dado-blade set

· Bar clamps

· Spring clamps

· Sanding station

· Wood chisels

· Combination square

Shopping list

☐ (1) $^6/_4 \times 6^1/_2$ in. × 2 ft. maple

☐ (1) $^3/_4 \times 8$ in. × 4 ft. maple

☐ (1) $^1/_4$ in. × 2 ft. × 2 ft. maple or birch plywood

☐ 1 × 1 in. × 2 ft. walnut scrap

☐ (2) 95° solid-brass jewelry box hinges

☐ Wood glue

☐ $^3/_4$-, $^1/_2$-in. brads

☐ Wide masking tape or plastic packing tape

☐ Finishing materials

Jewelry Box

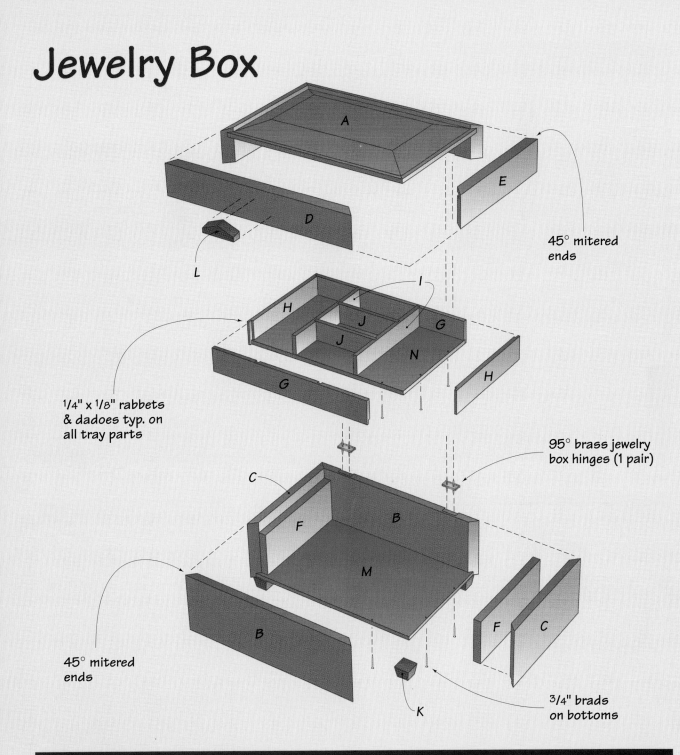

45° mitered ends

L

1/4" x 1/8" rabbets & dadoes typ. on all tray parts

H

I

J

J

G

N

G

H

95° brass jewelry box hinges (1 pair)

C

F

B

M

B

F

C

45° mitered ends

K

3/4" brads on bottoms

Jewelry Box Cutting List

Part	No.	Size	Material
A. Lid	1	3/4 × 7 3/8 × 11 1/2 in.	Maple
B. Box sides	2	1/2 × 4 × 12 in.	"
C. Box ends	2	1/2 × 4 × 8 in.	"
D. Lid sides	2	1/2 × 2 × 12 in.	"
E. Lid ends	2	1/2 × 2 × 8 in.	"
F. Tray supports	2	1/2 × 3 × 7 in.	"
G. Tray sides	2	1/4 × 1 1/2 × 10 5/8 in.	"

Part	No.	Size	Material
H. Tray ends	2	1/4 × 1 1/2 × 6 7/8 in.	Maple
I. Tray dividers	2	1/4 × 1 1/4 × 6 5/8 in.	"
J. Tray dividers	2	1/4 × 1 1/4 × 4 1/4 in.	"
K. Feet	4	1 × 1 × 3/4 in.	Walnut
L. Handle	1	1/2 × 2 × 3/4 in.	"
M. Box bottom	1	1/4 × 7 1/2 × 11 1/2 in.	Maple plywood
N. Tray bottom	1	1/4 × 6 5/8 × 10 5/8 in.	"

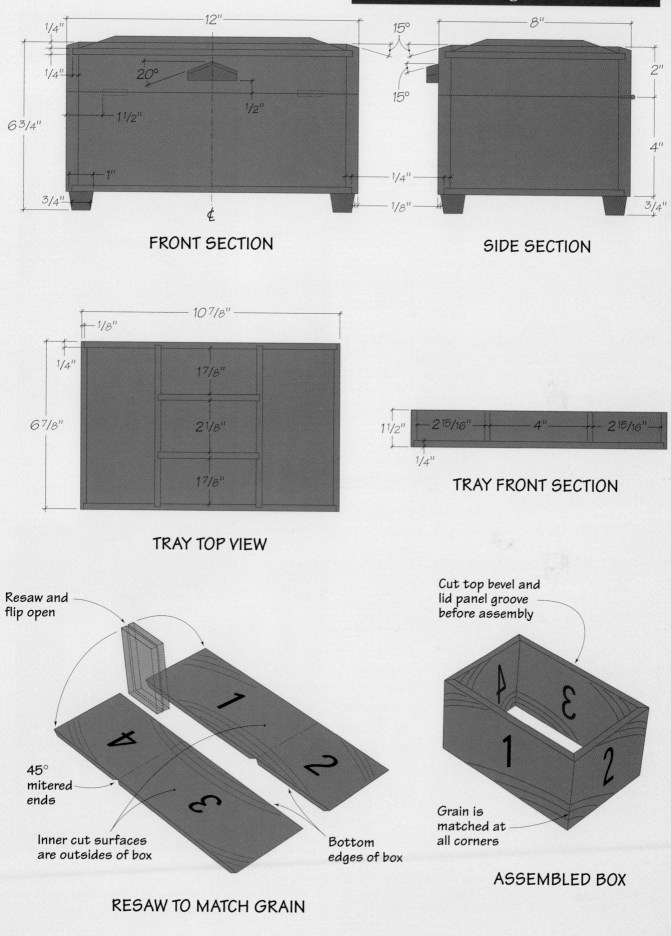

FRONT SECTION

SIDE SECTION

TRAY TOP VIEW

TRAY FRONT SECTION

RESAW TO MATCH GRAIN

Resaw and flip open

45° mitered ends

Inner cut surfaces are outsides of box

Bottom edges of box

ASSEMBLED BOX

Cut top bevel and lid panel groove before assembly

Grain is matched at all corners

MAKE AND ASSEMBLE THE BOX

The box and lid sides and ends are resawn and cut from one piece of maple to give a four-corner grain match (two sides have continuous grain and two are butt- or end-matched). A prominent grain pattern will show off the four-way match better than an all-over pattern like bird's-eye, but a bit of figure or curl to the wood will add a richness that is welcome in just about any woodworking project.

❶ Cut the lid panel to size, according to the dimensions given in the *Cutting List,* page 206.

❷ Install a vertical-style panel raising router bit in the router table. Fasten a tall auxiliary fence to the router table. If you have an adjustable-speed router, set the speed to about 13,000 rpm. Using a featherboard to secure the lid panel, rout the shape, removing about ⅛ in. of material with each pass until you reach the desired profile. The finished panel should have a ¼ × ¼-in. lip around the edge that will fit into the groove in the lid **(See Photo A).** NOTE: *Using a panel raising bit in a router table is an easy and safe way to cut a raised panel. The tall auxiliary fence provides a secure bearing surface for the panel, and the featherboard keeps the panel tight against the fence as it passes the cutter.*

❸ Plane the 6/4 stock for the box sides and ends to 1¼ in. thick. Joint one long edge and rip the stock to 6¼ in., then cross-cut to 21 in. in length. (This piece comprises the box sides and ends and the lid sides and ends, which will be cut apart later after the box is assembled.)

❹ Mark a centerline along the ripped edge, dividing the board in two. With the jointed edge riding on the saw table, resaw the board on a band saw **(See Photo B).** Use a resaw jig to guide the workpiece.

❺ Plane the two resawn board halves to ½ in. thick. It is important to label the four lid and four box parts on the two boards at this point. Use the illustrations on the bottom of page 207 as a guide.

PHOTO A: Rout the raised-panel face of the lid, taking off only about ⅛ in. at a time. Do this by starting with the router fence nearly flush to the edge of the bit, and move the fence further into the bit for each pass. Removing too much material in one pass could burn the lid panel or prematurely dull the router bit.

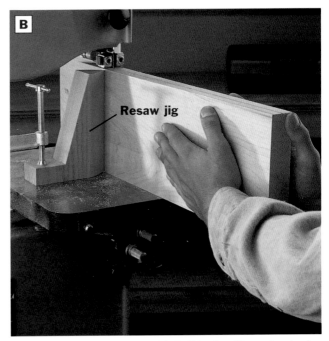

PHOTO B: Resaw the maple stock in half for the sides and ends of the box, using a marked centerline as a guide for the blade. A shop-made resaw jig clamped to the saw table will help square the board to the table and keep the blade tracking along the cutting line.

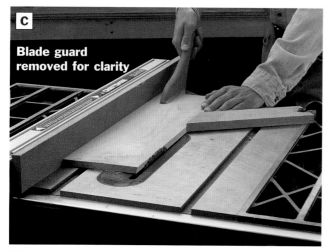

PHOTO C: Cut a 15° bevel into the top edges of the two resawn box boards. Use a featherboard and pushstick for accuracy and safety.

PHOTO D: Cut the bottom rabbet into the lower edge of the box sides. Attach an auxiliary wood fence if you use a table saw and dado-blade set to cut these rabbets.

PHOTO E: Cut the sides to length on the table saw, mitering the ends at the same time. Use a miter gauge set to exactly 90° to feed the stock through the blade.

PHOTO F: Apply glue to the mitered faces and use tape to hold the corner joints together while the glue sets. Tack the box bottom panel into its rabbet. The lid panel dado gets no glue.

❻ Set your table saw blade to 15° and cut a bevel on the lid edges of both resawn workpieces (**See Photo C**).

❼ Cut a ¼ × ¼-in. dado along the edge of both resawn boards, ¼ in. down from the top of the beveled edge. Then cut a ¼-in.-deep rabbet for the box bottom along the opposite long edge of each board (**See Photo D**). To do this, first fasten an auxiliary wood fence to the saw fence to keep the dado blade from damaging the metal fence.

❽ Install a combination table saw blade and tilt it to 45°. Test the angle cut on some scrap stock to be sure it is exact. Then use a miter gauge to feed the workpieces as you cut the four sides to length, with a 45° miter at each end (**See Photo E**).

❾ Cut the plywood bottom to size. Set the bottom panel into the rabbets on the box ends and sides, and the lid panel in the groove near the bevel. Check the fit of the mitered corners. NOTE: *The lid panel is narrower than the bottom panel to allow the lid to expand across the grain.* Disassemble the box, and sand the inside faces of all the parts, as well as the top surface of the lid panel.

❿ Arrange the box side and end pieces end-to-end, with their outside faces up and the grain aligned. With the mitered edges pressed tightly together, run a strip of wide masking tape or clear plastic packing tape along each of the three corner joints and burnish it. Flip the assembly over and spread wood glue into both members of each miter joint (use no glue for the lid or bottom panels to allow

PHOTO G: Apply bar clamps across the box length and width to ensure tight miter joints. Wood cauls between the box and the clamp jaws will help distribute clamping pressure.

PHOTO H: Rip the box and lid into two pieces on the table saw, with the box bottom against the saw fence. Raise the blade to ⅝ in. and cut one end, then cut adjacent sides, working your way around the box.

PHOTO I: Glue the tray supports to the inside ends of the box. Butt them against the box bottom and hold them tight with spring clamps.

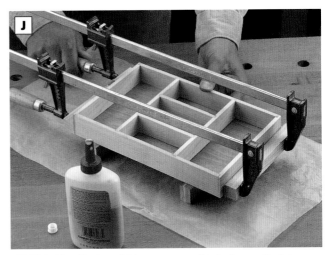

PHOTO J: After the tray dividers are assembled, glue up the tray sides and ends and tack the tray bottom in place with brads.

for wood movement). Roll the assembly into a box with the bottom panel and lid in place, and tape the last joint closed **(See Photo F).**

⓫ Use bar clamps clamped across the width and length of the jewelry box to further close the miters **(See Photo G).** Allow the glue to dry, remove the clamps and tack the bottom panel into the rabbet with ¾-in. brads.

⓬ Remove the tape, working carefully to avoid tearing away the wood grain at the corners. If it's difficult to do this, soften the adhesive with a heat gun. Apply mineral spirits with a rag to remove any tape adhesive residue.

⓭ With the box bottom against the table saw

fence, rip the lid from the box, starting on an end and cutting clockwise around the box side panels **(See Photo H).** *CAUTION: Be sure to support the lid on the last cut, but be careful not to pinch the blade between the lid and the box as you make the cut, which could cause the saw to kick back.*

⓮ Cut the two tray supports to size. Sand the inside face and top edge of each support, and glue the supports to the inside faces of the box ends with the lower edges butted against the bottom panel **(See Photo I).**

ASSEMBLE THE TRAY

⓯ Surface-plane ¾-in. stock down to ¼ in. for the tray parts. Rip- and cross-cut the tray sides, ends, dividers and bottom to size. *CAUTION: Use care when cutting these small workpieces to size, especially if you cut them on a table saw. If you make the cuts on a table saw, start with stock that is long enough to keep your hands a safe distance away from the blade.*

16 Cut ¼-in.-wide × ⅛-in.-deep dadoes in the long tray dividers and the tray sides, as shown in the *Tray (Top View)* illustration, page 207. Then, cut ⅛-in.-deep, ¼-in.-wide rabbets in the ends of both tray ends. Cut ⅛-in.-deep, ¼-in.-wide rabbets along the bottom inside edges of the tray ends and sides to accept the tray bottom. Sand all the tray parts smooth with 150- to 180-grit sandpaper.

17 Glue and clamp the center tray divider unit together and let the glue dry. Then glue and clamp the tray sides and ends to the assembled dividers with the divider ends set in the dado grooves **(See Photo J)**. Drill pilot holes and use ½-in. brads to fasten the tray bottom in place.

ADD THE HINGES, FEET & HANDLE

18 Cut a 1 × 1 × 12-in. blank of walnut for the jewelry box feet. Cross-cut one end square and mark a line around it, ¾ in. from the end. Starting at this line, bevel the four faces of the foot so they taper to ¾ in. square at the end of the blank. Sand the foot tapers on a stationary disk sander **(See Photo K),** then cut off the foot. Repeat this procedure for the remaining three feet.

19 Cut a piece of walnut to ½ in. thick × ¾ in. wide × 2 in. long for the handle and square the ends. Divide one long edge in half and draw 20° beveled lines from this point to either short end of the handle blank. Cut along these angle lines with a band saw to create a five-sided shape that matches the handle on the *Front View* illustration, page 207. Designate a front face to the handle and bevel the edges from the back face toward the front to give the handle a sleeker profile and mimic the leg tapers.

20 Finish-sand the feet, handle, outsides of the box and tray with 180-grit sandpaper. Because maple is dense and closed-grained, the maple box needs to be sanded with fine paper—220-grit—to remove fine scratches; otherwise they'll show up in the finish. This finishing step is particularly important if you plan to apply a wood stain to the jewelry box.

PHOTO K: For safety and to maintain control over the workpiece, sand the tapers on a long walnut blank, then cut off a foot and repeat for the other three feet.

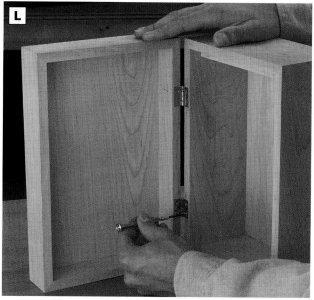

PHOTO L: Measure and cut the hinge mortises with a wood chisel, then install the brass jewelry box hinges to attach the lid to the box.

21 Mark out the hinge leaf mortises on the lid and box, and cut the mortises with a sharp wood chisel. Install the hinges, drilling pilot holes for the screws first **(See Photo L).**

22 Glue and clamp the feet to the bottom of the box, ⅛ in. in from the corners. Glue and clamp the handle onto the lid (See *Front Section,* page 207).

FINISHING TOUCHES

23 Apply a clear finish to show off the natural beauty of the maple and walnut—we used three coats of Danish oil.

Inlaid Tea Tray

Impress your guests and cut down on the number of trips you make to the kitchen when you build this generously sized serving tray. The finger-jointed corners are attractive as well as sturdy, and the decorative veneer inlay adds a sophisticated touch.

Vital Statistics: Inlaid Tea Tray

TYPE: Serving tray

OVERALL SIZE: 17W by 3H by 24L

MATERIAL: Cherry, cherry plywood, veneer inlay

JOINERY: Finger, biscuit, dado joints

CONSTRUCTION DETAILS:

· Tray bottom made of two sheets of ¼-in. cherry plywood laminated together and surrounded by a mitered and biscuited cherry frame

· Decorative veneer inlay on tray bottom installed into a shallow rabbet cut around the perimeter of the top plywood panel

· Frame ends attach to sides with finger joints

FINISH: Satin tung oil or polyurethane

Building time

PREPARING STOCK
1 hour

LAYOUT
2-3 hours

CUTTING PARTS
4-5 hours

ASSEMBLY
2-3 hours

FINISHING
1 hour

TOTAL: 10-13 hours

Tools you'll use

· Table saw
· Dado blade
· Power miter saw
· Router table with ½-in. straight bit
· Scroll saw
· Drum sander or drill press and drum sander attachment
· Biscuit jointer
· Clamps

Shopping list

☐ (1) ½ × 8 in. × 6 ft. cherry

☐ (1) ¼ in. × 2 ft. × 2 ft. cherry plywood

☐ #20 biscuits

☐ ¹⁄₃₂ × ½ in. × 6 lineal ft. decorative veneer inlay strip

☐ Wood glue

☐ Finishing materials

Inlaid Tea Tray

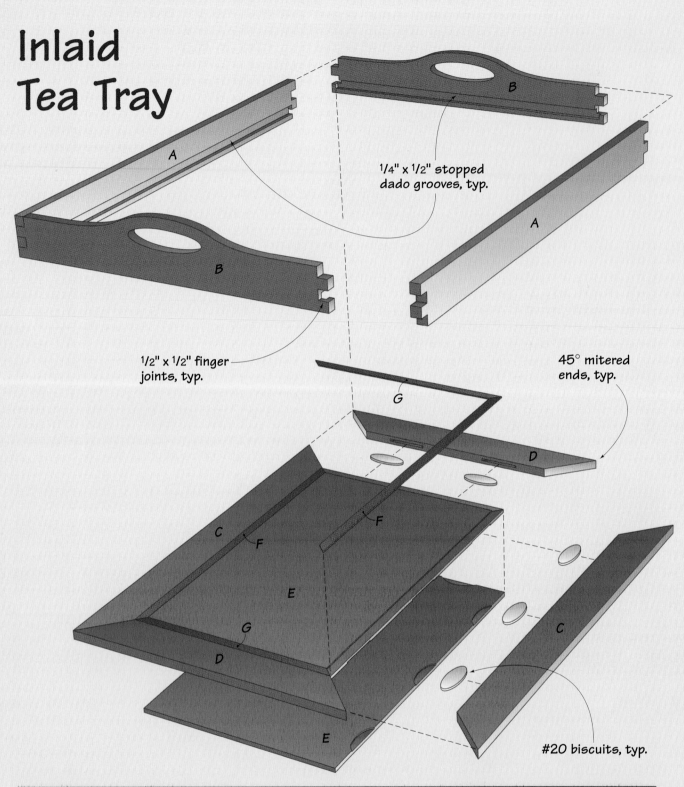

1/4" x 1/2" stopped dado grooves, typ.

1/2" x 1/2" finger joints, typ.

45° mitered ends, typ.

#20 biscuits, typ.

A

B

A

B

G

D

F

C

F

E

G

D

E

C

Inlaid Tea Tray Cutting List

Part	No.	Size	Material
A. Tray sides	2	$1/2 \times 2 \times 24$ in.	Cherry
B. Tray ends	2	$1/2 \times 3 \times 17$ in.	"
C. Frame sides	2	$1/2 \times 2 1/4 \times 23 7/16$ in.	"
D. Frame ends	2	$1/2 \times 2 1/4 \times 16 7/16$ in.	"

Part	No.	Size	Material
E. Bottom panels	2	$1/4 \times 11 15/16 \times 18 15/16$ in.	Cherry plywood
F. Long inlays	2	$1/32 \times 1/2 \times 20$ in.	Veneer strips
G. Short inlays	2	$1/32 \times 1/2 \times 13$ in.	"

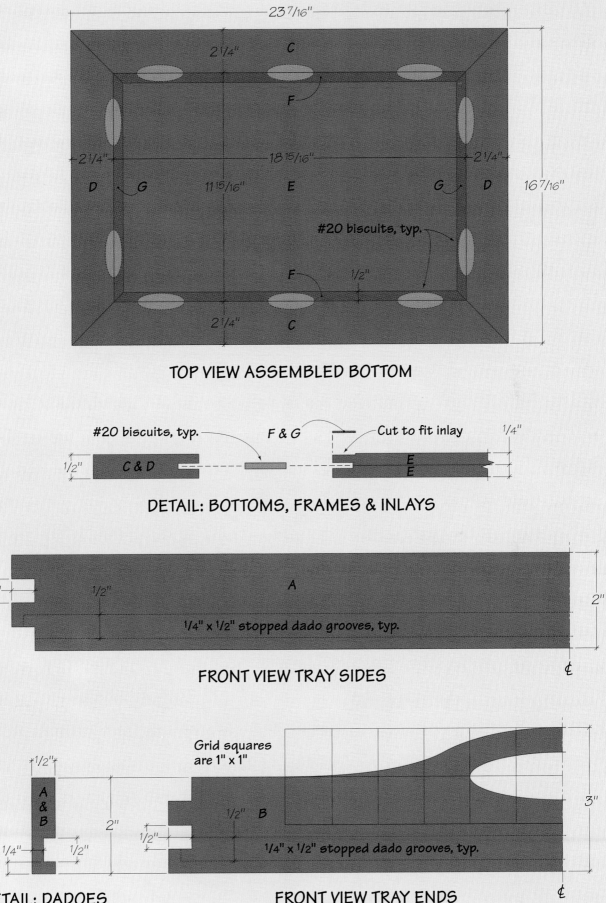

23 7/16"

2 1/4" C

F

2 1/4" 18 15/16" 2 1/4"

D G 11 15/16" E G D

#20 biscuits, typ.

16 7/16"

F 1/2"

2 1/4" C

TOP VIEW ASSEMBLED BOTTOM

#20 biscuits, typ. F & G Cut to fit inlay 1/4"

1/2" C & D E E

DETAIL: BOTTOMS, FRAMES & INLAYS

1/2" 1/2" A 2"

1/4" x 1/2" stopped dado grooves, typ. ¢

FRONT VIEW TRAY SIDES

1/2" Grid squares are 1" x 1"

A & B 2" 1/2" B 3"

1/4" 1/2" 1/2" 1/4" x 1/2" stopped dado grooves, typ. ¢

DETAIL: DADOES   **FRONT VIEW TRAY ENDS**

MAKE THE TRAY SIDES & ENDS

❶ Rip and cross-cut workpieces for the tray sides and ends, according to the dimensions given in the *Cutting List,* page 214.

❷ Mark the tray ends for the handles and finger joints. Start by drawing a 1 × 1-in. grid pattern on the tray ends, then transfer the curved handle profile and cutout shown in the *Front View Tray Ends* drawing, page 215, onto the parts. Next, lay out the finger joints. Mark ½ × ½-in. finger joints on the tray ends and sides **(See Photo A).** Notice on the exploded view drawing (page 214) that the fingers on the tray sides match, and the fingers on the tray ends match. In order to interlock, the fingers start on the top edges of the tray sides and on the bottom edges of the tray ends.

❸ Lay out the bottom grooves. The plywood bottom will fit into ½-in.-wide, ¼-in.-deep dadoes cut into both the tray sides and ends. Lay out these dado cuts on the inside faces of the tray parts, ¼ in. up from the bottom edges. The grooves on both sets of parts must stop ¼ in. from the ends of the workpieces, or you'll cut through the closest fingers.

❹ Cut the finger joints: Set up a ½-in.-wide dado blade on the table saw and raise it ½ in. above the saw table. Attach a tall auxiliary fence to the miter gauge to support the workpieces as you cut them on-end. Then stack the tray sides together and clamp them to the miter gauge,

PHOTO A: Lay out the finger joints on the ends of the tray side and end pieces. Use a combination square to mark the joints. Draw X's on the waste areas.

PHOTO B: Mill the finger joints with a ½-in.-wide dado blade. Attach an auxiliary wood fence to the miter gauge to hold the workpieces securely. Since the fingers match on like workpieces, clamp them in pairs to cut the fingers in both parts at once. NOTE: *Work carefully when setting up these cuts—even slightly misaligned cuts can produce poorly fitting finger joints.*

PHOTO C: Cut the bottom panel grooves in the tray sides and ends on the router table. When cutting these stopped dadoes on the tray sides and ends, mark the leading and trailing edges of the bit on the router fence so you know where to start and stop the cuts.

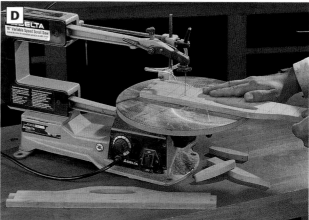

PHOTO D: Cut the curved handle profiles and cutouts on the scroll saw. You'll need to drill an access hole for the blade first, in order to start the handle cutout.

checking to be sure they are square to the saw table. Cut away the waste between the fingers. Follow the same procedure for cutting the tray end fingers (**See Photo B**).

5 Rout grooves for the bottom panel. Install a ½-in. straight bit in the router table, and align the bit and fence to follow your bottom dado layout lines on the tray sides and ends. Then mark the leading and trailing edges of the router bit on the fence, and use these references to start and stop the dadoes as you cut them in the tray parts (**See Photo C**). Square the ends of these stopped dadoes with a chisel.

6 Cut the handle profiles and cutouts on the tray end pieces with a scroll saw (**See Photo D**).

7 Sand the tray side and end pieces smooth. A drum sander works well for sanding the profiles.

BUILD THE BOTTOM

8 Rip and cross-cut the frame side and end pieces to width and length. Cut 45° miters on the ends of these four parts with a miter saw (**See Photo E**).

9 Cut and glue the plywood bottom panels together to create a ½-in.-thick blank. Spread glue on one face of each panel, and laminate them together. Sandwich the glue-up between clamps and long cauls to distribute clamping pressure evenly and produce a tight glue joint (**See Photo F**).

10 Lay out and cut #20 biscuit slots to join the frame sides and ends to the bottom panel (**See**

PHOTO E: Rip and cross-cut the frame end and side pieces to size, then miter-cut the ends of the parts to 45°.

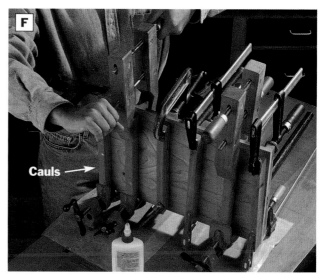

PHOTO F: Laminate two ¼-in. plywood sheets together to form the bottom panel. Clamp up the plywood on both sides with long wood cauls to press the sheets tightly together until the glue dries.

PHOTO G: Lay out and cut #20 biscuit slots to join the frame side and end pieces to the bottom panel. Clamp the parts in a bench vise to hold them securely when you cut the slots.

PHOTO H: Rout a shallow rabbet around the top face of the bottom panel for the veneer inlay strips. Install a ½-in. straight bit in your router table to cut this 1⁄32-in.-deep rabbet. Practice on scraps first and test the fit of the strips in the rabbet.

PHOTO I: Miter-cut the corners of the decorative inlay strips using the 45° fence on a combination square and a sharp utility knife. Hold the knife as square to the inlay as you can when making the cuts, so the mitered joints will meet flush.

PHOTO J: Install the inlay strips on the bottom panel rabbets. Glue one piece at a time to the plywood, and press it firmly in place with a couple of clamps and a wood caul. Cover the inlay with wax paper before clamping on the caul to keep the parts from sticking together.

Photo G). Plan for two biscuits on each end piece and three per side piece. Cut all the slots.

⑪ Rout a ½-in.-wide, ¹⁄₃₂-in.-deep rabbet around the top face of the bottom panel for the decorative veneer inlay strips. Use a straight bit in the router table to make these cuts **(See Photo H).**

⑫ Cut and fit the bottom panel inlay strips. Instead of cutting these strips all at once, you'll get better results if you work your way around the bottom panel, cutting one piece at a time, then fitting and cutting the adjacent strip. Trim 45° miters on the ends of the inlay strips with a sharp utility knife and a combination square **(See Photo I).** For best visual effect, try to cut the corner joints so the inlay pattern continues around the corners without abrupt breaks in the pattern. NOTE: *Most decorative inlay strips have a pattern repeat for seaming and cornering.*

⑬ Glue the inlay strips to the bottom panel: Install the pieces one at a time in the shallow rabbets. Clamp the inlay in place with a wood caul protected by wax paper, in case the glue seeps through the inlay. Allow the glue to dry before removing the caul and moving on to the next strip **(See Photo J).**

⑭ Install the frame side and end pieces on the bottom panel: Spread glue on the mating surfaces of the parts and into the biscuit slots. Insert the biscuits and clamp up the assembly **(See Photo K).** A frame clamp or strap clamp works well for holding the mitered corners closed while the glue dries. Then sand the bottom assembly smooth.

PHOTO K: Attach the frame sides and ends to the inlaid bottom panel with glue and biscuits. Dry-fit the parts together first with the biscuits in place. Once the pieces are glued and fitted, install a frame clamp around the assembly and tighten.

PHOTO L: Spread glue onto mating surfaces of the finger joints, slip the bottom into its grooves and clamp up the tray. Install clamps both lengthwise and widthwise to hold the finger joints closed in two directions.

ASSEMBLE THE TRAY

⑮ Dry-fit the tray sides and ends around the bottom panel assembly with the bottom panel inserted in its grooves. Then disassemble the parts, spread glue in the gaps between the fingers, and fit the tray together **(See Photo L).** Do not glue the bottom panel into its grooves so it can "float" freely. Clamp up the tray both lengthwise and widthwise, and measure diagonally from corner to corner to be sure the tray is square. Adjust the clamps to make corrections.

FINISHING TOUCHES

⑯ Smooth the entire project with 220-grit paper, easing all the edges lightly as you go. Apply three coats of clear tung oil to the tray. Sand between coats with 320-grit wet/dry paper or #0000 steel wool, and remove the dust with a tack cloth. If your tray will be used to serve beverages, topcoat with three layers of polyurethane varnish instead of tung oil, to protect it from moisture stains.

Spice Shelves

Get those jars of spices and seasoning out of a dark cupboard and onto this handsome oak spice holder. Two lower shelves are designed to accommodate full-size shakers, while the top shelf stores taller containers and bottles. Chamfered back slats and lap-jointed front rails lend a fine woodworking air to this deceptively simple piece.

Spice Shelves

Vital Statistics

TYPE: Wall-hung spice shelf unit

OVERALL SIZE: 14³/₁₆W by 22H by 4D

MATERIAL: Red oak

JOINERY: Butt joints reinforced with glue and finish nails; glued dado and lap joints

CONSTRUCTION DETAILS:

· Project constructed from pre-milled ¼- and ½-in.-thick stock

· Back panel "V-grooves" are formed by chamfering the edges of the back slats before glue-up

· Shelf dadoes are gang-routed into the sides using a simple shop-made jig

FINISH: Danish oil

BUILDING TIME: 6-8 hours

Shopping List

☐ (4) ½ × 3½ in. × 4 ft. red oak*

☐ (1) ¼ × 1¼ in. × 4 ft. red oak*

☐ 1¼-in. finish nails

☐ Wood glue

☐ Finishing materials

☐ Picture-hanging hardware

* See page 225 for more information on buying pre-milled thin lumber

Spice Shelves: Step-by-step

MAKE THE BACK PANEL

❶ Cross-cut the four back slats to length: Arrange the slats together on edge to form a panel with pleasing grain pattern. Label the order of the slats in the panel.

❷ Mill the back slat chamfers with a router and a piloted chamfering bit: Set the bit to a depth of ⅛ in. Rout only the "show-side" edges of the slats that will touch each other once the back panel is glued up. The two outermost edges are not chamfered (**See Photo A**).

❸ Glue up the back panel: Spread wood glue along the mating edges of the chamfered back slats and clamp them together.

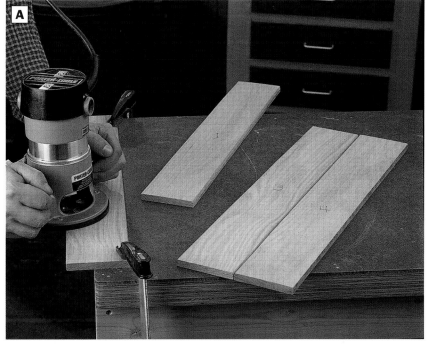

PHOTO A: Rout chamfers along the mating edges of the back slats with a piloted chamfering bit set to a cutting depth of ⅛ in. It's a good idea to label the slats first so you profile only the edges that will meet once the panel is glued up.

Spice Shelves

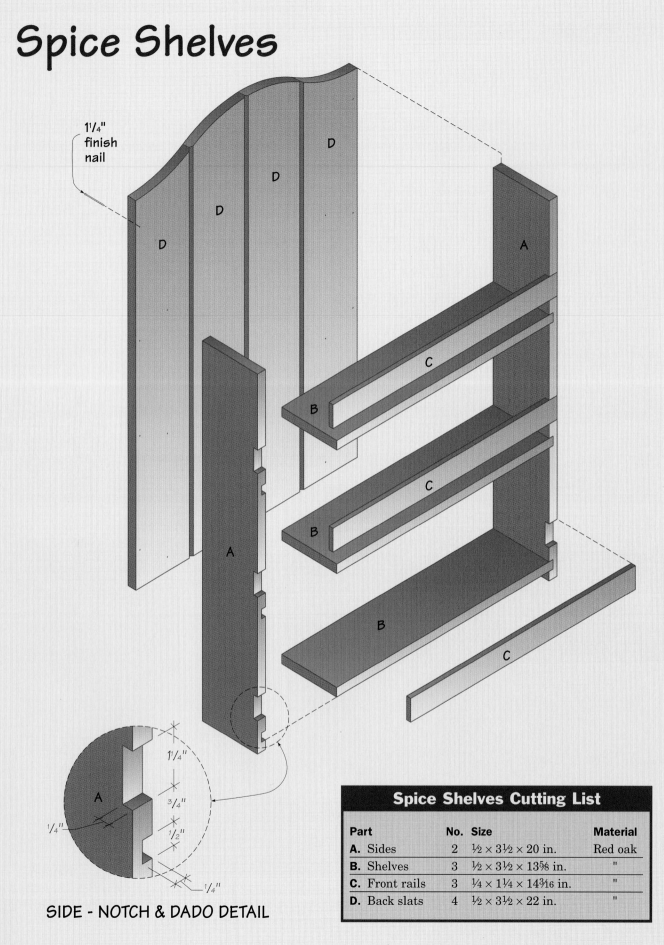

1¼" finish nail

D
D
D
D
A
B
C
B
C
B
C
A

SIDE - NOTCH & DADO DETAIL

A
1¼"
¾"
½"
¼"
¼"

Spice Shelves Cutting List

Part	No.	Size	Material
A. Sides	2	½ × 3½ × 20 in.	Red oak
B. Shelves	3	½ × 3½ × 13⅝ in.	"
C. Front rails	3	¼ × 1¼ × 14³⁄₁₆ in.	"
D. Back slats	4	½ × 3½ × 22 in.	"

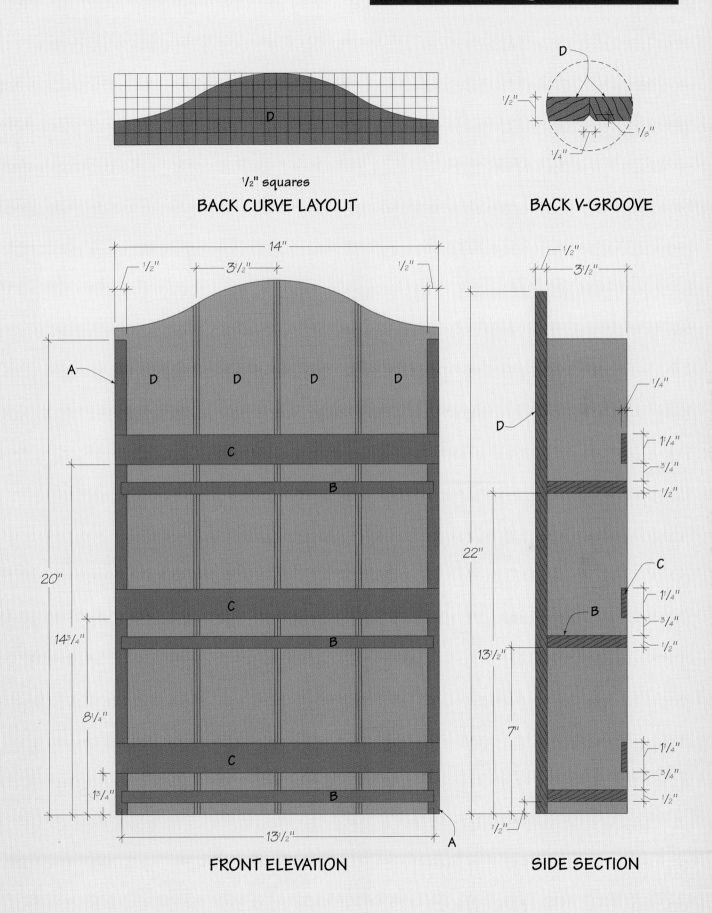

½" squares

BACK CURVE LAYOUT

BACK V-GROOVE

FRONT ELEVATION

SIDE SECTION

PHOTO B: Glue and clamp the slats together to form the back panel. Clamp scrap cauls across the slats to hold the panels flat. Apply just enough clamping pressure to close the joints.

PHOTO C: Enlarge the *Back Curve Layout* grid pattern on page 223 to make a template for drawing the profile at the top of the back. Cut the profile to shape with a jig saw.

PHOTO D: Create a simple shop-made jig out of plywood to gang-rout shelf dadoes across the sides. Guide the router base along a removable fence, and rout each dado clear across both the jig and sides.

PHOTO E: Spread glue on the mating surfaces of the shelves and sides, and assemble these parts. NOTE: *In this photo, the rail notches in the sides are facing down.*

Also clamp a pair of scrap cauls across the panel to help keep it flat (**See Photo B**).

❹ Create a full-size paper template of the *Back Curve Layout,* page 223, and use the template to trace the top profile onto the back panel. Trim the top profile to shape with a jig saw (**See Photo C**).

❺ Sand the back panel smooth with 150-grit paper. It's easier to sand this panel now before assembly.

MAKE THE SIDES

❻ Cross-cut the sides to length. Lay out the shelf dadoes on these workpieces, positioning them according to the *Side Section* drawing, page 223.

❼ Rout shelf dadoes in the sides. We routed the

dado grooves across both sides at once with a simple shop-made jig. The jig is comprised of a ¾-in. plywood panel about 12 in. wide and 24 in. long, sized so that both side panels can lie side by side and flat on it. Strips of ½-in.-thick plywood were glued (not nailed) around the panel to hold both side panels securely and to serve as backup support for minimizing bit tearout. We then screwed a fence across the jig to guide the router base for cutting the dadoes. With the jig clamped to your worksurface and the sides in place, rout dado grooves across the full jig and both sides at your shelf layout marks, moving the jig fence accordingly for making each dado cut (**See Photo D**).

❽ Lay out and cut the ¼-in.-deep, 1¼-in.-wide notches in the sides that will house the three front

PHOTO F: Dry-fit the front rails in their notches in the sides. The rails should fit flush with the front edges of the sides. Once they do, glue and clamp the front rails in the notches.

PHOTO G: The back is secured with glue and nails. Before attaching, mark a line across the back at each shelf to serve as guides for locating the fasteners. Drill pilot holes for the finish nails, and set the heads so they will not scratch the wall once the shelf unit is hung.

rails. See the *Front Elevation* drawing, page 223, for marking the notch locations, then carefully cut the notches with a sharp wood chisel.

9 Smooth the sides with 150-grit sandpaper.

ASSEMBLE THE PROJECT

10 Dry-fit the shelves in the side dadoes to check the fit of the parts. Widen or deepen the dadoes as needed with a chisel and sandpaper.

11 Apply glue to the ends of the shelves and into the dadoes, then assemble the shelves and sides with clamps. Tighten the clamps just enough to seat the shelves in the dadoes (**See Photo E).**

12 Cut the front rails to length and dry-fit them in their notches on the sides. Adjust the fit of the parts as needed by chiseling out more waste from the notches. The rails should fit flush with the front edges of the sides.

13 Spread glue into the notches and install the rails, clamping the parts together (**See Photo F).**

14 Fasten the back panel to the project: Turn the project facedown on your worksurface. Set the back in place with the chamfered face down and mark shelf centerlines across the back for locating finish nails. Spread glue on the back edges of the sides and shelves, and set the back panel in place. Install the back with 1¼-in. finish nails driven through pilot holes in the shelves and sides (**See Photo G).**

FINISHING TOUCHES

15 Apply the finish of your choice. We wiped on three coats of Danish oil.

16 Attach picture hanger hardware that will allow the spice rack to hang close to the wall.

Pre-milled lumber options

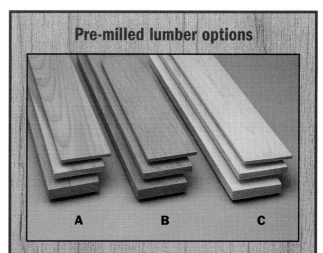

A   B   C

To build this spice rack as designed, you'll need to buy lumber that is pre-milled to ¼- and ½-in. thicknesses unless you have access to a power planer. Most home centers will carry a limited assortment of woods milled to these thicknesses, in addition to the usual ¾-in.-thick stock. Depending on where you shop, you may find such woods as poplar (A), red oak (B) and pine (C), as well as other woods like cherry, maple and walnut. Look in the craft or hobby sections of the store to find these specialty thicknesses, and expect to pay higher prices.

Crosscut Trivets

While it may look like 14 separate sticks have been glued together in a grid pattern to form these trivets, the truth is you can cut the whole trivet in one part from a single piece of wood. There's no gluing or assembly involved—just a little milling on the router table. Thanks to the 'woven' design, these trivets effectively disperse heat to protect tables and countertops from hot dishes. They make unique gifts, and you can build them in a snap from any hardwood species you like.

Vital Statistics: Crosscut Trivets

TYPE: Trivets

OVERALL SIZE: 6½W by ¾H by 6½L

MATERIAL: Hardwood

JOINERY: None

CONSTRUCTION DETAILS:

· Trivet is milled from a single piece of stock

· No glue-up, assembly or finishing required

· Lattice cuts can be made with a router and ½-in. straight bit or table saw and dado blade

· Four cuts are made at each router fence setting, and there are three fence settings in all to mill this size trivet

FINISH: None

Building time

PREPARING STOCK
¼ hour

LAYOUT
¼ hour

CUTTING PARTS
½ hour

ASSEMBLY
None

FINISHING
None

TOTAL: 1 hour

Tools you'll use

· Router table with ½-in. straight bit or table saw with dado blade

· Sander

Shopping list

☐ (1) ¾ × 6½ × 6½ in. hardwood

Crosscut Trivets

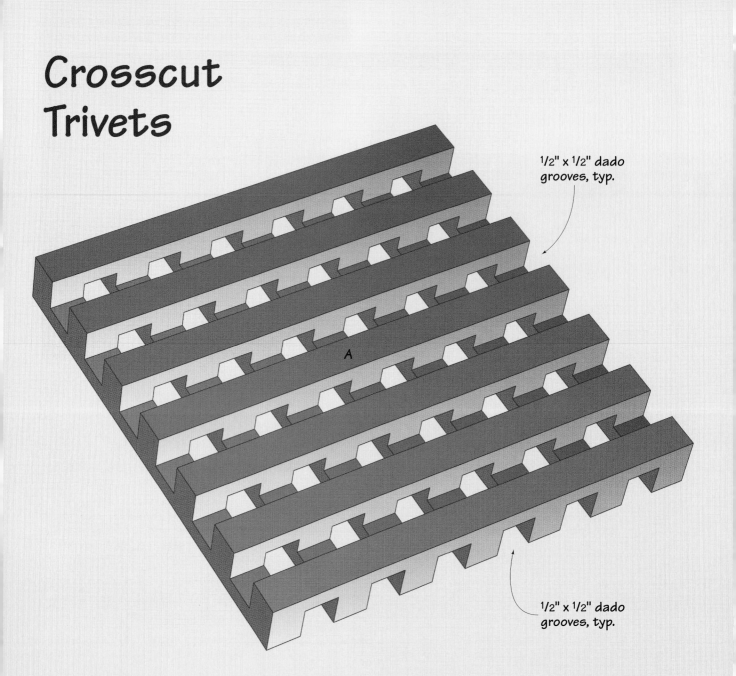

1/2" x 1/2" dado grooves, typ.

1/2" x 1/2" dado grooves, typ.

A

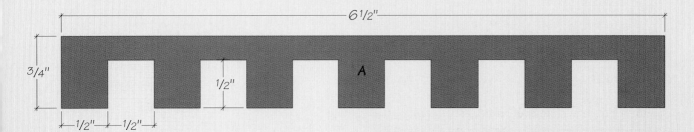

6 1/2"

3/4"

1/2"

1/2"   1/2"

A

Crosscut Trivets Cutting List

Part	No.	Size	Material
A. Trivet	1	3/4 × 6 1/2 × 6 1/2 in.	Hardwood

Crosscut Trivets: Step-by-step

Straight, tight-grained plain-sawn stock such as oak or cherry will produce nicer cross-grain cuts, but experiment with a variety of hardwoods to produce an interesting collection of these unique trivets. Mahogany, maple and walnut are other good wood choices. We routed the lattice-style pattern with a straight bit to produce square, flat-bottomed grooves.

❶ Rip and cross-cut a 6½ × 6½-in. blank of ¾-in. cherry. Sand the faces and edges smooth and flat.

❷ Install a ½-in. straight bit in the router. Use a freshly sharpened or new carbide-tipped bit for best results. NOTE: *You could also make all of the following cuts on the table saw with a dado blade.*

❸ Make the first round of passes: Set your router table fence ½ in. from the bit, with the bit raised to ³⁄₁₆ in., and cut along one face of the blank with the grain. Then rotate the trivet 180° and make a second groove on the same face. Flip the workpiece over, rotate it 90° and make a third pass. Finally, rotate the piece 180° and cut a fourth groove.

❹ With the fence at the same setting, raise the bit to ³⁄₈ in. and repeat the same sequence of cuts you made in Step 3 to cut deeper grooves. After you've made these passes, raise the bit another ¹⁄₁₆ in. to ⁷⁄₁₆ overall, and make four more passes to cut clear through the groove intersections **(See Photo A).**

❺ Move the fence 1½ in. from the bit and repeat the bit-raising milling process to cut four more grooves. Then set the fence position for the third and final round of cuts to 2½ in. from the bit. Complete these grooves to finish the latticed pattern **(See Photo B).**

❻ Sand lightly to ease the cut edges. Do not apply a finish if the trivets will be used beneath hot cookware, or the finish could melt.

PHOTO A: Make the first series of grooves with the router fence set ½ in. away from a ½-in. straight bit raised to ³⁄₁₆ in. Cut two parallel grooves into one face, then flip the workpiece and cut two grooves in this face that are perpendicular to the grooves in the opposite face. Raise the blade to ³⁄₈ in. and then ⁷⁄₁₆ in., cutting progressively deeper grooves until the intersections between the grooves open up.

PHOTO B: Reposition the fence at 1½ in. and 2½ in. from the bit for the second and third rounds of cuts. Continue milling the grooves in three passes, raising the bit after each, until the trivet is completed.

Knife Storage Block

One of the most useful accessories in any cook's repertoire, a solid-wood knife block keeps blades safely at hand and neatly stored while protecting their sharpened edges. This knife block is sized to fit on countertops beneath wall cabinets, and it's easy to build. Slots for the knives are simply dadoed into one face of each strip before assembly. The knife block is made of beech, a tough, beautiful wood commonly used for kitchen accessories.

Vital Statistics: Knife Storage Block

TYPE: Knife block

OVERALL SIZE: $7\frac{5}{8}$W by $8\frac{5}{8}$H by $10\frac{3}{4}$L

MATERIAL: Beech

JOINERY: Face-glued laminations, butt joints reinforced with screws

CONSTRUCTION DETAILS:

· Slots for knives are cut into one face of the block laminations to make alignment easy during glue-up

· Can be built with standard $\frac{3}{4}$-in.-thick stock if you choose to use a more common hardwood, like maple, for this project

· Block designed to hide the bottom open ends of the knife slots

· Legs fasten to the block with screws

FINISH: Clear satin polyurethane

Building time

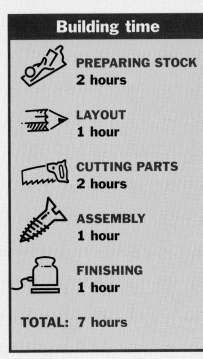

PREPARING STOCK
2 hours

LAYOUT
1 hour

CUTTING PARTS
2 hours

ASSEMBLY
1 hour

FINISHING
1 hour

TOTAL: 7 hours

Tools you'll use

· Table saw
· Planer
· Jointer
· Band saw, scroll saw or jig saw
· Drill/driver
· Clamps

Shopping list

☐ (8) $\frac{4}{4} \times 4$ in. $\times$ 10 ft. beech

☐ (1) $\frac{4}{4} \times 6$ in. $\times$ 2 ft. beech

☐ #8 $\times 1\frac{1}{4}$-in. flathead wood screws

☐ Moisture-resistant wood glue

☐ Finishing materials

Knife Storage Block

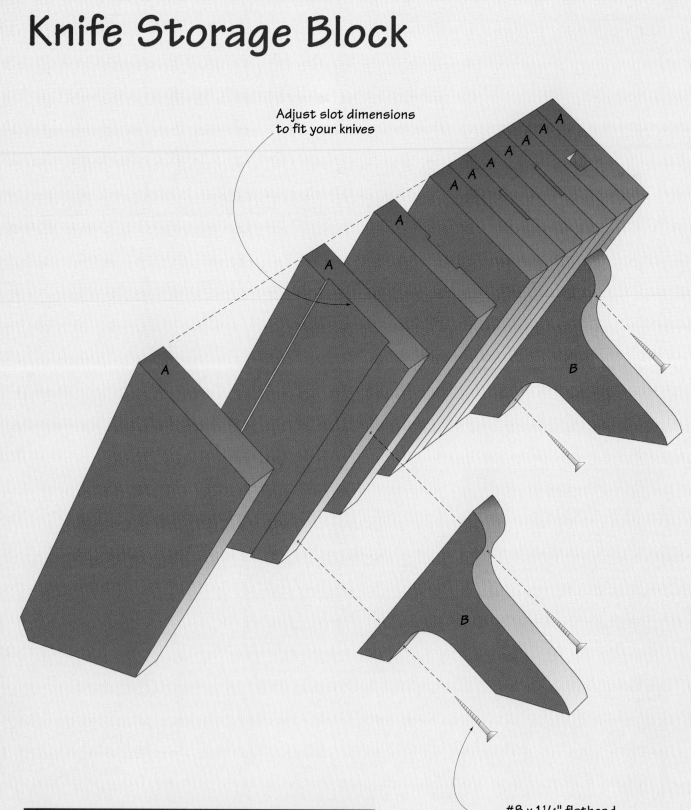

Adjust slot dimensions
to fit your knives

#8 x 1¹/4" flathead
wood screws, typ.

Knife Storage Block Cutting List			
Part	No.	Size	Material
A. Block laminations	10	¾ × 3½ × 12 in.	Beech
B. Feet	2	¾ × 4¾ × 7¼ in.	"

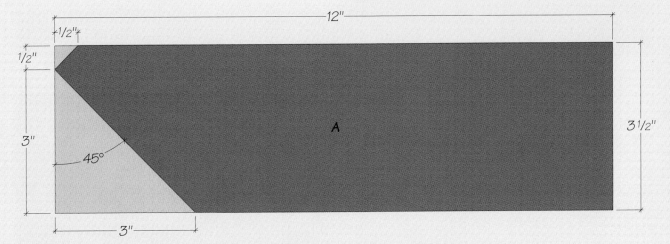

SIDE VIEW BLOCK LAMINATIONS

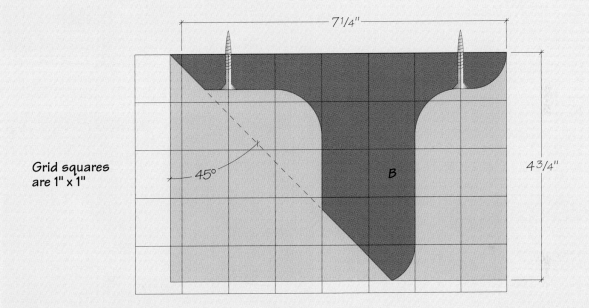

Grid squares are 1" x 1"

SIDE VIEW FEET

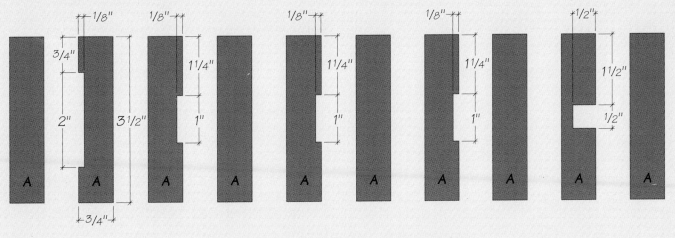

END VIEW BLOCK LAMINATIONS

PREPARE THE STRIPS

❶ Plane all of the 4/4 beech stock down to ¾ in. thick. Beech is an excellent choice for this project, as its tight grain will resist warping. Choose quartersawn stock if possible, which is less likely to expand and contract dramatically in response to changes in humidity. Be sure the faces of the stock are flat.

❷ Rip stock for the strips to width. Make these rip cuts on the table saw with the blade set to 3½ in., then flatten and smooth the cut edges on the jointer.

❸ Cross-cut 10 strips to length. Lay out the groove locations on the strips using the *End View Block Laminations* drawing on page 233 as a guide. The widths and depths of these dado cuts will vary, depending on the dimensions of your knife blades.

❹ Mill grooves into the strips. Make these cuts with either a dado head in your table saw or a straight bit and fence on a router table (**See Photo A**). If you want to include a hole for holding a sharpening rod, cut a square groove for it now, along with the rest of the knife slots.

❺ Lay out and cut the angled ends on each of the strips, according to the dimensions given on the *Side View Block Laminations* drawing, page 233. Cut these angles on the table saw with the miter gauge set to 45° (**See Photo B**). Cut away the larger angled portion first, then reset the miter gauge to 45° in the opposite direction to nibble away the smaller angle.

SHAPE THE FEET

❻ Lay out and cut the two feet to shape: Cut blanks for the feet to 8 in. long and 5 in. wide, with the grain running lengthwise. Draw a 1 × 1-in. grid onto one workpiece, and draw the *Side View Feet* profile shown on page 233 onto the blank. Trim this leg to shape on a band saw, scroll saw or with a jig saw (**See Photo C**). Use the leg as a pattern for tracing the profile onto the second leg blank, and cut it to shape. Then clamp the legs together and gang-sand them on the drum sander so they match.

PHOTO A: Cut the knife slots into one face of the strips using a dado blade on the table saw (as shown), or on a router table with a straight bit and fence.

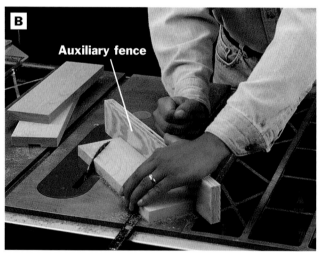

PHOTO B: Mark and trim the angled ends of the strips on the table saw with workpieces supported by the miter gauge set to a 45° angle. Attach a piece of scrap to the miter gauge to serve as an auxiliary fence. Doing so provides better workpiece support and control.

GLUE UP THE BLOCK

❼ Keeping glue out of the knife grooves will be your biggest challenge when gluing up so many strips at once. Here's a solution to help remedy the problem: Cut strips of ⅛-in.-thick scrap wood to fill each knife slot dado. Make these pieces fit snugly but not tightly. They should be able to slide easily into and out of the dadoes when the block is clamped together. Coat each filler strip with paraffin wax to repel glue.

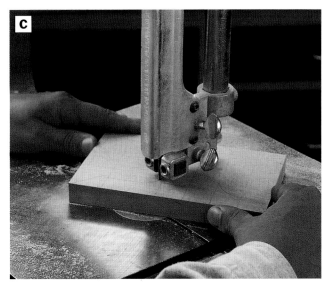

PHOTO C: Lay out and cut one foot to shape on the band saw. Use this workpiece as a template for drawing and cutting the second leg to shape. Then clamp the legs together and sand both smooth at one time.

PHOTO D: After your clamps have squeezed the excess glue from the assembly, but before the glue starts to set, remove the wax-coated filler strips in the knife slots. Once the glue dries, sand the block smooth.

8 Dry-fit the 10 strips together and temporarily clamp them. Check to be sure that all the knives fit into their grooves. They should be loose enough to facilitate easy removal, yet snug enough so the fit isn't sloppy. You may even want to mark the configuration of the strips so they'll be easy to organize once you start the gluing process.

9 Glue and clamp the strips together. First, spread an even coat of glue onto both faces of the inner 8 strips and on the inside face of the two outside strips. Then set the waxed filler strips into the knife slots. NOTE: *Apply a thin, even coating of glue. The strips will be more likely to slip out of alignment when you clamp them if the glue is too thick, because it will act like a lubricant.* Assemble the block laminations into a block. Alternate bar or pipe clamps above and below the block to distribute clamping pressure evenly, and gradually tighten the clamps until the joints between the laminations just close. Tap the workpieces with a mallet, if necessary, to keep the edges and ends even. Wipe up glue squeeze-out with a wet rag, and remove the filler strips before the glue has a chance to set to keep the strips from sticking **(See Photo D).**

10 Sand the block thoroughly after the glue has dried to remove all traces of excess glue, working your way up to 220-grit paper.

FINISHING TOUCHES

11 Install the legs on the block: Drive 1¼-in. flat-head wood screws through countersunk pilot holes in the legs and into the block to attach the parts. Align the parts so the bottom front corners of the legs are even with the bottom end of the block **(See Photo E).**

12 Seal the block with several coats of clear polyurethane varnish. Or leave the block natural if you prefer.

PHOTO E: Drive flathead wood screws through the feet and into the bottom of the knife block. Drill countersunk pilot holes for the screws first, to make screw installation easier and to recess the screw heads.

Display Coffee Table

Coffee tables are supposed to create an environment that invites conversation, so what better furniture project than a table that is itself a conversation piece? This design will not only showcase your woodworking talents, but also display collectibles or memorabilia where they can be studied and appreciated.

Don't be afraid to change the dimensions of the table. For instance, you can change the height of the tabletop to be level with or slightly below your sofa cushions. Or adjust the depth or overall size of the display box to accommodate whatever collection you might have.

Display Coffee Table

Shopping List

- [ ] 6 bf of $^{10}/_4$ cherry
- [ ] 10 bf of $^5/_4$ cherry
- [ ] 3 bf of $^4/_4$ cherry
- [ ] (1) $^1/_2 \times 24 \times 48$-in. cherry-veneer plywood
- [ ] (1) $^1/_4 \times 16^5/_8 \times 34^5/_8$-in. glass
- [ ] (24) #20 plate-joining biscuits
- [ ] (3) $1^1/_2 \times 2$-in. brass butt hinges

- [ ] (20) #4 $\times$ $^3/_4$-in. brass flathead wood screws
- [ ] (1) #8 $\times$ $^1/_2$-in. brass flathead wood screw
- [ ] Wood glue
- [ ] 120- and 220-grit sandpaper
- [ ] Finishing materials

Display Coffee Table: Planning

PREPARING STOCK

Although cherry was chosen as the material for this table, you can use any hardwood. We used $^{10}/_4$ stock planed to $2^1/_4$ in. for the legs and $^5/_4$ stock, which we planed to 1 in., for the aprons and top frame. For the molding strips, stops and support bar, we used $^4/_4$ stock. The bottom is $^1/_2$-in. cherry-veneer plywood.

① Begin by milling your stock to thickness. If you don't have access to a thickness planer, ask your lumber supplier to plane the lumber or check with a local woodworking shop. Many small shops will do this for an hourly fee.

The safest and most efficient way to make the molding strips is to first rip a board that's at least 3 in. wide. Then, mold the board edges with a $^1/_4$-in. cove bit on the router table. Finally, rip the molded edges off the board on the table saw **(See Photo A).**

② Rip and cross-cut the apron stock to the finished dimensions. While you're at it, cross-cut the molding strips to the same length.

③ Use the router table and a $^3/_8$-in. cove bit to cut the molded edge along the bottom edge of each apron piece. Cut the grooves for the bottom in the apron stock with the table saw and a dado blade.

CASE JOINERY

The molding strips are more than just decorative details. The one attached to the back apron is mortised for the top hinges, so it's important that the glue joint between the apron and molding be strong.

④ Apply glue to one of the strips and to the edge of its matching apron. Position the strip so it's flush with the apron's top edge and apply clamps every 2 to 3 in. **(See Photo B).** Repeat the pro-

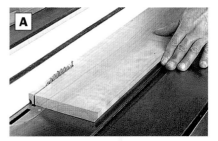

PHOTO A: Rip the molding strips from the board edges. Then plane the cut edges and repeat the molding/ripping process.

PHOTO B: Cut the molding strips to length; then attach them flush to the top of the apron with glue and spring clamps.

cedure for the remaining pieces. Scrape off any squeezed-out glue from around the joint once it's dry.

⑤ The leg-to-apron joint is strong and easy to make. Rip and cross-

Display Coffee Table

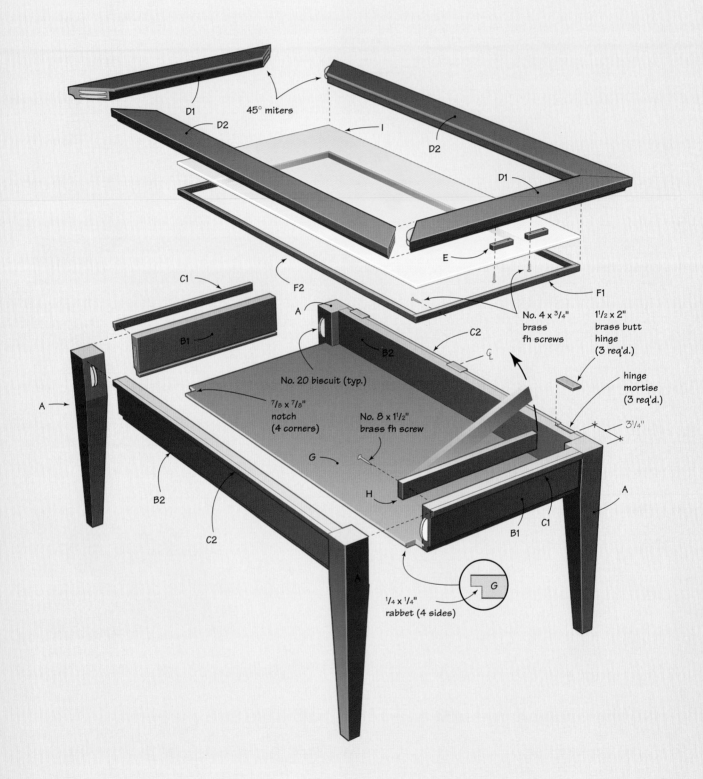

45° miters

D1

D2

I

D2

D1

E

No. 4 x ³/₄"
brass
fh screws

1¹/₂ x 2"
brass butt
hinge
(3 req'd.)

F2

F1

C1

B1

A

A

C2

B2

C̶

No. 20 biscuit (typ.)

hinge
mortise
(3 req'd.)

³¹/₄"

A

⁷/₈ x ⁷/₈"
notch
(4 corners)

No. 8 x 1¹/₂"
brass fh screw

B2

G

H

A

C1

A

C2

B1

G

A

¹/₄ x ¹/₄"
rabbet (4 sides)

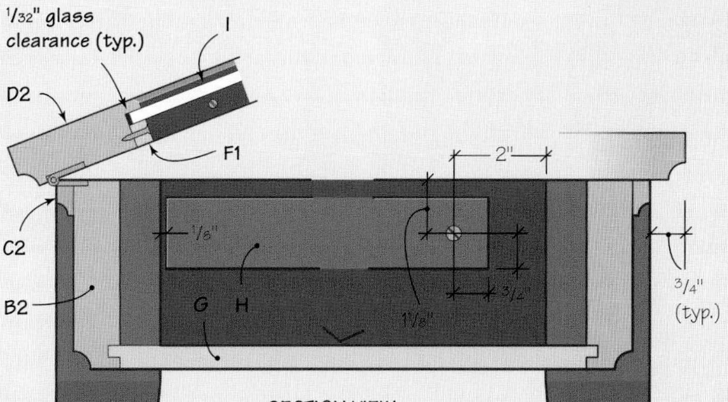

1/32" glass clearance (typ.)
I
D2
F1
C2
B2
1/8"
G
H
2"
1 1/8"
3/4"
3/4" (typ.)

SECTION VIEW

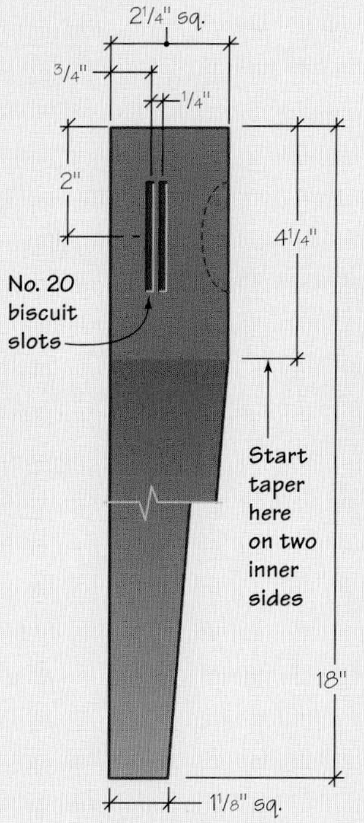

2 1/4" sq.
3/4"
1/4"
2"
4 1/4"
No. 20 biscuit slots
Start taper here on two inner sides
18"
1 1/8" sq.

LEG DETAIL

Display Coffee Table Cutting List

Part/Description		No.	Size	Material
A	Legs	4	2¼ × 2¼ × 18 in.	Cherry
B1	Aprons	2	1 × 4 × 16 in.	"
B2	Aprons	2	1 × 4 × 34 in.	"
C1	Molding strips	2	⅜ × ¾ × 16 in.	"
C2	Molding strips	2	⅜ × ¾ × 34 in.	"
D1	Top frame	2	1 × 3 × 22 in.	"
D2	Top frame	2	1 × 3 × 40 in.	"
E	Locating blocks	2	⅜ × 7⁄16 × 2 in.	"
F1	Glass stops	2	⅜ × ½ × 16¾ in.	"
F2	Glass stops	2	⅜ × ½ × 34 in.	"
G	Bottom	1	½ × 18¼ × 34¼ in.	Cherry ply
H	Support bar	1	⅝ × 1½ × 14⅝ in.	Cherry
I	Top	1	¼ × 16⅝ × 34⅝ in.	Glass

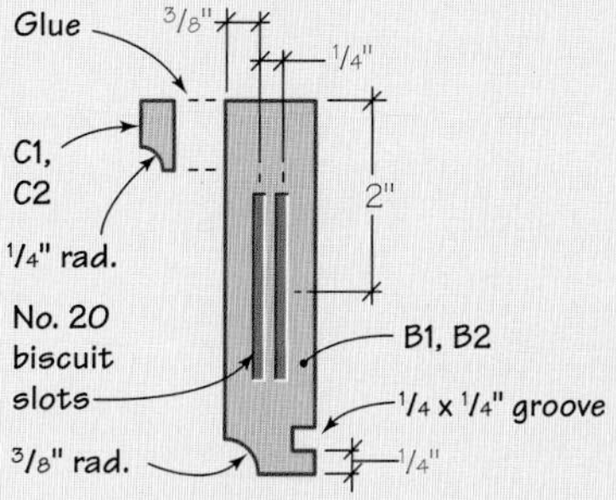

Glue
3/8"
1/4"
C1, C2
1/4" rad.
2"
No. 20 biscuit slots
B1, B2
1/4 x 1/4" groove
3/8" rad.
1/4"

APRON DETAIL

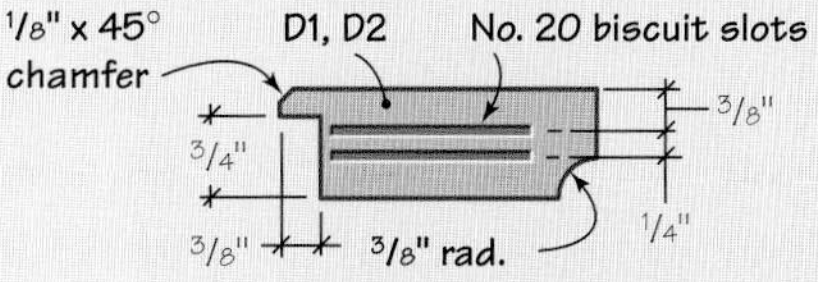

1/8" x 45° chamfer
D1, D2
No. 20 biscuit slots
3/8"
3/4"
3/8"
3/8" rad.
1/4"

FRAME DETAIL

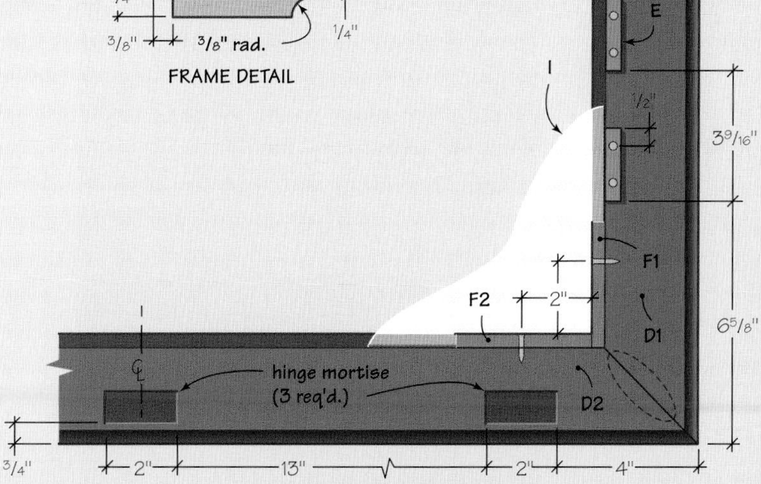

E
I
1/2"
3 9/16"
F1
F2
2"
D1
6 5/8"
hinge mortise (3 req'd.)
D2
3/4"
2"
13"
2"
4"

FRAME DETAIL — BOTTOM VIEW

PHOTO C: The table saw and rip fence make a good worksurface and stop when cutting the biscuit slots in the legs.

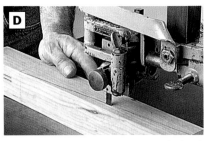

PHOTO D: Rough-cut the leg tapers on the band saw, keeping outside the line. Then, smooth the surface with a sander or a hand plane.

PHOTO E: Slide the bottom into the apron grooves; then glue and clamp the remaining leg/apron assembly in place.

cut the leg blanks to size, then lay out the plate-joining slots. Note that there are two #20 plate-joining biscuits, spaced ¼ in. apart, in each joint. Use the plate joiner to cut the slots in both the legs and apron ends. You can use your plate joiner's fence to locate the slots or make spacer blocks to use under the tool's base as we did **(See Photo C).** The legs and aprons will require blocks of different thickness (your plate joiner's base-to-blade distance is also a factor). Use scrap lumber to test the locations of the slots and adjust the spacer thickness before cutting the actual table parts.

❻ Lay out the leg tapers; then use the band saw to make the cuts **(See Photo D).** Be sure to saw on the waste side of the layout line. If you don't have a band saw, you can use either a table saw and a taper jig or a jig saw with a long blade.

❼ Use a hand plane or belt sander to remove the saw marks and refine the leg profiles. Take care not to extend the taper into the top part of the leg where it joins the apron.

❽ Cut the bottom panel to finished size. Lay out the notch in each corner for leg clearance; then make the cuts with a jig saw or back saw. Next, rout the

rabbet on the bottom of the panel using an edge guide and straight bit.

It's a good idea to sand the parts with 120- and 220-grit paper before you assemble them. Although assembly inevitably causes some small scratches, touching up minor flaws is much easier than doing extensive sanding after assembly. Dust all parts thoroughly after sanding.

BASE ASSEMBLY

❾ Begin the base assembly by joining leg pairs to the long aprons. Apply glue to both the biscuits and slots; then position the parts together and clamp. Check for square by measuring diagonally in both directions across the assembly.

❿ Next, join the two short aprons to one of the long assemblies—the easiest way is upside down on your workbench. Slide the bottom panel into the apron grooves without glue **(See Photo E),** then install the second long apron/leg assembly. Check for square and make any necessary adjustments. Let the glue cure fully (six to 12 hours) before removing the clamps.

MAKING THE TOP

⓫ Rip the top frame stock to width, but leave the pieces several inches long. Use a straight

bit and edge guide to rout the rabbet for the glass (you could also use a router table or a table saw). Make the cut in two or three passes so you don't overload the router or tear out the wood grain. Use a router table and a chamfer bit to cut the small bevel along the top inside edge of each piece.

⓬ Cut the frame parts to finished length with a miter saw or a table saw and miter gauge. Lay out and cut the two biscuit slots in the ends of each frame piece. Position the slots so that they're not exposed when you cut the cove on the bottom outside edge of the frame **(See Photo F).**

⓭ Dry-fit the top frame to check for square before gluing and clamping **(See Photo G).** After the glue sets, rout the ⅜-in. cove around the bottom edge of the frame. Routing after assembly ensures that the coves will match perfectly at the corners.

PHOTO F: Locate the biscuit slots so they're not exposed by the glass rabbet or the ⅜-in. cove that are cut after assembly.

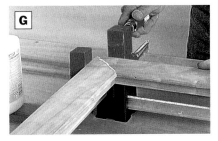

PHOTO G: Use bar clamps across the length and width of the top during glue-up. Adjust the clamps to align the miters.

PHOTO H: Rout the butt-hinge mortises with a straight bit; then clean up the corners and edges with a sharp chisel.

PHOTO I: Inset the top mortises so the top has a uniform overhang. Use the same methods to cut these mortises.

HINGE INSTALLATION

⑭ Lay out the locations of the hinges on the top edge of the table base using a sharp utility knife. Remove most of the waste from each mortise with a router and straight bit. Guide the router by hand to within ¹⁄₁₆ in. of the layout lines; then clean the mortise with a sharp chisel **(See Photo H)**. Or cut the mortise entirely with a chisel by making a series of closely spaced ¹⁄₈-in.-deep parallel cuts down the length of the mortise, then paring away the waste.

⑮ Test the fit of the hinge in its mortise and adjust the depth of the recess until the hinge is flush with the surrounding wood. If you cut too deeply, use a veneer shim under the hinge to achieve a flush relationship.

⑯ Mark the mortise locations in the tabletop; then cut them using the same techniques **(See Photo I)**. Note that these mortises are set back from the top edge to allow the top to overhang the table base. This isn't a typical butt-hinge mortise, but it allows the top to open a full 90° for access to the interior.

⑰ Bore the screw holes and temporarily install the hinges using steel screws, which are less likely to strip out or snap **(See Photo J)**. Save the brass screws for final assembly.

FINISHING DETAILS

⑱ Cut the support bar. Then, bore a clearance hole and countersink for the screw. (Another way to support the top is to use a ¼-in.-dia. brass rod that's stored in a groove routed into the top edge of the apron.) Attach the bar to the side apron and adjust the tension by tightening the screw **(See Photo K)**. Attach the locating blocks for the support bar to the underside of the top frame.

⑲ Remove the top frame from the base; then cut the glass stops. Drill clearance holes and countersinks in the stops for #4 × ¾-in. flathead wood screws. Then use a ¼-in. spacer to position the stops so you can bore pilot holes in the frame. Install the stops temporarily to check the fit **(See Photo L)**. Don't install the glass yet—it's best to do this after finishing.

⑳ Sand the top frame to 220 grit. Dust off all surfaces thoroughly, then wipe them down with a tack rag before finishing. We applied three coats of satin polyurethane, thinning the first coat with one part thinner to six parts finish. The next day I sanded lightly with 320-grit paper before applying an undiluted coat. We rubbed out the cured finish of the third coat with 0000 steel wool. When the finish is dry, reattach the top and the support bar and install the glass top.

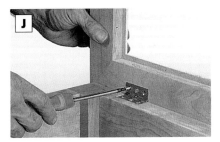

PHOTO J: Use steel screws to test-fit the hinges and thread the pilot holes. Brass screws are soft and easily damaged.

PHOTO K: Adjust the support bar tension by tightening or loosening the screw. Remove the bar for finishing.

PHOTO L: Bore clearance holes in the glass stops; then bore pilot holes in the frame before test-fitting the stops.

Treasure Chest

The traditional blanket chest is more than just a place to store blankets. It's become the standard place where many Americans accumulate life's treasures and in the process, it has become a treasure in its own right. For hundreds of years, people have handed down dovetailed chests like this one from one generation to the next.

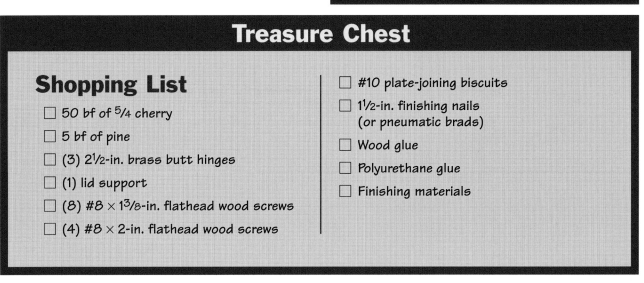

Treasure Chest

Shopping List

- ☐ 50 bf of ⁵⁄₄ cherry
- ☐ 5 bf of pine
- ☐ (3) 2½-in. brass butt hinges
- ☐ (1) lid support
- ☐ (8) #8 × 1³⁄₈-in. flathead wood screws
- ☐ (4) #8 × 2-in. flathead wood screws
- ☐ #10 plate-joining biscuits
- ☐ 1½-in. finishing nails (or pneumatic brads)
- ☐ Wood glue
- ☐ Polyurethane glue
- ☐ Finishing materials

Treasure Chest: Planning

WHY DOVETAILS?

Before the advent of central heating and air conditioning, the dovetail was the woodworker's joint of choice for building cases because furniture had to endure a wide range of temperature and humidity. Dovetailed cases continued to hold together even after expansion and contraction caused glue failure. With modern climate control and superior glues, dovetails are no longer a structural imperative, but there is no denying they can transform an ordinary chest into an heirloom-quality treasure.

If you're intimidated by doing this seemingly precise work by hand, remember that until just a few generations ago woodworking was done only with hand tools. Practice on some scrap pieces first and you'll find that it takes more patience than skill to chop a dovetail by hand. And if you're still not sold on doing the work with hand tools, but you like the look of dovetails, there are a number of commercially available through-dovetail jigs for routers that will dramatically speed up your work. The down side is that these jigs can cost a hefty sum, making them impractical unless you cut dovetails with some regularity.

DEALING WITH STOCK

We used cherry to build this chest, but you can use almost any furniture-grade wood. You'll get the best results if you mill your own stock (if you can't, it's okay to use ¾-in. stock, but you'll have to modify the dimensions of the bottom and base). Start with ⁵⁄₄-in. (1¼-in.) rough stock to ensure that you'll wind up with ⅞-in.-thick milled stock. Let the wood acclimate to your shop's environment for about a week before you start milling. Be sure to mill extra pieces to set up cuts. When gluing up the top, front, back and side panels, use plate-joining biscuits to help align and join the boards. And to minimize the visual transitions between

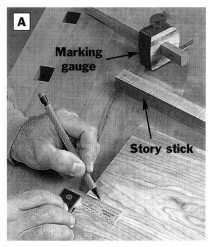

PHOTO A: To ensure consistency, mark the pins using a story stick (in background); then extend the layout marks with a square.

boards, try to match the grain at the joint line. Also, be aware of wood color and avoid defects such as knots and pitch pockets. You might also consider making a drop-in aromatic cedar bottom out of ¼-in. tongue-and-groove cedar closet liner, which is available at home centers.

MARK & CUT DOVETAILS

One of the first and most important steps when cutting dovetails

Treasure Chest

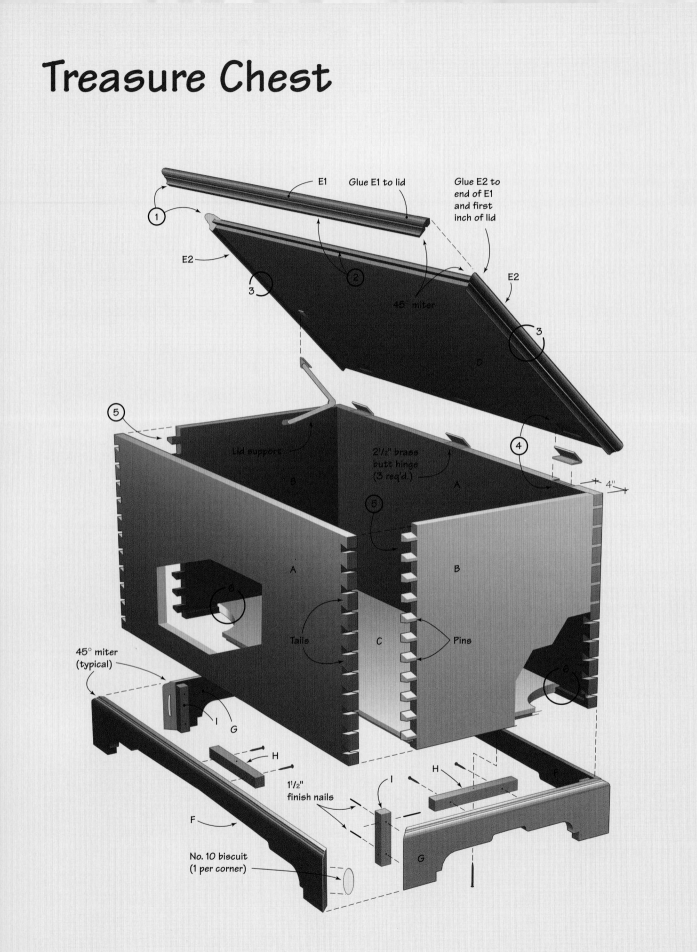

E1

Glue E1 to lid

Glue E2 to end of E1 and first inch of lid

E2

E2

3

3

45° miter

D

1

2

5

Lid support

2½" brass butt hinge (3 req'd.)

A

4

4"

4

B

A

B

6

6

C

Tails

Pins

45° miter (typical)

I

G

H

1½" finish nails

I

H

H

I

F

G

No. 10 biscuit (1 per corner)

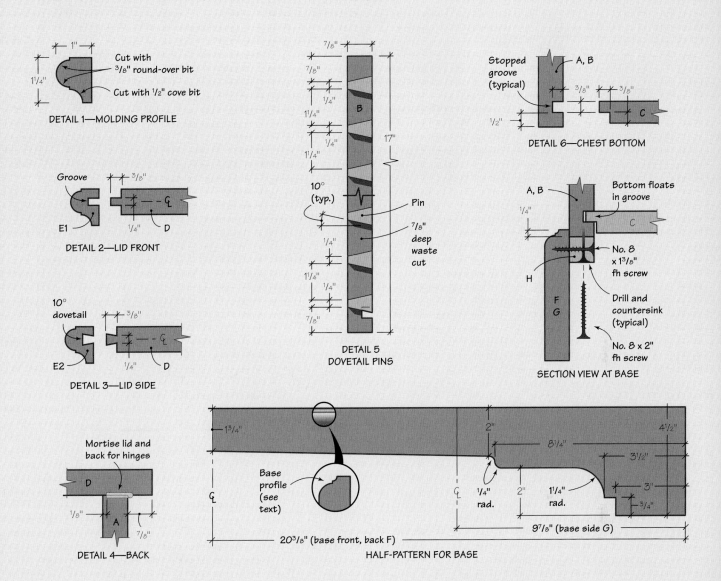

DETAIL 1—MOLDING PROFILE

DETAIL 2—LID FRONT

DETAIL 3—LID SIDE

DETAIL 4—BACK

DETAIL 5
DOVETAIL PINS

DETAIL 6—CHEST BOTTOM

SECTION VIEW AT BASE

HALF-PATTERN FOR BASE

Treasure Chest Cutting List

Part/Description		No.	Size	Material
A	Front/back*	2	7⁄8 × 17 × 39 in.	Cherry
B	Sides*	2	7⁄8 × 17 × 18 in.	"
C	Bottom*	1	3⁄4 × 167⁄8 × 377⁄8 in.	Pine
D	Lid*	1	7⁄8 × 191⁄4 × 393⁄4 in.	Cherry
E1	Front molding	1	1 × 11⁄4 × 41 in.	"
E2	Side moldings	2	1 × 11⁄4 × 197⁄8 in.	"
F	Base front/back	2	7⁄8 × 41⁄2 × 403⁄4 in.	"
G	Base sides	2	7⁄8 × 41⁄2 × 193⁄4 in.	"
H	Cleats	4	7⁄8 × 7⁄8 × 8 in.	"
I	Corner blocks	4	7⁄8 × 7⁄8 × 41⁄4 in.	"

*Must be assembled from narrower stock.

is to label all of the case parts to avoid confusion. Corners must mate perfectly, so you can't mix them up. We make masking tape labels (front, back, up, left, right, etc.) and leave them on until the case is fully assembled. You can use the pin layout in the drawing or figure out your own spacing. For instance, if you don't want to do quite so much cutting, increase the spacing between pins (to make larger tails) or vary the size of the pins or tails for a random appearance. However, the tails on the top and bottom should be one-half to three-quarters the width of the rest of the tails. If you make them too wide, they'll look clumsy; if they're too narrow, they can break off easily when you assemble the chest. When in doubt, don't make them any less than ¾ in. wide.

We made the narrowest part of the pins ¼ in. wide so it would be practical to remove the waste between the tails (where the pins fit) with a ¼-in. chisel. Some woodworkers like smaller pins because they look more refined, but they're more prone to breaking, and removing the waste between the tails is sure to try your patience.

We've found that one of the best ways to ensure accurate and consistent joints is to use a story stick **(See Photo A).** This is simply a piece of stock that's the same width and thickness as the panels and has the dovetail layout drawn on it. To use it, just transfer the marks on the stick directly to the workpiece—no measuring, no mistakes.

It's a good practice to lay out the joinery so the ends of the pins

PHOTO B: Extend the pin marks on the end grain by setting a T-bevel to 10°. Mark with a fine pencil or a utility knife.

PHOTO C: Cut on the outside of the line with a pull saw or a dovetail saw. Mark the waste with an "X" to prevent mistakes.

and tails protrude about 0.001 in. after assembly. This is so you can sand or plane the end grain perfectly smooth and flush with the front of the panels. To get the right amount of projection, set up the mark for the shoulder line with a piece of stock that's the same thickness as the panel stock. Then add the width of a .05 pencil line (the line is always smaller than the diameter of the lead). Mark the shoulder line with a combination square and pencil or with a marking gauge. When you begin cutting the shoulders with a chisel, be sure to cut to the outside of the line **(See Photo D).**

Cutting the cheeks of the pins and tails requires the greatest amount of skill and patience. You'll get a lot of practice cutting pins first **(See Photo C),** but cutting between the tails (where the tails go) is where accuracy really counts. We use a small Japanese panel saw to make the cuts. A good European-style dovetail saw will also do the job.

These specially designed back saws make quick work of the task at hand. Fine, crosscut teeth and minimal tooth set produce smooth, even cuts with very little tearout. Be sure the workpiece is securely clamped, and try to keep the saw perpendicular to the edge of the work. Once the cut is started, let the saw find its own path. Careful, controlled strokes, rather than heavy downward pressure on the blade, will yield the best results. If the blade wanders, don't try to force it back onto the line. A sharp chisel works well to straighten any crooked pin cheeks after you've chipped away all the waste and before you lay out the tails **(See Photo E).**

❶ Use the pins to determine the position of the tails by laying out mating parts. First, use the inside of the pins to mark the tail locations on the outside of the front **(See Photo G).** After the edges have been marked, connect them and the inside marks with a pencil line **(See Photo H).**

PHOTO D: Make shallow cuts on the shoulder lines. Don't cut too deep or the chisel will drift off the line.

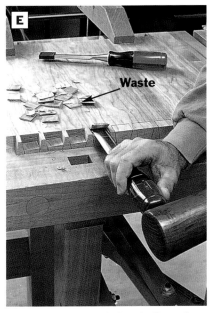

Waste

PHOTO E: Alternately chisel on the line and chip out the waste (shown) until you're about two-thirds through. Finish from the other side.

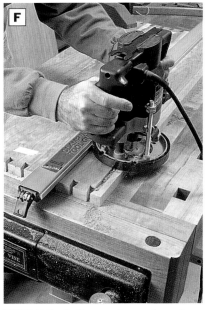

PHOTO F: The bottom requires a stopped groove in all four case sides. If you rout through, the groove will show on the outside.

2 Next, stand the side piece on edge in its correct orientation in order to mark the inside of the front and to trace fully around the pins (See Photo I). Be sure to keep the workpieces properly aligned throughout the layout, as even the slightest shift will cause mismatched joints down the road.

Cutting the cheeks of the tails is one of woodworking's more tedious and time-consuming techniques. Take extra care to cut precisely along the layout lines in order to give your joints the most refined appearance possible. Don't get frustrated with the process; remember that the result will be one of the most attractive, secure styles of joinery available.

3 Once you've cut all the tails and pins, you'll probably need to adjust the fit. The joints should slide together easily without being forced. If a few of the parts require some fine-tuning, pare pins and tails as necessary with

a sharp chisel. Don't worry if you remove a little too much. You can always glue slivers or a piece of veneer back on before the final assembly.

More joinery

4 Rout the stopped grooves for the bottom in the front, back and sides (See Photo F). To make setting up the fence for the router easier, use a ¼-in.-thick hardboard spacer cut to a width that's equal to the distance from the edge of the workpiece to the fence. For consistent spacing, hold the spacer against the fence and the edge of the work, then lock down the fence. Be careful not to rout through the ends of the workpiece, which would expose the dado on the outside of the chest.

5 Cut the bottom ¹⁄₁₆ to ⅛ in. smaller in length and width than the size of the opening (in the grooves) to allow for seasonal wood movement. Cut it for a tighter fit in the summer and a looser fit in the winter.

6 Trim the lid to size only after fitting the case together (without glue) to determine its exact size. Allow ¹⁄₁₆ in. overhang on each side and ⅛ in. on the front edge. Remember to add to your dimensions the tongue for the front molding and the dovetail for the side moldings.

Lid moldings

Make the lid moldings with a router table or a shaper if you have one. Don't attempt to make these cuts with a handheld router. Set up your router table with appropriate guards and featherboards. Be sure to have extra stock, because you'll probably need to make several practice cuts when setting up.

7 First, cut the lower ⅜-in. radius (middle cut); then make the bottom ½-in. cove cut; finally, cut the top ⅜-in. radius (See *Detail 1,* page 245).

Note that there's a difference in how the front molding and side

PHOTO G: Mark the tails layout with the pins of the mating part. First, mark the outside of the front with the inside of the pins.

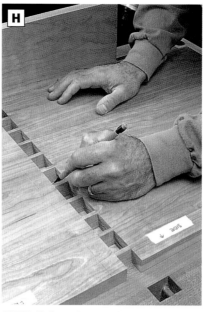

PHOTO H: Keep the workpieces aligned and mark the edges; then connect the edge and inside marks with pencil lines.

PHOTO I: Mark the inside of the front by standing the side on its edge (oriented correctly); then trace around the pins.

moldings are attached to the lid. The molding on the front is attached with a tongue-and-groove joint and glue. However, the moldings on the sides run perpendicular to the lid's grain, so they must allow for the lid's expansion and contraction. Any molding that is solidly glued, screwed or nailed to the lid can cause it to split. To prevent this, We used a sliding dovetail to attach the side moldings. The joint is glued only at the front miter and about 1 in. behind it (apply glue only on the lid side of the joint or glue will be spread along the entire length of the molding). This allows the lid to slide freely in the molding.

8 You can use a table saw (as we did) or a router table to cut both sides of the joint. Practice with scrap first to get the fit right. The molding should fit snugly but slide easily on the lid dovetail. When making the groove, first cut it straight in order to remove most of the stock and to establish the depth;

then tilt the blade (or change the bit) to cut the 10° angle on both sides of the groove. Now you're able to cut the lid dovetail to fit.

MAKING THE BASE
As with the lid, you should wait until you've assembled the case (either glued or not) before you size the base parts. The front, back and sides can fit tightly against the case because there's no cross-grain wood movement to worry about.

9 When making the parts, rout the top profile first on your router table. Any piloted edge-forming bit such as a cove-and-bead or an ogee bit will work. Next, cut the miters. You'll need a miter saw with a fairly substantial capacity or a table saw and a cutoff box.

10 Make a hardboard half-pattern for the base relief cuts; then use it to trace the design onto the workpieces (the pattern is the same for the front, back and sides). Cut out the pattern on the workpieces with a band saw or

jig saw and sand the edges smooth. Because of the shape of the decorative contours, an oscillating spindle sander works particularly well for this job.

ASSEMBLY & FINISHING
We used polyurethane glue to assemble the case because it has a long open time and it only needs to be applied to one side of the joint **(See Photo J).** Also, it has very little tack, which is key in getting the dovetails to slide together easily.

Because the bottom is held in a stopped groove, the assembly sequence is very important for the case to go together properly.

11 First, attach the bottom to the sides (standing all three pieces on edge works best); then slip on the front, followed by the back. Tapping the joints together lightly with a soft mallet and a scrap block will secure the fit and further distribute the glue within the dovetails **(See Photo K).** Plywood cauls at each joint

PHOTO J: Use a brush to apply polyurethane glue to the mating surfaces of the pins (apply glue to all surfaces if you use wood glue).

PHOTO K: Lightly tap the sides together with a mallet and block, but be careful to keep the pieces from jamming.

PHOTO L: Clamp the case behind the joints using plywood cauls. Check for square by measuring the case diagonally.

will apply even pressure after clamping up the case, while measuring the diagonals of the assembly is a good way to check for square (**See Photo L**). Once the glue has cured, you can trim the protruding ends of the pins and tails with a hand plane or sand them flush.

⓬ Install all of the hardware before finishing to check the fit and make adjustments. Be sure to remove the hardware before finishing, though. If you plan on installing a lock, keep in mind that the lid will expand and contract, so the latching mechanism must accommodate this play.

⓭ Though cherry is a wood that's prone to blotching when stained, thorough sanding and careful stain application will help to prevent it. In order to properly prepare the surface, we sanded with progressively finer grits up to 220. Instead of staining the entire chest at once, we applied oil-based pigment stain to one surface at a time and

quickly wiped off the excess. This piecemeal technique helped prevent pools and runs that can cause blotching.

⓮ For adequate protection, a project like this needs a film finish; avoid using an oil finish. We applied six coats of semi-gloss wiping varnish to all the surfaces of the chest. Wiping varnish is simply regular alkyd or polyurethane varnish that's been thinned with mineral spirits. You can either buy it mixed or make

your own in the shop, as we did. The advantage of wiping rather than brushing is that you'll get a finish that looks like it's been sprayed. To remove dust nibs and achieve the smoothest possible finish, sand with 320-grit or finer paper between coats and rub out the final coat with 0000 steel wool. After both the base and case have been finished to a desirable look and texture, join the two pieces with screws through the cleats previously attached to the base (**See Photo M**).

PHOTO M: Finish the case and base separately before joining them with 2-in. wood screws.

Desktop Book Rack

Need a gift idea for a college student you know? You'll be the wise gift giver when you present this Arts-and-Crafts inspired desktop book rack. Made of red oak and decorated with authentic wedge-pinned through tenons, this useful project takes up little more desktop than a legal notepad and keeps important books within arm's reach.

Desktop Book Rack

Vital Statistics

TYPE: Desktop book rack

OVERALL SIZE: 19L by 9½H by 7½D

MATERIAL: Red oak

JOINERY: Through tenons pinned with wedges

CONSTRUCTION DETAILS:

· Mortises in sides cut out with a jig saw and squared with a chisel

· Square holes in through tenons for wedges drilled out first, then squared with a chisel

FINISH: Stain, varnish

BUILDING TIME: 3-4 hours

Shopping List

☐ (1) 1 × 8 in. × 2 ft. red oak

☐ (1) ½ × 4 in. × 4 ft. red oak*

☐ Wood glue

☐ Finishing materials

*Most lumberyards and building centers carry a limited selection of ½-in. and ¼-in.-thick hardwood. For more on buying pre-milled thinner stock, see page 225.

Desktop Book Rack: Step-by-step

MAKE THE SIDES, BACK & SHELF

1 Cross-cut workpieces for the sides, back and shelf, sized according to the *Cutting List,* page 252.

2 Lay out and cut the sides to shape: Make a full-size paper grid drawing of the sides, according to the *Side Layout* drawing, page 252. Cut out the paper shape and use it as a template for drawing the sides onto the side workpieces. Cut out the sides with a jig saw.

3 Rip-cut the back and shelf to width. Mark and cut the through tenons on the ends of the back and shelf pieces. Refer to the *Tenon Layout* drawing, page 252, to mark the shape of the tenons and wedge holes on the ends of the back and shelves. Cut the through tenons to shape **(See Photo A).**

PHOTO A: Lay out and cut the two sides, back and shelf pieces to shape. Since the back and shelf parts are identical, clamp them together and gang-cut both with a jig saw.

CUT THE WEDGE HOLES & MORTISES

4 Drill out the waste from the four tenon wedge holes with a sharp ½-in.-dia. brad point bit.

5 Cut out the mortises in the sides for the back and shelf tenons. First bore ½-in.-dia holes at the ends of each mortise **(See Photo B).** Then saw out the rest

Desktop Book Rack

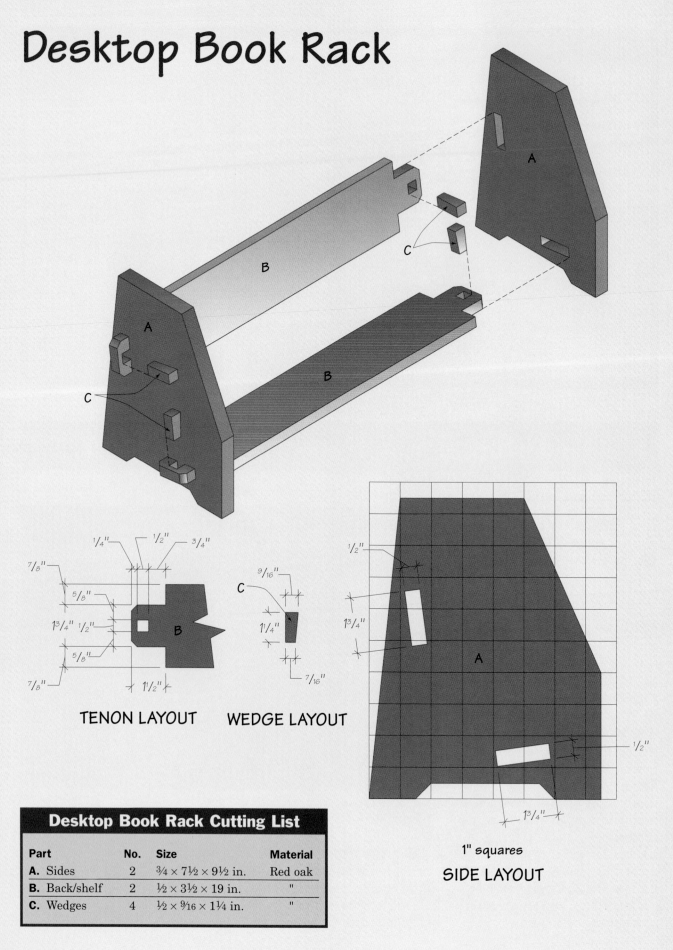

TENON LAYOUT

WEDGE LAYOUT

1" squares

SIDE LAYOUT

Desktop Book Rack Cutting List

Part	No.	Size	Material
A. Sides	2	¾ × 7½ × 9½ in.	Red oak
B. Back/shelf	2	½ × 3½ × 19 in.	"
C. Wedges	4	½ × 9⁄16 × 1¼ in.	"

PHOTO B: Drill out the centers of the wedge holes in the tenons with a ½-in. bit. Use the same bit for boring holes in the ends of the mortises in the sides. If you align the parts carefully and clamp them together, it's possible to drill through both parts at once.

PHOTO C: Clean out the remaining waste from the mortises in the sides with a jig saw. Square up the wedge holes and the ends of the mortises with a sharp chisel and a file.

PHOTO D: Lay out and cut four tenon wedges from ½-in.-thick stock. Cut the wedges a little wider than necessary so you can sand them as needed for a good fit in the wedge holes.

PHOTO E: Assemble the sides, back and shelf with clamps, then glue and insert the wedges into the wedge holes. Tap the wedges snug with a wood mallet. Wipe away excess glue before it dries.

of the waste in between the holes. Square up the wedge holes and the mortises with a sharp ½-in. chisel, then clean up the cutouts with a narrow file **(See Photo C).**

ASSEMBLE & FINISH THE BOOK RACK

❻ Make the wedges: Refer to the *Wedge Layout* drawing, page 252, for marking the wedge shapes on a strip of ½-in.-thick stock. NOTE: *Lay out the wedges so the grain runs lengthwise.* Cut out the wedges with a jig saw so they are slightly wider than your layout lines **(See Photo D).**

❼ Dry-fit the book rack together. The tenons should seat fully into the mortises when you interlock the parts. Adjust the fit of the mortises and tenons by sanding the tenons a little at a time. Aim for a snug, but not forced, fit of the tenons in the mortises.

❽ Dry-fit the wedges into their holes in the tenons with the angled edges of the wedges facing the book rack sides. The wedges should overhang the tenons evenly when fully inserted. Sand the wedges until they fit properly.

❾ Disassemble the book rack and sand all the parts smooth. Reassemble, this time gluing the wedges into the tenons **(See Photo E).** Wipe off excess glue immediately with a damp rag.

❿ Wipe or brush on your choice of stain, followed by a clear topcoat. We wiped on two coats of Danish oil.

Mission Table

Working in a kitchen is a lot like working in a shop. No matter how many worksurfaces and storage spaces you have, you can always use more. This Arts-and-Crafts-style rolling island fits the bill because it provides a nearly 2 × 4-ft. top, three drawers and a large shelf. It works equally well as a kitchen island, a baker's cart or a sideboard for the dining room.

Bakers will appreciate the granite top because it stays cool, which makes it ideal for rolling out pie crusts. Even if you don't bake, the top and shelf provide an extra 16 sq. ft. of surface area. With plenty of clearance, the shelf is particularly useful for storing large countertop appliances.

Mission Table

Shopping List

- ☐ 20 bf ⁶/₄ quartersawn white oak
- ☐ 10 bf ⁸/₄ quartersawn white oak
- ☐ ¼ × 24 × 48-in. birch plywood
- ☐ ³/₄ × 24 × 48-in. oak plywood
- ☐ (2) ½ × 30 × 60-in. Baltic birch plywood
- ☐ (1) ³/₄ × 23½ × 47-in. granite top
- ☐ (4) 2-in. locking casters
- ☐ (3) pairs 18-in. drawer slides
- ☐ (2) 3⅛-in. drawer pulls
- ☐ (1) 3³/₄-in. drawer pull
- ☐ (16) #8 × 2-in. flathead wood screws
- ☐ (7) #8 × 1-in. flathead wood screws
- ☐ ⅝-in. pneumatic brads
- ☐ 1-in. pneumatic brads
- ☐ Wood glue
- ☐ Polyurethane glue
- ☐ Finishing materials
- ☐ Silicone caulk

Mission Table: Planning

If our island design is too large for your kitchen, you can scale back the width and eliminate a drawer and still retain the look. However, if you have the urge to simplify the joinery—don't. The joinery was designed so that the island could withstand the rigors of being rolled around and worked on. Don't substitute stub tenons or biscuits for the island's 1-in.-long tenons or you'll sacrifice much of its durability.

LOCATING MATERIALS

Purchase all the materials—including the top and casters—before you start this project. To help keep costs down, we used the polished granite top from a cast-iron bistro table purchased at a home furnishings retail outlet. The price of the entire piece was less than what we would

PHOTO A: To ensure plumb caster stem holes, use a drilling guide made from a piece of scrap leg stock and ¼-in. plywood.

PHOTO B: A fence and two boxes clamped together provide accuracy and support for routing leg mortises.

have paid at a local countertop supplier for just the granite. Other suitable top options include marble and solid-surfacing materials such as Corian.

Quartersawn white oak is the wood of choice for this project because it's the species most often associated with American Arts-and-Crafts furniture. You

Mission Table

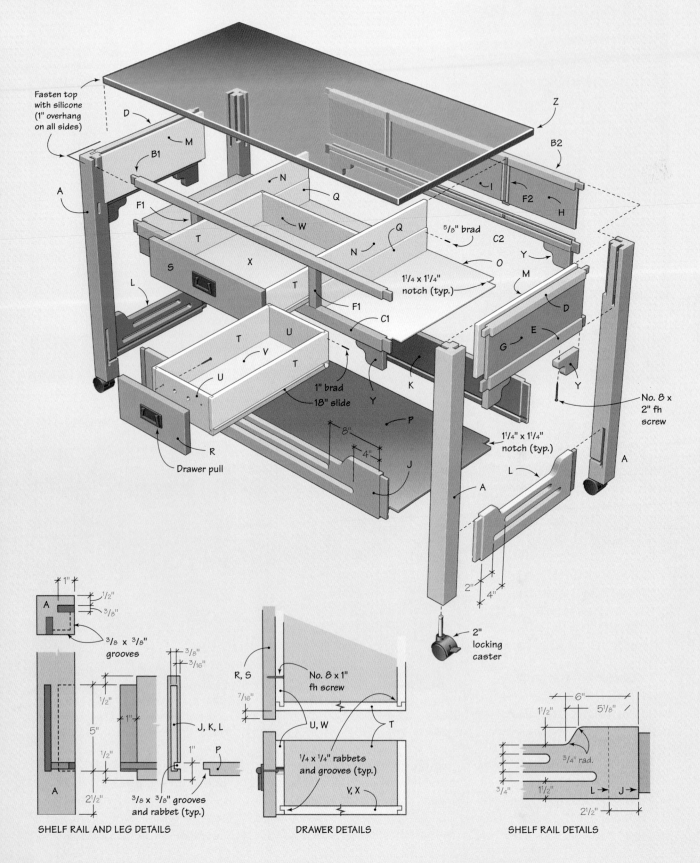

Fasten top with silicone (1" overhang on all sides)

D

M

B1

A

F1

N

Q

W

T

S

X

T

L

F1

Q

N

C1

O

⁵/₈" brad

1¹/₄ x 1¹/₄" notch (typ.)

C2

I

F2

H

B2

Z

Y

M

D

G

E

Y

No. 8 x 2" fh screw

T

U

V

U

1" brad 18" slide

Y

K

P

J

8"

4"

1¹/₄ x 1¹/₄" notch (typ.)

A

L

2"

4"

A

R

Drawer pull

2" locking caster

SHELF RAIL AND LEG DETAILS

A

1"

1/2"

3/8"

³/₈ x ³/₈" grooves

5"

1/2"

1"

1/2"

A

2¹/₂"

3/8"

3/16"

J, K, L

1"

P

³/₈ x ³/₈" grooves and rabbet (typ.)

DRAWER DETAILS

R, S

7/16"

No. 8 x 1" fh screw

U, W

T

¹/₄ x ¹/₄" rabbets and grooves (typ.)

V, X

SHELF RAIL DETAILS

6"

5¹/₈"

1¹/₂"

³/₄" rad.

1¹/₂"

3/4"

L

J

2¹/₂"

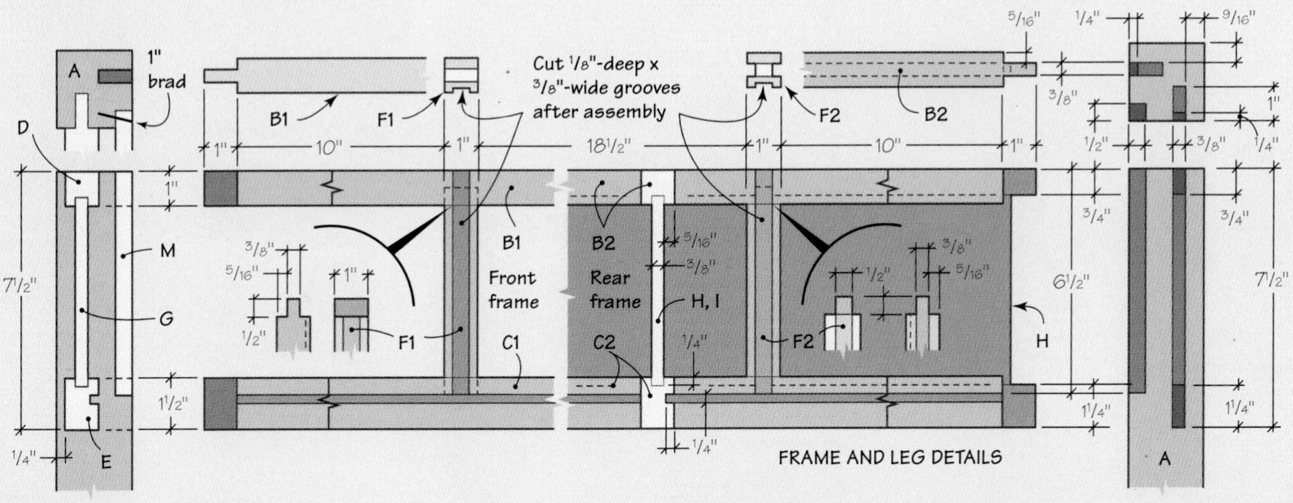

A
1" brad
D
B1
F1
Cut 1/8"-deep x 3/8"-wide grooves after assembly
F2
B2
1"
10"
18 1/2"
5/16"
1/4"
9/16"
3/8"
1/2"
7 1/2"
M
G
E
Front frame
Rear frame
C1
C2
H, I
H
6 1/2"
3/4"
1 1/2"
1 1/4"
FRAME AND LEG DETAILS

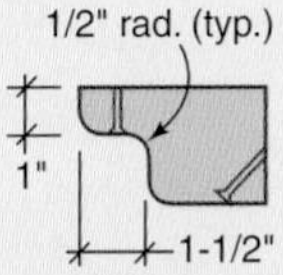

1/2" rad. (typ.)
1"
1-1/2"

BRACKET—Y

Mission Table Cutting List

Part/Description	No.	Size	Material
A Legs	4	2¼ × 2¼ × 31¾ in.	White oak
B1 Front top rail	1	1 × 1 × 42½ in.	"
B2 Rear top rail	1	1 × 1 × 42½ in.	"
C1 Front center rail	1	1 × 1½ × 42½ in.	"
C2 Rear center rail	1	1 × 1½ × 42½ in.	"
D Side top rails	2	1 × 1 × 19 in.	"
E Side center rails	2	1 × 1½ × 19 in.	"
F1 Front stiles	2	1 × 1 × 6 in.	"
F2 Rear stiles	2	1 × 1 × 6 in.	"
G End panels	2	⅜ × 5½ × 17½ in.	"
H Small back panels	2	⅜ × 5½ × 10½ in.	"
I Center back panel	1	⅜ × 5½ × 19 in.	"
J Front shelf rail	1	¾ × 6 × 42½ in.	"
K Rear shelf rail	1	¾ × 6 × 42½ in.	"
L Side shelf rails	2	¾ × 6 × 19 in.	"
M Drawer slides	2	½ × 6½ × 18 in.	Birch ply
panels			
N Dividers	2	½ × 6½ × 19¼ in.	"
O Dust cover	1	¼ × 19½ × 43 in.	"
P Shelf	1	¾ × 20 × 43½ in.	"
Q Spacers	4	¼ × 3 × 19 in.	"
R Small drawer faces	2	¾ × 4⅞ × 9⅞ in.	White oak
S Center drawer face	1	¾ × 4⅞ × 18⅜ in.	"
T Drawer sides	6	½ × 4¼ × 18 in.	Birch ply
U Small drawer fronts/backs	4	½ × 4¼ × 8½ in.	"
V Small drawer bottom	1	½ × 8½ × 17½ in.	"
W Center drawer front/back	2	½ x 4¼ x 17 in.	"
X Center drawer bottom	1	½ × 17 × 17½ in.	"
Y Corner brackets	8	¾ × 4 × 2½ in.	White oak
Z Top	1	¾ × 23½ × 47 in.	Granite

PHOTO C: Define the rail tenon shoulders using a table saw cutoff box with a stop-block clamped to the rear fence.

PHOTO D: Cut the grooves in the rails for the dust cover and shelf with a router table and a straight bit.

PHOTO E: Remove the waste from the tenon cheeks by pushing the work across the router bit with a miter gauge.

won't find this wood at your local home center, but rather at lumberyards that cater to the cabinetmaking trade.

Remember that the size of the casters will affect the height of the island. We used double-wheel, locking stem casters rated at 90 pounds each. Stem casters are less obtrusive than those that mount with a plate, and the locks prevent the island from wiggling when you perform certain kitchen functions, such as rolling dough. Also, the relatively small wheels of these casters don't look out of scale on the island's legs. If you have a wood or tile floor, casters with a soft urethane wheel (rather than nylon) will roll more smoothly and quietly with considerably less damage to the floor surface.

MILLING MATTERS

This project requires a fair amount of woodworking experience because the joinery is complex and must be made precisely. You'll have to mill most of the parts to size from rough stock, so you'll need a jointer and a planer. They don't have to be particularly large machines; small benchtop models will do the job just fine.

Precision parts are the key to this project. Remember to mill all pieces of the same thickness at the same time. Even small variations in thickness and squareness can lead to big joinery and assembly problems later on. To keep the distinctive quarter-sawn faces most visible, plan your milling operations carefully. On all the legs, matching quartersawn sides should face the front and back, giving the island a unified look and allowing for uniform staining.

Because it's unlikely that you'll find $^{10}\!/_4$ or $^{12}\!/_4$ stock, you'll need

to glue boards together to make the legs. To do this, mill $^6\!/_4$ rough stock that's at least 5 in. wide to 1¼ in. thick. Next, crosscut the milled boards so they're at least 1 in. longer than the finished leg; then rip them in half. Here's the trick to grain-matching the legs: Assemble the boards by simply folding them together along the cut line. Once the blanks are glued, you can joint and plane them to the finished size.

We were unable to get $^4\!/_4$ (1-in.-thick) rough stock to mill the ¾-in. parts, so we had to resaw $^6\!/_4$ stock (although milled ¾-in. stock is generally available, it is seldom flat enough). If you need to resaw stock, your band saw should have a 6-in. minimum resaw capacity and accept at least a ½-in. skip-tooth blade. Use a short, tall fence to guide the stock through the blade. Even a wide, resawing blade may wander at times as it naturally

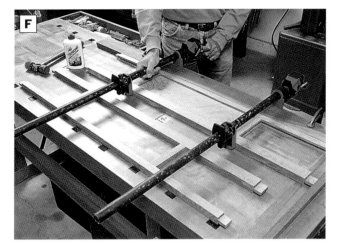

PHOTO F: Before routing grooves for the dividers, glue together the front and back rail assemblies.

PHOTO G: Gang the front and back rail assemblies to rout the centered grooves in the stiles.

PHOTO H: Cut the shelf rail curve to within 1/16 in. of the pattern line; complete the cut using a template and a flush-trim bit.

tries to follow the wood grain. Minimize this action by holding the workpiece tightly against the fence. If you detect some flex in the blade, the board may require some planing after it has been cut.

LEG WORK

1 The legs are the hubs for most of the other parts, so start with leg joinery. First, cut the legs and all the other oak parts to length. To avoid confusion and mistakes, carefully lay out all the joints and label the parts. Don't cut any of the plywood parts yet; their size may require some minor tweaking to achieve a good fit.

2 Orient and label each leg for its position and grain direction. Once you've measured and marked one set of joints, transfer the layout to a story stick and use it to mark the remainder of the like joints. This step prevents measuring errors.

3 Although there are several good ways to cut mortises, when working with a wood as hard as white oak, we prefer to remove most of the waste with a narrow bit and finish with a plunge router and a chisel. We restrain the workpiece on the drill press table with fences on both sides to prevent it from wandering. Then we rout the remaining waste in a few passes using a simple routing fixture (**See Photo B**). Make the mortises about 1/16 in. deeper than the length of the tenons to prevent the tenons from bottoming out and to provide a relief channel for excess glue.

4 Routing leaves the mortise ends radiused. Whether you square them with a chisel or leave them rounded makes no difference in the joint's

strength. Of course, if you leave them rounded you'll have to round the corresponding tenon edges to fit. After you rout the mortises, leave the fence in the same position and rout the panel grooves. Routing the grooves in the legs for the bottom shelf is a simple job, but it can be an awkward balancing act if your router is too big. A router with a small base and low center of gravity is less prone to tipping as you work across the leg. Clamp a fence to the leg to guide the router for these cuts.

TENON TACTICS

To be strong, tenons must fit just right—not too tight and not too loose. (The cure for a sloppy-fitting tenon is to glue veneer to both cheeks and then recut.) Of course, you should always cut the mortises first. Use some scraps to make test cuts so you can sneak up on the right size without sacrificing workpieces. When cutting tenons, abide by

PHOTO I: Make successive passes to cut the decorative grooves. Two fences prevent the router base from drifting.

PHOTO J: Keep order by organizing parts and clamps. Use polyurethane glue for a longer open time.

the rule of thirds: A tenon should be roughly one-third the thickness of the workpiece.

❺ We usually cut the tenon shoulders on the table saw first **(See Photo C).** The saw provides a clean, square edge and defines which faces you must cut away later to make the tenon cheeks. The blade's cutting depth should be close to the level of the cheeks, but it doesn't have to be perfect.

❻ Cutting the tenons on a router table produces smooth, uniform results. Guide the work with a miter gauge and make multiple full-depth passes across the bit **(See Photo E).** Use the router table fence as a stop to prevent the bit from cutting beyond the shoulder line.

ASSEMBLY STRATEGIES

❼ Sand all the parts before you assemble them. It saves time, and the finished project looks better. You should only need to do touch-up sanding after assembly. Before you sand, fill voids and defects with a water-based wood putty, which will take

stain better than a solvent-based product.

We prefer to remove mill marks and blemishes with a cabinet scraper before sanding. It's faster, produces less dust and is more effective than sanding at removing planer marks. After scraping, do a quick round of hand-sanding with 150-grit paper.

❽ Assemble the front and back rail ladders first **(See Photo F).** Don't forget to install the center back panel in its grooves, and be sure the assembly is square by measuring its diagonals.

❾ Rout the grooves for the dividers after assembling the ladders **(See Photo G).** You'll save time and end up with more consistent grooves if you gang-rout the assemblies.

❿ We used wood glue to assemble the rail ladders because there were few parts. However, polyurethane glue, with its long open time, is a better choice for the complex main assembly **(See Photo J).** You'll need about 20 minutes to do the job. Polyurethane glue has the added advantage of acting as a lubricant when fitting tight joints, whereas wood glue will cause the wood to swell and grab. Regardless of the glue you use, dry-fit the parts with clamps first. Any joints that don't fit properly will be easy to spot.

⑪ Decorative shelf rails accentuate the Arts-and-Crafts design. After transferring the shape onto the workpiece, cut the curves using either a band saw or a jig saw (though the latter will have a difficult time working through solid white oak). Be sure to cut 1/16 in. outside the mark. This will allow you to complete the cut more accurately with a flush-trim bit in your router **(See Photo H).** The piloted bit rides along the edge of the template to ensure proper contours of consistent dimensions.

⑫ To highlight the style further, we added grooves to the shelf rails. Two fences secured the workpiece for this operation, while stopblocks at each end made sure we didn't go too far **(See Photo I).** Multiple passes are necessary in order to rout completely through the rails. Be sure to place a scrap piece below the rail to act as an auxiliary worksurface so you don't end up with an unwanted decorative groove in your bench as well.

DRAWERS & FINISHING

⑬ Assemble the island before you make the drawers and cut the dividers to fit. To simplify drawer construction, we made all the parts out of 1/2-in. Baltic birch plywood and made the fronts and the backs the same. With only three drawers to make, we found the table saw to be the fastest and most accurate tool for cutting the grooves and dadoes.

⑭ The boxes are assembled with glue at each corner dado-rabbet joint. A carpenter's square can be a helpful guide to guarantee that each joint maintains a perpendicular relationship. Use clamps to hold the drawer together while it dries **(See Photo K),** and measure diagonals to ensure a square assembly.

⑮ The drawer faces are flush to the frame, but require a 1/16-in. gap on all sides. To achieve the necessary spacing, place shims at each corner. Hold the face securely while driving the screws from inside the drawer **(See Photo L).**

⑯ Finishing this project is easy because oak generally stains evenly without blotching. However,

PHOTO K: Use clamps to draw the drawer box joints together before nailing and to adjust the sides until they're square.

PHOTO L: When installing the drawer face, use 1/16-in.-thick shims to maintain even spacing around the front.

you should quickly wipe off excess stain to keep the wood from looking muddy. When you choose a stain, consider how the color will look with the granite top and the hardware. We used a brown-mahogany stain to get a look that's similar to that of traditional ammonia-fumed Arts-and-Crafts furniture. Any film finish (varnish, lacquer, water-based or shellac) will work as a topcoat. Keep in mind, as attractive as this piece looks, it is intended for use in the kitchen and will take a beating from time to time.

⑰ The final step is to glue down the top with a thin bead of silicone caulk along the edges. Be careful not to use too much or it can ooze onto the finished wood.

Magazine Rack

Keep magazines and other periodicals neatly organized and within easy reach when you display them in this wall-mounted oak magazine rack. Two compartments provide ample storage space, yet the rack only projects 3½ in. at its widest point from a wall. For a decorative touch, we use pre-milled oak door stop to make the slats.

Magazine Rack

Vital Statistics

TYPE: Magazine rack

OVERALL SIZE: 24L by 20H by 3⅞D

MATERIAL: Red oak, oak door stop molding

JOINERY: Butt joints reinforced with glue and screws

CONSTRUCTION DETAILS:
- Divider receives a lap joint to fit around back rail
- Brass assembly screws are driven into countersunk pilot holes, but the screwheads are left exposed for a decorative touch

FINISH: Varnish

BUILDING TIME: 2-3 hours

Shopping List

- ☐ (1) 1 × 4 in. × 10 ft. red oak
- ☐ (2) ⅜ × 1¼ in. × 8 ft. oak door stop molding
- ☐ #8 brass flathead wood screws (1-, 1½-, 3-in.)
- ☐ Wood glue
- ☐ Finishing materials

Magazine Rack: Step-by-step

CUT THE PARTS

❶ Crosscut two 20-in. pieces of oak for the side pieces and one 19¼-in. strip for the divider.

❷ Draw the shapes of the sides. Refer to the *Side Layout* drawing, page 264, to lay out the profiles of these parts. Use a compass to scribe 1-in.-radius curves on the top outside corners.

❸ Cut the sides to shape with a jig saw, and smooth the cut edges with a file.

❹ Lay out and cut the divider. The overall shape of the divider matches the sides, but the divider is ¾ in. shorter and has a notched cutout at the top to wrap around the back rail. Use one of the side pieces to trace the divider shape. See the *Divider Layout* drawing, page 264, to mark the ¾-in.-deep, 3-in.-long cutout. Cut out the divider with a jig saw (**See Photo A**).

PHOTO A: Cut the sides and divider to shape with a jig saw. It's easiest to cut these parts if you clamp each workpiece to your worksurface. Drill clearance holes in the corners of the divider notch to provide clearance for turning the blade when making the bottom notch cut.

Magazine Rack

Attach to wall using suitable wall anchors & 3" brass screws with finish washers

1½" brass flathead wood screws

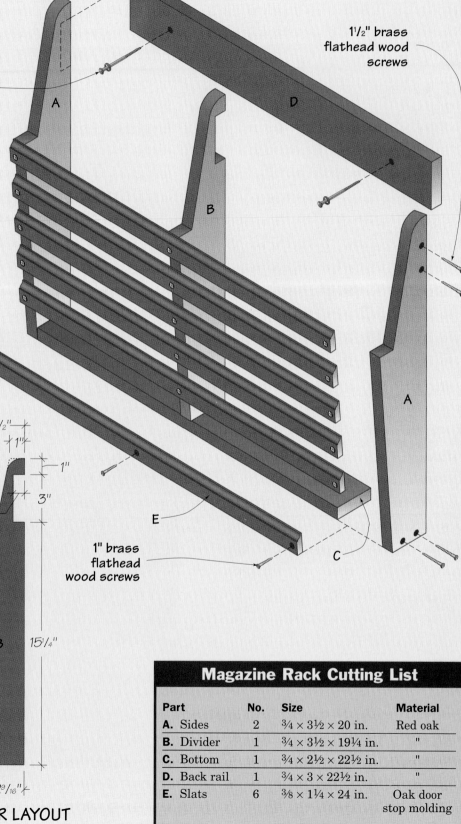

SLAT PROFILE

1¼"

E

³⁄₈"

1" brass flathead wood screws

A

D

B

A

C

E

SIDE LAYOUT

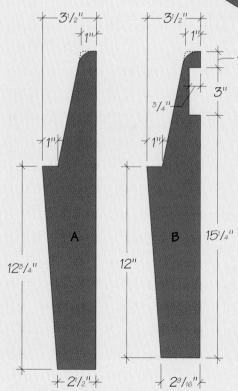

3½"

1"

A

12¾"

1"

2½"

DIVIDER LAYOUT

3½"

1"

1"

3"

³⁄₄"

1"

B

15¼"

12"

2⁹⁄₁₆"

Magazine Rack Cutting List			
Part	No.	Size	Material
A. Sides	2	³⁄₄ × 3½ × 20 in.	Red oak
B. Divider	1	³⁄₄ × 3½ × 19¼ in.	"
C. Bottom	1	³⁄₄ × 2½ × 22½ in.	"
D. Back rail	1	³⁄₄ × 3 × 22½ in.	"
E. Slats	6	³⁄₈ × 1¼ × 24 in.	Oak door stop molding

5 Rip and cross-cut the bottom and back rail to size. Cross-cut the six slats to length.

6 Sand all the parts smooth.

ASSEMBLE THE MAGAZINE RACK

7 Test the fit of the back rail in the divider notch, then fasten the back rail to the divider with glue and a couple of countersunk 1-in. screws, driven through the back rail into the divider notch.

8 Install the sides and bottom on the back rail and divider: The sides overlap the ends of the back rail, and the top edge of the back rail is inset 1 in. down from the top ends of the sides. The bottom fits between the sides, flush with their bottom ends and against the bottom end of the divider. Spread glue on the mating surfaces of these joints, clamp the parts in place and attach them with pairs of countersunk 1½-in. flathead wood screws **(See Photo B).**

9 Apply finish to all surfaces of the magazine rack assembly and slats **(See Photo C).**

10 Install the slats: Arrange the slats on the rack so their profiled edges face up. The top slat should be even with the 1-in. notches on the sides and divider. The bottom slat is flush with the bottom of the project. Space the remaining four slats evenly (1¹⁄₁₆-in. spaces between slats). Attach the slats to the sides and divider with countersunk 1-in. brass screws, one screw per joint **(See Photo D).**

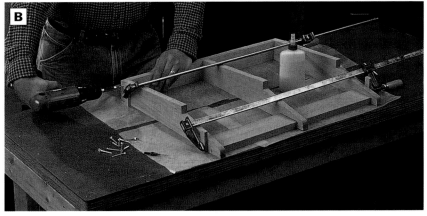

PHOTO B: Glue and clamp the sides to the ends of the bottom and upper rail. Reinforce these joints with countersunk 1½-in. brass wood screws.

PHOTO C: Apply finish to the rack assembly and the slats before installing the slats. Prefinishing the parts while they're fully accessible is easier and faster than waiting until after the slats are installed.

PHOTO D: Attach the slats to the front edges of the sides and divider with countersunk 1-in. brass wood screws. Lay out the slats so they're spaced evenly apart on the rack.

Kid's Wall Clock

Kids will find it tougher to lose track of time when it's marked on the belly of their favorite animal or storybook character. We're providing three animal patterns here, but the simple plywood clock back design could be adapted to any shape you like.

Kid's Wall Clock

Vital Statistics

TYPE: Wall clock

OVERALL SIZE: Varies with clock shape

MATERIAL: Plywood

JOINERY: None

CONSTRUCTION DETAILS:

· Clock shapes made by tracing around a full-size template

· Hole for clock insert cut with a hole saw and drill

FINISH: Primer and paint

BUILDING TIME: 1-2 hours

Shopping List

☐ (1) $3/4$ in. × 2 × 4 ft. birch plywood

☐ (1) $1/4$ in. × 2 × 4 ft. hardboard

☐ Spray mount adhesive

☐ (1) $4^3/8$-in.-dia. battery-powered quartz clock insert

☐ Two-part epoxy (optional)

☐ Picture-hanging hardware

☐ Finishing materials

Kid's Wall Clock: Step-by-step

MAKE A CLOCK BACK TEMPLATE

❶ The easiest way to draw the shape of the clock back onto your plywood is to begin with a full-size paper pattern and trace the shape. You can make a more durable template by gluing your paper pattern to a piece of hardboard, as we show here.

❷ Choose and enlarge a grid drawing shown in the technical art, page 268, on a photocopier to produce a full-size paper pattern.

❸ Mount the paper pattern to a piece of hardboard. We used spray mount adhesive, available at craft stores (**See Photo A**). You could also apply the pattern to the hardboard with a thin coat of white glue or double-sided tape.

PHOTO A: Enlarge the grid drawing about 400% of its original size to create a full-size paper template for tracing the shape of the clock back. We adhered the paper pattern onto a piece of hardboard to make the template more rigid, then cut out the template shape.

Kid's Wall Clock

TEDDY BEAR PATTERN

All grid squares are 1". Enlarge to 400% to create a full-size pattern.

DOG PATTERN

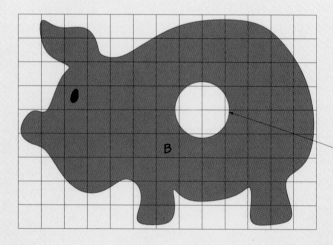

PIG PATTERN

Size hole for clock insert according to manufacturer's specifications.

Kid's Wall Clock Cutting List			
Part	No.	Size	Material
A. Teddy bear	1	$\frac{3}{4} \times 11 \times 13$ in.	Plywood
B. Pig	1	$\frac{3}{4} \times 9 \times 13$ in.	"
C. Dog	1	$\frac{3}{4} \times 11 \times 14$ in.	"

PHOTO B: Trace the template shape onto a piece of plywood, then cut out the clock back with a jig saw.

PHOTO C: Bore a clock insert hole with a hole saw chucked in a drill. Support the cut from beneath with a backer board.

4 Cut the hardboard template to shape with a jig saw, and smooth the cut edges with sandpaper.

MAKE THE CLOCK BACK

5 Cut a piece of plywood to size for the clock back, according to the *Cutting List,* page 268.

6 Trace the clock back shape onto the plywood using your full-size template **(See Photo B).**

7 Cut out the clock back shape with a jig saw and fine-toothed blade.

8 Fill any voids in the edges of the plywood clock back with wood putty, and sand the workpiece smooth when the putty dries.

9 Prime and paint the clock back. Add details like eyes, nose and mouth with an artist's brush.

INSTALL THE CLOCK INSERT

10 Cut out the clock insert hole. An easy way to do this is to first set the template in place over the clock back and drill a small pilot hole through the center of the clock pattern. Use this as a centerpoint on the clock back for cutting the clock insert hole with a hole saw **(See Photo C).**

11 Install the clock insert in the clock back. Glue the insert to the clock back permanently, if you wish, with two-part epoxy.

FINISHING TOUCHES

12 Attach sturdy picture-hanging hardware to the clock back so the clock hangs evenly.

Clock inserts

Most home centers and woodworking supply catalogs sell an assortment of battery-powered quartz clock inserts. There also are companies that specialize in clock-making supplies, and you can find their catalogs advertised in woodworking magazines. The style of the clock faces, hands and overall dial shapes vary widely, as do the diameters of holes you'll need to cut for inserting them into your project. It's a good idea to buy the clock insert ahead of time so you can have it on hand as you plan your clock project.

Building Blocks

Play blocks are timeless toys, and they make a great gift. They're also a good solution for using up those odds and ends of hardwood that accumulate in every woodshop. This design includes all the popular shapes of store-bought block sets, and building them is as easy as it looks.

Building Blocks

Vital Statistics

TYPE: Play blocks

OVERALL SIZE: Varies by block shape

MATERIAL: Hardwood (we used maple), hardwood dowel

JOINERY: None

CONSTRUCTION DETAILS:

· Curves in arched blocks cut with 3-in.-dia. hole saw

FINISH: Child-safe enamel paint (For other options, see Child-safe Woods & Finishes, below)

BUILDING TIME: 5-6 hours

Shopping List

☐ (1) 1 × 4 in. × 8 ft. maple

☐ (1) 1 × 4 in. × 4 ft. maple

☐ (1) 1-in.-dia. × 3-ft. hardwood dowel

☐ Finishing materials

Building Blocks: Step-by-step

LAY OUT & CUT THE BLOCKS

❶ Follow the dimensions given in the technical drawings, page 272, to lay out the assorted block shapes. If you build this project with the quantity and size of lumber specified in the *Cutting List,* you'll be able to construct the full set of 56 pieces. We've sized the block shapes so you can lay many of them out side by side or in groups of two or four to maximize lumber. With this in mind, draw all the shapes.

❷ Cut out the blocks. A number of the block shapes are small once they're completed, so organize your cutting sequence to allow enough extra lumber to clamp and cut the parts safely.

❸ Cut the arch shapes. You could cut these curves with a jig saw, but we used a 3-in. hole saw instead to produce smooth arch shapes **(See Photo A).**

❹ Mark and cut the dowel rod for making the long and short cylinders. Clamp the dowel securely if you cut the cylinders with a jig saw. You may find it easier to cut these parts with a fine-toothed hand saw instead.

Child-safe woods & finishes

This play blocks project may seem like the perfect way to clean out your shop scrap bin, but keep a few things in mind: Not all wood types are suitable for making toys for small children. Softwoods like cedar or redwood can splinter if a child chews on them. Treated lumber is manufactured with harmful chemicals that shouldn't be ingested, as are sheet goods like plywood and particleboard. Avoid exotic species as well: some contain natural oils that may irritate skin and eyes. Better wood alternatives for toys are hardwoods like maple, birch and poplar. They resist splintering, contain no potentially harmful chemicals and take finishes well.

Speaking of finishes, most wood finishes are safe for children once they are fully dry, but if you plan to paint these blocks, choose paint that's labeled "child-safe" on the can. If a clear finish is what you're after, topcoat the blocks with shellac or water-based polyurethane. You could also simply wipe them with mineral oil, available at all drugstores.

Building Blocks

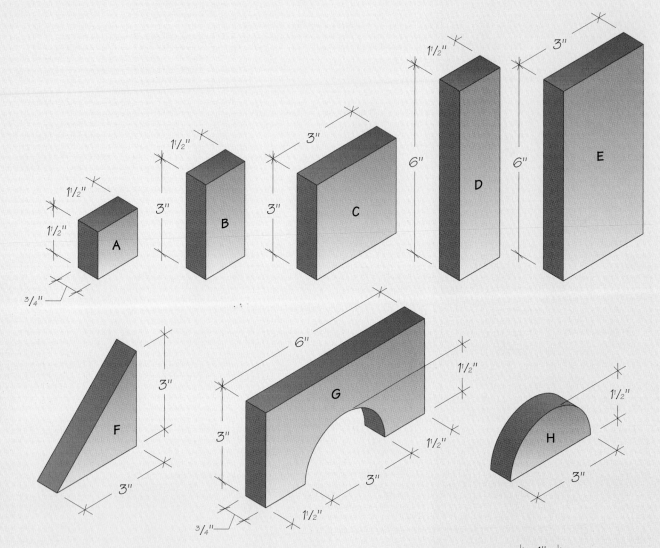

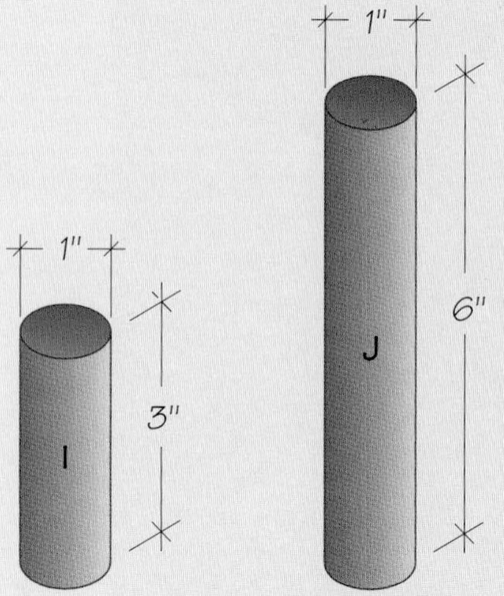

Building Blocks Cutting List

Part	No.	Size	Material
A. Small squares	8	¾ × 1½ × 1½ in.	Hardwood
B. Small rectangles	6	¾ × 1½ × 3 in.	"
C. Medium squares	8	¾ × 3 × 3 in.	"
D. Medium rectangles	6	¾ × 1½ × 6 in.	"
E. Large rectangles	8	¾ × 3 × 6 in.	"
F. Triangles	4	¾ × 3 × 3 in.	"
G. Arches	4	¾ × 3 × 6 in.	"
H. Semicircles	4	¾ × 1½ × 3 in.	"
I. Short cylinders	4	1-in.-dia. × 3 in.	Dowel
J. Long cylinders	4	1-in.-dia. × 6 in.	"

PHOTO A: Lay out and cut the block shapes. Arrange the parts on your boards to maximize the lumber. We cut the curved profiles of the arch blocks with a 3-in. hole saw.

PHOTO B: Sand the blocks thoroughly to remove all sharp corners, edges and any splinters.

FINISHING TOUCHES

5 Sand the blocks thoroughly with 150-grit sandpaper. Remove all sharp corners and edges **(See Photo B)**.

6 Apply the finish. We sprayed on a coat of primer first, followed by two coats of child-safe enamel paint in assorted primary colors **(See Photo C)**. Sand lightly between coats of paint to smooth the surfaces further.

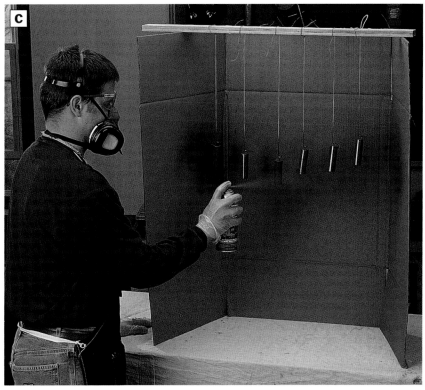

PHOTO C: Finish the blocks. We used primer and child-safe enamel spray paint. To make spraying easier, we hung the blocks with thumbtacks and string attached to a scrap of wood and suspended over a cardboard spraying shield. Wear a respirator if you use a spray finish.

Schoolhouse Desk

Long before there were classrooms equipped with computers and Internet access, there were one-room schoolhouses outfitted with a chalkboard and rows of single-unit desks. These desks recall a simpler era when children needed a sturdy surface on which to practice their reading, writing and arithmetic. Today, a desk like this still functions for doing schoolwork at home, but kids will also find it the perfect place to color, draw or paint. There's even a shelf below the desktop to store their supplies. Best of all, the whole project is made from a single sheet of 4 × 8 plywood.

Schoolhouse Desk

Vital Statistics

TYPE: Desk

OVERALL SIZE: 26W by 34L by 26H

MATERIAL: Birch plywood

JOINERY: Butt joints reinforced with glue and screws

CONSTRUCTION DETAILS:

· All the parts are cut from a single 4 × 8-ft. sheet of plywood

· Create a cutting diagram on the plywood for all project parts first, to minimize waste

FINISH: Primer and paint

BUILDING TIME: 4-6 hours

Shopping List

☐ (1) $^{3}/_{4}$ in. × 4 × 8 ft. birch plywood

☐ Drywall screws (1$^{1}/_{4}$-, 2-in.)

☐ Wood glue

☐ Finishing materials

Schoolhouse Desk: Step-by-step

LAY OUT & CUT THE PARTS

❶ Refer to the *Cutting List* on page 276 to lay out the project parts on the plywood sheet. Creating a cutting diagram now will economize your cutting and help to minimize waste. Mark each project part with the letter that corresponds to the *Cutting List,* to help you identify the parts once they're cut.

❷ Cut the parts to size. Support the plywood on sawhorses while you cut out the parts with a circular saw. Guide your cuts with a straightedge clamped to the plywood so the saw follows the layout lines accurately. Make the longest cuts first to break the plywood sheet into more manageable portions (**See Photo A**).

PHOTO A: Draw a cutting diagram on the plywood sheet to lay out the project parts. Mark each part with a letter that corresponds to the *Cutting List* on page 276 to help identify them. Clamp a straightedge in place to guide the saw as you cut the parts to size.

Schoolhouse Desk

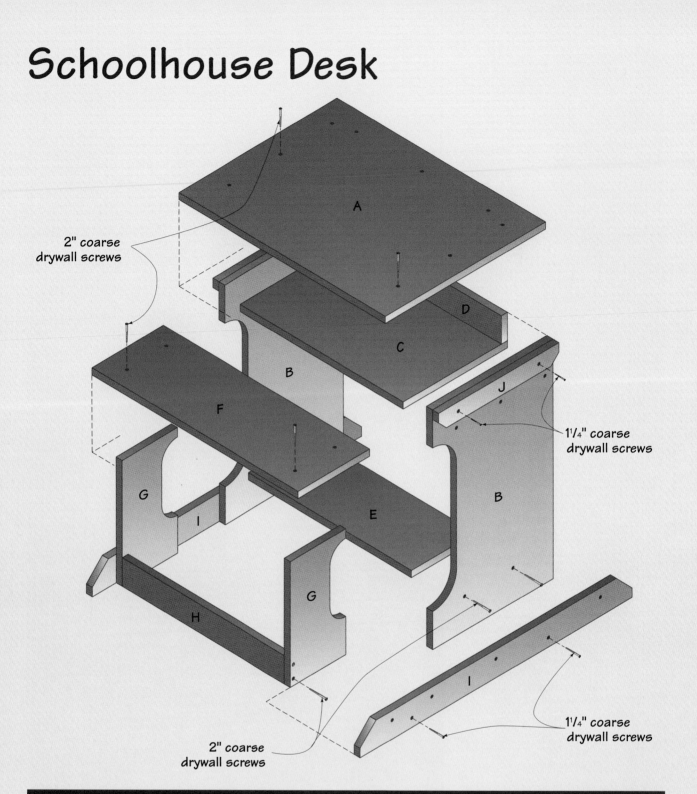

2" coarse
drywall screws

1¹/₄" coarse
drywall screws

1¹/₄" coarse
drywall screws

2" coarse
drywall screws

Schoolhouse Desk Cutting List

Part	No.	Size	Material	Part	No.	Size	Material
A. Desktop	1	¾ × 20 × 26 in.	Birch plywood	**F.** Bench seat	1	¾ × 9 × 26 in.	Birch plywood
B. Desk legs	2	¾ × 15 × 25¼ in.	"	**G.** Bench legs	2	¾ × 7 × 13¼ in.	"
C. Shelf	1	¾ × 13 × 20½ in.	"	**H.** Bench stretcher	1	¾ × 3 × 20½ in.	"
D. Shelf back	1	¾ × 3 × 20½ in.	"	**I.** Runners	2	¾ × 3 × 34 in.	"
E. Footrest	1	¾ × 8 × 20½ in.	"	**J.** Desktop cleats	2	¾ × 2 × 15 in.	"

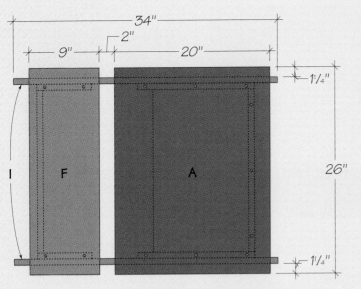

PLAN VIEW

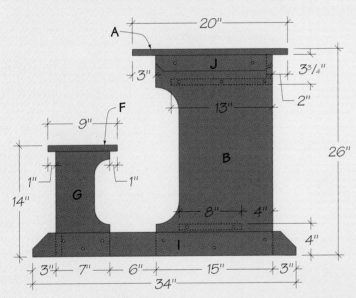

SIDE ELEVATION

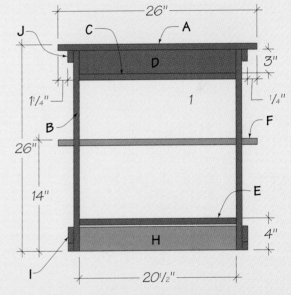

FRONT ELEVATION

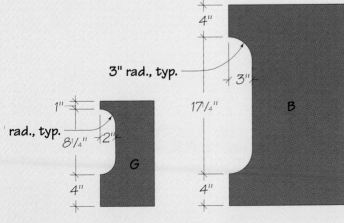

BENCH LEG LAYOUT   DESK LEG LAYOUT

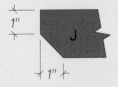

TOP CLEAT END LAYOUT

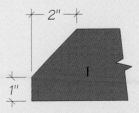

RUNNER END LAYOUT

PHOTO B: Lay out the curves on the bench legs. Set your compass to draw a 2-in. radius to draw the arcs. Connect the layout lines with a straightedge.

BUILD THE BENCH

❸ Make the bench legs: Refer to the *Bench Leg Layout* drawing, page 277, to draw curved cutouts along one long edge of each bench leg. Scribe the curves with a compass set to draw a 2-in. radius. Connect the curves with a straightedge **(See Photo B).**

❹ Cut the bench legs to shape: Secure each workpiece with clamps to your worksurface to hold it while you cut, and follow your layout lines with a jig saw to make the bench leg cutouts **(See Photo C).**

❺ Assemble the legs and bench stretcher: See the *Exploded View*

drawing, page 276, for information on arranging the bench stretcher between the two bench legs. Notice that the stretcher aligns with the back bottom corner of the legs. Spread glue on the ends of the stretcher, clamp it in place between the legs and attach the parts with countersunk 2-in. drywall screws driven through the legs and into the stretcher.

❻ Install the bench seat: Position the bench seat on the ends of the legs opposite the stretcher. The seat should overhang the legs 2 in. on the sides and 1 in. over the front and back edges. Lay out leg centerlines for screws on the top face of the seat. Drill countersunk pilot holes along these lines, apply glue to the top ends of the legs and secure the seat to the legs with 2-in. drywall screws **(See Photo D).**

ASSEMBLE THE DESK

❼ Attach the shelf back to the shelf: Orient the parts so one long edge of the shelf overlaps the shelf back, forming an "L" shape. Spread glue on the mating surfaces of these parts and clamp them facedown on your workbench so the clamps overhang the bench. Drill countersunk pilot holes through the shelf and into the shelf back. Fasten the parts with 2-in. drywall screws **(See Photo E).**

❽ Mark and cut the curved cutouts in the desk legs, according to the *Desk Leg Layout* drawing, page 277. To draw the shape, scribe the 3-in.-radius curves with a compass, and connect the curves with a straight line. Make the cutouts with a jig saw.

PHOTO C: Clamp each bench leg to your workbench and cut to shape with a jig saw. Be sure your clamps don't interfere with the path of the saw.

❾ Mark both faces of the desk legs to determine where they will attach to the shelf, shelf back and footrest. The *Side* and *Front Elevation* drawings on page 277 show the locations of these parts. Draw part outlines as well as screw locations on the legs **(See Photo F).**

❿ Attach the shelf assembly to the desk legs: Arrange the parts upside down on your workbench. This will ensure that the top edge of the shelf back and the top of the legs will be flush. It's helpful to place a couple 3-in.-wide scrap blocks under the front edge of the shelf for support. Spread glue on the ends of the shelf assembly and secure the shelf between the legs with a clamp or two. Attach the legs to the shelf and shelf back with 2-in. drywall screws, driving the fasteners at the marked screw locations.

⓫ Attach the footrest to the desk legs: Spread glue on the ends of the footrest and align it with the marks on the insides of the legs. Support the footrest with 3¼-in.-wide scraps of wood from beneath and clamp it in place. Drive countersunk 2-in. screws through the legs and into the footrest **(See Photo G).**

⓬ Position the desktop on the desk legs, and mark it for installation: Set the desktop on the legs so it overhangs the legs 2 in. on the back and sides but 3 in. on the front. Outline the shapes of the legs and shelf back on the top and bottom faces of the desktop with a pencil and straightedge to determine the screwhole positions.

⓭ Attach the desktop: Move the

PHOTO D: After the bench stretcher is secured between the legs, fasten the bench seat with glue and countersunk 2-in. drywall screws.

PHOTO E: Spread glue along one edge of the shelf back and clamp it flush with the back edge of the shelf. Attach the parts with countersunk 2-in. drywall screws.

PHOTO F: Lay out the shelf and footrest positions on both sides of both desk legs. See the *Side Elevation* drawing, page 277, to position these parts.

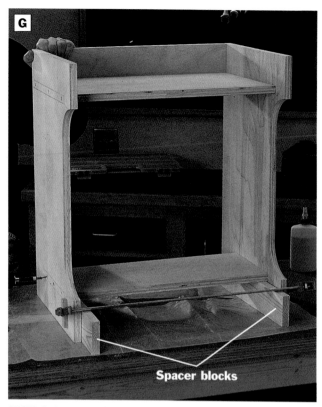

PHOTO G: Install the footrest with glue and screws. Insert a couple of 3¼-in.-wide spacer blocks beneath the footrest to hold it in position temporarily while you screw it in place.

PHOTO H: Install the desktop on the legs and shelf back with glue and countersunk 2-in. drywall screws. Mark the positions of the legs and shelf back on the desktop for locating the screws.

PHOTO I: Mark the angled ends of the runners and cut the corners with a circular saw. Support your straightedge from beneath with a wood scrap clamped to the workbench.

project to the shop floor so you can work at a comfortable height. Spread glue on the top edges of the legs and shelf back, and set the desktop in position. Hold the desktop steady while you drill countersunk pilot holes for the screws. Secure the top with 2-in. drywall screws (**See Photo H**).

⓮ Mark and cut the angled corners on the desktop cleats and runners to match the *Top Cleat* and *Runner End Layout* drawings, page 277 (**See Photo I**). Guide the saw against a clamped straightedge. Because of the narrow width of these cleats and runners, you may need to support the straightedge with a piece of scrap before making the cuts.

FINISHING TOUCHES

⓯ Fill all the screwholes and any edge voids in the bench and desk. Sand the bench, desk, top cleats and runners smooth (**See Photo J**).

⓰ Prepare all project surfaces for paint with a coat of primer.

⓱ Determine the paint scheme for your desk. If you choose multiple colors, mask off the necessary areas with tape and apply one color at a time. Be

PHOTO J: Once you've filled all the screwholes and any voids in the ply-wood, sand the bench and desk before you prime and paint. A random-orbit sander and 150-grit sandpaper will make this a quick task.

PHOTO K: Fasten the runners to the bench and desk legs with coun-tersunk 1¼-in. drywall screws. Hold the parts together with clamps while you drive the screws. Stagger the screw pattern.

sure that each color has dried completely before taping it off and painting another area.

⑱ Fasten the desktop cleats to the desk legs: Clamp the cleats in place so their angled corners face down. Drill countersunk pilot holes through the cleats and into the legs. Install the cleats with a couple of 1¼-in. drywall screws.

⑲ Attach the runners to the bench and desk: Clamp the runners along the bottom ends of the bench and desk legs so the angled ends of the run-ners face up. Position the parts so the ends of the runners overhang the bench and desk by 3 in. (See the *Side Elevation* drawing, page 277). Drive a staggered row of 1¼-in. drywall screws through the runners to fasten the parts together **(See Photo K).**

⑳ Fill the screwhead holes in the desktop cleats and runners with wood putty and sand smooth. Touch up these spots with paint to complete the project **(See Photo L).**

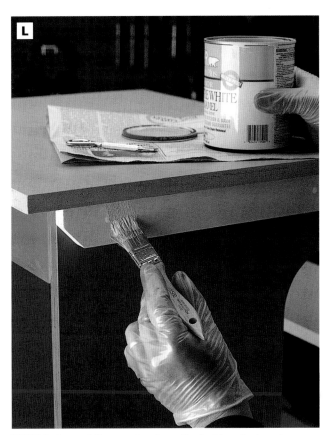

PHOTO L: Conceal the screwheads on the desktop cleats and run-ners with wood putty and paint.

Double-drawer Chessboard

This project proves that some toys simply aren't just for kids. With its walnut case, delicate moldings and brass hardware, this chessboard project will be the perfect complement to your cherished chess set. Our design features a pair of drawers for storing chess pieces during and after a game, and the walnut-and-maple checkered top is easier to build than you might think.

Vital Statistics: Double-drawer Chessboard

TYPE: Chessboard

OVERALL SIZE: 16W by 16D by 3¾H

MATERIAL: Walnut, maple, walnut and maple veneers

JOINERY: Dado, rabbet and butt joints

CONSTRUCTION DETAILS:

· Playing surface is composed of self-stick veneer squares on an MDF panel, to minimize wood movement

· Top and bottom pieces attach to front, back and sides with biscuits

· Drawer faces are cut from front and back pieces so the grain will match when the drawers are closed

FINISH: Satin polyurethane

Building time

PREPARING STOCK
4 hours

LAYOUT
3-4 hours

CUTTING PARTS
6 hours

ASSEMBLY
4-6 hours

FINISHING
2 hours

TOTAL: 19-22 hours

Tools you'll use

· Table saw

· Scroll saw

· Miter saw (optional)

· Biscuit joiner

· Drill/driver

· Clamps

· Router table with ¼-in. bead bit

· J-roller (or rolling pin)

Shopping list

☐ (1) ½ × 8 in. × 6 ft. walnut

☐ (1) ½ × 4 in. × 4 ft. maple

☐ (1) ½ × 2 ft. × 4 ft. MDF

☐ (1) ¼ in. × 2 ft. × 2 ft. birch plywood

☐ (1) 1/40 × 2 ft. × 2 ft. walnut self-stick veneer

☐ (1) 1/40 × 2 ft. × 2 ft. maple self-stick veneer

☐ (2) ½-in.-dia. brass knobs

☐ (2) #6 x 1¼-in. machine screws

☐ #0 biscuits

☐ Wood glue

☐ Finishing materials

Double-drawer Chessboard

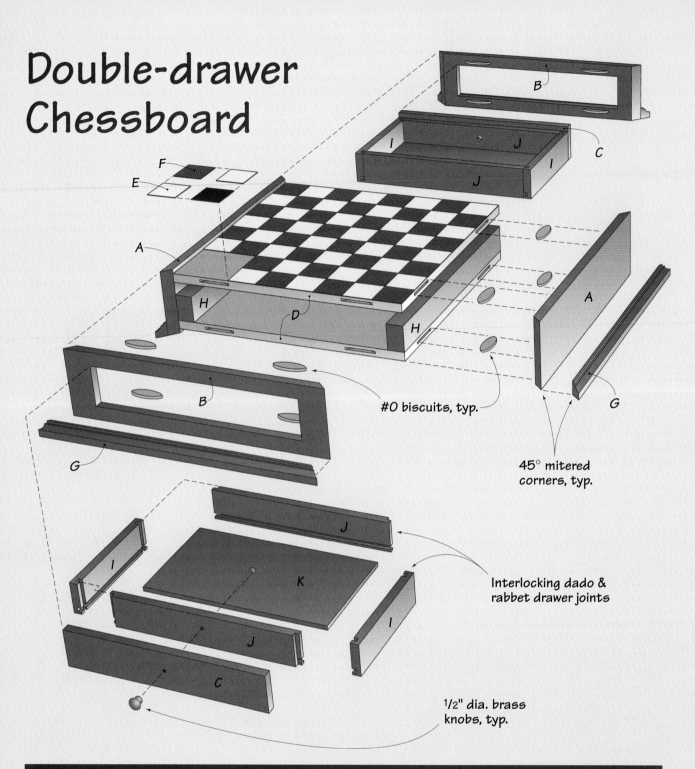

#0 biscuits, typ.

45° mitered corners, typ.

Interlocking dado & rabbet drawer joints

1/2" dia. brass knobs, typ.

Double-drawer Chessboard Cutting List

Part	No.	Size	Material
A. Sides	2	$\frac{1}{2} \times 3\frac{3}{4} \times 15$ in.	Walnut
B. Front & back	2	$\frac{1}{2} \times 3\frac{3}{4} \times 15$ in.	"
C. Drawer faces	2	$\frac{1}{2} \times 2\frac{3}{16} \times 11\frac{15}{16}$ in.	"
D. Top & bottom	2	$\frac{1}{2} \times 14 \times 14$ in.	MDF
E. Light squares	32	$\frac{1}{40} \times 1\frac{3}{4} \times 1\frac{3}{4}$ in.	Maple veneer
F. Dark squares	32	$\frac{1}{40} \times 1\frac{3}{4} \times 1\frac{3}{4}$ in.	Walnut veneer

Part	No.	Size	Material
G. Molding	4	$\frac{1}{2} \times \frac{3}{4} \times 16$ in.	Walnut
H. Drawer guides	2	$1 \times 1\frac{1}{2} \times 14$ in.	Scrap
I. Drawer sides	4	$\frac{1}{2} \times 1\frac{7}{8} \times 7$ in.	Maple
J. Drawer fronts & backs	4	$\frac{1}{2} \times 1\frac{7}{8} \times 11\frac{7}{16}$ in.	"
K. Drawer bottoms	2	$\frac{1}{4} \times 6\frac{1}{2} \times 11\frac{7}{16}$ in.	Birch plywood

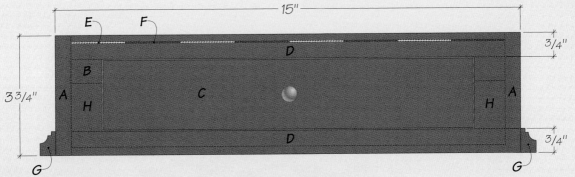

FRONT VIEW

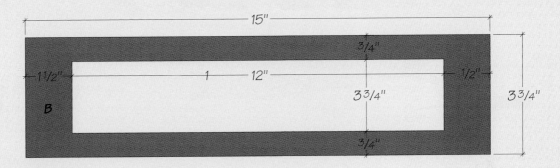

DETAIL: FRONT & BACK (B)

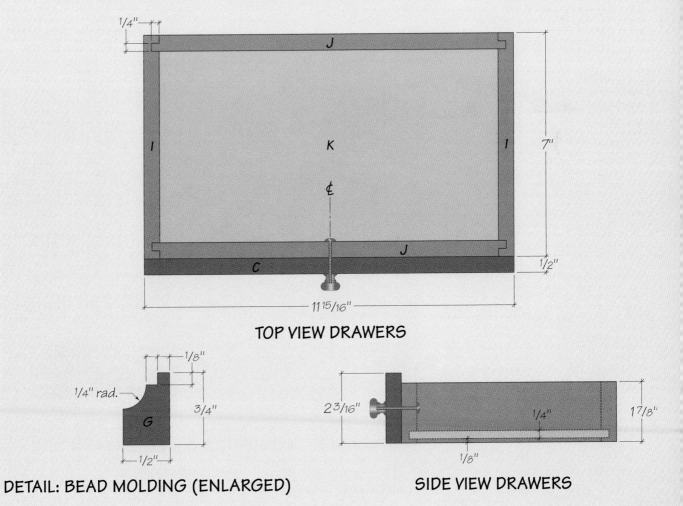

TOP VIEW DRAWERS

DETAIL: BEAD MOLDING (ENLARGED)

SIDE VIEW DRAWERS

BUILD THE FRONT, BACK & SIDES

❶ Cut the chessboard sides, front and back pieces to size from ½-in.-thick walnut. Rip stock for all four parts to 3¾ in. wide. Cross-cut the parts to length on the table saw with the blade set to a 45° angle **(See Photo A).** This way, your crosscuts will also form the miters on the ends of the parts.

❷ Lay out and cut the drawer faces from the front and back workpieces: Use the dimensions shown in the *Detail: Front & Back* drawing on page 285 to draw your cutting lines. Drill tiny starter holes at all four corners of each drawer face. Cut out the drawer faces with a scroll saw and the narrowest fine-tooth blade you have, keeping your cuts as straight as possible **(See Photo B).** The goal here is to produce drawer faces that are about ¹⁄₁₆-in. smaller all around than the openings into which they fit. This way, once the drawers are assembled and installed, the grain pattern will match across the front and back of the chessboard.

MAKE THE TOP

❸ Cut the medium-density fiberboard (MDF) top to size: Rip and cross-cut the panel accurately; once you assemble the chessboard, the edges of the top will fit flush with the front, back and sides. If the panel is out of square, the mitered corners around the chessboard will not close properly. To ensure the panel is square, measure its

PHOTO A: Cross-cut the front, back and side pieces to length on the table saw with the blade tilted to 45°. Since all four parts are the same length, you can use the saw fence as an index to establish the length of the parts, as we show here. CAUTION: *If you use this method, the blade must tilt away from the fence, and the waste piece must fall away on the side of the blade opposite the fence. Otherwise, the waste piece or the workpiece could become trapped between the blade and the fence and result in kickback.*

PHOTO B: After drilling starter holes at all four corners of both drawer faces, carefully cut out the faces from the front and back workpieces. The faces are cut from the front and back parts so the wood grain will match when the drawers are closed.

diagonals. If the board is square, the diagonal measurements will be equal.

❹ Draw a layout grid on the top panel. Use a pencil and straight-edge to divide the top into four equal quadrants. You'll lay out the veneer squares starting from the center, and these layout lines will help keep the veneer aligned.

❺ Cut the 64 veneer squares: Draw 32 squares on both the maple and walnut veneer. Use a steel straightedge and a sharp utility knife to trim the 1¾-in. squares to size (See Photo C). Hold the blade vertically as you cut, or the edges of the squares won't mate tightly later. Use one square as a template to check the dimensions of the rest of the squares.

❻ Lay out and adhere the veneer squares to the top: First, dry-assemble the squares on the top panel to check the fit of the parts. Then install four squares around the centerlines by removing the protective backing paper from each and pressing them into place. Be sure the MDF is free of all traces of dust before you begin, so the veneer will lay perfectly flat. Orient the first four squares in an alternating pattern of maple and walnut. You can either keep the grain running the same direction for all the veneer, or run the maple and veneer grains perpendicular to one another, whichever look you prefer. Then proceed to mount the rest of the squares, working out from the center and using your layout lines as alignment guides (See Photo D). Keep the joints tight between the squares.

PHOTO C: Lay out and cut the chessboard squares from walnut and maple self-stick veneer. Make 32 of each, using a straightedge and utility knife to cut them out. Hold the blade vertically as you cut so that the edges will be square and fit tightly together.

PHOTO D: Divide the MDF top panel into four layout quadrants with a straightedge and pencil. Then begin to install the veneer squares, starting with a group of four at the center. Work outward from the center, in all four directions, fitting the squares as tightly together as you can. Use a J-roller or rolling pin to press the back of each square firmly in place.

❼ Press the veneer squares down firmly. Use a J-roller (a countertop laminating tool) or a kitchen rolling pin to ensure good adhesion of the veneer squares, especially along the edges and corners of each square. When all the squares are in place, give the whole top a light sanding with 400-grit paper installed on a random-orbit sander. Don't use an orbital sander—it will make scratches across the grain.

ASSEMBLE THE CARCASE
❽ Cut the bottom MDF panel for the bottom to size. Be sure its dimensions match the top panel.

PHOTO E: Assemble the top and bottom, front, back and sides with #0 biscuits and glue to form the carcase. Protect the perimeter of the veneer top from glue squeeze-out with masking tape. Be sure the carcase is square when you clamp by measuring the diagonals. When the diagonal measurements match, the carcase is square. Adjust the clamps, if needed, to adjust for square.

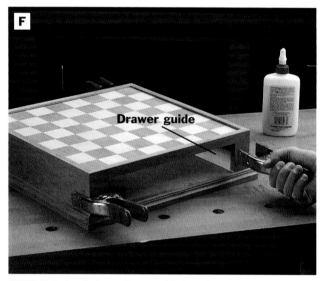

PHOTO F: Cut and glue a drawer guide into the recesses on either side of the drawer openings. Clamp the guides from both sides of the chessboard while the glue dries.

9 Dry-assemble the top, bottom, sides, front and back to check the fit of the parts. Be sure the chess board grid is oriented correctly: there should be a white square on the right corner above each drawer opening. The miter joints must close tightly. If they don't, sand the edges of the top and bottom panels a little at a time to improve the fit of the miter joints.

10 Cut slots for #0 biscuits to join the carcase parts. Biscuits will make aligning the carcase parts easier during glue-up. Refer to the drawing on page 284

for locating the approximate positions of the biscuit slots. Notice that you'll cut two slots into each edge of the top and bottom pieces as well as the mating slots in the front, back and side pieces. When you cut the slots, index your biscuit joiner so that the top and bottom panels are flush with the top and bottom edges of the drawer cutouts. You may want to cut a test slot on scrap to check your joiner's depth-of-cut setting.

11 Assemble the carcase: Protect the veneered face of the top panel from glue squeeze-out by covering the perimeter with masking tape. Spread glue along the mating surfaces of the joints and into the biscuit slots, insert biscuits and clamp up the carcase. Check the assembly for square **(See Photo E),** and wipe away excess glue. Remove the masking tape after the glue stops squeezing out and before it dries.

12 Rout and install the bead molding around the base of the carcase. The safest way to mill this narrow molding is to rout the long edge of a length of ½-in.-thick stock, then trim the profiled edges off the board to form the molding. Set up your router table with a ¼-in.-radius bead bit, and rout the molding in two passes of increasing depth. Rip-cut the ¾-in.-tall moldings from the board. Miter-cut four strips to length, and attach the molding around the carcase with glue and clamps.

BUILD THE DRAWERS

13 The first step in building the drawers is to cut a pair of spacers to act as drawer guides. These are simply scrap stock, ripped to width, trimmed to length and glued into the recesses on each side of the drawer openings **(See Photo F).** Rip them about ⅟16 in. narrower than flush so they set back slightly from the ends of the drawer openings. This will allow a bit of room for drawer play.

14 Cut the drawer fronts, backs and sides to size: Rip and cross-cut these maple parts on the table saw.

15 Cut the rabbets in the drawer front and back pieces. These rabbet cuts will form a tongue on each end of the workpieces. The tongues will fit into dadoes that you'll cut in the drawer sides to form strong, interlocking joints. To make the rabbet cuts, attach a sacrificial wood fence to your table saw's rip fence, and set your dado blade to ½ in. wide. Start the saw and raise the blade so that it cuts ¼ in. into the sacrificial fence. Stop the saw and reset the fence so that ¼ of the blade protrudes beyond the fence, forming a ¼ × ¼-in. rabbet cut setup. Hold a workpiece against the miter gauge and sacrificial fence, then slide the miter gauge over the blade to cut each rabbet **(See Photo G).** You could also cut these rabbets on the router table with a straight bit.

16 Cut dadoes into the drawer sides to receive the drawer front and back tongues as well as the drawer bottom. All of the dado cuts are ¼ in. wide and ¼ in. deep. Reset your dado blade and saw fence accordingly to make the tongue dadoes, then the drawer bottom dadoes.

17 Glue up the drawer boxes. Dry-assemble the parts to check their fit. Then spread glue onto the mating surfaces of the corner joints but not into the drawer bottom dadoes. The drawer bottoms should float freely in their grooves, without glue, to allow for wood movement. Assemble the parts and clamp the drawers.

18 Attach the walnut drawer faces to the drawer fronts. First, check the fit of the drawer boxes in their openings, and sand as needed until the boxes slide easily in and out. Spread glue on the drawer fronts. Set the drawer face against the drawer fronts and align each drawer face on the drawers so the bottom and ends of the drawer face are flush with the bottom and sides of the drawer boxes. Hold the drawer faces in place with spring or C-clamps until the glue dries.

FINISHING TOUCHES

19 Sand the entire project (except the veneered grid) with 220-grit paper. Use a tack cloth to remove any residual dust, then apply three coats of satin polyurethane varnish.

PHOTO G: Attach a sacrificial wood fence to your table saw's rip fence, and use it to establish the ¼ × ¼-in. dado blade reveal for cutting rabbets on the ends of the drawer front and back pieces. Cut the rabbets with the workpieces held against both the miter gauge and the sacrificial fence.

PHOTO H: After applying three coats of satin polyurethane, install the knobs on each drawer. Although we don't show it here, you may also want to add catches or turnbuckles for holding the drawers closed for transport.

20 Install the drawer knobs. Locate the centers of the drawer faces, and drill pilot holes through the faces and drawer fronts for the knob screws. Screw the knobs in place **(See Photo H).**

DESIGN NOTE: *This chessboard was not designed to be portable or frequently transported. If you are likely to move yours around a lot, be sure to hold both drawers closed as you carry it in order to keep them from sliding out of their openings. Or you may want to add magnetic catches, ball catches or small turnbuckles to secure the drawers closed.*

Domino Set

Somewhere around 1720, dominoes found their way to Europe by way of the silk route from China. Sets dating back some 600 years earlier have been discovered in Eastern Asia. But the game most of us know as "Dominoes" is an American version with its roots in the early 20th century. Also known as Muggins or Five Up, the basic game requires just 28 tiles. Follow our project plans to build a set of hand-made walnut and maple dominoes, along with a handy storage box.

Vital Statistics: Domino Set

TYPE: Dominoes and box

OVERALL SIZE: Dominoes: 1W by $1^1/_{32}$H by 2L

Storage box: $5^1/_4$W by $1^5/_8$H by $8^1/_4$L

MATERIAL: Walnut, self-stick maple veneer, Plexiglas

JOINERY: Laminated butt joints, miters and dadoes

CONSTRUCTION DETAILS:

· Maple veneer and walnut emulate traditional ivory and ebony dominoes

· Several simple shop jigs are employed to improve accuracy and safety when machining small domino tiles

· Drilling through the maple veneer produces walnut-colored dots on the dominoes

· Storage box outfitted with a sliding lid

FINISH: Satin polyurethane varnish

Building time

PREPARING STOCK
2 hours

LAYOUT
3-4 hours

CUTTING PARTS
2 hours

ASSEMBLY
4-5 hours

FINISHING
1 hour

TOTAL: 12-14 hours

Tools you'll use

· Table saw

· Jointer

· Power miter saw (optional)

· Drill press with $3/_{16}$-in. twist bit

· Frame clamp

Shopping list

☐ (1) $1/_{40}$ in. × 2 ft. × 2 ft. self-stick maple veneer

☐ (2) $1/_4$ × 2 in. × 3 ft. walnut

☐ (1) $1/_2$ × 2 in. × 3 ft. walnut

☐ (1) $1/_4$ × 6 × 12-in. birch plywood

☐ (1) $1/_8$ × $4^1/_2$ × $7^7/_8$ in. Plexiglas

☐ Wood glue

☐ Finishing materials

Domino Set

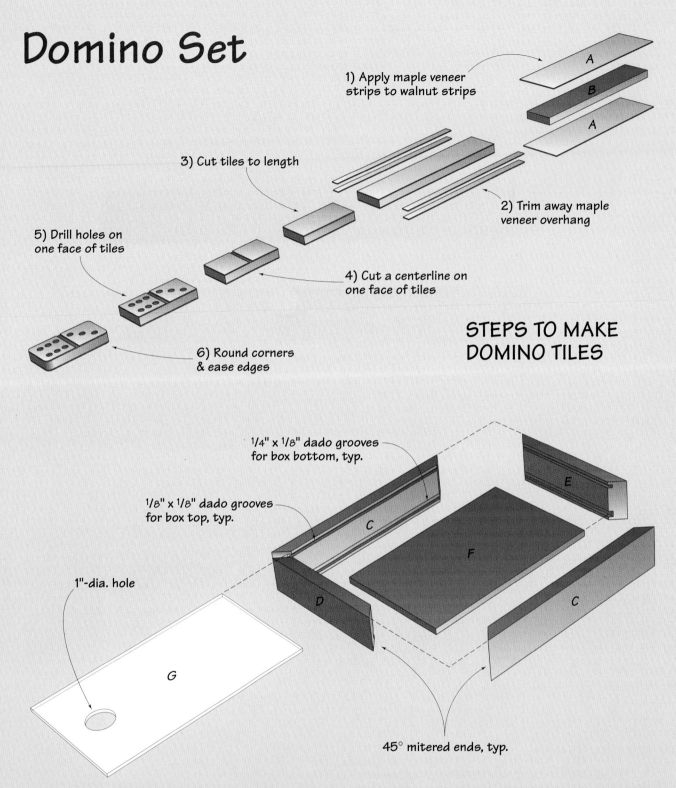

1) Apply maple veneer strips to walnut strips

A

B

A

2) Trim away maple veneer overhang

3) Cut tiles to length

4) Cut a centerline on one face of tiles

5) Drill holes on one face of tiles

6) Round corners & ease edges

STEPS TO MAKE DOMINO TILES

1/4" x 1/8" dado grooves for box bottom, typ.

1/8" x 1/8" dado grooves for box top, typ.

1"-dia. hole

45° mitered ends, typ.

C E D F C G

Domino Set Cutting List								
Part	**No.**	**Size**	**Material**		**Part**	**No.**	**Size**	**Material**
A. Domino faces	2	1/40 × 1½ × 72 in.	Maple veneer		**E.** Box back	1	½ × 1⅝ × 5¼ in.	Walnut
B. Domino cores	1	¼ × 1 × 72 in.	Walnut		**F.** Box bottom	1	¼ × 4½ × 7½ in.	"
C. Box sides	2	½ × 1⅝ × 8¼ in.	"		**G.** Lid	1	⅛ × 4½ × 7⅞ in.	Plexiglas
D. Box front	1	½ × 1⅜ × 5¼ in.	"					

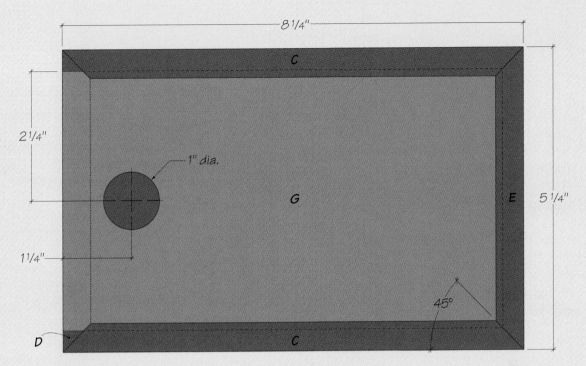

TOP VIEW

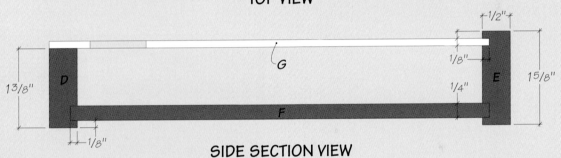

SIDE SECTION VIEW

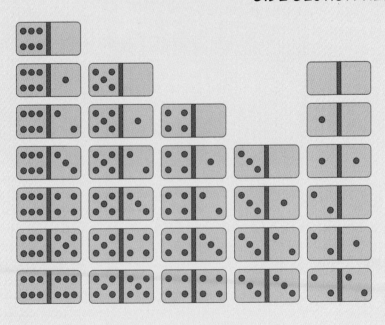

SET OF 28 DOMINO TILES

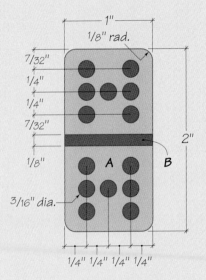

TILE HOLES & CENTERLINE

MAKE THE DOMINO BLANKS

To replicate the look of ivory tiles with inlaid ebony dots, adhere two strips of self-stick maple veneer onto a walnut core, then drill through the veneer on one face of each domino to expose the walnut beneath, producing patterns of dots on the maple.

❶ Rip-cut the ¼-in. walnut stock to 1 in. wide for the domino cores: To make a standard set of 28 dominoes, start with two 36-in.-long strips of 1-in.-wide walnut, which will provide enough material for making a few extra dominoes in case of errors. Since the long walnut edges of each domino will show, remove any saw kerf marks left on the edges of the walnut by running the strips on-edge over a jointer.

❷ Apply the maple veneer to both faces of the long walnut strips: Peel off the protective paper that covers the veneer's adhesive backing and press the veneer firmly into place on the walnut. To make most efficient use of the veneer, align the edge of the veneer sheet with the edge of each walnut strip when you bond the two together. Then trim the veneer cleanly along the edge of the walnut with a sharp utility knife (**See Photo A**).

❸ Cross-cut the domino tiles to length. Clamp a stopblock to the fence of a power miter saw, 2 in. from the blade, and cut the long walnut and maple strips into as many 2-in. domino tiles as you can (**See Photo B**). To minimize tearing out the wood, install a sharp carbide-tipped crosscut blade or ply-wood-cutting blade in the saw to make these cuts.

CUT THE CENTERLINES

❹ Cut centerlines across one face of each domino. Make these cuts on the table saw. Since the tiles are too small to hold against the miter gauge safely by hand, you'll need to build a simple jig to hold the dominoes in place while you cut them. The jig consists of a hold-down made from a piece of ¾-in.-wide scrap with a notch cut along one edge. Screw the hold-down to an auxiliary fence on the miter gauge. The notch should face the saw table and be just large enough to hold one domino at a time securely against the saw table. Set your table

PHOTO A: Peel off the protective paper that covers the adhesive backing of the maple veneer and adhere it to the ¼-in.-thick walnut strips. Trim the veneer to fit the walnut with a sharp utility knife.

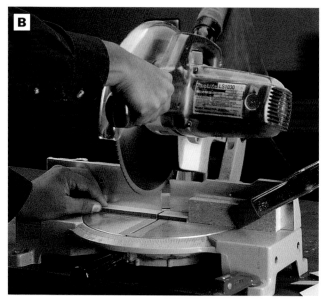

PHOTO B: Cross-cut the laminated strips into individual domino tiles using a stopblock clamped to the fence of a power miter saw. Set the block 2 in. from the blade, and cut the dominoes one after the next.

saw blade height so the blade will just trim through the veneer layer on the domino. Practice on a spare domino first, so you are sure the hold-down is attached accurately to the miter gauge. Then cut the centerlines one by one, slipping a domino blank into the hold-down and sliding the miter gauge over the saw blade (**See Photo C**). Cut a centerline across one face of each domino tile only.

MARK & DRILL THE DOTS

❺ Lay out the dot patterns on your dominoes. See the full-size domino and dot patterns shown on page 293 for layout guides. To make locating the dots easier, we used the printed pattern to make a marking template from clear Plexiglas. We drilled ¹⁄₁₆-in.-dia. holes through the plastic at each dot and mounted the Plexiglas template to a wood jig, sized to hold one domino. We marked for the dots by pressing a finish nail through the appropriate holes in the template and into the maple veneer (See Photo D).

❻ Drill the dots: Install a ³⁄₁₆-in.-dia. twist bit in the drill press, and clamp a fence to the drill press table. (A twist bit is a better choice for drilling the dots than a brad-point bit because it produces a smooth-bottomed hole without leaving a spur mark.) Align the fence for boring the center row of dots first. When drilling the dots, bring the tip of the drill bit down until it just touches the veneer and makes a tiny dimple on the wood. Do not pierce

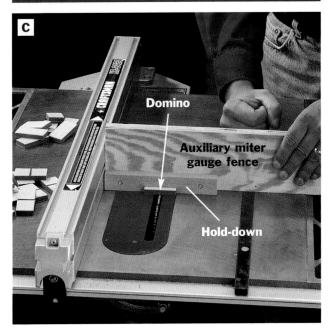

PHOTO C: To trim the domino centerlines, fasten a notched hold-down to an auxiliary fence mounted on the table saw miter gauge. The hold-down keeps your hands a safe distance from the blade and aligns each domino accurately to make the shallow centerline cut. Cut a centerline across one face of each domino.

PHOTO D: Mark the dot locations on the domino blanks, using the *Tile Holes & Centerline* pattern drawing on page 293 as a guide. For greater precision, we built a simple jig with a clear Plexiglas top drilled with ¹⁄₁₆-in.-dia. holes at each dot location. We pressed a finish nail through the appropriate holes in the Plexiglas to mark each dot pattern.

PHOTO E: Drill shallow holes through the maple veneer and just into the walnut core to create the domino dots. Set the depth stop to keep the bit from drilling too deeply. Clamp a fence to the drill press table so the rows of dots will line up lengthwise along the dominoes. Work carefully when drilling to hit your dot locations precisely.

PHOTO F: Cut the ¼-in.-wide groove for the box bottom using a dado blade in the table saw. Then install a ⅛-in.-kerfed blade in the saw and cut a groove for the sliding lid along the opposite long edge of the workpiece. Cutting these grooves now allows you to work more safely with a long workpiece and ensures that the grooves will align perfectly when you assemble the box later.

PHOTO G: Cut the box sides and ends to length. We set a power miter saw to 45° so that the parts would be both cut to length and also mitered for assembly. Accuracy is especially critical if you perform both of these operations in one step.

the veneer. Use this depression as a guide to shift the domino until the bit hits your dot mark. Set the depth stop on the drill press so that the bit goes through the top (maple) layer and barely enters the middle (walnut) core. Once the center rows of dots are drilled, reset the fence to drill the two outside rows of dots, and drill these dots on all of the dominoes (**See Photo E**). (NOTE: *You don't need to change the fence setting in order to drill both outside rows. Just flip the dominoes end-for-end.*)

MAKE THE BOX

7 Cut the plywood box bottom to size.

8 Rip a 30-in. length of ½-in.-thick walnut stock to 1⅝ in. wide for the box sides and ends. Then set up a ¼-in.-wide dado blade in your table saw to plow the groove for the box bottom. Make a test cut on some scrap and check the fit of the plywood bottom in the groove (some ¼-in. plywood is quite a bit shy of its nominal thickness). Then plow the groove ⅛ in. from one long edge of the workpiece (**See Photo F**).

9 Cut a ⅛-in.-wide groove ⅛ in. in from the other long edge of the walnut box workpiece for the sliding lid. Here, the groove should be slightly wider than the Plexiglas is thick; you want the top to be able to slide freely, but not loosely. Test-fit the Plexiglas box lid in the groove; if it barely slides with the protective film in place, it will be a good fit once the film is removed (don't remove it yet).

10 Miter-cut the box sides, front and back to length. A power miter saw works best for this operation, but you could make these cuts on a table saw as well. Since the 45° miter cuts will serve as the cuts that mark the length of the parts, measure carefully when you cut the angles (**See Photo G**).

11 Dry-fit the box sides and ends. Check the fit of the miter joints and sand the joints, if needed, to improve the fit.

12 Trim the box front to 1¼ in. wide along the lid edge. The cut will trim off the lid groove on this part. This way, the lid will slide over the box front once the box is assembled. Then glue up the miter joints and clamp the box together with the bottom inserted in the ¼-in. groove (**See Photo H**).

⓭ Sand the edges and ends of the Plexiglas lid with emory or wet/dry sandpaper, and drill a 1-in.-dia. hole 1¼ in. from one end to serve as a finger catch. Drill the hole with a sharp bit on the drill press at a slow speed to keep the plastic from cracking or chipping.

⓮ Sand the entire project with 220-grit paper, and round the corners of the dominoes. Then apply three coats of clear satin polyurethane varnish to all wood surfaces. Spray-on polyurethane works well for finishing these small parts.

PHOTO H: Glue and clamp the box parts together, with the box bottom in place. We used a frame clamp, which holds all four corners of the box together and squares up the assembly as well. If you use a different clamping method, adjust the clamps until the box is square.

Dominoes rules of play

The most common game of dominoes is called Five-up, Muggins or sometimes All-Fives. It is played with the standard double-six set of 28 dominoes you've just made in this project. Two to four people can play, and you should have a pen and paper handy to track their individual scores.

Turn all the dominoes facedown on a flat surface. Each player then takes a tile (also known as a bone) to see who goes first. The one with the most dots starts, and the order of play goes clockwise around the table. Each player draws five tiles from the pile after returning the initial ones to the pile and shuffling the tiles around.

The first player can play any tile to get things started. The next player must then match either end of that tile (for example, if the initial tile has a four and a five, the second player can butt a four to the four or a five to the five).

When someone plays a double (with the same number of dots on each side of the line), this is placed crosswise at the end of the chain. Up to four dominoes can butt against this double: two continuing the chain in its original direction, and two more lead off at right angles.

If a player doesn't have a play to make, he or she must continue to draw tiles and keep them until a play can be made. A player can also decide against playing a tile he or she already has, in order to draw from the pile instead.

Points are awarded as a round progresses to players who form unions of tiles that total up to a multiple of five. However, a player only gets the points if he or she claims them before the next player takes a turn.

The first player to use up all of his or her tiles scores points from the tiles that remain in the other players' piles. These totals are rounded off to the nearest five (round 2 down and 3 up). If play comes to a stop because nobody has a playable domino, all the players add up their remaining tiles. The player with the lowest total scores points from the tiles that remain in all the other players' piles.

There are numerous variations of these rules, and no hard and fast "right" way to play. Several versions can be found in books on games at your local library or through searches on the Internet. Individual families, clubs or social groups often have "house" rules, too.

Booster Bench

There's no denying that youngsters love to do things themselves. Bring sink faucets and higher bookshelves down to
their level with the aid of this booster bench. It also makes a
great seat for story time. Build one with a 4-ft.-long piece of
1 × 8 in just a couple hours.

Booster Bench

Vital Statistics

TYPE: Booster bench

OVERALL SIZE: 16L by 6¾H by 7¼D

MATERIAL: Pine

JOINERY: Butt joints reinforced with glue and screws

CONSTRUCTION DETAILS:

· Entire project can be built from one 4-ft. board

· Countersunk screwheads can be concealed with wood putty

FINISH: Primer and paint

BUILDING TIME: 1-2 hours

Shopping List

☐ (1) 1 × 8 in. × 4 ft. pine

☐ Wood glue

☐ #8 × 2-in. flathead wood screws

Booster Bench: Step-by-step

MAKE THE STRETCHER & LEGS

❶ Rip and cross-cut a 2½-in.-wide, 12½-in.-long board for the stretcher. To draw the stretcher arch, use a photocopier to enlarge the curved grid shown on the *Stretcher Layout* drawing, page 300, until the squares are ½ in. Cut out your paper pattern and use it as a template for drawing the stretcher arch on the pine blank.

❷ Cross-cut two 6-in. lengths of pine for the legs.

❸ Draw the leg shapes, using the *Leg Layout* grid drawing, page 300, as a guide. Make another paper template and use it to draw the leg arches (**See Photo A**).

❹ Cut the arches in the stretchers and legs with a jig saw. Smooth the curved cuts with a file.

MAKE THE TOP

❺ Cross-cut a 16-in. board for the bench top.

❻ Lay out and draw 1-in. radius corners on the top workpiece. Cut the corners, and smooth the curved cuts with a file.

PHOTO A: Draw arched profiles on the stretcher and legs. Full-size paper templates are helpful for drawing these curved shapes.

Booster Bench

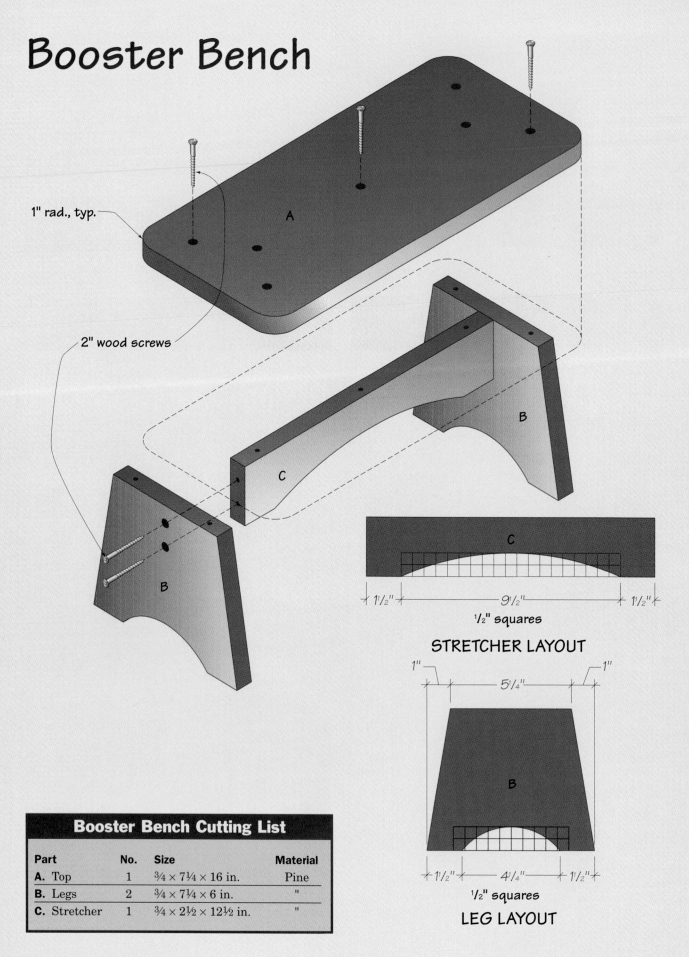

1" rad., typ.

2" wood screws

A

B

C

B

B

C

1½"   9½"   1½"

½" squares

STRETCHER LAYOUT

1"   5¼"   1"

B

1½"   4¼"   1½"

½" squares

LEG LAYOUT

Booster Bench Cutting List

Part	No.	Size	Material
A. Top	1	¾ × 7¼ × 16 in.	Pine
B. Legs	2	¾ × 7¼ × 6 in.	"
C. Stretcher	1	¾ × 2½ × 12½ in.	"

PHOTO B: Glue and clamp the stretcher between the legs so the top ends and edges of the parts are flush. Fasten the parts with countersunk 2-in. flathead wood screws.

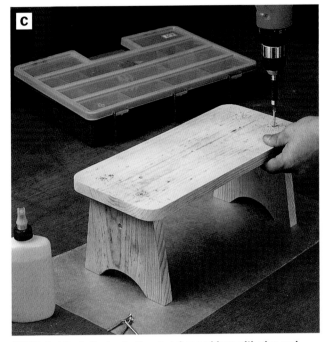

PHOTO C: Attach the top to the stretcher and legs with glue and screws. Lay out the stretcher and leg locations on the top first, for locating the screws.

ASSEMBLE THE BENCH

7 Sand all of the stool parts smooth.

8 Assemble the stretcher and legs: Draw centerlines on the legs for locating the stretcher and pairs of attachment screws. Spread glue on the ends of the stretcher and clamp it in place between the legs. Drill countersunk pilot holes through the legs and into the stretcher, then fasten the parts with 2-in. flathead wood screws (**See Photo B**).

9 Install the top: Center the top over the legs and stretchers, and mark centerlines on the top for driving screws into the legs and stretcher. Spread glue on the mating parts, and drive countersunk flathead wood screws through the top to join the parts (**See Photo C**).

10 Finish the bench: Fill the screwhead recesses with wood putty, and sand smooth. Apply primer and glossy paint (See *Wood & Finish Options*, right).

Wood & finish options

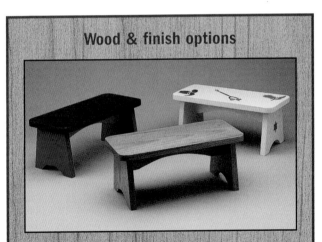

We used solid pine for building the booster bench shown on these pages, but any 3/4-in.-thick lumber you have on hand would work just as well. One attractive option would be to build a bench from oak or another hardwood with attractive grain pattern. In this case, counterbore the screws and install matching oak plugs to cover the screwheads. Then finish with your choice of stain and topcoat. Paint-grade plywood also could be used to build this bench, followed by a coat of paint and maybe a few brightly painted stencils. Another successful painting scheme is to simply select a few glossy primary colors or maybe the favorite colors of the child who'll use the bench. Let creativity be your guide.

Rocking Horse

Build this trustworthy steed for a little cowpoke in your life, and you'll create a rocking toy that could well get passed down for generations to come. This rocking horse is made from standard-dimension pine available at any lumberyard or home center. With safety in mind, the design sports a wide base, shallow rocker curve, rounded edges and concealed fasteners.

Vital Statistics: Rocking Horse

TYPE: Rocking Horse

OVERALL SIZE: 20W by 36L by 28H

MATERIAL: Pine

JOINERY: Biscuits, dadoes, butt joints

CONSTRUCTION DETAILS:

· Rocking horse's wide, angled stance and gradual rocker profile make it less likely to tip

· Wide pine parts are edge-glued from narrower stock

· All edges are eased with ¼-in. roundover profiles or sandpaper

· Screwheads are capped with wood buttons or concealed underneath the rocker for safety

FINISHING OPTIONS: Clear water-based polyurethane varnish; could also be finished with child-safe paint

Building time

PREPARING STOCK
1-2 hours

LAYOUT
2-3 hours

CUTTING PARTS
4-6 hours

ASSEMBLY
2-3 hours

FINISHING
1-2 hours

TOTAL: 10-16 hours

Tools you'll use

· Jointer

· Table saw

· Jig saw, band saw or scroll saw

· Biscuit joiner

· Drill/driver and 1-in.-dia. spade bit

· Right-angle drilling guide

· Belt sander

· Router and ¾-in. straight bit, ¼-in. roundover bit

· Straightedge, bevel gauge or adjustable protractor gauge

· Bar or pipe clamps

· Compass

· Hammer and nailset

Shopping list

☐ (1) 1 × 6 in. × 8 ft. pine

☐ (1) 1 × 10 in. × 8 ft. pine

☐ (1) 1 × 12 in. × 8 ft. pine

☐ 1-in.-dia. × 36-in. pine doweling

☐ 4d finish nails

☐ #8 flathead wood screws (1¼-, 2-in.)

☐ ⅜-in.-dia. wood buttons

☐ #20 biscuits

☐ Wood glue

☐ Finishing materials

Rocking Horse

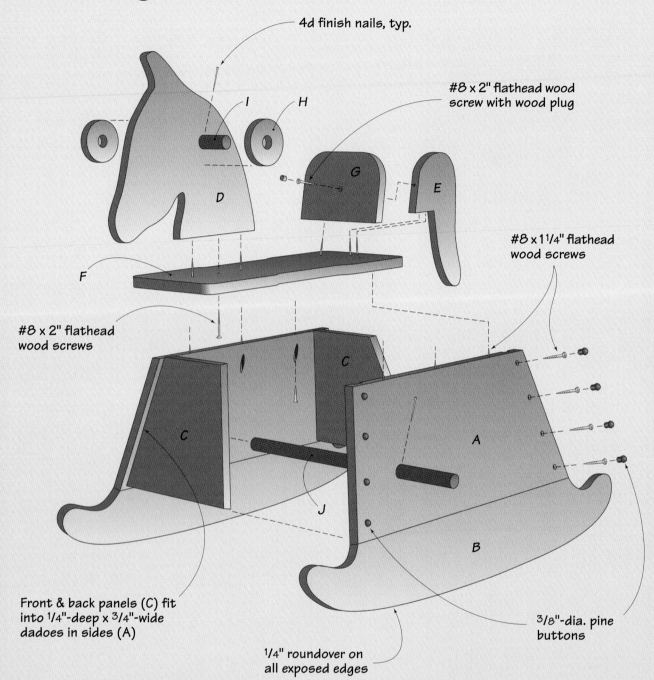

4d finish nails, typ.

#8 x 2" flathead wood screw with wood plug

I

H

G

E

D

F

#8 x 1¼" flathead wood screws

#8 x 2" flathead wood screws

C

C

A

J

B

Front & back panels (C) fit into ¼"-deep x ¾"-wide dadoes in sides (A)

3/8"-dia. pine buttons

¼" roundover on all exposed edges

Rocking Horse Cutting List

Part	No.	Size	Material	Part	No.	Size	Material
A. Sides	2	¾ × 10¼ × 24 in.	Pine	**F.** Seat	1	¾ × 9¼ × 22 in.	Pine
B. Rockers	2	¾ × 5 × 34¾ in.	"	**G.** Seat back	1	¾ × 5½ × 8⅜ in.	"
C. Front, back	2	¾ × 11¼ × 10 in.	"	**H.** Collars	2	¾ × 3¼ × 3¼ in.	"
D. Head	1	¾ × 13¼ × 14 in.	"	**I.** Handle	1	1-in. dia. × 6 in.	Pine dowel
E. Tail	1	¾ × 6 × 11½ in.	"	**J.** Footrest	1	1-in. dia. × 19½ in.	"

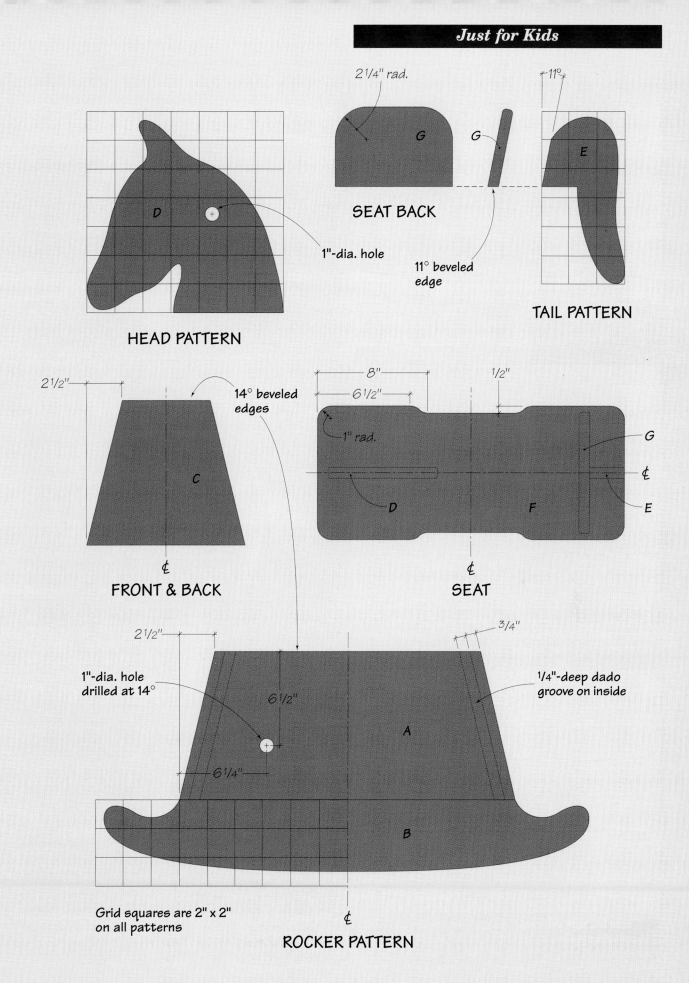

2¼" rad.

11°

SEAT BACK

G

G

E

1"-dia. hole

11° beveled edge

TAIL PATTERN

D

HEAD PATTERN

2½"

14° beveled edges

C

¢

FRONT & BACK

8"

6½"

½"

1" rad.

G

D

F

¢

E

¢

SEAT

2½"

3/4"

1"-dia. hole drilled at 14°

6½"

A

¼"-deep dado groove on inside

6¼"

B

Grid squares are 2" x 2" on all patterns

¢

ROCKER PATTERN

MAKE THE SIDES & ROCKERS

1 Edge-joint and edge-glue panels for the sides, front and back, head and tail. Rip- and cross-cut these panels to the final sizes given in the *Cutting List,* page 304.

2 On one of the two sides, make a reference mark for the footrest hole 6½ in. from one edge (we'll call this the top edge) and 6¼ in. from the closer end. The intersection of these lines marks the center-point for the hole. Mark the footrest hole on the other side, measuring from the opposite end you chose for the first side piece. The resulting footrest marks should mirror one another.

3 Lay out the angled ends of the sides by measuring 2½ in. from each end along the top edges of both side panels and drawing reference marks. Draw a straight line from each mark to the bottom corner of the closer end **(See Photo A).** Cut along the angled lines and smooth the sawn edges with sandpaper.

4 Cut dadoes on the inside faces (the face opposite the footrest marks) of the sides along the angled ends you cut in Step 3. Install a ¾-in. straight bit in a table-mounted router and set the bit depth to ¼ in. Set the fence ¾ in. from the bit. Use an angled pushblock to guide each side panel over the bit **(See Photo B).** You could also cut these dadoes on the table saw with a dado-blade set.

5 Joint one edge of the rocker stock and cut to size. Join the rockers to the sides. Lay the sides on your workbench so the dadoes face up. Set the jointed edge of a rocker against the bottom edge of each side so the rocker overhangs the side evenly on both ends. Mark four biscuit locations along the joint between the side panels and the rockers **(See Photo C).** Cut #20 biscuit slots at your reference marks, then spread wood glue along the mating parts of the joint, insert biscuits into the biscuit slots, and glue and clamp the rockers to the sides.

6 Cut a 14° bevel along the top edge of each side assembly on the table saw, with the blade tilted to 14°. Cut the bevels with the dado side of the work-

PHOTO A: Lay out the angled ends of the side pieces and draw lines from the top edges to the bottom corners. Note the opposite locations of the footrest "X"s on the two side pieces.

PHOTO B: Cut ¾-in.-wide, ¼-in.-deep dadoes on the inside faces of the side panels with a ¾-in. straight bit in the router. Use an angled pushblock to guide the workpiece and a featherboard to secure the workpiece against the router table.

PHOTO C: Mark centerlines for biscuit slot locations to join the sides to the rockers. Make sure the sides are centered on the rockers. Assemble the parts with #20 biscuits and glue.

piece facing up. NOTE: *If you cut these bevels on the table saw, set your saw fence so the blade just clips the corner across the board's thickness; it should not shorten the overall height of the sides.*

❼ Drill the footrest holes through the side panels at the footrest reference marks you made in Step 2. Chuck a 1-in.-dia. spade bit in a drill that is mounted in a right-angle drill guide and set the drill guide angle to 14° **(See Photo D).** Drill test holes first.

❽ Lay out the rocker curves using the grid pattern on page 305 as a reference. Cut out the rocker shapes with a jig saw or a band saw.

❾ Smooth the edges of the rockers with a belt sander. We clamped the two side panels together in our bench vise and gang-sanded them **(See Photo E).** Gang-sanding ensures that the rocker curves will match. Then round-over all the side assembly edges, except the beveled top edge, using a router and a ¼-in.-radius roundover bit.

MAKE THE FRONT & BACK

❿ Rip- and cross-cut the front and back glued-up panels to size. On one end of each panel (we'll call this the top end), make reference marks 2½ in. from either edge, and draw a line connecting these marks to the closer bottom corners (similar to the side layouts you did in Step 3).

⓫ Cut a 14° bevel along the top ends of the front and back, just as you did on the top edges of the sides in Step 6 **(See Photo F).**

⓬ Cut the angled sides of the front and back pieces using a jig saw or band saw. Round over the bottom edge of both workpieces with a router and ¼-in. roundover bit. The edges of the angled sides and top end should remain square. Finish-sand the rocking horse sides, front and back.

⓭ Attach the sides to the front and back with wood glue and four #8 × 1¼-in. flathead wood screws per joint **(See Photo G).** The front and back should fit into the side dadoes so the ends and edges of the four parts align at the top of the glued-up assembly where the seat will attach. Drill counterbored pilot holes for the screws, to accept ⅜-in.-dia. pine buttons.

D

Backer board

PHOTO D: Drill 1-in.-dia. holes for the footrest at a 14° angle through the sides, using a right-angle drill guide. Place a backer board beneath the workpiece to prevent tearout.

E

PHOTO E: Clamp the side assemblies together and gang-sand both rockers. Sanding the rockers side-by-side ensures that the rockers will match and gives the belt sander a wider surface on which to ride.

F

Blade guard removed for clarity

PHOTO F: Cut a bevel along the top edge of the front and back pieces with the table saw blade tilted at 14°. Use a featherboard clamped to the saw table and a pushstick to guide the workpieces.

PHOTO G: Attach the sides to the front and back with glue and four #8 × 1¼-in. screws per joint. Drill counterbored pilot holes for the screws to accept ⅜-in.-dia. buttons.

PHOTO H: Round-over the edges of the seat, seat back, tail, head and collars with a ¼-in. roundover bit in the router (See inset photo). Since the parts would be difficult to clamp, set the parts on a high-friction router mat to keep them stationary during routing.

Roundover bit

PHOTO I: Attach the head and tail to the seat, driving screws up through the bottom of the seat. Fasten the seat back to the tail. Use #8 × 2-in. flathead wood screws and glue.

ADD THE HEAD, TAIL & SEAT PARTS

⓮ Enlarge the head and tail patterns on page 305 to full size and transfer the patterns onto the stock for the head and tail. Mark the centerpoint for the handle on the head piece. Cut along the outlines for the head and tail with a jig saw, band saw or scroll saw, and sand the cut edges smooth. Drill a 1-in.-dia. hole for the handle through the head piece.

⓯ Cut the seat board to size from 1 × 10 pine and mark the seat board for the shaped recesses and rounded corners that are shown in the drawing on page 305. Cut the seat board to shape and sand the edges smooth.

⓰ Cut the seat back to size from 1 × 6 pine. Cut an 11° bevel along one edge of the seat back on the table saw. Lay out and cut the 2¼-in.-radius corners on the edge opposite the bevel edge. Smooth the cut edges with sandpaper.

⓱ Cut two 3¼-in.-square blanks for the handle collars. Connect the diagonal corners of each workpiece with straight lines, and mark the centerpoint where the lines intersect. Draw a 3¼-in.-dia. circle around these centerpoints with a compass. Drill a 1-in.-dia. hole through the centerpoint of each collar for the handle, and cut the circular collars to shape. Finish-sand the collars.

⓲ Round-over the edges of the seatboard, collars, seat back, head and tail with a router and a ¼-in. roundover bit, except for the bottom edge of the head and seat back where each will attach to the seat, as well as the two straight edges of the tail **(See Photo H).** Finish-sand all of these parts.

⓳ Attach the head and tail to the seat with glue and #8 × 2-in. flathead wood screws, driven through clearance holes in the underside of the seat **(See Photo I).** Use the seat diagram on page 305 as a guide for positioning the head and tail. Position the head 1 in. back from the front end of the seat. Spread glue along the beveled edge of the seat back and set the seat back into place on the seat so it rests against, and is centered on, the tail. On the seat back, measure up 2¼ in. from the seat and drill a counterbored pilot hole through the seat back into the tail. Attach the two parts with a 2-in. screw, cover the screwhead with a pine plug, and cut the plug off flush when the glue dries.

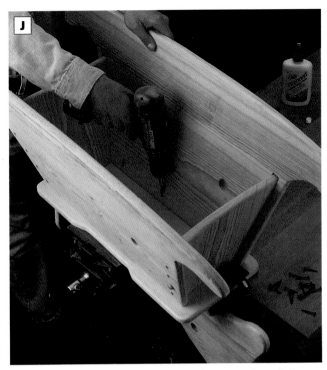

PHOTO J: Center the base on the bottom of the seat. Spread glue on the mating surfaces and drive #8 × 1¼-in. flathead wood screws up into the seat, through counterbored pocket holes, to attach the parts.

PHOTO K: Secure the footrest and the handle dowels with 4d finish nails driven at angles into the adjoining panels. Set the nails below the wood surface with a nailset. Glue the handle collars to the head.

20 Attach the base to the seat with glue and six #8 × 1¼-in. flathead wood screws. Clamp the seat assembly upside down in a bench vise and center the base on the bottom of the seat. Drill countersunk pocket holes through the base and into the seat to fasten the parts together (**See Photo J**).

FINISHING TOUCHES

21 Cut the dowels to length for the handle and footrest, and round-over the ends with sandpaper. Finish-sand the dowels.

22 Install the footrest through the holes in the base and install the handle through the hole in the rocking horse head. Adjust both dowels so they protrude evenly on both sides. Lock the dowels in place with 4d finish nails driven at an angle. Set the nailheads below the surface of the dowels with a nailset (**See Photo K**). Slip the handle collars over the handle ends in the head and glue and clamp the collars to each side of the head.

23 Glue pine buttons into the counterbored holes in the rocker base to conceal the screwheads.

24 Finish-sand any rough surfaces and apply three coats of water-based polyurethane or another child-safe finish (**See Photo L**).

PHOTO L: Finish-sand any remaining rough edges and apply three coats of clear polyurethane varnish to all wood surfaces.

Doll Cradle

Every young doll lover should have a cradle to rock toy babies to sleep. Here's a classic design that's a snap to build. Its proportions will fit most popular doll sizes. The cradle features dowels between the rockers on each side, so little ones can use their feet to rock the cradle. The cloverleaf-style cutouts add a touch of good luck for make-believe moms and dads.

Vital Statistics: Doll Cradle

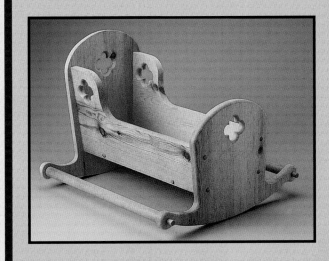

TYPE: Doll cradle

OVERALL SIZE: 18W by 19½L by 14¾H

MATERIAL: Pine

JOINERY: Glued, screwed and plugged butt joints

CONSTRUCTION DETAILS:

- Cloverleaf cutouts are created on the drill press
- Outside edges of headboard and footboard as well as cutouts are routed with ¼-in. roundover bit
- Ends of dowels are tenoned on the table saw to fit into round holes in the rocker ends
- Screws are counterbored and covered with button plugs

FINISH: Non-toxic clear varnish or paint

Building time

PREPARING STOCK
1 hour

LAYOUT
2 hours

CUTTING PARTS
3-4 hours

ASSEMBLY
2-3 hours

FINISHING
1 hour

TOTAL: 9-11 hours

Tools you'll use

- Table saw
- Band saw
- Drill/driver
- Clamps
- Router with ¼-in. roundover bit
- Drill press
- Drum sander or drill press drum sanding kit
- 1-in. Forstner bit

Shopping list

- ☐ (1) ¾ × 10 in. × 10 ft. knotty pine
- ☐ (1) 1-in.-dia. × 4-ft. dowel
- ☐ #8 × 1½-in. flathead wood screws
- ☐ ⅜-in.-dia. wood buttons
- ☐ Wood glue
- ☐ Finishing materials

Doll Cradle

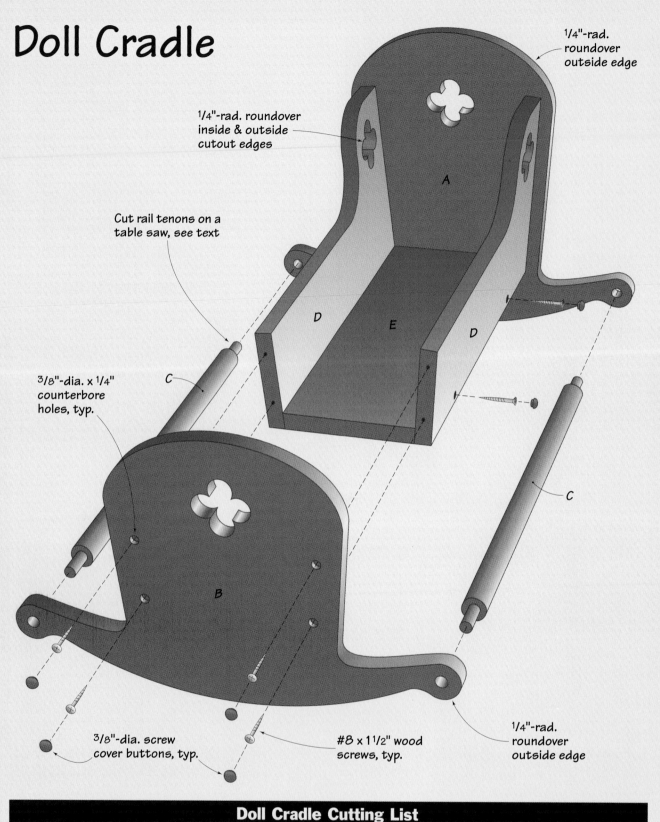

1/4"-rad. roundover outside edge

1/4"-rad. roundover inside & outside cutout edges

Cut rail tenons on a table saw, see text

3/8"-dia. x 1/4" counterbore holes, typ.

A

D

E

D

C

C

B

3/8"-dia. screw cover buttons, typ.

#8 x 1 1/2" wood screws, typ.

1/4"-rad. roundover outside edge

Doll Cradle Cutting List								
Part	**No.**	**Size**	**Material**		**Part**	**No.**	**Size**	**Material**
A. Headboard	1	3/4 × 18 × 14 3/4 in.	Knotty pine		**D.** Sides	2	3/4 × 9 1/4 × 18 in.	Knotty pine
B. Footboard	1	3/4 × 18 × 11 in.	"		**E.** Bottom	1	3/4 × 6 × 18 in.	"
C. Rails	2	1-in. dia. × 20 1/2 in.	Dowel					

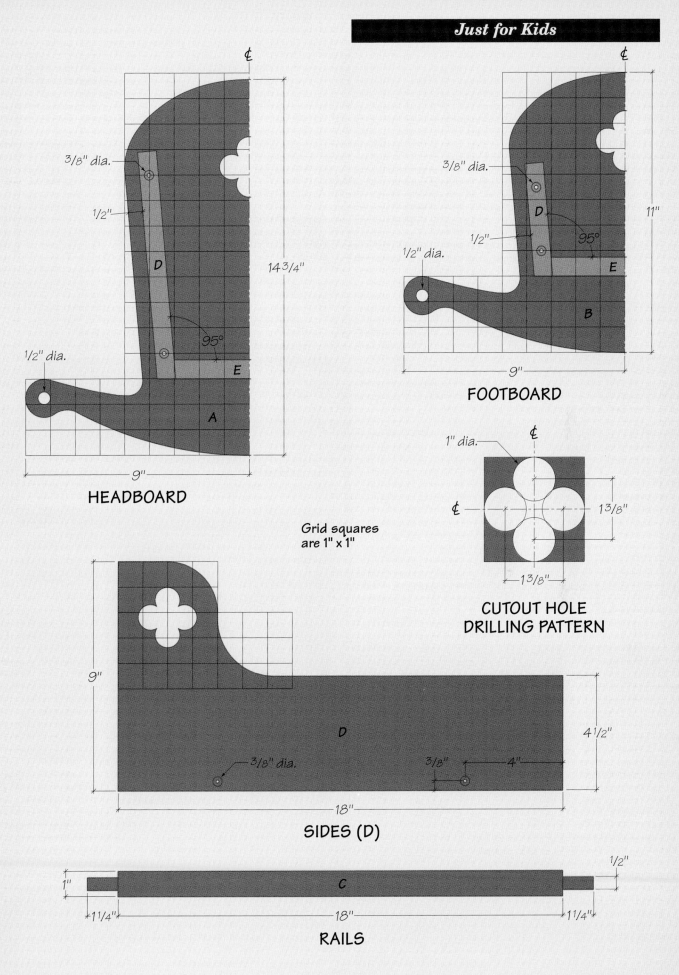

3/8" dia.

1/2"

D

95°

E

1/2" dia.

A

14 3/4"

9"

HEADBOARD

3/8" dia.

D

1/2"

95°

E

1/2" dia.

B

11"

9"

FOOTBOARD

Grid squares
are 1" x 1"

1" dia.

1 3/8"

1 3/8"

**CUTOUT HOLE
DRILLING PATTERN**

9"

D

3/8" dia.

3/8"

4"

4 1/2"

18"

SIDES (D)

1/2"

1"

C

1 1/4"

18"

1 1/4"

RAILS

BUILD THE HEADBOARD & FOOTBOARD

❶ You'll need 18-in.-wide stock for the headboard and footboard. To make blanks for these parts, first joint flat one long edge of your 1 × 10 pine stock. Cross-cut two 14¾-in. lengths for the headboard and two 11-in. pieces for the footboard. Edge-glue and clamp the pairs of boards to form 18½-in.-wide blanks. After the glue dries, sand the blanks smooth.

❷ Cut out the headboard and footboard: Transfer the *Headboard* and *Footboard* patterns on page 313 to your blanks. Cut the headboard and footboard to shape with a band saw or jig saw.

❸ Smooth the edges: Clamp the headboard and footboard together so the edges of the rockers are flush, and gang-sand the rockers on a drum sander **(See Photo A).** This way, the rocker profiles will match. Remove the clamps and sand the rest of the edges. Then, rout around one edge of the headboard and one edge of the footboard with a ¼-in. roundover bit.

❹ Drill holes in the rockers for the rails. Stack the headboard and footboard again so the edges of the rockers are flush, and mark the rail hole locations on the ends of the rockers. Bore ½-in.-dia. holes through both rockers at once on the drill press.

MAKE THE SIDES & BOTTOM

❺ Cut out the sides and bottom: Rip and cross-cut the side and bottom panels to size on the table saw. Then tilt the blade 5° and bevel-cut one long edge of the side panels. Cut the same 5° bevel along both long edges of the bottom. Be careful when bevel-cutting the bottom—the beveled edges need to mirror one another so the sides will cant away from the bottom when the doll cradle is assembled (See the exploded view drawing on page 312).

❻ Cut the top curved profiles in the sides: Transfer the *Sides* grid drawing on page 313 to one of the side panels. Since these profiles match on both side panels, stack the sides together and cut the curves into both workpieces at once on the band saw with the gridded piece on top. Sand the cut edges smooth.

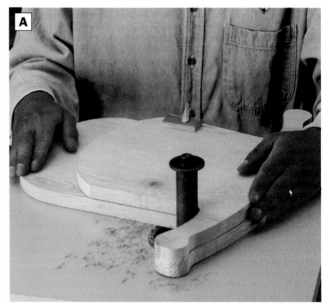

PHOTO A: After the headboard and footboard have been band-sawn to shape, clamp the pieces together so the rockers are flush. Smooth the rocker profiles on the drum sander until they'll match. Then unclamp the parts and smooth the rest of the cut edges.

PHOTO B: Bore four holes to create the cloverleaf cutout pattern in the sides, headboard and footboard. Avoid tearout by clamping a scrap backer board to the drill press table.

DRILL THE CUTOUTS

❼ Drill cutouts in the headboard, footboard and sides: Mark the location of the cutouts on these parts. Then use the *Cutout Hole Drilling Pattern*, page 313, to find the centerpoints for drilling the

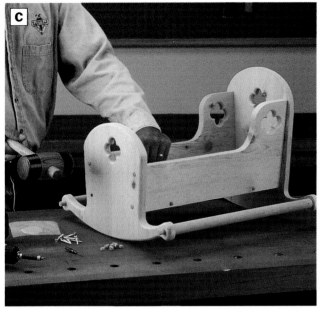

PHOTO C: Assemble the cradle parts with glue and flathead wood screws. Drill counterbored pilot holes to recess the screwheads. Then cover these screwheads with button-style wood plugs. Tap the plugs into their counterbores until they seat fully.

Cutting round tenons

This end of ¾-in. dowel against saw fence

Cutting round dowel tenons is a simple task on the table saw. However, it's a good idea to practice the technique first before milling your actual workpieces to get the feel of it. First, set the fence the length of the dowel, minus the length of the tenon, away from the blade. Adjust the blade height to ¼ in. Set the dowel against the saw fence with the tenon end closest to the blade. Feed the dowel into the blade with the dowel held against the miter gauge. When you've cut about halfway across the dowel thickness, stop the miter gauge and slowly rotate the dowel one complete turn against the miter gauge fence. Repeat this process, resetting the fence a little less than ⅛ in. further away from the blade to remove more waste. The goal is to work your way to the end of the dowel until all waste is removed from the tenon area. CAUTION: *Keep a firm grasp on the dowel at all times, especially when rotating it into the blade.*

---

four holes that make up each cutout. Bore holes for the cutouts through the cradle parts with a 1-in.-dia. Forstner or spade bit on the drill press **(See Photo B)**.

8 Ease the edges of the cutouts: Rout around both edges of each cutout on the headboard, footboard and sides with a ¼-in. piloted roundover bit. Sand these edges to remove any saw marks and router burns.

MAKE THE RAILS
9 Cut tenons on the ends of the rails. Cross-cut the dowel rails to length first, then cut 1¼-in.-long, ½-in.-dia. round tenons on both ends of each rail (See *Cutting Round Tenons,* right). Smooth the tenons with a file and sandpaper, and check their fit in the holes in the rockers. The rails should swivel easily.

ASSEMBLE THE PARTS
10 Sand all the doll cradle parts with 220-grit sandpaper. Then dry-fit the pieces together to check their fit, and adjust as necessary.

11 Glue and screw the cradle together. Refer to the drawings on page 313 to mark pilot holes for attaching the headboard and footboard to the sides, as well as attach the sides to the bottom. Join the sides to the bottom first with glue and 1½-in. flat-

head wood screws driven into counterbored pilot holes. Be sure the sides overlap the edges of the bottom piece. The sides should flare outward. Then set this assembly between the headboard and footboard and slip the rails into their holes in the rockers. Fasten these parts with counterbored wood screws and glue.

FINISHING TOUCHES
12 For a decorative touch, cover all exposed screwheads with ⅜-in. button-style wood plugs, secured with glue **(See Photo C)**.

13 Topcoat the cradle with a clear child-safe finish. We used three coats of satin polyurethane.

Funtime Toy Box

Playroom cleanup tasks will be much easier when kids can "feed" their toys to this whimsical whale toy box. You won't need a whale-sized budget to build this toy box either—all it takes is one sheet of plywood, some rope and a little paint. Rope handles make the lid easy to remove, and the absence of hinges means little fingers will be safe from pinching.

Funtime Toy Box

Vital Statistics

TYPE: Toy box

OVERALL SIZE: 36L by 28H by 21½W

MATERIAL: Birch plywood

JOINERY: Butt joints reinforced with glue and screws

CONSTRUCTION DETAILS:

· The whale shapes are drawn to shape using a 1-in.-square grid pattern marked directly on the plywood

· Both whale sides are cut to shape with the gridded plywood pattern on top

FINISH: Primer and paint

BUILDING TIME: 4-6 hours

Shopping List

☐ ¾ in. × 4 × 8 ft. plywood

☐ Drywall screws (1¼-, 2-in.)

☐ ¾-in.-dia. × 2-ft. nylon rope

☐ Wood glue

☐ Finishing materials

Funtime Toy Box: Step-by-step

MAKE THE WHALE SIDES
To draw the whale profile, you could create a full-size paper template and trace the shape. It's more practical, however, to simply create a grid directly on the plywood, then use the grid drawing shown in the technical art, page 318, to mark points on your plywood grid for drawing the shape.

❶ Cut workpieces for the whale sides according to the *Cutting List,* page 318.

❷ Create a 1-in. square grid pattern on one of the two whale sides using a long T-square or straightedge and a pencil (**See Photo A**).

❸ Use a photocopier to enlarge the *Whale Side Layout* drawing on page 318 for easier reference

PHOTO A: Create a full-size grid with 1-in. squares on one of the whale side blanks with a long T-square or straightedge and pencil.

Funtime Toy Box

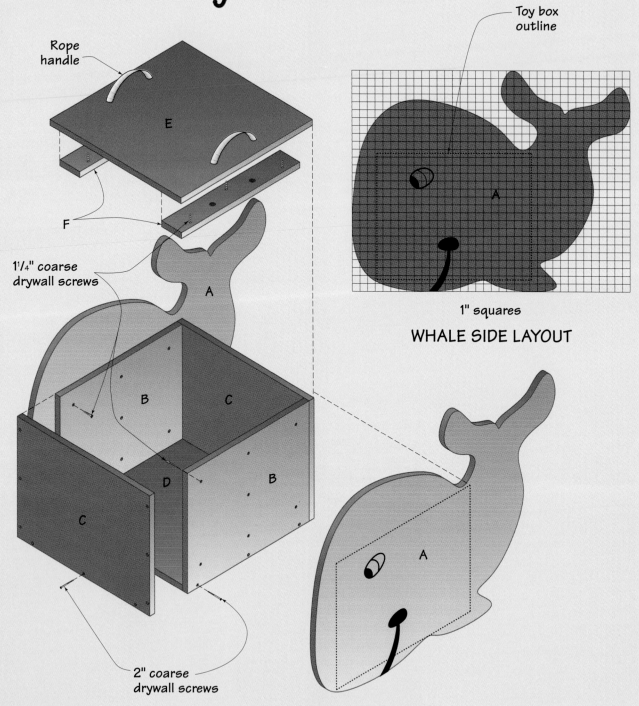

Rope handle

Toy box outline

E

F

1¼" coarse drywall screws

A

B

C

D

B

C

A

2" coarse drywall screws

1" squares

WHALE SIDE LAYOUT

A

Funtime Toy Box Cutting List

Part	No.	Size	Material	Part	No.	Size	Material
A. Whale sides	2	¾ × 28 × 36 in.	Plywood	**D.** Box bottom	1	¾ × 18½ × 18½ in.	"
B. Box sides	2	¾ × 18½ × 15¼ in.	"	**E.** Box lid	1	¾ × 19¾ × 20 in.	"
C. Box front/back	2	¾ × 20 × 15¼ in.	"	**F.** Lid battens	2	¾ × 3 × 18¼ in.	"

when marking your grid.

❹ Mark points on the plywood grid squares that correspond to points on the paper reference to form a "dot-to-dot" pattern of the full-size whale profile. Connect the points with a solid pencil line to draw the whale shape. Follow the same procedure for drawing the whale eye **(See Photo B).**

❺ Cut the whale sides to shape: Stack the gridded whale side on top of the unmarked whale side. Elevate the workpieces off your worksurface with scrap 2 × 4s. Gang-cut both blanks to shape with a jig saw, keeping the workpieces aligned **(See Photo C).** Adjust the supports as needed to keep the cutting path clear.

ASSEMBLE THE BOX

❻ Cut the box sides, front, back and bottom to size.

❼ Build the box: Arrange the box sides, front and back around the box bottom so the front and back panels overlap the ends of the side panels. Apply glue to the mating surfaces of the box and clamp the box together. Reinforce the joints with countersunk 2-in. drywall screws **(See Photo D).**

BUILD THE LID

❽ Cut the plywood lid panel and two battens to size.

❾ Attach the battens to the lid. Lay out the positions of the battens on the lid so the battens are parallel to the 20-in.-long edges of the lid panel. Inset the battens ⅞ in. from the ends of the lid and ¾ in. in from the edges. Spread glue on the battens and drive 1¼-in. drywall screws through the battens into the lid to secure the parts.

PHOTO B: Transfer layout points onto your plywood grid using an enlarged copy of the technical grid drawing as a reference. Connect the "dots" to draw the whale shape. Mark outlines for the eye and mouth as well.

PHOTO C: Stack the side with the grid drawing on top of the other side to gang-cut both whale side workpieces to shape. Raise the workpieces above the worksurface with scraps to provide clear space for the saw blade as you cut.

PHOTO D: Once you've glued and clamped the box sides, front and back around the box bottom, drill countersunk pilot holes and reinforce the joints with 2-in. drywall screws.

Scrap

PHOTO E: Drill through the lid and battens for the rope handles. Use a spade bit of the same diameter as the rope you've chosen. Back up the hole you're drilling with scrap to reduce tearout.

PHOTO F: Paint the primary project color first on the whale sides, but leave the mouth and the black and white areas of the eye as primer only. Paint the mouth black. Then cut out regions of your paper eye template and use the template as a guide for finishing the eye details. A fine-tipped artist's brush is helpful for painting the small details.

⑩ Drill pairs of holes in the lid for the rope handles: Locate each pair of holes 2 in. in from the long edges of the lid, spaced about 6 in. apart. Bore holes through the lid and battens (**See Photo E**).

PAINT THE TOY BOX

⑪ Fill the screwhead recesses and any plywood voids with wood putty. Sand the parts smooth.

⑫ Trace a paper template of the eye shape off of the gridded plywood whale side to use as a guide.

⑬ Prime and paint the lid, toy box and whale sides with the primary project color.

⑭ Paint the mouth and eye details. Cut out regions of the paper eye template as needed to help you paint the black and white eye areas (**See Photo F**).

FINISHING TOUCHES

⑮ Fasten the toy box to the whale sides: Center the toy box between the whale sides, using the *Whale Side Layout* drawing, page 318, as a guide. Support the toy box from beneath with scrap, and clamp the parts together. Drive 1¼-in. screws through the box and into the sides (**See Photo G**).

⑯ Make the handles: Cut two 10-in. lengths of nylon rope, tape the ends and thread the rope through the lid holes. Secure the handles with knots tied under the lid battens (**See Photo H**). Singe the ends of the rope with a flame to minimize fraying.

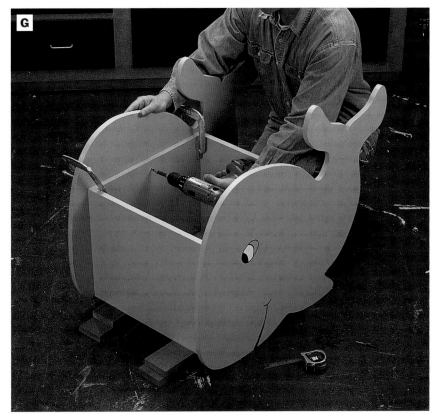

PHOTO G: Elevate the box on scrap blocks to attach the whale sides. Once you've positioned the parts properly, hold them in place with clamps and protective clamp pads. Attach the toy box to the whale sides with 1¼-in. drywall screws driven from inside the box.

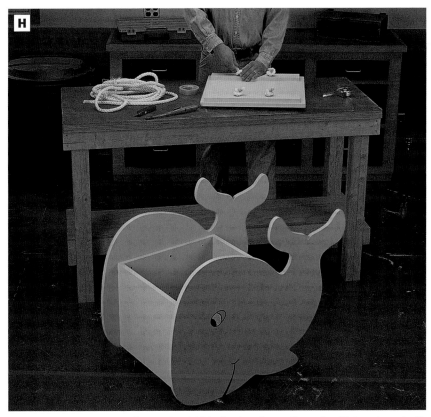

PHOTO H: Cut the rope handles to about 10 in. long, and wrap the ends with tape to make it easier to feed the ends through the lid holes. Insert the ropes in the lid and knot the ends.

Planters

Deck plants provide a graceful transition from the distinctly indoor space of your home to the distinctly outdoor space of your yard. Attractive planters filled with flowers, herbs and shrubs can transform your deck into a cozy and inviting outdoor "room." These planters are designed to be used either as enclosures for potted plants or to be lined with landscape fabric and filled with dirt. We built these planters for a cedar deck; for best results, build yours from the same material as your deck.

Vital Statistics: Planters

TYPE: Deck and railing planters

OVERALL SIZE: Railing planter: $7\frac{1}{4}$W by $35\frac{1}{4}$L by $7\frac{1}{4}$H

Deck planter: 16W by $20\frac{1}{2}$L by $15\frac{1}{8}$H

MATERIAL: Cedar, exterior plywood

JOINERY: Butt joints reinforced with galvanized finish nails and screws

CONSTRUCTION DETAILS:

· Railing planter fits over standard 2 × 6 railing cap

· Recessed bottoms and weep holes improve air circulation and drainage on both planters

FINISHING OPTIONS: UV protectant sealer, exterior paint or leave unfinished to weather naturally to gray

Building time

PREPARING STOCK
0 hours

LAYOUT
1-2 hours

CUTTING PARTS
1-2 hours

ASSEMBLY
2-3 hours

FINISHING
1-2 hours

TOTAL: 5-9 hours

Tools you'll use

· Circular saw

· Jig saw

· Drill/driver

· Clamps

· Hammer

· Nailset

Shopping list

☐ (3) 1 × 8 in. × 8 ft. cedar

☐ (1) $\frac{3}{4}$ × 12 × 12 in. exterior plywood

☐ Galvanized deck screws ($1\frac{1}{4}$-in.)

☐ Galvanized finish nails (2-in.)

☐ UV protectant sealer

Planters

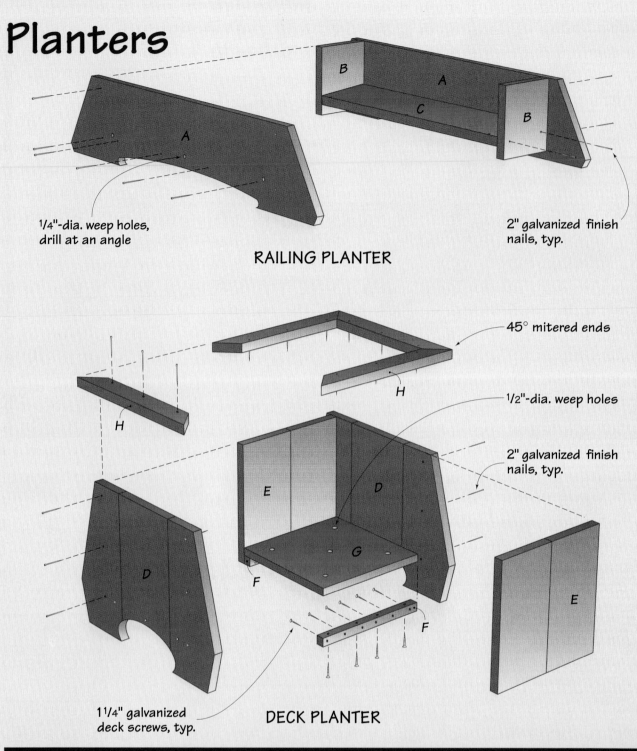

¼"-dia. weep holes, drill at an angle

2" galvanized finish nails, typ.

RAILING PLANTER

45° mitered ends

½"-dia. weep holes

2" galvanized finish nails, typ.

1¼" galvanized deck screws, typ.

DECK PLANTER

Planters Cutting List

Part	No.	Size	Material	Part	No.	Size	Material
Railing Planter				**Deck Planter**			
A. Sides	2	⅞ x 7¼ x 35¼ in.	Cedar	**D.** Sides	2	⅞ × 20½ × 14¼ in.	Cedar
B. Ends	2	⅞ x 5½ x 6½ in.	"	**E.** Ends	2	⅞ × 12 × 12 in.	"
C. Bottom	1	⅞ x 5⁷⁄₁₆ x 24 in.	"	**F.** Cleats	2	⅞ × ⅞ × 12 in.	"
				G. Bottom	1	¾ × 12 × 12 in.	Exterior plywood
				H. Crown	4	⅞ × 2 × 16 in.	Cedar

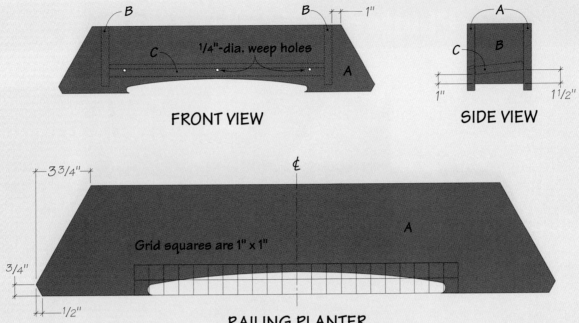

B ⌐ B ⌐ 1"

C ¼"-dia. weep holes A

FRONT VIEW

A ⌐ C B 1" 1½"

SIDE VIEW

3¾"

₵

Grid squares are 1" x 1" A

3/4"

1/2"

RAILING PLANTER

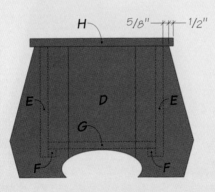

H 5/8" 1/2"

E D E

G

F F

FRONT VIEW

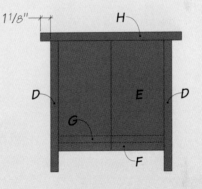

1⅛" H

D E D

G

F

SIDE VIEW

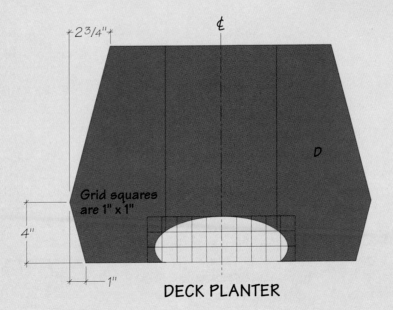

2¾"

₵

Grid squares are 1" x 1"

D

4"

1"

DECK PLANTER

Cedar lumber is typically sold with one side rough and one side smooth. This feature provides you the opportunity to choose which surface to emphasize in the finished planters. For these planters, we held the rough side out because we wanted a casual, rustic look. If you prefer, you can achieve a more refined look simply by building your planters with the smooth surface out. If you intend to paint your finished planters, we recommend building with the smooth side out.

RAILING PLANTER
CUT OUT THE PARTS

❶ Make a template for marking the two side profiles. Cut a piece of hardboard or stiff cardboard to size, 7¼ in. by 35¼ in., for use as a pattern. Following the *Railing Planter* drawing on page 325, mark the angles on the ends and the curved cutout profile on the bottom edge. Cut the template to shape with a jig saw and sand the cuts smooth.

❷ Trace the profile from the template onto the side workpieces.

❸ Cut out the sides. Clamp the blanks securely to your workbench and cut the profiles with your jig saw (See Photo A).

❹ Cut the ends and bottom to size, according to the dimensions in the *Cutting List* on page 324.

ASSEMBLE THE PLANTER

❺ Attach the ends to the bottom. The bottom is sloped to route seepage water away from

PHOTO A: Lay out and cut a template for making the sides of the railing planter, then use this template to draw the shapes on the side workpieces. Cut out the shapes with a jig saw.

your deck railing cap. Refer to the *Side View* drawing, page 325, and mark the slope of the bottom piece on the inside faces of the ends. Drill pilot holes in the ends. Clamp the bottom in place between the ends, and attach the parts with 2-in. galvanized finish nails (See Photo B).

❻ Attach the sides. Lay the end/bottom assembly on your workbench. Center the first side piece on the assembly left-to-right with all top edges flush. Clamp it in place. Note that the lower edges of the end pieces are ¾ in. above the lower edges of the sides; this allows the planter to rest on the railing cap while the sides overlap it for stability.

Attach the side by driving galvanized finish nails through the side into the ends and the bottom. Use a nailset to recess the nailheads. Follow the same procedure to position and attach the remaining side.

❼ Drill the weep holes. Clamp the assembled planter to your worksurface with the deeper side of the compartment facing up. Drill three angled ¼-in.-dia. weep holes through the side of the planter into the deepest corner of the compartment (See Photo C). Position the weep holes so they are just above the bottom piece inside the planter.

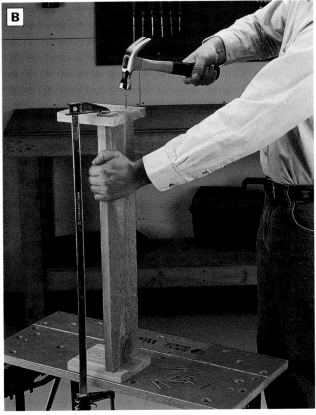

PHOTO B: Mark the slope of the bottom piece on the planter end pieces, then attach the ends to the bottom with galvanized finish nails. Clamp the pieces to help hold them steady during assembly.

PHOTO C: Fasten the planter sides to the ends and bottom with nails, then drill three angled ¼-in.-dia. weep holes through the side where the bottom of the planter slopes to its lowest point.

DECK PLANTER
MAKE THE SIDE PANELS

Each side panel is composed of three boards, which are held together during the construction process by a temporary cleat.

❶ Cut six pieces of 1 × 8 cedar to 14½ in. long (you'll need three pieces for each side).

❷ Cut two temporary cleats (not shown on the *Cutting List*) 13½ in. long from scrap wood.

❸ Build the sides. Lay groups of three boards facedown on your workbench in two groups. Center a temporary cleat left-to-right along the top edge of each group of boards, and fasten each panel together by driving 1¼-in. wood screws through the cleat into the boards.

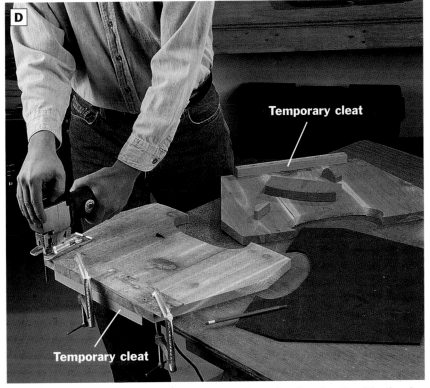

PHOTO D: Assemble two blanks for the deck planter sides using three lengths of 1 × 8 cedar per blank, fastened together with a temporary cleat. Mark the profiles on the side pieces with a template, then cut the sides to shape. You'll remove the temporary cleats later.

PHOTO E: Clamp pairs of 6-in.-wide boards for the end panels and fasten each panel together with a cleat. Use 1¼-in. galvanized screws to join the parts. These two cleats are permanent parts of the planter.

PHOTO F: Cut the bottom piece to size, drill five weep holes through the bottom for drainage, and fasten it to the cleats on the end pieces with countersunk screws. Attach the bottom so it will rest on the cleats when the planter is finished.

❹ Make a template for marking the profiles of the two sides. Cut a piece of hardboard or stiff cardboard 14¼ in. wide by 20½ in. long. Following the *Deck Planter* drawing on page 325, mark the angles on the ends and the shape of the curved cutout along the bottom edge. Cut the template to shape with a jig saw and sand the cut edges smooth.

❺ Trace the profile from the template onto the side panels. Draw on the face of the panels that does not have the cleats. Clamp each panel securely to your workbench and cut the parts with a jig saw **(See Photo D).**

MAKE THE ENDS & BOTTOM

The end panels are each composed of two boards fastened together with a permanent cleat.

❻ Rip a 4-ft., 1-in. length of 1×8 cedar to 6 in. wide. Cut the ripped board into four 12-in. lengths. Lay each pair of boards facedown on your workbench and clamp them together with the ends flush.

❼ Cut two pieces of scrap left over from Step 6 to ⅞ × ⅞ × 12 in. to form two cleats. Drill countersunk pilot holes in the cleats.

❽ Assemble the end panels by positioning a cleat flush with the bottom edges of each pair of boards and fastening the parts with 1¼-in. galvanized deck screws, screwing through the cleats into the end panels **(See Photo E).**

❾ Cut the bottom to size from ¾-in. exterior plywood. Draw intersecting lines from corner to corner to use as a guide for locating and drilling five ½-in.-dia. weep holes.

ASSEMBLE THE PLANTER

10 Attach the end panels to the bottom. Clamp the bottom in place between the ends so it will rest on top of the cleats when the planter is right-side-up. Drill through the cleats from below to fasten the bottom **(See Photo F).**

11 Attach the sides. Position the first side panel on the end/bottom assembly so it is centered left-to-right and the top edges are all flush. Drive 2-in. galvanized finish nails through the side panel into the ends and the bottom, using a nailset to drive the nails below the surface of the wood. Attach the remaining side in the same fashion **(See Photo G).**

12 Unscrew and remove the temporary cleats from the side panels.

13 Cut the four crown pieces. Rip cedar stock to 2 in. wide. Measure your planter to verify the length of the crown pieces. The inside edges of the crown should sit flush with the inside of the planter when installed. Cut the pieces to length with the ends mitered at 45°.

14 Attach the crown pieces to the planter with finish nails **(See Photo H).**

FINISHING TOUCHES FOR BOTH PLANTERS

15 Break all edges with sandpaper and check that all nailheads are set. You may choose to leave the planters unfinished, apply the same finish as you have on your deck, or topcoat with paint.

PHOTO G: Fasten the sides to the end/bottom assembly by nailing through the sides and into the ends and bottom. Drill pilot holes before you drive the nails to keep the cedar from splitting. Once both sides are attached, remove the temporary cleats.

PHOTO H: Install the four crown pieces around the top of the planter with nails. Lay out and cut the crown pieces so they are mitered on the ends and fit flush with the inside of the planter.

Daytripper Chair

This two-part chair is made up of two interlocking and removable substructures that nestle one inside the other for easy storage or portability. When set up, it is as handsome as it is sturdy and comfortable. This chair will be equally at home on your deck, on the sidelines of the soccer field or in your living room, if you're ever in need of extra seating.

See pages 336-343 for plans on how to build a matching table to accompany this Daytripper Chair project. The table folds down to nearly flat for storage and transport.

Vital Statistics: Daytripper Chair

TYPE: Daytripper chair

OVERALL SIZE: 23W by 30L by 30½H

MATERIAL: Red oak, pressure-treated pine

JOINERY: Butt joints reinforced with galvanized deck screws

CONSTRUCTION DETAILS:

· Back and seat supports built from treated lumber for strength

· Oak plugs conceal screws in slats

· Handle integrated into top two back slats

· Chair disassembles for ease of storage and transport

FINISHING OPTIONS: Danish oil or a penetrating UV protectant sealer, exterior latex paint

Building time

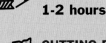

PREPARING STOCK
0 hours

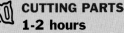

LAYOUT
1-2 hours

CUTTING PARTS
1-2 hours

ASSEMBLY
4-6 hours

FINISHING
2-3 hours

TOTAL: 8-13 hours

Tools you'll use

· Band saw or jig saw

· Circular saw or power miter saw

· Router with ⅛-in. roundover bit, ½-in. straight bit

· Drill/driver

· Drill press

· ⅜-in. plug cutter

· Compass

· Mallet

· Clamps

Shopping list

☐ (1) ¾ × 10 in. × 8 ft. pressure-treated pine

☐ (1) ¾ × 8 in. × 8 ft. pressure-treated pine

☐ (2) ¾ × 4¾ in. × 8 ft. red oak

☐ Galvanized deck screws (1½-in.)

☐ Moisture-resistant wood glue

☐ Danish oil or penetrating UV protectant sealer

☐ Latex primer

☐ Exterior latex paint

Daytripper Chair

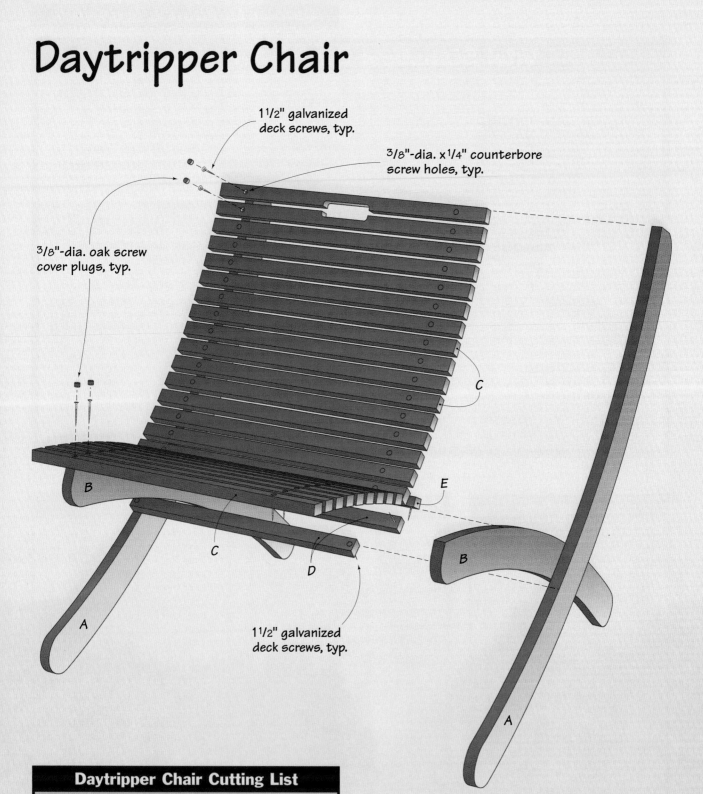

1 1/2" galvanized deck screws, typ.

3/8"-dia. x 1/4" counterbore screw holes, typ.

3/8"-dia. oak screw cover plugs, typ.

B

C

A

C

D

E

B

A

1 1/2" galvanized deck screws, typ.

Daytripper Chair Cutting List

Part	No.	Size	Material
A. Back supports	2	$3/4 \times 7^5/8 \times 41$ in.	Treated pine
B. Seat supports	2	$3/4 \times 5^5/8 \times 32^1/2$ in.	"
C. Slats	25	$3/4 \times 1 \times 23$ in.	Red oak
D. Inner crossbar	2	$3/4 \times 2 \times 19$ in.	"
E. Outer crossbar	1	$3/4 \times 1 \times 17$ in.	"
F. Short crossbar	1	$3/4 \times 1 \times 17$ in.	"

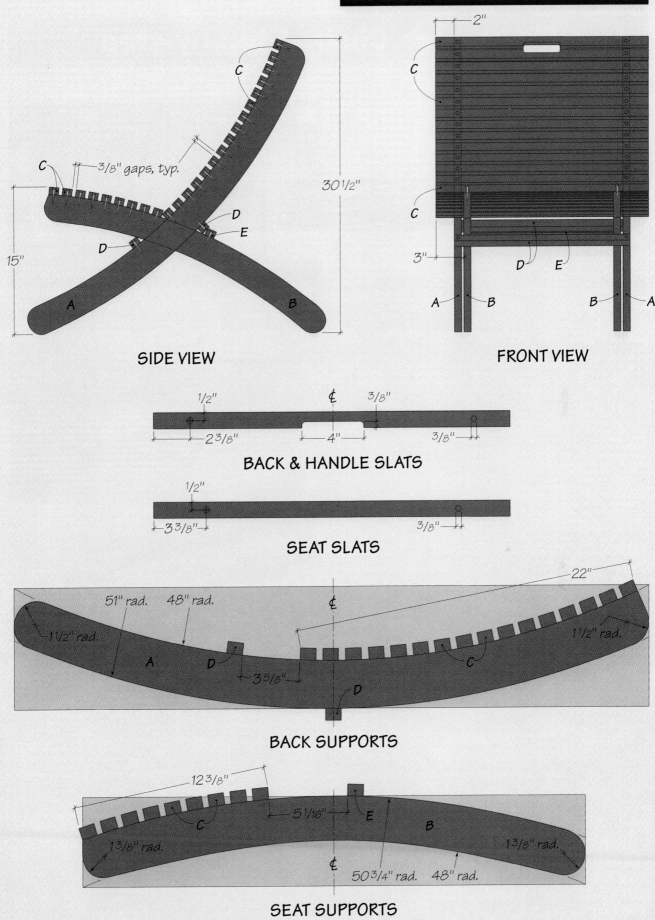

C

3/8" gaps, typ.

C

30 1/2"

D

E

15"

D

A

B

SIDE VIEW

2"

C

C

3"

D

E

A   B   B   A

FRONT VIEW

1/2"   ℄   3/8"

2 3/8"   4"   3/8"

BACK & HANDLE SLATS

1/2"

3 3/8"   3/8"

SEAT SLATS

22"

51" rad.   48" rad.   ℄

1 1/2" rad.   1 1/2" rad.

A   D   C

3 5/8"

D

BACK SUPPORTS

12 3/8"

5 1/16"   E

C   B

1 3/8" rad.   1 3/8" rad.

50 3/4" rad.   48" rad.

℄

SEAT SUPPORTS

CUT OUT THE PARTS

① Cut two back supports and two seat supports to size and shape. To ensure identical pairs, use templates made from ¼-in. hardboard to trace profiles onto the workpieces **(See Photo A).** Follow the dimensions shown in the *Back Supports* and *Seat Supports* drawings, page 333. Before cutting out the back supports, measure and mark the centerline to use later as a reference line for crossbar installation.

② Paint the supports. Sand the surfaces and edges well. Apply a coat of latex primer, then two coats of exterior latex paint. Transfer the centerline reference mark on the back supports to the painted surfaces.

③ Make the slats and crossbars. Cut blanks to length from ¾-in. oak stock. Set the fence on your table saw to rip the 1-in.-wide slats and crossbars. Re-set the fence to cut the 2-in.-wide, inner long crossbar.

④ Drill counterbored pilot holes in the back slats and seat slats for attaching these parts to the supports later. Designate 16 slats as the back slats and the remaining nine slats for the seat. Drill a pilot hole 2⅜ in. from each end of the back slats, so the counterbore portion of each hole is ⅜ in. deep. This is easiest to do using a depth setting on a drill press. At the same drill press depth setting, drill a pilot hole 3⅜ in. from each end of the seat slats.

⑤ Make the crossbars. Cross-cut the two long crossbars and the short crossbar to length from the 1-in. stock you ripped in Step 3. Drill counterbored pilot holes for screws ⅜ in. from each end.

⑥ Rout a ⅛-in. roundover on the edges and ends of one face of the slats and crossbars **(See Photo B).** The proportions of these parts are too narrow to rout "freehand" with a router, so shape these parts on a router table with a pin-style guide installed.

⑦ Rout a "handle" in the adjoining edges of two back slats (See *Back & Handle Slats*, page 333), using a ½-in. straight bit in the router table and cutting a ⅜ × 4-in. centered notch in both slats **(See Photo C).**

PHOTO A: Create seat and back support templates from hardboard, and use these templates to draw the profiles on the back and seat support workpieces (use treated lumber, not plywood as shown). Cut out the parts with a jig saw.

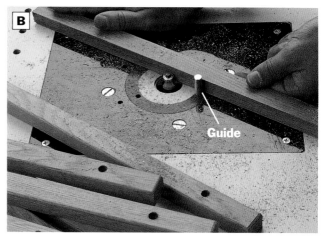

PHOTO B: Ease the edges and ends of the slats and crossbars with a ⅛-in. roundover bit in the router table. Use a pin-style guide on the router table to help control the workpieces as you machine them.

ASSEMBLE THE BACK

⑧ Cut two 17½-in.-long spacers from scrap, and clamp them between the back supports to hold the supports in place. Use a carpenter's square to verify that the ends of the supports are even with one another. Set the assembly concave-side-up.

⑨ Attach the back slats. Screw the top slat in place, holding the upper edge flush with the top corners of the back supports and the handle profile facing inward. Measure from the attached slat (See *Back Supports* drawing, page 333) and mark the location of the lowest back slat. Screw this slat in place.

⑩ Verify the spacing of the remaining back slats

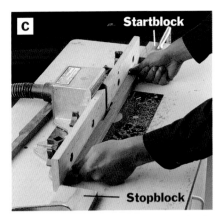

PHOTO C: Make handle cutouts in two back slats using a router table and straight bit. Install start- and stopblocks to limit the length of cut when routing these recesses.

PHOTO D: When installing the back and seat slats to the supports, clamp scrap spacers between the supports to keep them aligned.

PHOTO E: Cover exposed screwheads on the slats and crossbars with oak plugs. Glue and insert the plugs, trim them and sand smooth.

between the top and bottom slats (about ½ in.). Attach these 15 back slats with 1½-in. galvanized deck screws, starting from the top with the slat that completes the handle cutout.

11 Install the inner long crossbar. Measure 3⅝ in. from the lowest back slat to position the crossbar. Screw the crossbar in place.

ASSEMBLE THE SEAT

12 Follow the same procedure as for the back assembly. Cut two spacers 15½ in. long, and clamp them between the seat supports.

13 Screw the front seat slat in place, with the edge flush with the top corners of the seat supports.

14 Measure 12⅜ in. from the attached seat slat, and mark the location of the last seat slat. Screw this slat in place.

15 Verify the spacing of the remaining seat slats (approximately ⅜ in.), and attach the rest of the slats with 1½-in. galvanized deck screws **(See Photo D).**

ASSEMBLE THE CHAIR

16 Plug all of the screw holes. Cut ⅜-in.-dia. oak plugs with a plug cutter. Glue and tap the plugs into place **(See Photo E).** Trim and sand the plugs flush.

17 Attach the outer long crossbar in place on the back support centerline you drew in Step 1.

18 Slide the seat into position between the back supports. Use C-clamps at the intersections of the

supports to hold the two assemblies in place. Mark the correct locations for the short crossbar **(See Photo F).** It should rest against the outer long crossbar. Attach the crossbar with galvanized deck screws. Then plug, trim and sand the crossbar screw holes.

FINISHING TOUCHES

19 Break all edges on the raw oak parts thoroughly with sandpaper. Mask off the painted surfaces of the supports, and cover the slats with Danish oil or a UV protectant sealer.

PHOTO F: Slide the seat assembly into the back assembly and use C-clamps to hold the chair together. Set the short crossbar against the lower long crossbar, mark its position, and install it with screws.

Daytripper Table

This folding table goes anywhere and stores easily, yet it has the look of fine furniture. Its contrasting base and top and its neatly plugged screw holes highlight both stylishness in conception and craftsmanship in construction. You can easily alter this versatile design to suit your decor by simply changing the species of wood for the top slats, the color of paint on the table subassembly or both.

See pages 330-335 for plans on how to build a matching chair to complement this Daytripper Table project. The chair pulls apart into two sections that nest one inside the other for storage.

Vital Statistics: Daytripper Table

TYPE: Folding table

OVERALL SIZE: 16W by 22L by 16H

MATERIAL: Red oak, exterior plywood

JOINERY: Butt joints reinforced with galvanized deck screws

CONSTRUCTION DETAILS:

· Legs made of plywood for strength

· Screws concealed with matching wood plugs on oak parts

· Table folds flat by way of pivot dowels on the stretchers and legs

FINISHING OPTIONS: Penetrating UV protectant sealer, exterior latex paint

Building time

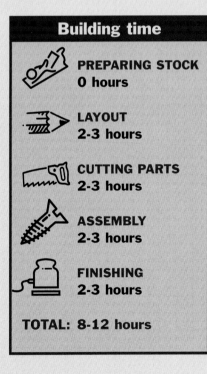

PREPARING STOCK
0 hours

LAYOUT
2-3 hours

CUTTING PARTS
2-3 hours

ASSEMBLY
2-3 hours

FINISHING
2-3 hours

TOTAL: 8-12 hours

Tools you'll use

· Band saw or jig saw

· Drill press

· Table saw

· Circular saw or power miter saw

· Compass

· Drill/driver

· Clamps

Shopping list

☐ (1) ³⁄₄ in. × 4 × 4 ft. exterior plywood

☐ (1) ³⁄₄ × 3¹⁄₂ in. × 8 ft. red oak

☐ (2) ³⁄₄-in.-dia. × 36-in. hardwood dowel

☐ (1) ¹⁄₄-in.-dia. × 36-in. hardwood dowel

☐ Galvanized deck screws (1¹⁄₂-in.)

☐ #6d galvanized finish nails

☐ UV protectant sealer

☐ Latex primer

☐ Exterior latex paint

Daytripper Table

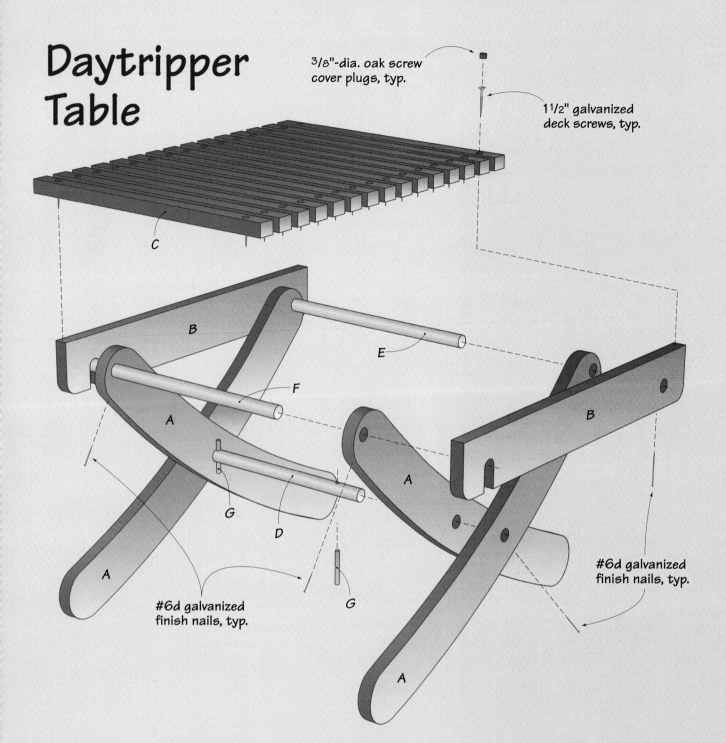

3/8"-dia. oak screw cover plugs, typ.

1 1/2" galvanized deck screws, typ.

C

B

E

F

A

G

D

A

G

#6d galvanized finish nails, typ.

B

A

#6d galvanized finish nails, typ.

A

Daytripper Table Cutting List

Part	No.	Size	Material
A. Legs	4	$3/4 \times 4 1/4 \times 25$ in.	Exterior plywood
B. Stretchers	2	$3/4 \times 3 \times 21 1/2$ in.	"
C. Slats	15	$3/4 \times 1 \times 16$ in.	Oak
D. Leg pivot dowel	1	$3/4$ dia. $\times 12 7/16$ in.	Hardwood
E. Table pivot dowel	1	$3/4$ dia. $\times 14 1/8$ in.	"
F. Table lock dowel	1	$3/4$ dia. $\times 14 1/8$ in.	"
G. Lock dowels	2	$1/4$ dia. $\times 1 1/4$ in.	"

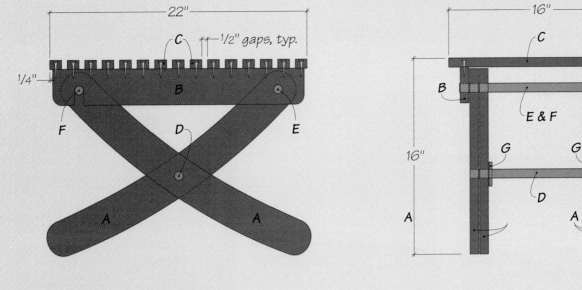

22"

C
1/2" gaps, typ.

1/4"

B

F   D   E

A   A

SIDE VIEW

16"

C

B   1"

E & F   B

G   G

16"

D

A   A

END VIEW

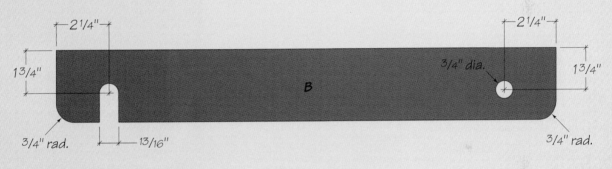

2 1/4"   2 1/4"

1 3/4"   3/4" dia.   1 3/4"

B

3/4" rad.   13/16"   3/4" rad.

STRETCHERS

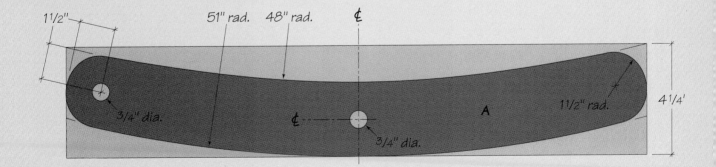

1 1/2"   51" rad.   48" rad.   ¢

3/4" dia.   ¢   1 1/2" rad.   4 1/4'

3/4" dia.   A

LEGS

MAKE THE LEGS

❶ Lay out one leg on a piece of 3/4-in. exterior plywood, cut it to shape, and use it as a template for the other three legs. To lay out the leg, draw two 3-in.-dia. circles with their centerpoints 22 in. apart. Mark the midpoint between the circles with a perpendicular line, for use later in locating the hole for the leg pivot dowel. Clamp the workpiece to your workbench and extend the perpendicular line you just drew onto the benchtop. Use this line as the pivot point for connecting the circles with a 48-in.-radius arc for the inner curve of the leg and a 51-in.-radius arc for the outer curve (See the *Legs* drawing, page 339). Drill a 1/16-in. locater hole through the centerpoints of the two dowel holes in the leg. Cut out the leg and sand the cut edges smooth.

❷ Trace the leg template onto three plywood leg blanks. Mark the centerpoints of the leg dowel holes by drilling through the locater holes in the template.

❸ Cut out the legs **(See Photo A),** and sand the profiles smooth.

❹ Drill the dowel holes in the legs **(See Photo B).** It is important that these holes be bored straight, so use a drill press or right-angle drill guide.

MAKE THE STRETCHERS & SLATS

❺ Cut the stretchers to size and shape. Start by cutting two plywood blanks to length and width. Mark the centerpoints of the

PHOTO A: Lay out and cut the four table legs on the band saw or with a jig saw. Since the profiles of the legs match, mark and cut one to serve as a template for tracing the profiles onto the other three leg blanks.

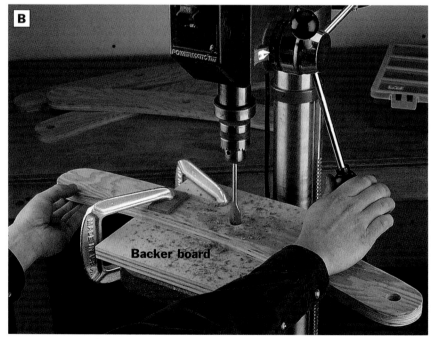

PHOTO B: Bore the 3/4-in.-dia. leg pivot and lock dowel holes in the legs. These holes must be drilled straight through the legs, or the dowels will be difficult to align during assembly. Bore the holes with a drill press, or mount your drill/driver in a right-angle drill guide. Set a backer board beneath each workpiece before you drill, to keep the bit from tearing out the wood as it exits.

pivot dowel hole and the hole
that will form the base of the
lock dowel slot on each stretcher
(See *Stretchers* drawing, page 339).
Draw the ¾-in. radiused corners
and cut them with your jig saw.

❻ Drill the dowel holes. Note
that the diameter of the hole
that will become the slot for the
table lock dowel is ¹³/₁₆ in., so
that the lock dowel can move
freely in and out of the slot. Use
a drill press or right-angle drill
guide to bore these holes as
straight as possible.

❼ Cut the lock dowel slots in the
stretchers **(See Photo C).** Use a
combination square to draw lines
from the outer edges of the ¹³/₁₆-
in. lock dowel hole to the edge of
the stretcher with the curved corners. Clamp the stretcher to your
worksurface, and cut along the
lines to make the slots.

❽ Finish the legs and stretchers. Fill any voids in the edges of
the plywood with wood putty or
auto body filler. Sand the parts
smooth. Prime the legs and
stretchers with a high-quality
latex primer. After the primer
dries, apply two coats of exterior
latex paint.

❾ Make the slats. Cross-cut six
16-in.-long blanks from red oak
stock. Set the fence on your table
saw 1 in. from the blade, and rip
the 15 slats to width.

❿ Drill counterbored pilot holes
in the slats. Make a right-angle
jig for your drill press to index
placement of the screw holes.
Clamp the jig in place so the
pilot holes are centered on the
slats and inset 1⅜ in. from the
ends **(See Photo D).** Set the
depth stop on the drill press so

PHOTO C: Connect the lock dowel hole with straight lines to the edge of each stretcher, forming the lock dowel slots. Clamp the legs to your worksurface and cut along these lines. The width of the slots should be ¹³/₁₆ in., to provide a loose fit for the ¾-in.-dia. lock dowel.

PHOTO D: Build a right-angle jig from scrap to help index placement of the counterbored holes in the ends of the slats. Clamp the jig to the drill press table so each slat is exactly aligned for drilling when you lay it in the jig. This way, there's no need to measure and mark each slat hole.

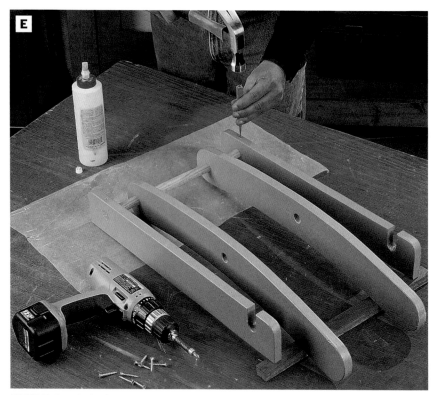

PHOTO E: Attach the first tabletop slat to the stretchers with screws. Lay the outer legs between the stretchers, and slide the table pivot dowel through the stretchers and outer legs. Pin the dowel in place with glue and finish nails driven into the dowel through the stretchers. Do not glue or nail the outer legs to the table pivot dowel.

PHOTO F: Install the inner legs between the outer legs, and insert the leg pivot dowel through the center dowel holes in the legs. Cut and insert the table lock dowel through the inner legs. Pin the table lock dowel to the inner legs and the leg pivot dowel to the outer legs with finish nails.

the counterbored portion of the holes is ¼ in. deep, to allow for inserting wood plugs later.

⑪ Round-over the edges and ends on one face of all the slats. The quickest method for doing this is to use a ⅛-in. piloted roundover bit in the router table. Or, you could ease these edges and ends with a sander instead.

ASSEMBLE THE TABLE
⑫ Attach the first slat to the stretchers to help establish their alignment during assembly. Start at the end with the lock dowel slot. Position the slat so it overhangs the outside faces of the stretchers by 1 in. and the ends of the stretchers by ¼ in. Fasten the slat in place with 1½-in. galvanized deck screws.

⑬ Install the table pivot dowel. Cut the dowel to length, and slip it through the end holes in the outer legs and stretchers. Assemble the parts so the concave profiles of the outer legs will face the tabletop slats. Fasten the dowel with glue and a #6d galvanized finish nail driven through each stretcher (**See Photo E**). Drill ¹⁄₁₆-in. pilot holes before driving the nails. Once fastened, the pivot dowel holds the tabletop frame in shape.

⑭ Attach the remaining table slats with screws. Start with the other end slat, overhanging it ¼ in. beyond the ends of the stretchers. Space the 13 intermediate slats ½ in. apart, with all ends lined up. Use spacers to help establish even gaps as you attach the slats.

⑮ Install the inner legs. With the table facedown on your work-surface, position the inner legs by setting them concave-side-down between the outer legs and sliding the leg pivot dowel through the center dowel holes in the legs.

16 Cut and fasten the table lock dowel to the inner legs. Space the inner legs by sliding them lightly against the inner faces of the outer legs. Insert the lock dowel through the end holes in the inner legs and position it so there is an equal overhang on each side. Fasten the lock dowel by drilling a pilot hole through the end of each leg and driving a finish nail into the dowel.

17 Fasten the leg pivot dowel. Drill a pilot hole into each outer leg, and drive a finish nail through the pilot hole into the dowel (**See Photo F**).

18 Install lock dowels through the leg pivot dowel. The lock dowels hold the inner legs in place against the outer legs. It's important to leave enough space between the two pairs of legs for easy movement when the legs are opened or closed. With the assembled table facedown on your worksurface, drill ¼-in.-dia. pilot holes through the pivot dowel (**See Photo G**). Cut the lock dowels to length, coat them with glue, and insert them.

FINISHING TOUCHES

19 Insert oak plugs with glue into the screw holes in the slats, let dry, and sand the plugged areas smooth. You could use wood filler instead of plugs, but the result will be less visually appealing.

20 Mask off painted surfaces of the table, and apply Danish oil or another clear exterior finish to the dowels and slats (**See Photo H**).

PHOTO G: Lock the inner legs in place by drilling and inserting ¼-in.-dia. dowels through the leg pivot dowel. Position the lock dowels to leave a slight bit of room between the legs, so they can move easily past one another without damaging the painted finish of the parts.

PHOTO H: Coat all raw wood, including the dowels, with Danish oil or another clear exterior-rated wood finish to protect the wood from UV rays and moisture exposure. Use masking tape to keep painted surfaces clean when you brush the slats and dowels with wood finish.

Basic Adirondack Chair

No piece of outdoor furniture conjures up an image of elegance and rugged outdoor comfort quite like the Adirondack chair. There are many variations of this American classic. This design features a straightforward concept and easy-to-work materials for a satisfying project that can be built in a day, yet provide years of enjoyment.

Vital Statistics: Basic Adirondack Chair

TYPE: Adirondack chair

OVERALL SIZE: $36\frac{1}{2}$W by 37D by $37\frac{1}{2}$H

MATERIAL: Cedar

JOINERY: Butt joints reinforced with galvanized deck screws

CONSTRUCTION DETAILS:

· Largely square, straight cuts can be made with simple hand or power tools

· Chair made entirely from dimension lumber

· Exposed screws throughout to enhance rustic appearance

FINISHING OPTIONS: Penetrating UV protectant sealer, exterior paint or leave unfinished to weather naturally to gray

Building time

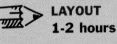

PREPARING STOCK
0 hours

LAYOUT
1-2 hours

CUTTING PARTS
2-4 hours

ASSEMBLY
2-4 hours

FINISHING
2-4 hours

TOTAL: 7-14 hours

Tools you'll use

· Jig saw or circular saw

· Drill/driver

· Tape measure

· Combination square

· Clamps

Shopping list

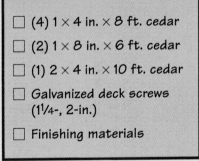

☐ (4) 1 × 4 in. × 8 ft. cedar

☐ (2) 1 × 8 in. × 6 ft. cedar

☐ (1) 2 × 4 in. × 10 ft. cedar

☐ Galvanized deck screws ($1\frac{1}{4}$-, 2-in.)

☐ Finishing materials

Basic Adirondack Chair

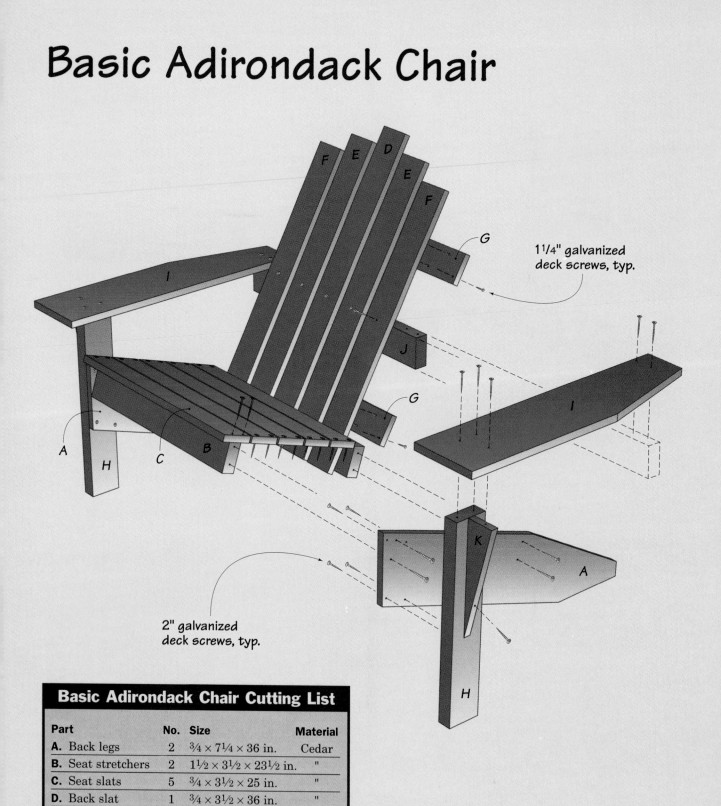

1¼" galvanized deck screws, typ.

2" galvanized deck screws, typ.

Basic Adirondack Chair Cutting List

Part	No.	Size	Material
A. Back legs	2	¾ × 7¼ × 36 in.	Cedar
B. Seat stretchers	2	1½ × 3½ × 23½ in.	"
C. Seat slats	5	¾ × 3½ × 25 in.	"
D. Back slat	1	¾ × 3½ × 36 in.	"
E. Back slats	2	¾ × 3½ × 34 in.	"
F. Back slats	2	¾ × 3½ × 32 in.	"
G. Back stretchers	2	¾ × 3½ × 19 in.	"
H. Front legs	2	1½ × 3½ × 21 in.	"
I. Arms	2	¾ × 7¼ × 30 in.	"
J. Back support	1	1½ × 3½ × 28 in.	"
K. Braces	2	¾ × 3 × 12 in.	"

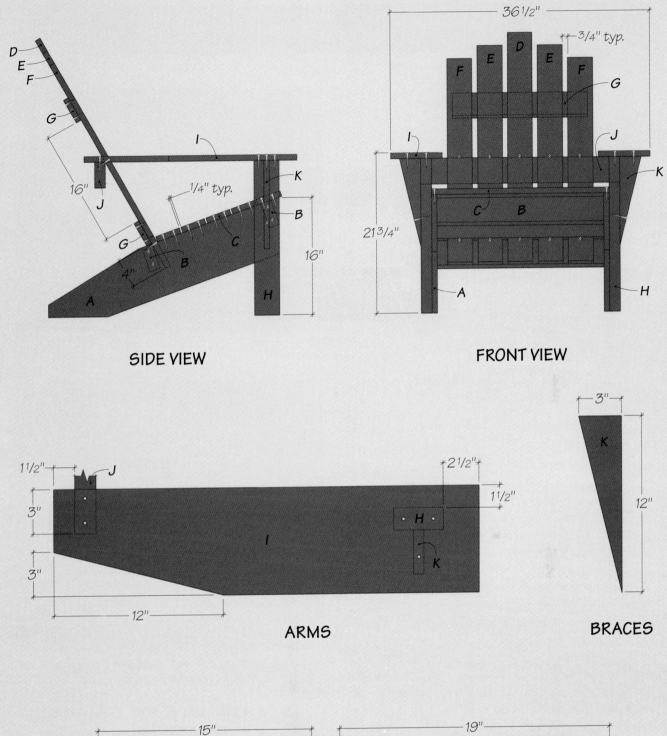

SIDE VIEW

FRONT VIEW

ARMS

BRACES

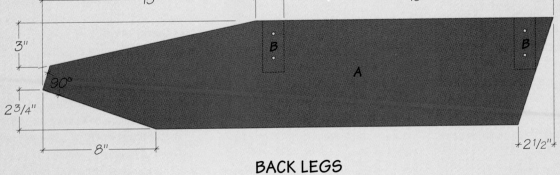

BACK LEGS

BUILD THE SEAT ASSEMBLY

❶ Cut the back legs to length from 1 × 8 stock. Follow the *Back Legs* drawing, page 347, to mark the angle cuts on the legs. Cut the leg angles with a jig saw or circular saw using a straightedge guide. Then cut the two seat stretchers to length.

❷ Attach the back legs to the seat stretchers. Position the face of the back stretcher 19 in. from the front ends of the legs and the leading edge of the front stretcher flush with the front ends of the legs. Mark the stretcher locations with a square, drill countersunk pilot holes through the legs and the stretchers, and fasten the parts with 2-in. galvanized deck screws **(See Photo A)**.

BUILD THE ARM ASSEMBLY

❸ Cut the front legs and the back support to length.

❹ Cut the arms and braces to size and shape. Mark for the angle cut on the back corner of each arm by measuring 12 in. along one long edge and 3 in. along the adjacent short end. Draw a line between these two points, and cut the angles with a jig saw guided by a straightedge. Save the triangular cutoff pieces; they'll become the arm braces.

❺ Measure and mark the positions of the front legs, braces, and back support on the arms (See *Arms* drawing, page 347). With the arms facedown on your workbench, use a combination square to mark the position of the front legs 2½ in. from the front of each arm and 1½ in. from the inside edges. Center and mark for a brace on the outside face of each leg. Then position the back support. It overlaps the inside edge of each arm by 3 in. and is inset 1½ in. from the ends.

❻ Build the arm assembly. Turn the arms faceup and drill countersunk pilot holes through the arms for attaching the legs and back support. Attach the front legs and back support with 2-in. deck screws driven through the arms. Attach the braces to the arms and legs with countersunk 2-in. deck screws **(See Photo B)**.

PHOTO A: Attach the back legs to the seat stretchers with 2-in. galvanized deck screws. Countersink the screwheads.

PHOTO B: Attach the back support, front legs and arm braces to the arm workpieces with 2-in. galvanized screws.

ATTACH THE ARM & SEAT ASSEMBLIES

Fastening the arm and seat assemblies together will require the use of temporary braces and clamps. Cut two 21-in. lengths of scrap for the temporary braces.

❼ Stand up the arm assembly and set the temporary braces beneath the arms to hold the arm assembly level. Position the seat assembly between the front legs so the front ends of the back legs are flush with the front edges of the front legs. Clamp the two assemblies together. The top corner of the

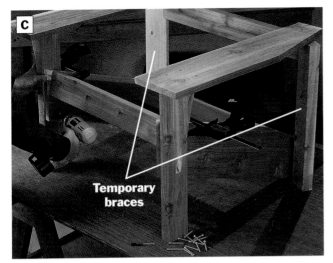

PHOTO C: Install the seat. Clamp the seat assembly between the front legs. You'll need to set temporary braces beneath the arms to hold them level. Attach the seat assembly to the front legs with deck screws.

PHOTO D: Arrange the back slats facedown on the bench, and fasten the back stretchers to the slats with 1¼-in. galvanized deck screws. Insert ¾-in. scrap spacers between the slats to make alignment easy.

back legs should be 16 in. up from the bottom of the front legs.

❽ Fasten the seat assembly to the front legs with countersunk 2-in. deck screws. Drive the screws through the back legs into the front legs **(See Photo C)**. Remove the temporary braces.

BUILD & ATTACH THE BACK

❾ Cut the back slats and the back stretchers to length. Assemble the back by laying the slats face-down on your workbench with the bottom edges flush. Position the stretchers so the lower stretcher is 4 in. from the bottom ends of the back slats, and there is 16 in. between the top and bottom stretchers. Drill countersunk pilot holes, and drive 1¼-in. deck screws through the stretchers into the slats **(See Photo D)**.

❿ Install the chair back. Attach the chair back by sliding it into position with the lower back stretcher resting on the rear seat stretcher. Drill countersunk pilot holes through the back slats into the rear seat stretcher and the back support. Attach the back with 2-in. deck screws.

ATTACH THE SEAT SLATS

⓫ Cut the five seat slats to length, and attach them to the back legs with 2-in. deck screws. Countersink the screw holes, and use ¼-in. hard-board spacers to hold the slats evenly apart as you fasten the slats **(See Photo E)**. NOTE: *You'll need to remove the chair arms one at a time to fasten the slats. Drive all the screws on one side of the seat,*

replace the arm, then remove the other arm and attach the slats.

FINISHING TOUCHES

⓬ Smooth all exposed chair surfaces and ease the corners with a sanding block. Apply the exterior sealer, stain or paint of your choice. Or leave the chair unfinished so it weathers naturally to gray.

PHOTO E: Set the seat slats in place and insert ¼-in.-thick hard-board spacers between the slats. Remove one chair arm for drill clearance and fasten the seat slats to the back leg. Once the slats are attached on one side, reinstall the arm, remove the other arm and fasten the slats to the other back leg. Then reinstall the arm.

Teak Cocktail Table

Impress guests at your next patio or deck party when you set their refreshments on this handsome cocktail table. Our cocktail table is made of teak—a dense, highly weather-resistant hardwood used in better-quality wood boatbuilding. The tabletop features spaced slats to provide for good drainage, as well as exposed splines around the edges. The overall design could be modified for a full-sized picnic table.

Vital Statistics: Teak Cocktail Table

TYPE: Cocktail table

OVERALL SIZE: 18 Dia. tabletop by 18H

MATERIAL: Teak

JOINERY: Mortise-and-tenon joints, floating tenons

CONSTRUCTION DETAILS:

· Table is made of weather-resistant teak, with brass and stainless-steel hardware and waterproof polyurethane glue so it can be used outdoors

· Tabletop rails are joined with spline tenons into an octagon shape and then cut round

· Slat tenons are pinned in place rather than glued to allow for wood movement

FINISHING OPTIONS: Finish with teak oil if the table will be used indoors. The wood can be left unfinished if it will be an outdoor piece, and the teak will age to a silvery gray. Otherwise, topcoat with a quality outdoor wood preservative with UV protectant to preserve the natural wood tones

Building time

PREPARING STOCK
2-3 hours

LAYOUT
3-4 hours

CUTTING PARTS
2-3 hours

ASSEMBLY
2-4 hours

FINISHING
1-2 hours

TOTAL: 10-16 hours

Tools you'll use

· **Planer**

· **Router table**

· **Router with piloted chamfer bit, V-groove bit, ¼-in. slot-cutting bit, ½-in. straight bit**

· **Power miter saw**

· **Band (strap) clamp**

· **Bar clamps**

· **Jig saw or band saw**

· **Table saw with tenon jig**

· **Drill press**

· **Drill/driver**

· **Wood chisels**

Shopping list

☐ (1) ¾ × 6 in. × 8 ft. teak

☐ (1) 1½ × 1½ in. × 6 ft. teak

☐ (4) brass "L" brackets, screws

☐ Polyurethane wood glue

☐ ½-in. stainless-steel brads

☐ Finishing materials

☐ Nylon glides

Teak Cocktail Table

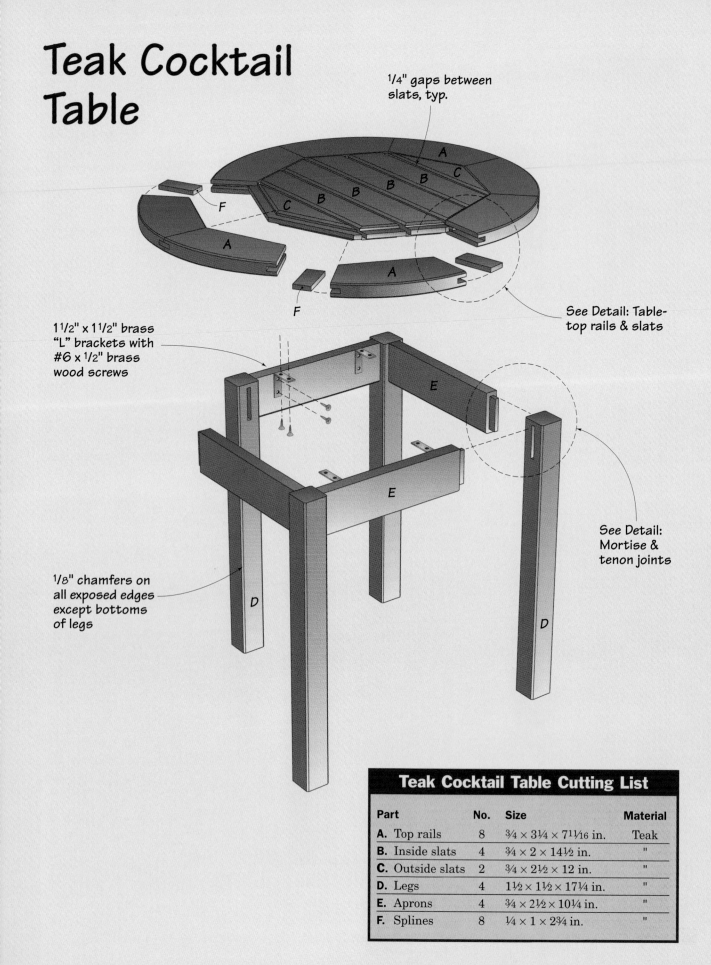

1/4" gaps between slats, typ.

A

B B C

C B B B A

F

A

F

See Detail: Table-top rails & slats

1 1/2" x 1 1/2" brass "L" brackets with #6 x 1/2" brass wood screws

E

E

D

See Detail: Mortise & tenon joints

1/8" chamfers on all exposed edges except bottoms of legs

D

Teak Cocktail Table Cutting List

Part	No.	Size	Material
A. Top rails	8	3/4 × 3 1/4 × 7 11/16 in.	Teak
B. Inside slats	4	3/4 × 2 × 14 1/2 in.	"
C. Outside slats	2	3/4 × 2 1/2 × 12 in.	"
D. Legs	4	1 1/2 × 1 1/2 × 17 1/4 in.	"
E. Aprons	4	3/4 × 2 1/2 × 10 1/4 in.	"
F. Splines	8	1/4 × 1 × 2 3/4 in.	"

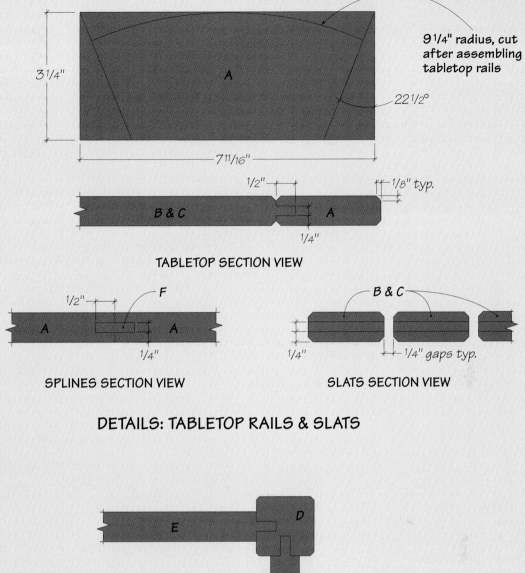

9 1/4" radius, cut after assembling tabletop rails

22 1/2°

3 1/4"

7 11/16"

A

1/2"

1/8" typ.

B & C

A

1/4"

TABLETOP SECTION VIEW

1/2"

F

A

A

1/4"

SPLINES SECTION VIEW

B & C

1/4"

1/4" gaps typ.

SLATS SECTION VIEW

DETAILS: TABLETOP RAILS & SLATS

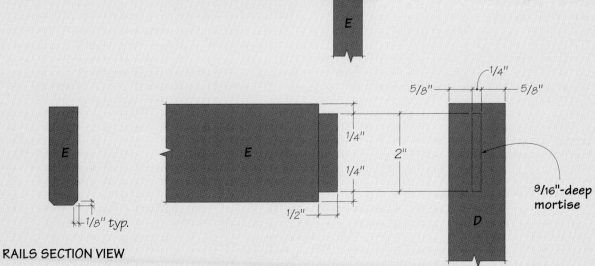

E

D

E

5/8"

1/4"

5/8"

E

1/4"

2"

1/4"

1/2"

9/16"-deep mortise

D

E

1/8" typ.

RAILS SECTION VIEW

DETAIL: MORTISE & TENON JOINTS
(LEG TO RAIL)

MAKE THE TABLETOP RAIL ASSEMBLY

❶ Surface plane your tabletop stock to ¾ in. thick and rip-cut to 3¼ in. wide. Rip enough teak stock to make all eight tabletop rails.

❷ Install a chamfer bit in the router table and cut a ⅛-in. chamfer along the top and bottom of one long edge of the tabletop rail workpieces.

❸ Install a ¼-in. piloted slot-cutting bit in the router table and set the bit height ¼ in. off the surface of the router table so the cutter will cut a centered ¼-in.-wide slot in the stock. Set the fence for a ½-in.-deep cut. Rout a slot along the chamfered edge of the stock (See Photo A).

❹ Set the blade of a power miter saw 22½° to the right of 0° and lock the angle setting. Cut this angle on a strip of scrap lumber to serve as a stopblock and flip it against the saw fence so its angle is opposite the blade angle. Set a length of tabletop stock against the saw fence with the slot against the fence and trim the workpiece near the end. Then flip the tabletop stock so the slot faces out. The scrap stock angle and the tabletop stock angle should now fit together to form a 45° angle. Interlock these parts and slide the tabletop stock/scrap block assembly along the saw fence until the blade will cut the tabletop stock piece at 7¹¹⁄₁₆, yielding a rail that's 7¹¹⁄₁₆ in. long on its edge with the slot on its narrow end. Fasten the stopblock to the saw table at this location (we used a screw) and cut the first tabletop rail (See Photo B). This setup will allow you to cut the tabletop rails one after the other without moving the stopblock.

❺ Cut seven more rails, being careful to keep the slot side on the short edge of each rail. To do this, you'll need to flip the stock over, cut off the end angle and flip the stock back with each new rail you cut.

❻ With the ¼-in. slot-cutter on the router table set at the same height as in Step 3, adjust the router table fence so the depth of cut is ½ in. Cut grooves along the mitered ends of each tabletop

PHOTO A: With a slot-cutting bit (See inset photo) in the router table, rout a ¼-in.-wide × ½-in.-deep groove into the edge of the tabletop rail stock. Use a featherboard to hold the stock against the fence.

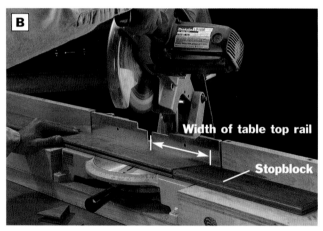

PHOTO B: Cut the tabletop rails to length with a 22½° angle on each end. Attach an angled stopblock to the saw table for consistent cuts.

PHOTO C: Rout spline grooves in the angled ends of the tabletop rails. Use a pushblock to aid in running the narrow pieces across the cutter and to back up the cut, preventing chipout.

PHOTO D: Glue the splines into the tabletop rail end grooves. Wipe the mating parts first with mineral spirits to remove the natural oils in the wood. Spread the glue evenly with a glue brush. Wear latex gloves and have mineral spirits and a rag handy to wipe up squeeze-out.

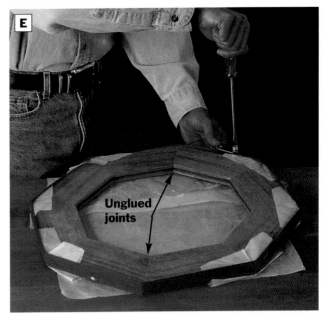

PHOTO E: Clamp the top rail assembly with a strap clamp, leaving two opposite joints unglued. Use wax paper around the glued corners to keep the strap from bonding to the wood.

rail (the grooves will house the splines). Use a piece of ¾-in. scrap with a 22½° angle cut on one side as a pushblock to guide the rails and keep them from chipping out at the back edge **(See Photo C).**

❼ Cut eight splines that are ¼ × 1 × 2¾ in. each. Then glue up the tabletop rails in two sections of four rails each. Wipe the mating surfaces with mineral spirits first, then apply polyurethane glue to the side grooves on each rail and insert the splines **(See Photo D).** The splines won't extend the full length of the joint, so align the splines flush with the bottom of the groove in the short side of each rail. NOTE: *Polyurethane glue cures by reacting with the moisture in the wood, so moisten the splines before assembling each joint.*

❽ After the two rail sections are assembled, fit them together with two splines (don't use glue) and clamp the tabletop together tightly with a strap clamp **(See Photo E).** You'll glue the two tabletop sections together later. Slip wax paper between the corners and the clamp's strap to keep glue squeeze-out from gluing the clamp to the rails. Let the setup dry thoroughly, then remove the clamp.

INSTALL THE SLATS

❾ Rip stock to width for the 2-in. inside and 2½-in. outside tabletop slats and cross-cut them to length.

PHOTO F: Insert ¼-in. spacers between the slats and clamp them together. Lay the rail assembly over the slats and trace the interior of the assembly onto the slats.

❿ On a flat surface, lay out the slats edge-to-edge, with the outside slats at the ends. Insert ¼-in. spacers to get the gaps between the slats **(See Photo F).**

⓫ Measure out ½ in. beyond the traced lines on all slats to allow for the length of the slat tenons, and draw new cutting lines using a straightedge or marking gauge. Remove the clamps and cut the slats one at a time along the cutting lines.

⓬ Install a ½-in. straight bit in the router table. Set the bit height to ¼ in. Adjust the fence to cut ½-in.-long tenons on the ends each slat **(See**

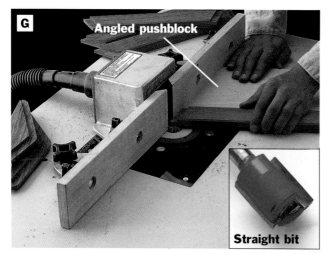

PHOTO G: Cut tenons into the angled ends of the slats with a ½-in. straight bit (See inset). Use an angled pushblock to guide the work.

PHOTO H: Rout ⅛-in. chamfers on the ends and edges of the slats using a V-groove bit in the router table. Use an angled pushblock to guide the workpiece.

PHOTO I: Glue and clamp the two halves of the tabletop rail assembly together with polyurethane glue and a strap clamp. Cover the glued corners with wax paper. Nail, rather than glue, the slats in place.

PHOTO J: Use a trammel to mark an 18-in.-dia. circle onto the underside of the tabletop, and cut it round with a band saw or jig saw.

Photo G). NOTE: *Use a piece of angled scrap as a pushblock to guide the slats and keep the bit from tearing out the slat ends.* Dry-fit the slats into the top rail assembly, again inserting the ¼-in. spacers. Trim the slat tenons, as needed, to fit.

⓭ Disassemble the tabletop pieces and chamfer the edges and ends of all the slats and tabletop rails on the router table **(See Photo H).** We used a veining (V-groove) bit in the router table to cut the chamfers, and used the fence as a guide. Finish-sand all parts for the tabletop.

⓮ Reassemble the tabletop and glue the final two splined joints. Use a band clamp to secure the assembly **(See Photo I).** Do not glue the slats. Instead, pin the joints through the center of each

tenon by nailing one ½-in. stainless-steel brad up into each tenon. This will allow the slats to expand and contract with changes in temperature and humidity, especially if the table is kept outside. Let the glue dry.

⓯ Lay the tabletop facedown. Place a ¼-in. spacer snugly into the gap between the two center slats, and measure and mark the centerpoint of the tabletop assembly onto the spacer. Pin a piece of scrap to the spacer to serve as a trammel, and scribe an 18-in.-dia. circle around the centerpoint **(See Photo J).** Cut out the tabletop along this cutting line with a jig saw or a band saw. Sand the edge smooth, and use a piloted chamfer bit to rout a ⅛-in. chamfer around the top and bottom edge of the tabletop.

PHOTO K: Drill out the leg mortises on the drill press to ½-in. depth. Clean up the waste from the shoulder of the mortises with a chisel.

PHOTO L: Glue and clamp the legs and rails together. Use clamp pads between the clamp jaws and mineral spirits to clean up squeeze-out.

MAKE THE LEG ASSEMBLY

16 Rip- and cross-cut the four legs and four aprons to size.

17 Lay out two ¼-in.-wide mortises in the top of each leg, centering them on two adjacent sides. The mortises should be 2 in. long, starting ¼ in. down from the top ends (See *Detail: Mortise & Tenon Joints,* page 353). Cut the ½-in.-deep mortises by drilling side-by-side ¼-in.-dia. holes on the drill press, then clean and square up the mortises with a wood chisel to the layout lines **(See Photo K).**

18 Use a table saw and a tenon jig or router and straight bit to cut a ¼-in.-thick × ½-in.-deep × 2-in.-long tenon on each end of all four leg rails.

19 Rout a ⅛-in. chamfer on all edges of the table legs and the two lower edges of each leg apron. Finish-sand these parts.

20 Glue and assemble the legs and leg rails with the rail chamfers facing the leg bottoms using polyurethane glue and clamps **(See Photo L).** Use clamp pads between the clamp jaws and legs, to protect the wood.

FINISHING TOUCHES

21 Lay the tabletop facedown and set the leg assembly on top of it. Attach the leg rails to the underside of the top with four brass L-brackets and ½-in. brass or stainless-steel screws **(See Photo M).** Drill pilot holes for the screws first.

PHOTO M: Attach the tabletop to the rails and legs using brass L-brackets. Drill pilot holes before driving the screws.

22 Finish the table with teak oil if you plan to use the table indoors. If the table will be used outdoors, you can leave it unfinished to weather to a silvery gray or topcoat it with wood preservative with UV protectant to retain the color of the wood. The natural oils in teak will resist rot and insects. Attach nylon glides to the foot bottoms so the legs won't absorb water through their ends.

Porch Glider

The gentle rocking motion of this two-person porch glider will make it one of your favorite summer spots. Built entirely of solid red oak, this charming piece of furniture is destined to become a family heirloom. Set it in a sheltered area, sit back and enjoy!

Vital Statistics: Porch Glider

TYPE: Porch glider

OVERALL SIZE: 27D by 59¾L by 35H

MATERIAL: Red oak

JOINERY: Butt joints reinforced with dowels or screws

CONSTRUCTION DETAILS:

· Many parts of the bench constructed with dowel joints for ease of construction and durability

· Bench suspended from stand by way of oak glider arms and pivoting hinges

· Screwheads concealed with matching oak plugs

FINISHING OPTIONS: Penetrating UV protectant sealer

Building time

PREPARING STOCK
1-2 hours

LAYOUT
3-4 hours

CUTTING PARTS
3-4 hours

ASSEMBLY
8-12 hours

FINISHING
2-4 hours

TOTAL: 17-26 hours

Tools you'll use

· Band saw

· Power miter saw or circular saw

· Table saw

· Drill press

· ⅜-in.-dia. plug cutter

· Drill/driver

· Drill bits (½-, 1-in.)

· Doweling jig

· Clamps

· Router with ¼-in. roundover bit

· Wooden mallet

· Flush-trimming saw

· Wrenches

· Combination square

Shopping list

☐ (1) 1½ × 8 in. × 4 ft. red oak

☐ (1) 1½ × 5½ in. × 4 ft. red oak

☐ (6) 1½ × 3½ in. × 8 ft. red oak

☐ (1) 1½ × 2½ in. × 4 ft. red oak

☐ (5) ¾ × 3 in. × 6 ft. red oak

☐ (2) ¾ × 2½ in. × 8 ft. red oak

☐ (1) ¾ × 1¾ in. × 6 ft. red oak

☐ (84) ⅜-in.-dia. × 2-in. fluted dowels

☐ Moisture-resistant wood glue

☐ Flathead wood screws (1½-, 2½-in.)

☐ (8) pivot hinges (available from Rockler Companies)

☐ UV protectant sealer

Porch Glider

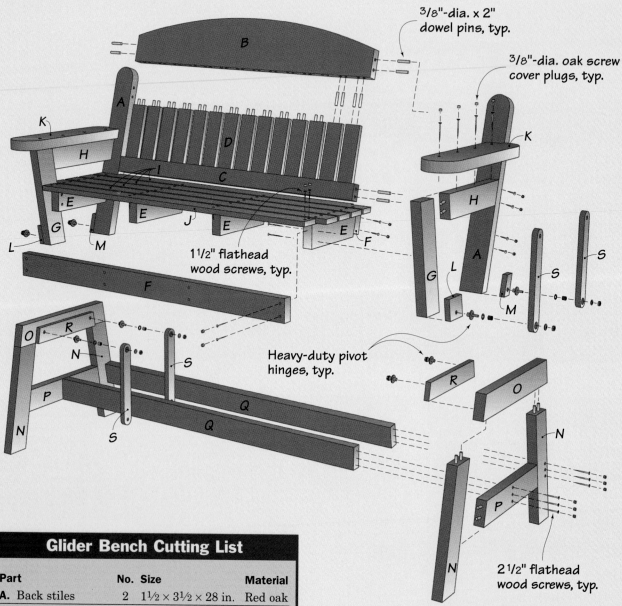

³/₈"-dia. x 2" dowel pins, typ.

³/₈"-dia. oak screw cover plugs, typ.

1¹/₂" flathead wood screws, typ.

Heavy-duty pivot hinges, typ.

2¹/₂" flathead wood screws, typ.

Glider Bench Cutting List

Part	No.	Size	Material
A. Back stiles	2	1¹/₂ × 3¹/₂ × 28 in.	Red oak
B. Upper back rail	1	1¹/₂ × 8 × 46¹/₄ in.	"
C. Lower back rail	1	1¹/₂ × 2¹/₂ × 46¹/₄ in.	"
D. Back slats	14	³/₄ × 2¹/₂ × 8³/₄ in.	"
E. Bench struts	4	1¹/₂ × 3¹/₂ × 12¹/₂ in.	"
F. Bench rails	2	1¹/₂ × 3¹/₂ × 50¹/₄ in.	"
G. Bench legs	2	1¹/₂ × 3¹/₂ × 16³/₈ in.	"
H. Arm supports	2	1¹/₂ × 3¹/₂ × 15¹/₂ in.	"
I. Bench slats	4	³/₄ × 3 × 53¹/₄ in.	"
J. Front bench slat	1	³/₄ × 3 × 50¹/₄ in.	"
K. Arm rests	2	1¹/₂ × 5¹/₂ × 23 in.	"
L. Bench leg blocking	2	³/₄ × 3 × 4¹/₁₆ in.	"
M. Back stiles blocking	2	³/₄ × 3 × 2³/₈ in.	"

Glider Stand Cutting List

Part	No.	Size	Material
N. Stand legs	4	1¹/₂ × 3¹/₂ × 18 in.	Red oak
O. End top rails	2	1¹/₂ × 3¹/₂ × 21¹/₄ in.	"
P. End bottom rails	2	1¹/₂ × 3¹/₂ × 18¹/₁₆ in.	"
Q. Stand stretchers	2	1¹/₂ × 3¹/₂ × 58¹/₂ in.	"
R. Spacers	2	³/₄ × 2¹/₂ × 14¹/₄ in.	"
S. Glider arms	4	³/₄ × 1³/₄ × 13¹/₈ in.	"

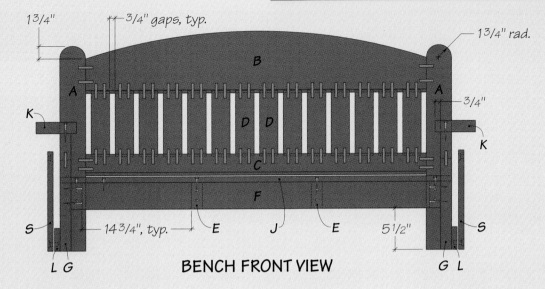

13/4"

3/4" gaps, typ.

13/4" rad.

3/4"

14 3/4", typ.

5 1/2"

BENCH FRONT VIEW

7/8"

6"

STAND FRONT VIEW

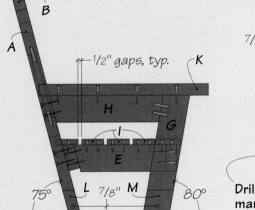

1/2" gaps, typ.

75°   7/8"   80°

BENCH SIDE VIEW

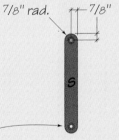

7/8" rad.   7/8"

Drill pivot hinge holes as per manufacturer's instructions

GLIDER ARMS

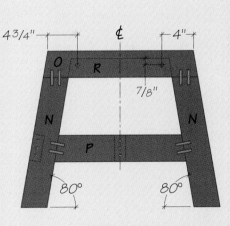

4 3/4"   ₵   4"

7/8"

80°   80°

STAND SIDE VIEW

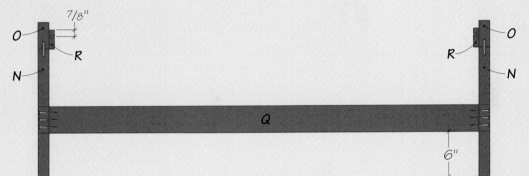

74 1/4" rad.

UPPER BACK RAIL

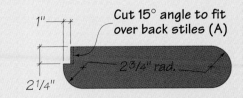

1"

Cut 15° angle to fit over back stiles (A)

2 3/4" rad.

2 1/4"

ARM RESTS

This porch glider is made up of two distinct structures joined together with glider arms and pivot hinges. The hinges we used are available from the Rockler Companies. You'll start by building the bench, then the glider stand. After both parts are constructed, you'll join them together. All the face screws in this piece are countersunk 1/4 in. and concealed with 3/8-in.-dia. matching oak plugs. Building the glider will require you to make many angled cuts. Assembly will go much more smoothly if you take the time to make these angled cuts precisely.

BUILD THE BACK ASSEMBLY

❶ Make the upper and lower back rails. Cut workpieces for both parts to length from 1½-in.-thick stock. Mark the arched profile on the upper back rail, using the *Upper Back Rail* drawing, page 361, as a layout guide. Cut the profile on your band saw (**See Photo A**). Sand the profile smooth, and save the curved waste pieces to use later as clamping cauls.

❷ Drill dowel holes for the back slats in the upper and lower rails. Clamp the rails together, face to face, holding the ends and dowel edges flush. Mark centerlines for drilling the dowel holes by measuring 1½ in. from one end of the rails to the center of the first hole, 1 in. from that mark to the center of the second hole and 2¼ in. from the second mark to the third hole. From that point on, alternate 1-, and 2¼-in. spaces. The final measurement at the other end should be 1½ in. Unclamp the rails and

PHOTO A: Cut the profile on the upper back rail to shape on the band saw. Save the curved cut-off pieces to use as cauls when you clamp the back rails and slats together later.

PHOTO B: A right-angle jig will make the job of drilling dowel holes in the slats quicker and more precise. Tip the drill press table vertically and clamp the jig in place so the bit aligns with the dowel locations on each slat. Flip the slats edgewise and endwise to drill all four holes.

drill the dowel holes, using a doweling jig as a guide. Each hole should be ⅝ in. deep, to allow clearspace at the bottom of the holes for glue.

❸ Make the back slats. Cut the 14 slats to length, then make a right-angle jig for your drill press to drill the dowel holes in the slat ends. The centerlines of the holes should be ¾ in. from each edge, leaving a 1-in. space between them. Tip your drill press table into the vertical position. Clamp the right-angle jig to the table with a slat in place, and adjust the jig position to achieve the correct hole position. Once the jig is set up, four dowel holes can be drilled in each back slat without changing the jig setting. Flip the slats edge-for-edge and end-for-end to drill the holes (**See Photo B**).

❹ Assemble the back rails and slats. Glue and insert two fluted dowels into one end of each of the back slats, then put a spot of glue in the holes in the lower back rail and on the mating surfaces of these joints. Tap the back slats into place against the rail with a wooden mallet. Insert glued dowels into the top ends of the slats, spread a thin layer of glue on the mating surfaces of the slats and the top back rail, and install this rail. Use the curved cutoffs from the upper rail as clamping cauls, and clamp up the back assembly (**See Photo C**).

❺ Make the back stiles. Cut the stiles to length, then bevel-cut the bottom ends of the stiles to 15°, using a power miter saw. Mark the arcs on the upper ends of the stiles and cut them with a jig saw.

❻ Drill pairs of matching dowel holes in the stiles and rails to join

PHOTO C: Assemble the upper and lower back rails and back slats with glue and dowels. Clamp the assembly together, using the waste pieces from Step 1 to make clamping the top rail easier. Alternate the clamps above and below the assembly to distribute clamping pressure evenly.

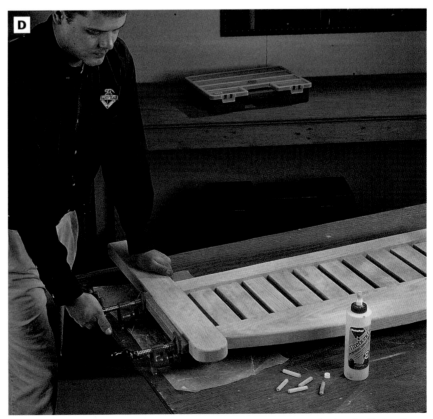

PHOTO D: Complete the back assembly by attaching the stiles to the back rails. Fasten the stiles to the ends of the rails with pairs of dowels and moisture-resistant wood glue.

PHOTO E: Build the bench frame by installing four struts between the front and back bench rails with glue and screws. In this photo, the bench frame is upside down. Notice that the beveled edge of the back rail lines up with the edges of the struts, leaving an offset on the other edge.

PHOTO F: Fasten the back assembly to the bench frame by driving countersunk screws through the stiles and into the back bench rail. Be sure the bottom beveled ends of the stiles are parallel with the bottom edges of the bench.

the rails to the back assembly. On your worksurface, lay the stiles in position against the ends of the upper and lower rails. The top corners of the top back rail should be 1¾ in. down from the tops of the stiles. Mark the dowel hole locations and use a doweling jig as a guide to drill the ⅜-in.-dia. dowel holes, two dowels per joint.

7 Attach the back stiles. Insert glued dowels into the holes, spread a thin coat of glue on the mating surfaces of the rails and stiles, and clamp the parts together (**See Photo D**). Protect the wood from clamp marks by using wooden cauls between the clamp jaws.

8 Ease the outer edges of the back frame assembly with your router and a ¼-in. roundover bit.

BUILD & ATTACH THE BENCH FRAME

9 Make the bench struts. Cut the struts to length. Then cut one end of each strut at a 75° angle across the width of the strut.

10 Cut both bench rails to length, and rip one edge of the back bench rail at a 15° angle on the table saw (See *Bench Side View,* page 361).

11 Build the bench frame. Mark the locations of the struts on the inner faces of the bench rails—two flush with the ends of the rails and the other two struts spaced 14¾ in. from the end struts. The beveled edge of the back bench rail should be flush with the tops of the struts when the bench is right-side-up. Drill pairs of countersunk pilot holes in the rails, and fasten the rails to the struts with wood glue and 2½-in. flathead wood screws (**See Photo E**).

⓬ Attach the back assembly to the bench frame. When attached, the bottom edge of the bench frame is parallel to the angled cut at the bottom end of the stiles and 5½ in. above it. Clamp the back in position against the bench, drill countersunk pilot holes, and screw the stiles to the back rail **(See Photo F)**.

BUILD & ATTACH THE ARM ASSEMBLIES

The arm assemblies consist of the bench legs and arm supports, joined together with dowels. When you attach the assemblies to the bench frame and back, be sure that the bottoms of the legs are even with the bottoms of the back stiles. Otherwise, the bench will not hang evenly later on when attached to the glider stand.

⓭ Cut the bench legs and arm supports to size, with their ends angled to 80°, as shown in the *Bench Side View* drawing, page 361.

⓮ Mark and drill dowel holes for connecting the arm supports and legs together. Lay out two dowels per joint. As before, butt the two mating parts together, draw a single line across the joint for each dowel, and drill straight holes for the dowels with a doweling jig **(See Photo G)**.

⓯ Connect the arm supports and legs. Insert glued dowels into the holes and spread glue on the mating surfaces. Use wooden cauls to protect the finished surfaces of the parts, and join the arm supports to the legs with clamps.

⓰ Fasten the arm assemblies to the bench. Use a square to make a mark 5½ in. up from the bottom of both legs. Clamp the arm assemblies in position, so your

PHOTO G: Join the bench legs to the arm supports with pairs of 2-in. fluted dowels. Use a doweling jig when you drill the holes to be sure that the dowel holes are drilled straight across the joints. Wrap a piece of tape around the drill bit to serve as a temporary depth stop.

PHOTO H: Fasten the arm assemblies to the bench by driving screws through the back stiles and into the arm supports. Screw from inside the bench to attach the end bench struts to the legs as well. Clamp the arm assemblies in place first, to make installing the assemblies easier.

PHOTO I: Cut the arm rests to shape, ease the edges with a router and roundover bit, then clamp them on top of the arm supports. Attach the rests to the supports with countersunk screws.

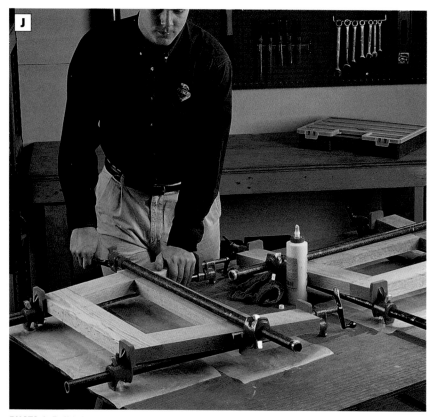

PHOTO J: Build the glider stand ends by attaching the top and bottom end rails to the stand legs with dowels and glue. The bottom rails fit between the legs, while the top rails overlap the top ends of the legs.

leg marks align with the bottom edges of the bench frame, and the backs of the arm supports rest against the back stiles. Drill countersunk pilot holes through the back stiles into the arm supports, and fasten the stiles to the supports with 2½-in. screws. Then drill pilot holes and drive screws from inside the bench through the outer bench struts and into the bench legs (**See Photo H**).

COMPLETE THE BENCH

17 Cut and position the bench slats. Cut the bench slats and the front bench slat to length. Ease the edges and ends on the top face of each slat with a router and ¼-in. roundover bit. Lay the slats in place on the bench frame so the back edge of the front slat is even with the back edge of the legs. Allow for ½-in. spaces between the slats. Mark the rear slat so it will notch around the back stiles. Cut out the notches on this slat with your jig saw.

18 Fasten the slats to the bench struts. Use two screws per strut location on the slats, centering the screws on the thickness of the struts. Drill countersunk pilot holes and fasten the slats in place with 1½-in. flathead wood screws.

19 Cut and attach the arm rests. Refer to the *Arm Rests* drawing, page 361, to lay out the shape of the parts. Cut the arm rests to size and shape with radiused ends and notched back corners. NOTE: *The easiest way to determine the 15° notch angle is to simply set each arm rest in position on the arm supports and mark the angle where the arm rests cross the back stiles.* Ease all the arm rest edges except the notched portion with a router and a ¼-in. roundover bit. Clamp the arm rests in place, drill countersunk pilot holes, and fasten them to the arm supports with 2½-in. flathead wood screws **(See Photo I)**.

20 Cut and attach the blocking pieces for the legs and stiles. Cut blanks to size for the four blocking pieces, hold them in place against the legs and stiles and mark the angle cuts. Cut the angles on a band saw. Apply an even coating of glue on the mating surfaces, clamp firmly and let dry completely. NOTE: *Since these parts are fastened with glue alone, it is important to build the best glue joints possible. Be sure the mating surfaces are flat and clean before gluing the joints.* Sand the edges flush and, if desired, ease the sharp edges with your router and a ¼-in. roundover bit.

BUILD THE STAND ENDS

21 Cut out the stand legs, top and bottom rails. Refer to the *Stand Side View* drawing, page 361, for details on determining the angled ends of these parts.

22 Drill pairs of dowel holes to attach the stand legs to the rails. Butt mating surfaces together, positioning the bottom rails 6 in. up from the bottoms of the legs. Mark the dowel locations and drill the holes with a doweling jig.

23 Assemble the stand ends. Insert glued dowels into the ends of the bottom rails, apply glue to the mating surfaces, and slide the legs into place over the dowels and against the bottom rails. Attach the top rails to the ends of the legs similarly. Clamp up the end assemblies **(See Photo J)**.

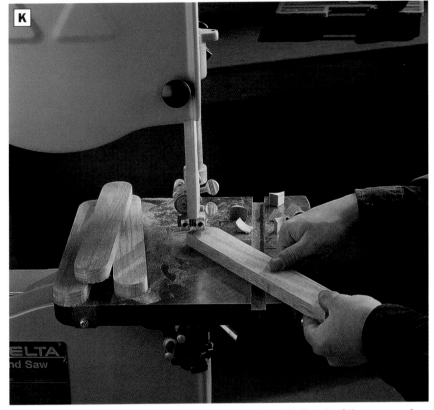

PHOTO K: Cut the four glider arms to shape on the band saw. Both ends of the arms receive ⅞-in.-radius curves. Sand the cut edges smooth and round them over with a router if you wish.

PHOTO L: Bore 5/16-in.-deep, 1-in.-dia. counterbores on both ends of the glider arms. Notice that the counterbores are on opposite faces of the arms. Then drill a ½-in.-dia. hole through the center of the counterbores all the way through the arms, to accommodate the pivot hinges.

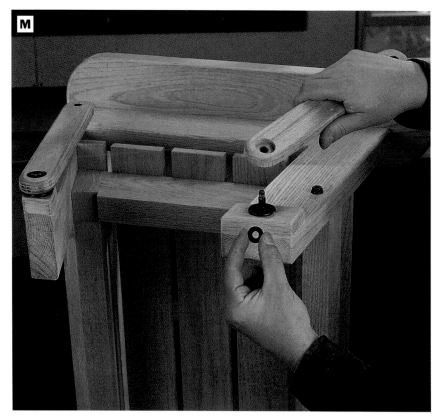

PHOTO M: Install pivot hinges to connect the glider arms to the blocking pieces on the bench. The hardware is essentially a shaft that slides inside a plastic bushing in the glider arms. The hinges press into holes in the blocking and hold the arms in place with washers and nuts.

PHOTO N: Set the bench on your worksurface so the glider arms hang freely. Attach the glider arms to the blocking pieces on the glider stand end assemblies with pivot hinges.

② Install the spacers. Cut the spacers to size and shape, and fasten them to the inside faces of the end assembly top rails with glue. The bottom edges of the spacers should be flush with the bottom edges of the end top rails.

MAKE THE GLIDER ARMS

㉕ Cut four blanks for the glider arms to length and width. Mark the $7/8$-in.-radius arc on the ends, and cut the arcs on your band saw **(See Photo K)**. Sand the cut edges smooth.

㉖ Drill the counterbored pivot hinge-mounting holes. Each of the hinge holes needs a $5/16$-in.-deep by 1-in.-dia. counterbore to recess the pivot hinge washer and nut. Drill the 1-in. counterbores first, then drill $1/2$-in.-dia. through holes at the center of the counterbores **(See Photo L)**. Note in the photo that the two holes in each arm are counterbored from opposite sides of the arms.

㉗ Attach the glider arms to the bench. Locate and drill the $1/2$-in.-dia. × $1/2$-in.-deep hinge holes in the blocking pieces at the ends of the bench. The holes should be centered across the width of the blocking pieces and $7/8$ in. up from the bottom of the blocking. Install the lower pivot hinges and connect the glider arms to the bench, according to the manufacturer's instructions **(See Photo M)**.

INSTALL THE BENCH IN THE GLIDER STAND

㉘ Attach the stand end assemblies to the glider arms. Locate and drill the $1/2$-in.-dia. × $1/2$-in.-deep hinge holes in the spacers attached to the end top rails. The *Stand Side View* drawing, page 361, identifies the exact location of the hinges on the glider stand spacers. Support the bench structure on a platform so the stand ends can rotate freely, and install the upper pivot hinges and glider arms **(See Photo N).**

㉙ Install the stand stretchers. Cut the stretchers to length, and round over the edges. Mark the position of the stretchers on the glider stand ends—one stretcher is centered on the bottom rails, and the other stretcher lines up with the back edge of the back legs. Clamp the stretchers in place between the stand ends, and drive 2½-in. screws through counterbored pilot holes to attach the parts **(See Photo O).**

FINISHING TOUCHES

㉚ Plug all the visible screw holes. Cut ⅜-in.-dia. oak plugs with a plug cutter mounted in your drill press. Spread glue on the plugs and tap them into the screw counterbores with a wooden mallet **(See Photo P).** Trim the plugs flush with the surrounding wood and sand smooth.

㉛ Sand the completed project thoroughly. Finish the glider with two coats of UV protectant sealer.

Shelter the glider

If you build this project from red oak, place the glider in an area sheltered from direct contact with moisture. Red oak, though durable, is not as weather-resistant as other woods. Should you desire to build the glider for an exposed location, use white oak, cedar, teak or Honduras mahogany instead. And be sure to use galvanized or stainless-steel screws as fasteners.

PHOTO O: Install stretchers between the end assemblies of the glider stand with 2½-in. countersunk flathead wood screws. Clamp the stand's ends to hold them stationary as you fasten the stretchers in place.

PHOTO P: Conceal all exposed screwheads with oak plugs. You could use oak dowel for making the plugs, but the preferred method is to cut the plugs from the face grain of a piece of oak stock. This way, the plugs will match the wood grain direction of the bench slats.

Full-shelter Doghouse

Keep a canine friend warm and dry in this sturdy doghouse. Our design features a dividing wall that provides complete shelter from wind and rain, and the shingled roof is removable for easier cleaning. In colder climates, you can even install sheet foam insulation beneath the floor for added warmth.

Full-shelter Doghouse

Vital Statistics

TYPE: Doghouse

OVERALL SIZE: 48L by 40W by 44H

MATERIAL: Exterior plywood, roofing materials

JOINERY: Butt joints reinforced with glue and screws

CONSTRUCTION DETAILS:
- Gussets beneath the roof panels strengthen the roof so it can be lifted off
- Roof sealed against weather with 15-pound building paper and asphalt shingles

FINISH: Exterior primer and paint

BUILDING TIME: 8-10 hours

Shopping List

- [ ] (3) ¾ in. × 4 ft. × 8 ft. exterior plywood
- [ ] (1) ¾ in. × 4 ft. × 4 ft. exterior plywood
- [ ] 2-in. deck screws
- [ ] Moisture-resistant wood glue
- [ ] 15-pound building paper
- [ ] Asphalt shingles
- [ ] Galvanized staples
- [ ] Roofing nails
- [ ] Finishing materials

Full-shelter Doghouse: Step-by-step

The proportions of this doghouse project are intended for housing medium to large dog breeds. Contact a dog breeder or your local branch of the Humane Society for information on suitable doghouse sizes for smaller dogs.

MAKE THE DOGHOUSE PARTS

❶ Cut two 40 × 40-in. pieces of plywood for the front and back panels. Follow the *Front Layout* drawing, page 372, to draw the angled roof profiles as well as the arch-top door opening. Cut the roof angles.

❷ Cut the door opening in the front with a jig saw. Start the cut by drilling a pilot hole in one corner of the door layout area, large enough to insert the saw blade for starting the cut (**See Photo A**).

PHOTO A: Draw the arch-top door opening on the doghouse front panel, and cut out the opening with a jig saw. Drill a starter hole in the cutout area first, so you can insert the saw blade to begin the cut.

Full-shelter Doghouse

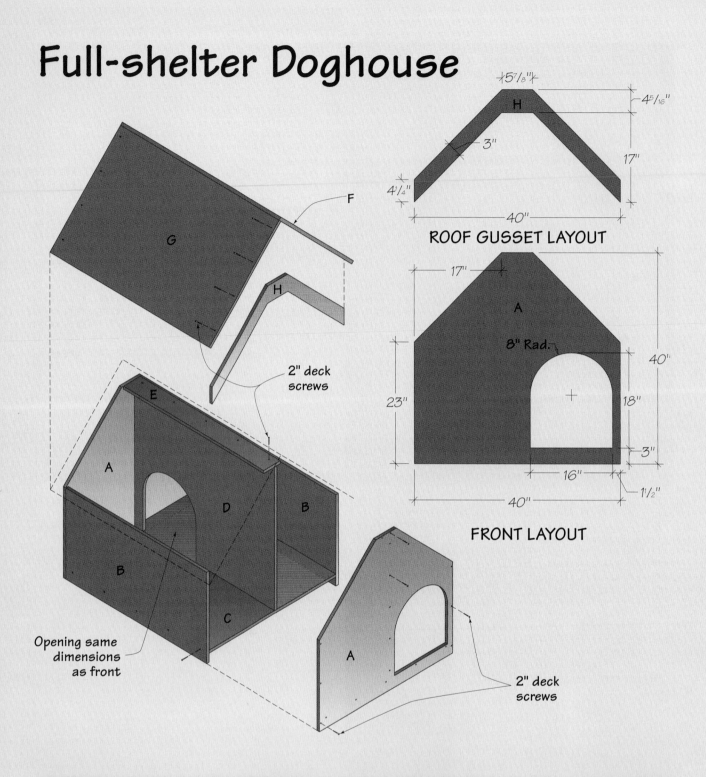

ROOF GUSSET LAYOUT

FRONT LAYOUT

2" deck screws

Opening same dimensions as front

2" deck screws

Full-shelter Doghouse Cutting List

Part	No.	Size	Material	Part	No.	Size	Material
A. Front/back	2	$3/4 \times 40 \times 40$ in.	Exterior plywood	**E.** Interior brace	1	$3/4 \times 5 \times 42\frac{1}{2}$ in.	Exterior plywood
B. Sides	2	$3/4 \times 42\frac{1}{2} \times 23$ in.	"	**F.** Roof (long)	1	$3/4 \times 48 \times 31$ in.	"
C. Bottom	1	$3/4 \times 38\frac{1}{2} \times 42\frac{1}{2}$ in.	"	**G.** Roof (short)	1	$3/4 \times 48 \times 30\frac{1}{4}$ in.	"
D. Interior divider	1	$3/4 \times 36\frac{1}{4} \times 42\frac{1}{2}$ in.	"	**H.** Roof gussets	2	$3/4 \times 21\frac{5}{16} \times 40$ in.	"

❸ Rip and cross-cut the two side panels, bottom and the interior brace to size.

❹ Make the interior divider: Cut a plywood workpiece to size, following the *Cutting List* dimensions on page 372. Lay the doghouse front panel on the divider workpiece and use the front door opening as a template for drawing a door on the divider. Locate the door so it's flush with the bottom edge of the divider and 2 in. from the end. Trace the door on the divider and cut the opening.

ASSEMBLE THE DOGHOUSE

❺ Fasten the front and back panels to the sides. Arrange the parts so the front and back overlap the ends of the side panels. Spread moisture-resistant wood glue on the ends of the sides and clamp the four parts together. TIP: *If you don't have clamps long enough to hold these parts together, stretch duct tape over the joints instead.* Drill countersunk pilot holes through the front and back and into the ends of the sides. Attach the parts with 2-in. deck screws.

❻ Install the bottom: Draw a reference line 3 in. up from the bottom edges of the doghouse assembly all the way around the inside of the structure. This line represents the top face of the doghouse bottom panel; it should align with the flat bottom edge of the front door. Slip the bottom panel into position and attach it with countersunk deck screws driven through the front, back and sides **(See Photo B).**

❼ Attach the interior divider: Draw vertical reference lines on the front and back panels for locating the divider inside the doghouse. Measure and mark these lines 20 in. in from the left side of the doghouse (when viewed from the front). Slide the interior divider into position so the divider door is positioned near the back of the doghouse. Secure the divider by driving 2-in. countersunk deck screws through the front, back and bottom panels.

❽ Install the interior brace: Set the interior brace so it caps the top edge of the divider and is centered on the short, flat top edges of the front and back panels. Drive 2-in. deck screws down through the brace into the divider as well as through the front and back panels to fasten the brace in place **(See Photo C).**

BUILD THE ROOF STRUCTURE

The doghouse roof is designed to be a removable

PHOTO B: Fasten the bottom panel in place between the front, back and side pieces with countersunk deck screws. Position the bottom 3 in. up from the bottom edges of the parts and so the top face is flush with the bottom of the door opening.

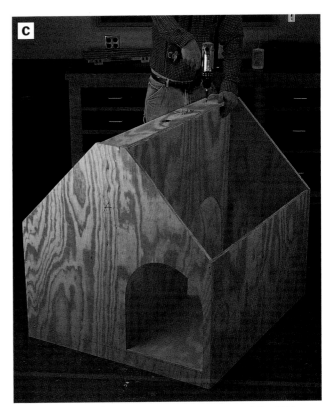

PHOTO C: Install the interior brace on the top edge of the divider and so it is centered on the short, flat top edges of the doghouse front and back. Fasten the parts with screws.

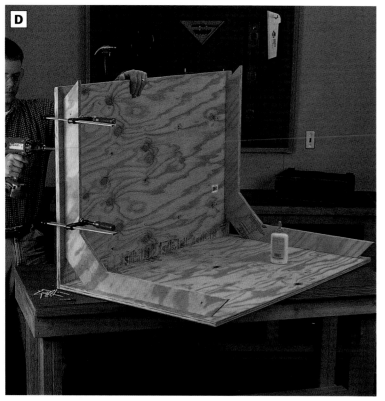

PHOTO D: Assemble the roof panels and gussets to form the roof structure. Allow for a 1-in. overhang between the ends of the roof and the gussets. Fasten the parts with glue and countersunk deck screws.

PHOTO E: Prime and paint the doghouse surfaces, inside and out. Seal the bottom edges with primer and paint, to keep the plywood from wicking up ground moisture.

unit, to make cleaning out the interior of the house easier. A pair of gussets beneath the roof panels stiffen the structure and hold the roof panels at 90° to one another.

❾ Rip and cross-cut the two roof sections. Follow the *Cutting List* dimensions carefully—the roof panels differ in width so one panel can overlap the other at the roof peak, once installed.

❿ Make the roof gussets: To lay out the gusset shape, mark a 20 × 40-in. rectangle on a plywood sheet, and follow the *Roof Gusset Layout* drawing, page 372, to draw the shape within this rectangle. Cut out the gusset with a jig saw or circular saw. Use the first gusset as a template for drawing the second gusset shape, then cut out the second gusset.

⓫ Assemble the roof panels: Spread glue along one long edge of the narrower roof panel, and set the wider roof panel against the first so it overlaps the glued edge and the parts meet at 90°. Drive countersunk 2-in. deck screws through the joint to fasten the roof panels together.

⓬ Install the gussets: Mark the inside faces of the roof panels with layout lines for gussets. The roof should overhang each gusset by 1 in. Spread moisture-resistant glue along the top long edges of the gussets, and clamp each gusset in place on the roof panels. Drive countersunk 2-in. deck screws through the roof panels and into the gussets **(See Photo D).**

APPLY FINISH

⓭ Sand the doghouse inside and out, as well as ease any sharp cut edges, especially around the doors.

⓮ Prepare the plywood for paint with a coat of exterior primer. Prime all surfaces, including the bottom edges of the doghouse that will come in contact with the ground. Topcoat with exterior paint **(See Photo E).**

PHOTO F: Staple a layer of building paper over the roof panels, then shingle the roof, starting from the bottom and working up to the peak.

PHOTO G: We stenciled the name of our project's future resident on the doghouse front.

SHINGLE THE ROOF

⑮ Cut and staple 15-pound building paper over the outer faces of the roof panels. Be sure the seams overlap at least 6 in. in the peak area to seal out leaks.

⑯ Install asphalt shingles over the building paper with roofing nails, just as you would shingle any roof. Start at the bottom and work your way up the roof, overlapping each course of shingles and staggering the shingle slots **(See Photo F).** Protect the roof peak with a row of overlapped shingle "ridge caps" nailed in place.

FINISHING TOUCHES

⑰ Stencil the dog's name on the project if you like, to add a personal touch **(See Photo G).**

⑱ In cold climates, install rigid foam insulation beneath the bottom panel (See *Adding insulation,* right).

Adding insulation

This doghouse project was designed to accept a sheet of 1-in.-thick rigid foam insulation below the bottom panel. Rigid foam is a good choice because it is relatively inexpensive and unaffected by ground moisture. Measure and cut the insulation with a utility knife. Glue it in place with construction adhesive.

Garden Bench

Imagine sipping a glass of lemonade and relaxing on this cedar bench some lazy summer afternoon. All it takes is a good day in the shop to make this vision a reality. The bench is designed to be easy to build, so you won't spend hours cutting and sanding elaborate curved profiles. In fact, most of your cutting chores involve making simple crosscuts with a circular saw.

Garden Bench

Vital Statistics

TYPE: Outdoor bench

OVERALL SIZE: 58½L by 33H by 24½D

MATERIAL: Cedar

JOINERY: Butt joints reinforced with glue and screws

CONSTRUCTION DETAILS:

· Project parts are sized to match nominal lumber width and thickness dimensions

· Stainless-steel screws are recommended for assembling the bench in order to avoid black stains around the fastener heads over time

FINISH: Clear wood preservative; could also be left unfinished and allowed to "weather" naturally to a silvery gray color

BUILDING TIME: 6-8 hours

Shopping List

☐ (1) 1 × 6 in. × 8 ft. cedar

☐ (3) 1 × 6 in. × 10 ft. cedar

☐ (5) 2 × 4 in. × 8 ft. cedar

☐ (1) 2 × 6 in. × 8 ft. cedar

☐ #8 stainless-steel deck screws (2-, 2½-, 3-in.)

☐ Finishing materials (optional)

Garden Bench: Step-by-step

BUILD THE BENCH SEAT

❶ Cross-cut the seat frame front, back, ends and two stretchers to length, according to the *Cutting List* dimensions on page 378.

❷ Assemble the seat frame front, back and ends. Arrange these parts so the outside faces of the frame ends are flush with the ends of the frame front and back pieces. Clamp up the parts. Drill countersunk pilot holes through the frame front and back pieces into the frame ends, and fasten the parts with 3-in. deck screws.

❸ Install the two seat frame stretchers: Measure and mark stretcher locations so the stretchers are centered on the

PHOTO A: Build the bench seat frame by fastening the front, back, ends and two stretchers together with 3-in. countersunk deck screws.

Garden Bench

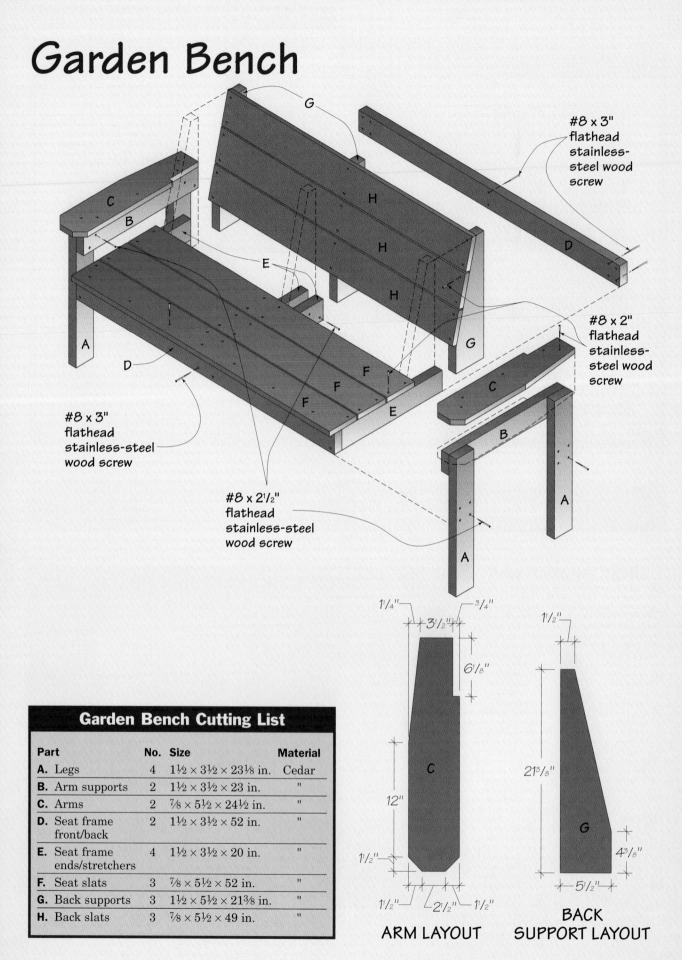

#8 x 3"
flathead
stainless-
steel wood
screw

#8 x 2"
flathead
stainless-
steel wood
screw

#8 x 3"
flathead
stainless-steel
wood screw

#8 x 2½"
flathead
stainless-steel
wood screw

ARM LAYOUT

BACK
SUPPORT LAYOUT

Garden Bench Cutting List

Part	No.	Size	Material
A. Legs	4	1½ × 3½ × 23⅛ in.	Cedar
B. Arm supports	2	1½ × 3½ × 23 in.	"
C. Arms	2	⅞ × 5½ × 24½ in.	"
D. Seat frame front/back	2	1½ × 3½ × 52 in.	"
E. Seat frame ends/stretchers	4	1½ × 3½ × 20 in.	"
F. Seat slats	3	⅞ × 5½ × 52 in.	"
G. Back supports	3	1½ × 5½ × 21⅜ in.	"
H. Back slats	3	⅞ × 5½ × 49 in.	"

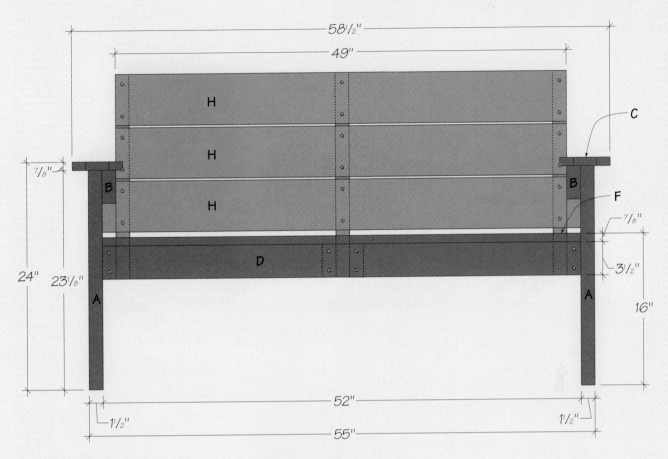

FRONT ELEVATION

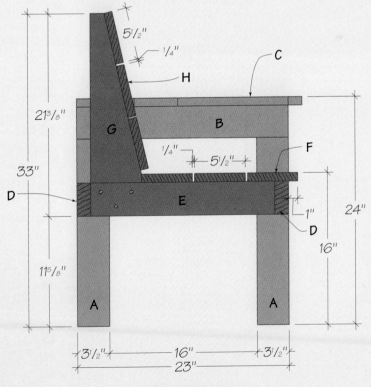

SIDE SECTION

PHOTO B: Install the seat slats on the bench seat frame with screws. Position the back seat slat 7 in. from the back of the seat frame. Insert ¼-in. temporary spacers between the slats before screwing the slats in place.

PHOTO C: Lay out the angled profile on the back support blanks with a straightedge.

PHOTO D: Cut the back supports to shape with your saw guided against a straightedge.

width of the frame and spaced 1½ in. apart (this spacing provides clearance for a seat back support later). Drive 3-in. countersunk deck screws through the seat frame front and back to secure the stretchers (**See Photo A**).

❹ Cross-cut three seat slats to length and fasten them to the seat frame. Arrange the seat slats so the ends are flush with the ends of the seat frame. Space the back slat 7 in. from the back of the frame, and insert ¼-in.-thick scrap spacers between the slats. Once the slats are positioned on the frame, the front slat should overhang the frame by 1 in. Drill countersunk pilot holes through the slats and into the seat frame members, and fasten the slats with 2-in. deck screws (**See Photo B**).

MAKE THE BENCH BACK

❺ Lay out the back supports: Cross-cut three back support blanks to a length of 21⅜ in. Draw the angled profile on each blank to match the *Back Support Layout* drawing, page 378 (**See Photo C**).

❻ Cut the back supports to shape. The easiest way to do this is to clamp each back support to your workbench so the cutting line overhangs the bench. Make the angled rip cuts with your saw guided against a clamped straightedge (**See Photo D**).

❼ Cross-cut three back slats to length.

❽ Assemble the bench back: Arrange the back supports on your workbench so they rest on their long back edges. Set the back slats in place on the back supports so the top slat on the bench back aligns with the top inside corners of the back supports. Separate the back slats with ¼-in. spacers. The ends of the back slats should be even with the outer back supports. Center the middle back support between the other two supports. Drive pairs of 2-in. deck screws through the slats at each back support location (**See Photo E**).

ATTACH THE SEAT & BACK

9 Slip the bench back supports inside the bench seat frame, behind the back seat slat and so the center seat stretchers "sandwich" the middle back support. Attach the bench seat and back assemblies by driving pairs of countersunk deck screws through the seat frame back and stretchers and into the back supports (**See Photo F**).

BUILD THE ARM & LEG ASSEMBLIES

10 Cross-cut the four legs and two arm supports to length.

11 Assemble the arm supports and legs: Lay an arm support on each pair of legs with the legs lying flat on the workbench and parallel to each other. Align each arm support so one edge is flush with the ends of the legs. Drive two countersunk screws through the arm supports at each leg to attach the parts and form two leg assemblies (**See Photo G**).

12 Fasten the leg assemblies to the bench seat: Clamp a leg assembly to each end of the bench seat so the outer edges of the legs are flush with the front and back of the seat. The arm supports should face inward. Adjust the parts so the seat slats are 16 in. up from the leg bottoms.

PHOTO E: Attach the back slats along the angled edges of the back supports with screws. Use ¼-in. spacers between the back slats to hold the slats apart.

PHOTO F: Fasten the bench back to the seat by slipping the back supports inside the seat frame and between the stretchers, then screwing through the seat frame back and stretchers into the back supports.

PHOTO G: Make the leg assemblies by fastening each arm support to a pair of legs. Drive pairs of 2½-in. countersunk deck screws through the arm supports and into each leg.

PHOTO H: Position and clamp the leg assemblies to the ends of the bench seat and attach the parts with screws. The arm supports should face inward.

Fasten the legs to the bench seat with four 2½-in. deck screws at each leg (See Photo H).

MAKE & ATTACH THE ARMS

⓮ Cross-cut two 24½-in. boards for the arms. Refer to the *Arm Layout* drawing, page 378, to draw the arm shapes on the blanks (See Photo I).

⓮ Clamp each arm workpiece to your worksurface, and cut out the arm shapes with a jig saw (See Photo J).

⓯ Position the arms on the arm supports so the back ends of the arms are flush with the back edges of the back legs. The long notch on each arm should wrap around the back supports, and the inside edge of the arms should overhang the arm supports by ¾ in. Attach the arms to the leg assemblies with 2-in. countersunk deck screws (See Photo K).

FINISHING TOUCHES

⓰ Sand all of the bench surfaces and ease the corners and edges with 100-grit sandpaper, especially the seat and back slats as well as the arms (See Photo L).

⓱ Brush on several coats of clear wood preservative, if you wish.

PHOTO I: Lay out the arm shapes on a pair of 1 × 6 cedar boards.

PHOTO J: Cut out the arms with a jig saw, with the workpieces clamped to your workbench.

PHOTO K: Position the arms on the leg assemblies and fasten them to the arm supports and the legs with screws.

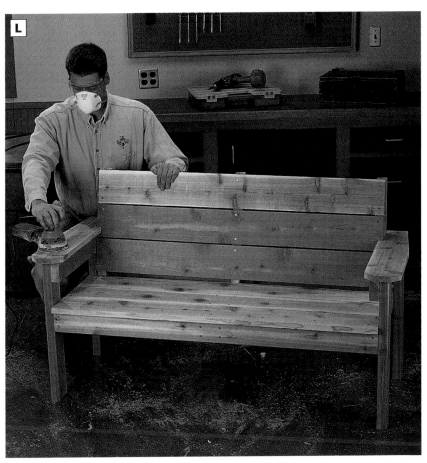

PHOTO L: Sand the bench smooth, especially the seat and back slats as well as the arms. Cedar dust can be a respiratory irritant, so wear a dust mask when sanding.

Potting Bench

The gardeners in your family will wonder how they ever got along without this versatile potting bench. Ruggedly built to withstand hard use, this bench features a rolling cart for potting soil or compost, a drawer for all those small tools and the convenience of a ready water supply and sink. Whether you're mixing soil, repotting plants or rinsing vegetables, this attractive bench will make your gardening work more enjoyable and efficient.

Vital Statistics: Potting Bench

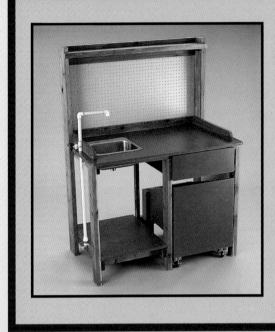

TYPE: Potting bench

OVERALL SIZE: 48W by 28½D by 63½H

MATERIAL: Cedar, exterior plywood, perforated hardboard

JOINERY: Butt joints reinforced with galvanized deck screws

CONSTRUCTION DETAILS:

· Countertop outfitted with removable bar sink

· Shop-made PVC plumbing system designed for garden hose hook-up

· Cart outfitted with rolling casters

FINISHING OPTIONS: Cedar parts topcoated with penetrating UV protectant sealer, exterior paint or leave unfinished to weather naturally to gray. Hardboard and exterior plywood finished with exterior latex primer and paint

Building time

PREPARING STOCK
0 hours

LAYOUT
3-4 hours

CUTTING PARTS
2-3 hours

ASSEMBLY
5-8 hours

FINISHING
3-5 hours

TOTAL: 13-20 hours

Tools you'll use

· Circular saw

· Jig saw

· Drill/driver

· Clamps

· Combination square

· Hacksaw

Shopping list

Plumbing parts:

☐ Stainless-steel bar sink

☐ ¾-in.-dia. PVC pipe (6 ft.)

☐ (2) strap clamps

☐ (2) 90° elbows

☐ PVC stop valve

☐ PVC female adaptor

☐ Hose thread to pipe thread transition fitting

☐ Angled hose fitting

☐ CPVC primer and cement

Shopping list

Bench materials:

☐ (2) 2 × 6 in. × 6 ft. cedar

☐ (1) 2 × 6 in. × 4 ft. cedar

☐ (6) 2 × 4 in. × 8 ft. cedar

☐ (4) 2 × 2 in. × 8 ft. cedar

☐ (1) 1 × 6 in. × 4 ft. cedar

☐ (1) 1 × 3 in. × 8 ft. cedar

☐ (2) ¾ in. × 4 × 8 ft. exterior plywood

☐ (1) ¼ in. × 4 × 4 ft. perforated hardboard

☐ (4) 2-in.-dia. casters

☐ Galvanized deck screws (1¼-, 1½-, 2-, 2½-in.)

☐ Latex primer and paint

☐ UV protectant sealer

Potting Bench

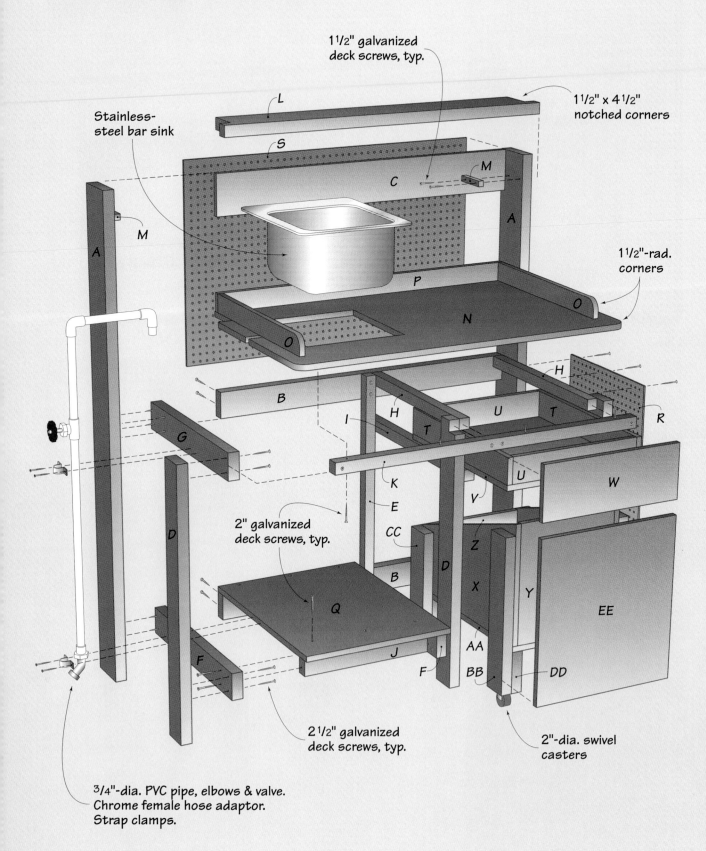

1½" galvanized
deck screws, typ.

1½" x 4½"
notched corners

Stainless-
steel bar sink

1½"-rad.
corners

2" galvanized
deck screws, typ.

2½" galvanized
deck screws, typ.

2"-dia. swivel
casters

¾"-dia. PVC pipe, elbows & valve.
Chrome female hose adaptor.
Strap clamps.

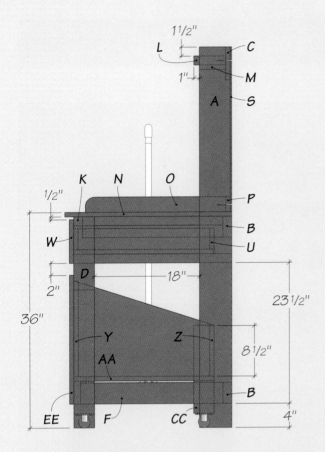

SIDE SECTION VIEW

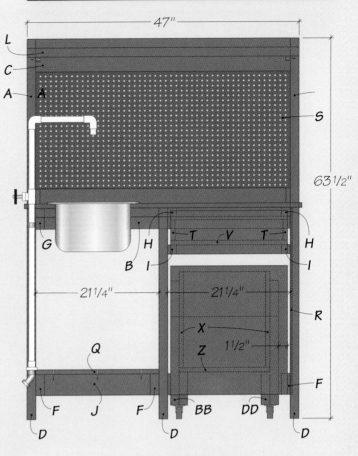

FRONT SECTION VIEW

Potting Bench Cutting List

Part	No.	Size	Material
A. Tall legs	2	$1\frac{1}{2} \times 5\frac{1}{2} \times 63\frac{1}{2}$ in.	Cedar
B. Back stretchers	2	$1\frac{1}{2}$ x $3\frac{1}{2} \times 44$ in.	"
C. Shelf stretcher	1	$\frac{3}{4} \times 5\frac{1}{2} \times 44$ in.	"
D. Front legs	3	$1\frac{1}{2} \times 3\frac{1}{2} \times 35\frac{1}{4}$ in.	"
E. Rear support	1	$1\frac{1}{2} \times 1\frac{1}{2} \times 35\frac{1}{4}$ in.	"
F. Lower stretchers	3	$1\frac{1}{2} \times 3\frac{1}{2} \times 24\frac{1}{2}$ in.	"
G. Upper stretcher	1	$1\frac{1}{2} \times 3\frac{1}{2} \times 24$ in.	"
H. Drawer stretchers	2	$1\frac{1}{2} \times 1\frac{1}{2} \times 24$ in.	"
I. Drawer slides	2	$1\frac{1}{2} \times 1\frac{1}{2} \times 27$ in.	"
J. Bottom stretcher (Front)	1	$1\frac{1}{2} \times 3\frac{1}{2} \times 18\frac{1}{4}$ in.	"
K. Top stretcher (Front)	1	$1\frac{1}{2} \times 1\frac{1}{2} \times 44$ in.	"
L. Shelf	1	$1\frac{1}{2} \times 5\frac{1}{2} \times 47$ in.	"
M. Shelf cleats	2	$\frac{3}{4} \times \frac{3}{4} \times 4\frac{1}{2}$ in.	"
N. Countertop	1	$\frac{3}{4} \times 28\frac{1}{2} \times 48$ in.	Exterior plywood
O. Side splashes	2	$\frac{3}{4} \times 2\frac{1}{2} \times 24$ in.	Cedar
P. Back splash	1	$\frac{3}{4} \times 2\frac{1}{2} \times 44$ in.	"
Q. Lower shelf	1	$\frac{3}{4} \times 27 \times 21\frac{1}{4}$ in.	Exterior plywood
R. Side panel	1	$\frac{1}{4} \times 18 \times 31\frac{1}{4}$ in.	Perforated board
S. Back panel	1	$\frac{1}{4} \times 27\frac{1}{2} \times 44$ in.	"
T. Drawer sides	2	$\frac{3}{4} \times 3\frac{1}{2} \times 24$ in.	Exterior plywood
U. Drawer ends	2	$\frac{3}{4} \times 3\frac{1}{2} \times 18\frac{3}{4}$ in.	"
V. Drawer bottom	1	$\frac{3}{4} \times 20\frac{1}{4} \times 24$ in.	"
W. Drawer face	1	$\frac{3}{4} \times 7\frac{1}{4} \times 20\frac{1}{4}$ in.	"

Cart Cutting List

Part	No.	Size	Material
X. Sides	2	$\frac{3}{4} \times 16 \times 24$ in.	Exterior plywood
Y. Front	1	$\frac{3}{4} \times 14\frac{1}{4} \times 16$ in.	"
Z. Back	1	$\frac{3}{4} \times 14\frac{1}{4} \times 8\frac{1}{2}$ in.	"
AA. Bottom	1	$\frac{3}{4} \times 15\frac{3}{4} \times 24$ in.	"
BB. Front legs	2	$1\frac{1}{2} \times 3\frac{1}{2} \times 20\frac{3}{4}$ in.	Cedar
CC. Back legs	2	$1\frac{1}{2} \times 3\frac{1}{2} \times 14\frac{3}{4}$ in.	"
DD. Leg cleats	4	$1\frac{1}{2} \times 3\frac{1}{2} \times 5\frac{1}{2}$ in.	"
EE. Face	1	$\frac{3}{4} \times 20\frac{1}{4} \times 21\frac{1}{2}$ in.	Exterior plywood

BUILD THE BENCH FRAME

1 Cut the following cedar parts to size: tall legs, front legs, drawer stretchers, drawer slides, upper stretcher and lower stretchers. Label each part in pencil to make the pieces easy to identify.

2 Build the left (plumbing) end assembly. As shown in the exploded drawing on page 386, the left end consists of a tall leg and a front leg joined by an upper stretcher and one of the lower stretchers. Install the upper stretcher flush with the top of the front leg, and inset it 1½ in. on both the front and back legs to allow space for the front top stretcher and the back stretcher. Install the lower stretcher 4 in. above the floor, and hold it in 1½ in. at the back and 1 in. at the front. Square up the assembly, drill countersunk pilot holes and fasten the parts with 2½-in. galvanized deck screws. When completed, the overall depth from the back edge of the tall leg to the front edge of the front leg should be 27 in.

3 Build the right end assembly. The right end consists of a tall leg, front leg, drawer stretcher, drawer slide and lower stretcher. Install the drawer stretcher just as you did for the upper stretcher in Step 2. Install the lower stretcher 4 in. above the floor, holding it in 1½ in. at the back and 1 in. at the front. Install the drawer slide 4¾ in. below the bottom edge of the drawer stretcher and flush with the outside edges of the legs. Fasten the whole assembly together with

PHOTO A: Build the right assembly by attaching a drawer stretcher, drawer slide and lower stretcher between a tall leg and front leg. Fasten the parts together with 2½-in. deck screws. Use a combination square to draw layout lines for the parts and to check the joints for square.

PHOTO B: Assemble the bench framework by attaching the two back stretchers, shelf stretcher and top front stretcher to the end assemblies. The ends of the stretchers should butt against the inside faces of the front and back legs. See Step 4 for exact stretcher placement.

deck screws driven into counter-sunk pilot holes **(See Photo A).**

❹ Connect the end assemblies with stretchers. Cut to size and attach the two back stretchers, shelf stretcher and the front top stretcher **(See Photo B).** When you install the shelf stretcher, inset it ¼ in. from the back edges of the tall legs to allow for the thickness of the back panel. Position the back stretchers 4 in. and 35¼ in. from the bottoms of the back legs.

❺ Build and install the middle support assembly. Cut the rear support, front bottom stretcher and remaining front leg to size. Cut a 1½ × 1½-in. notch in the top end of the front leg **(See Photo C).** Fasten the rear support, front leg, drawer stretcher, drawer slide and lower stretcher together with deck screws.

❻ Stand the support assembly you made in Step 5 in place, and position it by attaching the front bottom stretcher with deck screws **(See Photo D).** Complete the installation by screwing the support to the top front stretcher and both back stretchers.

❼ Build the benchtop. Cut the countertop to size (see *Cutting List,* page 387) from exterior plywood. Mark and cut a 1½-in.-radius arc on both front corners. Cut a 2 × 5½-in. notch on the back corners so the countertop fits around the tall legs and overhangs the bench by ½ in. on each end. Mark and cut a clearance slot in the left edge of the top, 1¼ in. wide by 1½ in. deep, for the plumbing assembly.

❽ Position the sink on the countertop so it is centered above the

PHOTO C: Notch the top front corner of the center front leg so it will fit around the top front stretcher. Then combine this leg with the rear support, drawer stretcher, drawer slide and lower stretcher to form the middle support assembly.

PHOTO D: Install the front bottom stretcher 3 in. back from the front ends of the lower stretchers to position the middle support assembly. Fasten the bottom stretcher in place, then attach the middle support assembly to the top front stretcher and back stretchers.

PHOTO E: Center the sink so it will hang over the storage area on the left side of the bench. Lay out the sink opening using the template provided by the manufacturer, and cut out the sink opening.

PHOTO F: Install the back splash and side splash pieces on the countertop, then fasten the countertop to the bench framework by driving screws through the stretchers from below and into the countertop.

PHOTO G: Fasten the perfboard side and back panels to the bench framework with 1½-in. galvanized deck screws. Be careful not to overdrive the screws when installing the perfboard.

open storage area on the left half of the bench. Mark and cut out the sink opening **(See Photo E).**

❾ Cut the lower shelf, side panel and back panel to size. Then prime and paint the countertop, lower shelf and the side and back panels.

❿ Cut out and attach the shelf cleats and the shelf to the tall legs. Position the cleats 3 in. from the tops of the tall legs, drill countersunk pilot holes and attach the cleats with 1½-in. galvanized deck screws. Notch the ends of the shelf (See drawing, page 386) to fit around the tall legs. Install the shelf with screws driven through the shelf stretcher from the back.

⓫ Cut out and attach the back and side splashes to the countertop. Clamp the back splash in place between the notches at the back of the countertop, and inset it ¼ in. from the back edge of the countertop to allow for the back panel. Drill countersunk pilot holes up through the bottom of the countertop and into the bottom edge of the back splash, then fasten it to the countertop with 2-in. galvanized deck screws. Round the top front corner of each side splash. Clamp the splashes in place and attach with screws.

12 Install the lower shelf to the back and bottom front stretchers with 2-in. deck screws.

13 Attach the countertop assembly to the bench with 2-in. screws **(See Photo F).**

14 Install the perfboard back and side panels **(See Photo G).**

BUILD THE DRAWER & CART

15 Cut the drawer sides, ends, bottom and face to size from ¾-in. exterior plywood.

16 Cut the plywood cart parts to size. To cut the angle on the cart sides, mark a point on each back edge 8½ in. from the bottom corner. Draw lines from each of these marks to the upper front corners **(See Photo H).** Cut the angles.

17 Prime all surfaces of the drawer and cart parts. Sand the surfaces and edges smooth first.

18 Assemble the drawer box. Apply glue to the ends of the end pieces, clamp the ends in place between the side pieces and assemble with 1½-in. galvanized deck screws **(See Photo I).** Position the drawer bottom, using it to square up the rest of the drawer structure. Fasten the bottom to the ends and sides with screws.

19 Assemble the cart box. As with the drawer, the ends are fastened between the sides, and the bottom piece fastens to the bottom edges of the ends and sides. Use countersunk 1½-in. screws for attaching the parts.

20 Paint the assembled drawer box and the loose drawer face, as well as the cart and the cart face. Apply two coats of exterior latex paint.

PHOTO H: Cut the cart's angled sides by measuring 8½ in. along one short edge of each side panel. Connect this point to the top corner on the opposite edge with a straightedge. Cut these parts to shape. Assemble the sides, ends and bottom panel to form the cart box.

PHOTO I: Glue and screw the drawer ends to the side pieces, driving the screws through countersunk pilot holes to keep the plywood from splitting. Then, fasten the drawer bottom to the bottom edges of this drawer frame. Use the bottom as a guide for squaring up the drawer.

PHOTO J: Clamp the drawer face to the front of the drawer box so the ends of the drawer face are flush with the drawer sides. The face should overhang the top and bottom of the drawer by 1½ in. Fasten the drawer face with 1¼-in. deck screws, driven from inside the drawer.

PHOTO K: Install the leg assemblies to the cart box with 1½-in. screws. The front legs should butt against the back of the cart face. Attach the rear legs so they are flush with the cart back.

PHOTO L: Attach casters to the cart leg and cleat assemblies. We used swiveling locking casters on the front legs and fixed casters on the back. If you plan to fill the cart with dirt, be sure the casters are sturdy.

㉑ Attach the drawer face. Center the face on the front of the drawer box, flush on the ends and over-hanging 1½ in. on both the top and the bottom edges. Clamp the face in position, drill countersunk pilot holes and attach the face from inside the drawer with 1¼-in. galvanized deck screws (See Photo J).

㉒ Attach the cart face. Note that the face is not centered on the cart: it overhangs 1½ in. on the left side, 3 in. on the right side and ½ in. at the top. Hold the face in position with spring clamps, and screw the face to the cart from inside the cart box.

㉓ Attach the cart legs and cart leg cleats. Cut the cart legs and cleats to size. Fasten the cleats to the legs with 2½-in. deck screws. Attach the legs to the cart with 2-in. deck screws (See Photo K).

㉔ Attach the casters to the legs and cleats (See Photo L). We used locking casters in the front so the cart stays in its place until you want to move it.

ADD THE PLUMBING

The sink is simply set loose into the countertop cutout. It can drain either directly into a 5-gallon pail, or you can use a hose clamp to attach a length of flexible tubing to the drain tail and route it to your desired location. The "faucet" is fabricated from PVC and metal parts (See *Plumbing Parts*, next page) that are available from any local building supply center.

㉕ Fabricate the PVC water supply and faucet assembly. Cut the three sections of straight piping to length with a hacksaw. De-burr the cuts with a utility knife or emery paper. Dry-fit the PVC assembly together to make sure the lengths are correct. Draw an alignment mark across the fitting and pipe at every joint with a permanent marker to help you make the proper alignments quickly, once the pieces are cemented together. Disassemble the pieces.

㉖ Build the plumbing assembly. Prepare the joint surfaces by scuffing with emery cloth. When you make the joints, wear gloves and be sure your work area is well ventilated. Make one joint at a time.

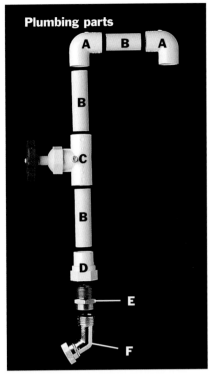

Plumbing parts

This plumbing system is designed to hook up to a garden hose for a water supply. To build it, you'll need: (A) 90° elbow; (B) ¾-in. PVC pipe; (C) PVC stop valve; (D) Female adaptor; (E) Hose thread to pipe thread transition fitting; (F) Angled hose connector.

Apply an even coat of PVC primer to both joint surfaces. Spread PVC cement onto the primed surfaces, following the directions on the can. Quickly slip the fitting and pipe together. Rotate the pieces a quarter turn to spread the glue evenly, and hold the parts in place with the marks aligned for approximately one minute **(See Photo M)**.

㉗ Attach the plumbing assembly to the bench. Position the assembly in the countertop notch, and secure the plumbing with strap clamps **(See Photo N)**.

FINISHING TOUCHES

㉘ Seal or paint the cedar parts of your bench as you like. No finish is actually required, but the cedar will turn gray if it isn't covered with a UV sealer.

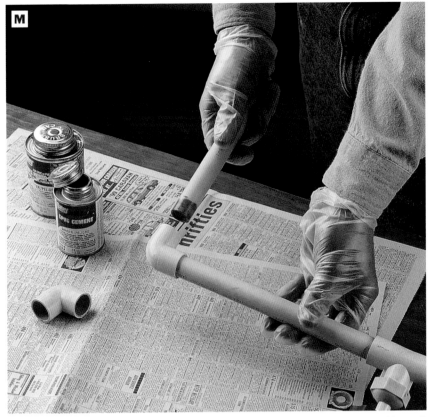

PHOTO M: Cut the straight pipe sections to length and dry-assemble the entire plumbing unit to check its fit on the potting bench. Then disassemble the PVC, prime the mating parts of each joint, and bond the PVC together with CPVC cement. Wear gloves when bonding the parts.

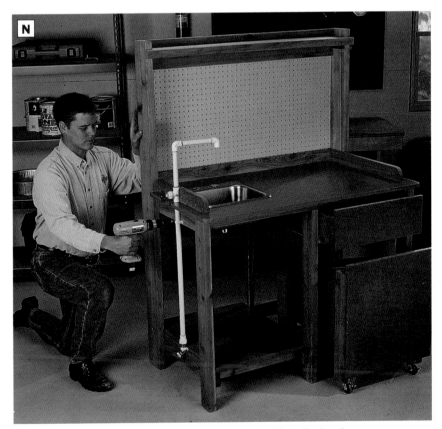

PHOTO N: Use strap clamps to attach the plumbing assembly to the bench.

Cedar Bird Feeder

Invite songbirds into your yard or garden with this aromatic cedar bird feeder.
Our design features a wide, protective roof to keep the feed dry, along with narrow perches to discourage larger predator birds. The feeder can be mounted to a post or hung from a branch, and you can build one in an afternoon.

Vital Statistics: Cedar Bird Feeder

TYPE: Bird feeder

OVERALL SIZE: 6W by 9¾H by 8L

MATERIAL: Aromatic cedar

JOINERY: Miters, screwed butt joints

CONSTRUCTION DETAILS:

· Lid hinges open on one side for cleaning and filling

· Plexiglas end panels are epoxied into shallow grooves in the sides

· Perches made of ¼-in. doweling

· Part ends are rounded over for finished look

FINISH: None

Building time

PREPARING STOCK
1 hour

LAYOUT
1 hour

CUTTING PARTS
2 hours

ASSEMBLY
2 hours

FINISHING
None

TOTAL: 6 hours

Tools you'll use

· Table saw

· Drill/driver

· Power miter saw (optional)

· Clamps

· Router table with ⅜-in. roundover bit

· Belt sander (optional)

· Drill press

· Hammer and nailset

Shopping list

☐ (1) ¾ × 6 in. × 4 ft. aromatic cedar

☐ (2) ⅛ × 3½ × 5⅞ in. Plexiglas

☐ ¼-in.-dia. hardwood dowel

☐ Two-part epoxy

☐ 4d galvanized finish nails

☐ ¾ × 4-in. brass jewelry box hinge

☐ Polyurethane glue

Cedar Bird Feeder

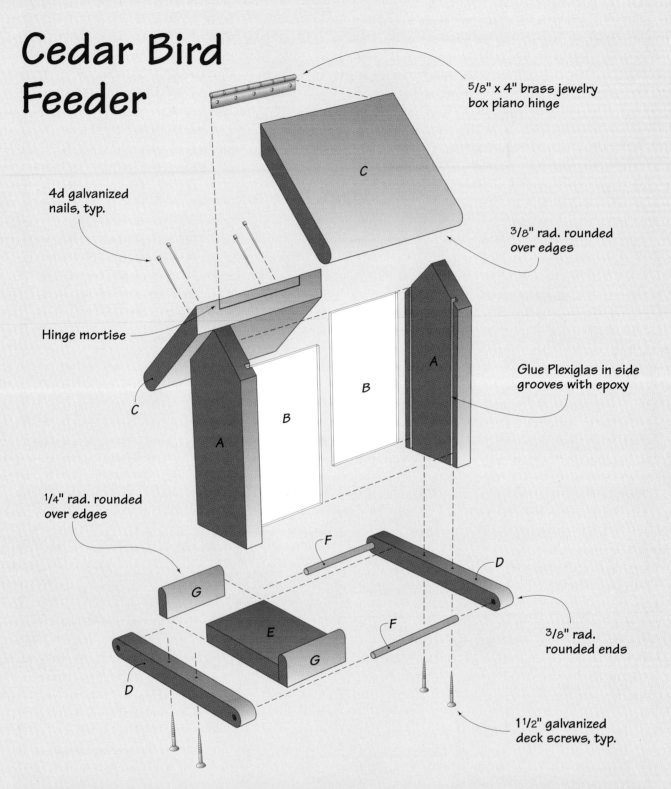

5/8" x 4" brass jewelry box piano hinge

4d galvanized nails, typ.

3/8" rad. rounded over edges

Hinge mortise

Glue Plexiglas in side grooves with epoxy

1/4" rad. rounded over edges

3/8" rad. rounded ends

1 1/2" galvanized deck screws, typ.

Cedar Bird Feeder Cutting List

Part	No.	Size	Material	Part	No.	Size	Material
A. Sides	2	3/4 × 3 × 8 in.	Cedar	**E.** Base plate	1	3/4 × 3 × 4 1/2 in.	Cedar
B. Ends	2	1/8 × 3 1/2 × 5 7/8 in.	Plexiglas	**F.** Perches	2	1/4 dia. × 4 1/2 in.	Hardwood dowel
C. Roof panels	2	3/4 × 6 × 5 1/8 in.	Cedar	**G.** Feed dams	2	1/2 × 1 1/4 × 3 in.	Cedar
D. Base strips	2	3/4 × 3/4 × 8 in.	"				

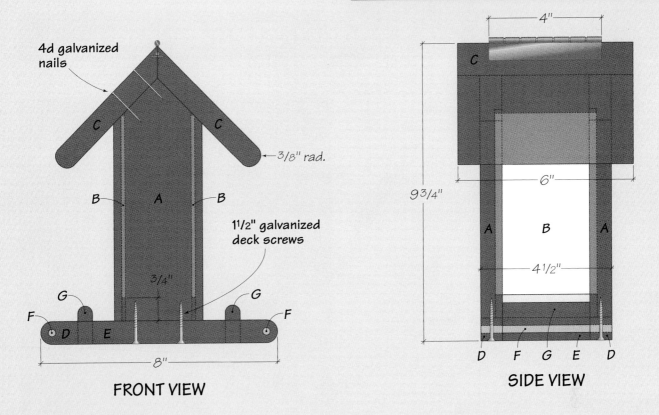

4d galvanized nails

3/8" rad.

C C

B A B

1 1/2" galvanized deck screws

3/4"

G G

F D E F

8"

FRONT VIEW

4"

C

9 3/4"

6"

A B A

4 1/2"

D F G E D

SIDE VIEW

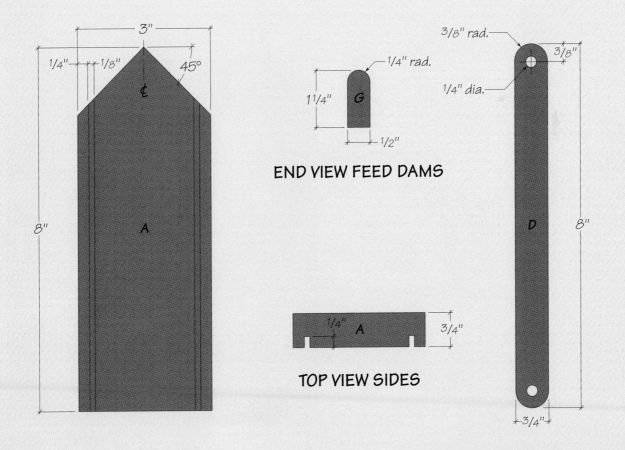

3"

1/4" 1/8" 45°

¢

A

8"

FRONT VIEW SIDES

1/4" rad.

1 1/4" G

1/2"

END VIEW FEED DAMS

1/4" A 3/4"

TOP VIEW SIDES

3/8" rad.

3/8"

1/4" dia.

D 8"

3/4"

FRONT VIEW BASE STRIPS

MAKE THE SIDES & ENDS

1 Lay out and cut the two sides to shape: Rip stock for the sides to 3 in. wide, and cross-cut the workpieces to 8 in. long. Form gables on one end of each side panel at the power miter saw with the blade turned 45° to the right or left **(See Photo A).** You can also make these gable cuts on the table saw with each workpiece held against the miter gauge, set at 45°. Align the cuts so the tip of the gable is centered on the width of the sides.

2 Cut grooves in the sides for the Plexiglas end panels. See the *Front View Sides* drawing on page 397 for positioning the grooves on the sides. Plow these ¼-in.-deep grooves on the table saw with a ⅛-in. kerf blade and the fence set ¼ in. from the blade.

3 Cut the Plexiglas end panels to size: To avoid scratching the panels, don't remove the clear film that covers the plastic for marking or cutting. Lay out the part shapes and cut the Plexiglas to size on the band saw with a fined-toothed blade **(See Photo B).** You can cut Plexiglas on the table saw also, but use a fine-toothed plywood-cutting blade or a blade intended to cut plastic and laminate. Otherwise, the Plexiglas will tend to chip as you cut. Gently sand the edges of each panel, then dry-fit them into the grooves in the cedar side pieces to be sure they fit. Widen the grooves if necessary on the table saw.

MAKE THE ROOF SECTIONS

4 Start by making a blank for both roof sections from one piece of stock. The board dimensions should be 6 in. wide and 10⅜ in. long. Round over both ends of the blank on the router table with a ⅜-in. roundover bit. NOTE: *Be careful when the router bit exits the board. Aromatic cedar is soft, and the end grain will tear out on the edges of the boards. Rout these bullnose profiles in several passes of increasing depth, which will also help minimize chipping and tearout.*

5 Split the roof blank in half to form the two roof sections. Since the roof sections meet at a 45° angle at the bird feeder peak, you'll cross-cut the roof blank in half at the table saw with the blade set at a 45°

PHOTO A: Trim the gable ends of the sides on a power miter saw with the blade swiveled to 45°. Center the gable peaks across the width of the workpieces.

PHOTO B: Measure and cut the Plexiglas end panels on the band saw with a fine-toothed blade. Leave the protective film on the plastic as you machine it, to minimize scratching.

PHOTO C: Tilt the table saw blade to 45° and cut the roof blank in half to form two roof sections. Take time to set up this cut accurately. Otherwise the roof section lengths won't match. One cut both trims the parts to length and forms the roof miter joint.

PHOTO D: Mark and cut the shallow hinge mortises into the beveled edges of the roof sections. Score along your mortise layout lines first with a utility knife, then pare out the mortise with a sharp chisel. Keep the mortise depth the same as the hinge leaf thickness.

bevel angle **(See Photo C).** Be careful when setting up this cut so you'll divide the roof blank equally.

6 Cut hinge mortises into the top bevels of the roof sections: The roof halves will be joined together with a single brass jewelry box hinge. In order to form a relatively tight miter joint at the bird feeder peak, you'll need to recess the hinge leaves into shallow mortises cut into the roof sections. Lay out the hinge location on each roof section by outlining the shape of the hinge leaves along the top edge of the roof bevels. Keep the knuckle of the hinge above the bevel edge, as shown in the *Side View* drawing, page 397. Clamp each roof section in a vise, and score along your mortise layout lines with a utility knife. Then pare away the material within your layout lines with a sharp chisel **(See Photo D).** The mortises shouldn't be deeper than the hinge leaves are thick.

BUILD THE BASE

7 Make the base strips: Rip a ¾-in.-wide stick of cedar to 16⅛ in. long on the table saw. Cross-cut the workpiece in half to form two 8-in.-long base strips. Round-over the ends of the strips with a wood rasp and random-orbit sander or on a stationary disk

sander. NOTE: *These ends are too narrow to round-over with a router without tearing out the wood.*

8 Drill holes through the ends of the base strips for the perches: Lay out the centerpoints for these perch holes on one base strip, ⅜ in. from each end. Stack the marked base strip on top of the other strip, and clamp them to your drill press table. Use a backer board beneath the base strips to keep from drilling into the drill press table. Chuck a ¼-in.-dia. bit in the drill press, and drill holes completely through both base strips **(See Photo E).** Dry-fit the perch doweling into the base strip holes to be sure it will fit.

9 Make the remaining base parts: Rip and cross-cut the base plate to size. Measure and cut the perch dowels to length at this time as well.

10 Assemble the base. Install the perches in one of the base strips, using a dab of polyurethane glue in each dowel hole. Apply a coat of polyurethane glue to the long edges of the base plate, and wet the mating surfaces of the base strips with a water-dampened rag. Squeeze a drop of glue into the dowel holes of the other base strip and assemble

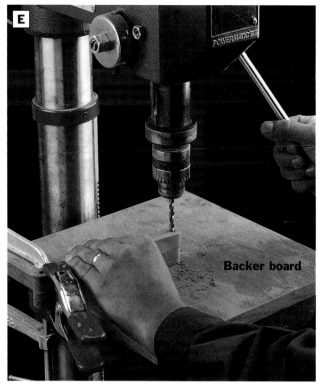

PHOTO E: Bore ¼-in.-dia. holes for the perches through both ends of the base strips. We stacked these parts and drilled both strips at once on the drill press.

PHOTO F: Assemble the base plate, base strips and perches with polyurethane glue. Clamp the parts together to keep the glue from forcing the joints open as it cures.

the base parts together, making sure the perches are properly seated in their holes **(See Photo F)**. Tap them gently, if needed, with a mallet. Polyurethane glue will foam and expand as it cures, so hold the base strips against the base plate with a couple of short bar clamps or large C-clamps until the glue cures. Clean up excess glue immediately with mineral spirits.

⓫ Make the feed dams: Since these parts are small, and one long edge of each receives a bullnosed profile, start from a piece of wide stock (6 in. wide or wider) and rout the bullnoses first before ripping and cross-cutting the dams to size. Routing wider stock will keep your hands a safe distance from the router bit. Round-over one long edge of the workpiece on the router table with a ⅜-in.-dia. roundover bit. Then rip and cross-cut the feed dams to size.

⓬ Install the feed dams on the bird feeder base. Attach the dams to the short ends of the base plate in between the base strips with polyurethane glue. Use a clamp to hold the dams in position until the glue cures. Again, clean up excess glue before it sets.

ASSEMBLE THE BIRD FEEDER

⓭ Install the clear end panels in the grooves in the

cedar sides: Spread a thin coat of two-part epoxy into each of the grooves in the sides, keeping the adhesive about 1 in. shy of the top and bottom of each groove. (Two-part epoxy is a good adhesive for bonding Plexiglas.) Remove the protective film from the Plexiglas, and slip the two end panels into their respective grooves, aligning them so they're approximately ¾ in. up from the bottoms of the sides **(See Photo G).**

⓮ Fasten the base to the sides: Apply a bead of polyurethane glue along the bottom edge of each side, then center the sides on the base strips. Drill countersunk pilot holes up through the bottom of the base strips and into the sides, and drive 1½-in. galvanized wood screws into the holes **(See Photo H).** Then drill a few ⅟₁₆-in.-dia. weep holes through the base, which will help keep the feed dry.

⓯ Assemble the roof: Mark and drill pilot holes for the brass screws that will attach the hinge to the roof sections. Install the hinge.

⓰ Fasten the roof to the side panels. Spread a bead of polyurethane glue along one gable edge of each side panel. Wet the mating surfaces of one of the roof sections and set the roof in place over the sides.

PHOTO G: Spread two-part epoxy into the grooves in the side panels, remove the protective film from the Plexiglas end pieces, and slide the end pieces into the grooves. The end pieces should stop ¾ in. from the bottoms of the sides.

PHOTO H: Attach the base to the sides with polyurethane glue and 1½-in. countersunk galvanized wood screws. Then drill a few small weep holes (smaller than the seed you'll put in the feeder) to allow any moisture to drain away, keeping the bird seed dry.

Be careful to align the roof so it overhangs the sides evenly. Drive a few galvanized 4d finish nails down through the glued roof section to fasten it to the sides **(See Photo I).** It's a good idea to drill pilot holes for these nails first, to keep the nails from splitting the sides. Then countersink the nailheads with a nailset.

Feeding songbirds

The type of food you provide in the feeder will in large part determine the bird species you attract. Dark-eyed juncos, for example, love millet, especially when it falls on the ground below the feeder. Sunflower seeds are a sure bet for bluejays, chickadees, cardinals, gold and purple finches, nuthatches, the tufted titmouse and pine siskens. Downy woodpeckers and blue jays also like an occasional meal of shelled peanuts. Regardless of the type of feed you use, experts agree that the feeder must be cleaned out regularly to keep the contents from molding. If the birds should consume molded seed, it can cause aspergillosis, a fatal illness for songbirds.

PHOTO I: Attach one half of the roof to the body of the bird feeder with polyurethane glue and galvanized 4d nails. The other roof section hinges open to allow easy access for filling and cleaning the feeder.

Up-and-Away Wind Chime

Nothing graces a summer evening like the sight of a brightly colored hot-air balloon overhead. This unique wind chime brings that simple pleasure home. Strong, bright colors and gentle chiming tones treat the senses as they announce the arrival of a cooling summer breeze. A charming gift, this simple project is made primarily from exterior plywood and rigid copper tubing as well as a few odds and ends from your fishing tackle box.

Vital Statistics: Up-and-Away Wind Chime

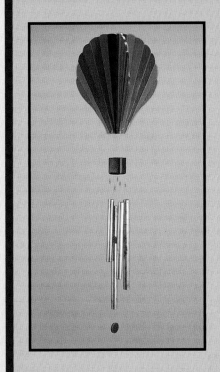

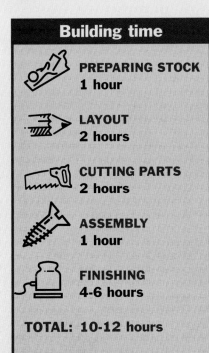

TYPE: Wind chime

OVERALL SIZE: 12½W by 12½D by 14¼L (balloon only)

MATERIAL: Plywood, pine

JOINERY: Half-lap joints

CONSTRUCTION DETAILS:

· The three-dimensional balloon is made of two plywood segments that interlock in a half-lap joint

· Basket made from a laminated block of pine with a 1½-in.-dia. hole drilled into the center

· Chimes, basket, clanger and sail are suspended from the balloon with monofilament fishing line and brass swivels

FINISH: Exterior latex primer, paint

Building time

PREPARING STOCK
1 hour

LAYOUT
2 hours

CUTTING PARTS
2 hours

ASSEMBLY
1 hour

FINISHING
4-6 hours

TOTAL: 10-12 hours

Tools you'll use

· Table saw

· Band, jig saw or scroll saw

· Drill press and 1½-in. Forstner bit

· Belt sander

· Drill/driver

· Hacksaw

· File

Shopping list

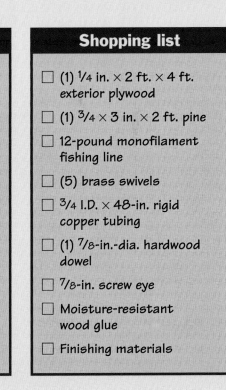

☐ (1) ¼ in. × 2 ft. × 4 ft. exterior plywood

☐ (1) ¾ × 3 in. × 2 ft. pine

☐ 12-pound monofilament fishing line

☐ (5) brass swivels

☐ ¾ I.D. × 48-in. rigid copper tubing

☐ (1) ⅞-in.-dia. hardwood dowel

☐ ⅞-in. screw eye

☐ Moisture-resistant wood glue

☐ Finishing materials

Up-and-Away Wind Chime

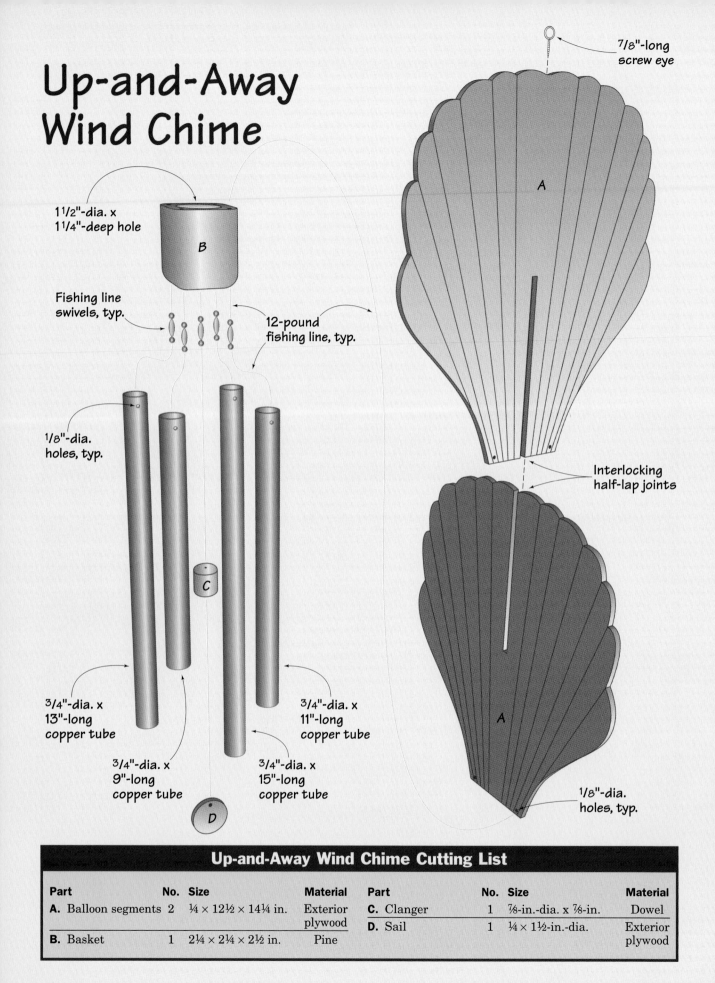

7/8"-long screw eye

1 1/2"-dia. x 1 1/4"-deep hole

B

Fishing line swivels, typ.

12-pound fishing line, typ.

1/8"-dia. holes, typ.

A

Interlocking half-lap joints

C

A

3/4"-dia. x 13"-long copper tube

3/4"-dia. x 11"-long copper tube

3/4"-dia. x 9"-long copper tube

3/4"-dia. x 15"-long copper tube

1/8"-dia. holes, typ.

D

Up-and-Away Wind Chime Cutting List

Part	No.	Size	Material	Part	No.	Size	Material
A. Balloon segments	2	1/4 × 12 1/2 × 14 1/4 in.	Exterior plywood	**C.** Clanger	1	7/8-in.-dia. x 7/8-in.	Dowel
B. Basket	1	2 1/4 × 2 1/4 × 2 1/2 in.	Pine	**D.** Sail	1	1/4 × 1 1/2-in.-dia.	Exterior plywood

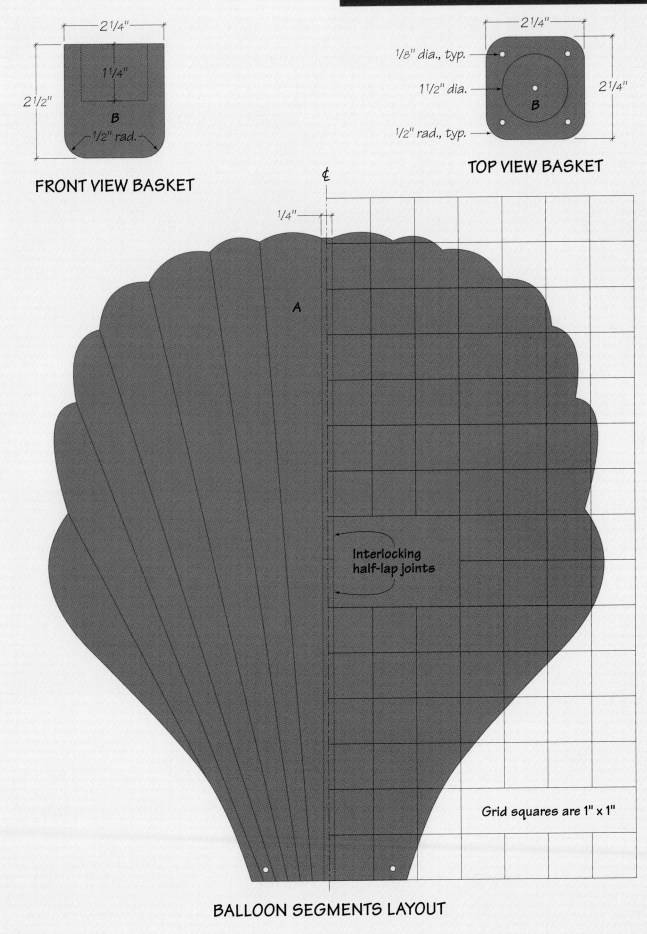

2 1/4"

1 1/4"

2 1/2"

B

1/2" rad.

FRONT VIEW BASKET

2 1/4"

1/8" dia., typ.

1 1/2" dia.

2 1/4"

B

1/2" rad., typ.

TOP VIEW BASKET

¢

1/4"

A

Interlocking
half-lap joints

Grid squares are 1" x 1"

BALLOON SEGMENTS LAYOUT

START WITH THE BALLOON

❶ Cut out and assemble the balloon. First, rip and cross-cut two 12½ × 14¼-in. pieces of plywood for the balloon segments. Enlarge the *Balloon Segments Layout* drawing on page 405 to make a full-size template for tracing the balloon parts. Then mark the locations of the half-lap slots on each workpiece. Set up your router table with a ¼-in. straight bit and adjust the fence so the bit lines up with the half-lap slots. Rout the slots into both balloon segments **(See Photo A).** Cut the balloon segments to shape with a band saw, scroll saw or jig saw. Sand the cut edges smooth, then slide the two segments together in the half-lap slots. When you are satisfied with the fit, disassemble the parts, spread moisture-resistant wood glue along the inside edges of the slots, and glue the balloon together.

❷ Drill a ⅛-in.-dia. hole near the bottom end of each quadrant of the balloon for attaching fishing line (See the *Balloon Segments Layout* drawing, page 405, when you mark these hole locations).

MAKE THE BASKET, CHIMES, CLANGER & SAIL

❸ Build the basket blank: Rip your ¾-in. pine stock to 2¼ in. wide and cross-cut three 8-in.-long strips. Face-glue the strips together to form a long blank for the basket. NOTE: *A long blank will be easier to clamp to the drill press table for boring the large hole.* Then rip-cut the blank so it is 2¼ in. square, and mark the centerpoint on one end of the blank. Flip your drill press table to vertical (90°), and clamp the blank so the end with the center-point faces up. Be sure the blank is square to the table. Chuck a 1½-in.-dia. Forstner bit in the drill press and line it up with the centerpoint on the end of the blank. Bore a 1¼-in.-deep hole. Unclamp the blank from the drill press and cross-cut the 2½-in.-long basket from the blank on the table saw or power miter saw. Next, drill five ⅛-in.-dia. holes through the bottom of the basket for attaching the chimes and clanger. Refer to the *Top View Basket* drawing on page 405 to mark the positions of these holes. Finally, secure the basket in a vise and round-over all sharp edges and corners with a belt sander so it resembles a basket.

PHOTO A: Notch the balloon segments for a half-lap joint on the router table. Rout these slots before cutting the balloon segments to shape, or you'll lose the straight edge to slide against the router fence.

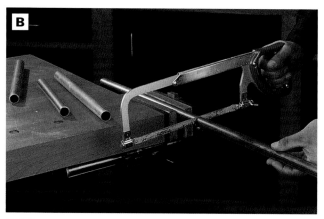

PHOTO B: Meaure and cut lengths of rigid tubing (we used copper) for the chimes. Clamp the tubing in a bench vise, and make these cuts with a hacksaw. Then file the cut edges smooth.

❹ Measure and cut the chimes to length. We used ¾-in.-dia. rigid copper tubing, available at any home center, for the chimes. You could also use hollow aluminum or brass tubing, which will produce distinctly different sounds. Cut four lengths of tubing to 9, 11, 13 and 15 in. for the chimes. Drill ⅛-in.-dia. holes about ¼ in. from one end of each chime through both walls of the pipes. You'll string the pipes to the basket through these holes. Then

PHOTO C: Prime the balloon and other wood parts first, then topcoat with exterior latex paint. Mask off areas where the color changes, and paint all like-colors at once.

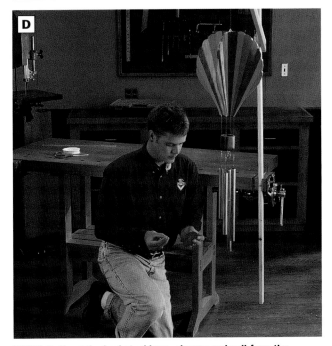

PHOTO D: Hang the basket, chimes, clanger and sail from the balloon with strong monofilament fishing line. Add brass swivels when you hang the chimes so the chimes can turn freely.

file the cut edges of the chimes smooth to remove any burrs. NOTE: *If you use copper tubing, it will eventually oxidize and turn a pleasing green color. If you prefer the copper color, spray on several coats of clear, spray-on lacquer to seal them.*

❺ Cross-cut a ⅞-in.-long piece of dowel for the clanger, and drill a hole through the middle. Lay out and cut a 1½-in.-dia. plywood circle for the sail, and drill a small hole through the sail near the edge. Sand these parts smooth.

PAINT THE WOOD PARTS

❻ Prime and paint the balloon, basket, clanger and sail. If you choose a multi-colored scheme like we did for our balloon, paint like-colored bands at the same time, masking them off from the other colored bands carefully **(See Photo C)**. Let each color dry completely before moving on to another color.

ASSEMBLE THE WIND CHIME

❼ Using two lengths of 12-pound fishing line, attach the basket to the balloon as follows: Tie one end of one line to a hole at the bottom of a balloon segment. Thread the line down through one of the bottom basket holes, across to the diagonal basket hole and up through to the opposite ballon segment hole. Tie off the line so the basket hangs about

3½ in. down from the balloon. Repeat this process with the other piece of fishing line, crisscrossing the line beneath the basket to cradle it and tying off to the remaining two balloon segment holes.

❽ Install the chimes. Use a brass swivel and two lengths of fishing line to hang each chime from the four bottom corner holes of the basket. Tie line from the chime to the swivel and from the swivel up through each basket hole, knotting it securely inside the basket. Plan for the chimes to hang about 4 to 6 in. from the bottom of the basket.

❾ Secure the clanger and sail by knotting and threading a 12-in.-long piece of fishing line down through the center basket hole, then tying off the clanger 9 in. down and attaching the round sail at the bottom of the line **(See Photo D)**.

HANGING INSTRUCTIONS

❿ Drill a pilot hole and insert a ⅞-in. screw eye into the top center of the balloon where the segments cross. Attach a stronger length of fishing line or heavy string to the screw eye, and hang the wind chime in a breezy but sheltered location.

Dial-A-Bird

Although you can't pick your family, you can choose your feathered friends with this unique birdhouse. A fellow woodworker designed this clever plan and passed it on to us. This birdhouse has a rotating dial with four holes of varying diameters drilled through it. The entrance hole you choose influences which species of birds are likely to take up residence. Build one for every bird lover on your gift list.

Vital Statistics: Dial-A-Bird

TYPE: Birdhouse

OVERALL SIZE: $7^3/_8$W by $8^1/_8$H by 10L

MATERIAL: Cedar

JOINERY: Rabbet, butt joints

CONSTRUCTION DETAILS:

· Sides fitted with rabbets on both ends to fit the front and back

· Sides cut $^3/_8$ in. short of roof members to provide for ventilation

· A bead of polyurethane glue along roof peak seals out leaks

FINISH: None

Building time

 PREPARING STOCK
1 hour

 LAYOUT
1-2 hours

CUTTING PARTS
1-2 hours

 ASSEMBLY
2-3 hours

FINISHING
None

TOTAL: 5-8 hours

Tools you'll use

· Planer

· Table saw

· Dado blade (optional)

· Band saw

· Clamps

· Router table with $^1/_2$-in. straight bit (optional)

· Drill press or drill/driver with $1^1/_8$-, $1^1/_4$-, $1^3/_8$- and $1^1/_2$-in. Forstner or spade bits

Shopping list

☐ (1) $^3/_4 \times 6$ in. $\times 6$ ft. cedar

☐ 4d galvanized finish nails

☐ (4) #8 × $1^1/_4$-in. galvanized deck screws

☐ (1) #8 × $^7/_8$-in. stainless-steel screw

☐ Polyurethane glue

Dial-A-Bird

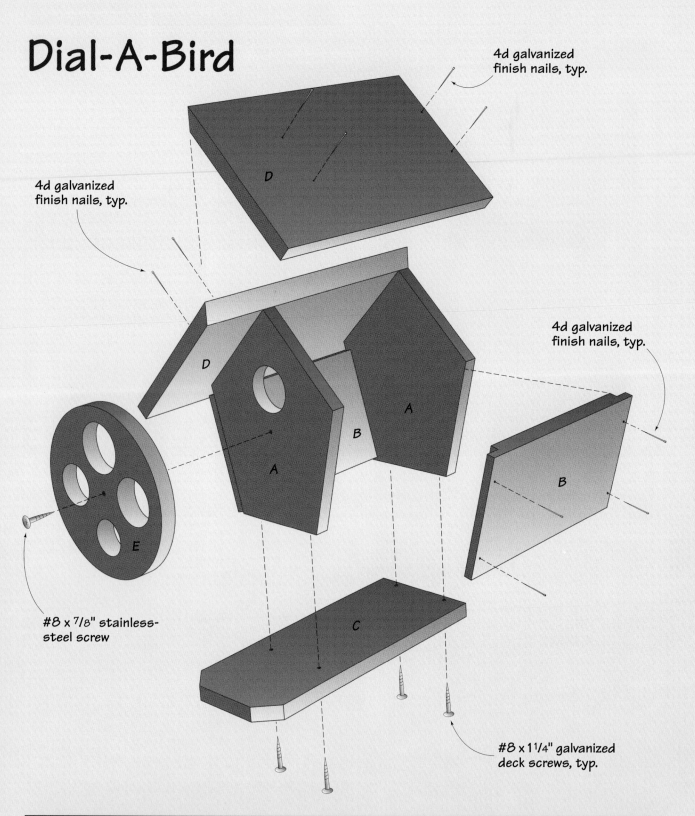

4d galvanized finish nails, typ.

4d galvanized finish nails, typ.

4d galvanized finish nails, typ.

#8 x 7/8" stainless-steel screw

#8 x 1 1/4" galvanized deck screws, typ.

Dial-A-Bird Cutting List

Part	No.	Size	Material	Part	No.	Size	Material
A. Front, back	2	$\frac{1}{2} \times 5\frac{1}{2} \times 6\frac{7}{8}$ in.	Cedar	**D.** Roof segments	2	$\frac{1}{2} \times 5\frac{1}{4} \times 9\frac{3}{8}$ in.	Cedar
B. Sides	2	$\frac{1}{2} \times 3\frac{7}{8} \times 7$ in.	"	**E.** Dial	1	$\frac{1}{2} \times$ 5-in.-dia.	"
C. Base	1	$\frac{1}{2} \times 3\frac{7}{8} \times 10$ in.	"				

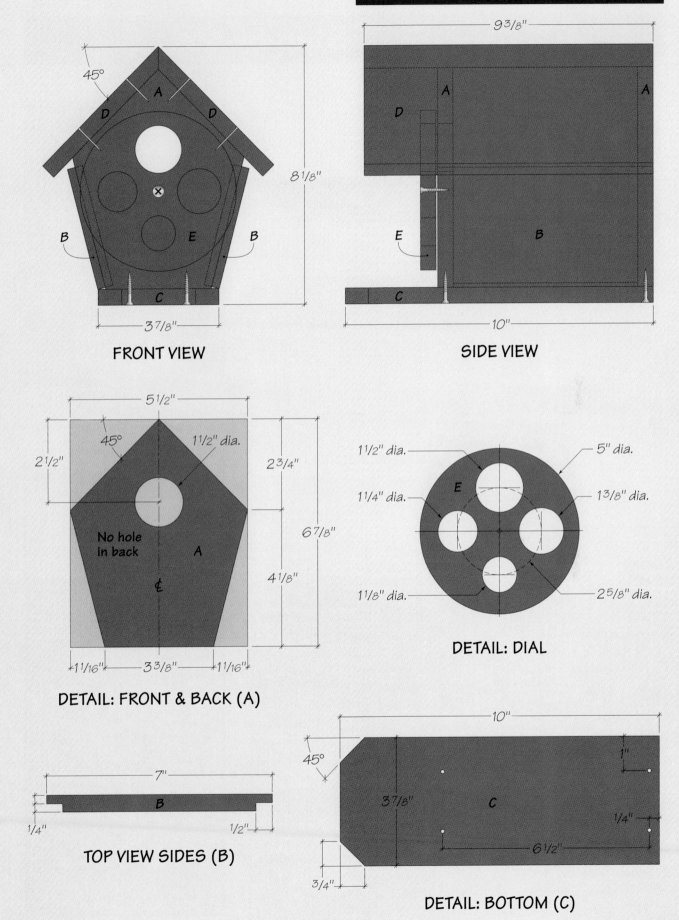

FRONT VIEW

SIDE VIEW

DETAIL: FRONT & BACK (A)

DETAIL: DIAL

TOP VIEW SIDES (B)

DETAIL: BOTTOM (C)

PREPARE THE STOCK

❶ Choose a cedar board that is knot-free and straight, and plane it down to ½ in. thick. If you don't have access to a power planer, resaw the board on your band saw (See page 43). You can also resaw on the table saw. To do this, stand the board on-edge and rip-cut both long edges with the blade raised to about 1½ in. Make additional rip cuts, raising the blade 1 in. with each pair of passes, until the final pass slices the board in two.

BUILD THE FRONT, BACK, SIDES & BASE

❷ Cut two 6⅞-in.-long blanks for the front and back. The front and back are the same shape and size, so you can lay out and cut both parts at once. Refer to the *Detail: Front & Back* drawing, page 411, to lay out the shape on one of these blanks. Stack the parts and cut both to shape on the band saw **(See Photo A).** Stay just outside your layout lines as you cut, and sand the sawn edges up to your layout lines. Then drill the 1½-in.-dia. hole through the front piece.

❸ Make the sides: Rip and cross-cut the sides to size according to the *Cutting List,* page 410. Notice on the *Top View Sides* drawing, page 411, that the front and back fit into rabbets in the sides. Cut these ¼-in.-deep, ½-in.-wide rabbets with a router table and straight bit or on the table saw with a dado blade.

❹ Rip and cross-cut the base to size. Then trim ¾ in. of material off the front corners of your base at 45° angles, and ease the sharp edges with sandpaper.

ASSEMBLE THE PARTS

❺ Attach the sides to the front and back: Spread polyurethane glue into the side rabbets, wet the mating edges of the front and back pieces with water, and set the parts together. Stretch strips of masking tape across the joints to hold the parts in place, then drive 4d galvanized finish nails through pilot holes in the sides to attach the parts. Set the nail-heads below the surface **(See Photo B).**

❻ Install the base: Drill counter-sunk pilot holes through the base and up into the front and back pieces. Fasten the parts with 1¼-in. galvanized deck screws, two screws into the front and two into the back. Don't glue the base in place—you'll need to remove it from time to time for cleaning.

MAKE & INSTALL THE ROOF

❼ Rip and cross-cut the roof segments to size. Then tilt your table saw blade to 45° and bevel-cut one long edge of each segment. The beveled edges will form a miter joint at the roof peak.

❽ Install the roof segments: Align the roof pieces so they are flush with the back of the house. Use polyurethane glue and 4d nails to attach the roof segments, setting the nailheads below the surface of the wood **(See Photo C).** The glue joint at the roof peak will seal the roof against leaks.

PHOTO A: Lay out and cut the front and back to shape. Since the parts are identically sized, gang-cut them on the band saw.

Recommended entry hole diameters by species

The four holes in the dial are sized to fit the following bird species:

1⅛-in. hole
• *Chickadee*
• *Prothonotary Warbler*

1¼-in. hole
• *Titmouse*
• *Red-breasted Nuthatch*
• *Downy Woodpecker*
• *House Wren*

1⅜-in. hole
• *White-breasted Nuthatch*
• *Tree & Violet-Green Swallows*

1½-in. hole
• *Eastern & Western Bluebird*
• *Mountain Bluebird*
• *Ash-throated Flycatcher*
• *Hairy Woodpecker*
• *Yellow-bellied Sapsucker*

PHOTO B: Attach the sides to the front and back with polyurethane glue and finish nails. Use strips of masking tape to hold the parts together while you drive and set the nails.

PHOTO C: Attach the roof halves to the house with polyurethane glue and galvanized finish nails. The roof is flush to the house back. Be sure to run a generous bead of glue along the peak to seal out leaks.

PHOTO D: Carefully lay out the hole locations on the dial, then use either spade bits or Forstner bits in the drill press to bore the four holes. Attach a backer board to the drill press table to minimize tearout on the dial.

BUILD THE DIAL

9 Cut out the dial and drill the access holes: Mark and cut the 5-in.-dia. dial on the band saw. Refer to the *Detail: Dial* drawing, page 411, to lay out the dial hole locations. It's important that the holes are located correctly, or they won't line up with the hole in the front of the birdhouse when the dial is installed. Drill the holes with Forstner or spade bits, using a scrap backer board on the drill press table (**See Photo D**) to avoid excessive tearout.

10 Attach the dial to the birdhouse with a ⅞-in. stainless-steel wood screw (**See Photo E**).

MOUNTING TIPS

Mount the birdhouse at least 6 ft. above the ground on a post, from a tree limb or attached to a wall. Unscrew the base after each season for cleaning.

PHOTO E: Fasten the dial to the birdhouse front with a single stainless-steel screw, driven into a countersunk pilot hole. Drill a pilot hole in the dial large enough to allow the dial to pivot on the screw, yet small enough to hold the screw securely in the front panel.

Woven Wood Deck Chair

Outdoor furniture should be as fun to build as it is functional to own—and this unique deck chair accomplishes both purposes. You'll build the chair frame and legs entirely from exterior plywood for durability, and assemble the major components with threaded metal inserts. Then, try your hand at weaving when you construct the seat and back lattice from bending plywood. As far as comfort is concerned, the woven seat and back provide just enough "give" to make cushions unnecessary. You could build several of these chairs and paint them in a variety of bright colors to add a festive flair to any patio or deck.

Vital Statistics: Woven Wood Deck Chair

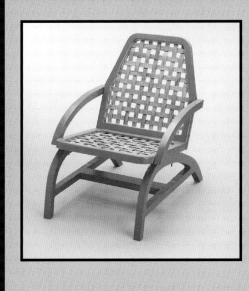

TYPE: Woven wood deck chair

OVERALL SIZE: 32H × 32D × 25W

MATERIAL: Exterior plywood, bending plywood

JOINERY: Butt joints reinforced with galvanized screws or threaded inserts and brass machine screws

CONSTRUCTION DETAILS:

· Threaded inserts allow the chair to be disassembled for storage

· Seat and back are woven from thin, bending plywood strips captured in rabbeted frames

· Frame parts laminated from two layers of ³/₄-in. plywood for strength

FINISHING OPTIONS: Exterior latex primer and paint, exterior spar varnish

Building time

PREPARING STOCK
0 hours

LAYOUT
4-5 hours

CUTTING PARTS
2-4 hours

ASSEMBLY
6-8 hours

FINISHING
2-3 hours

TOTAL: 14-20 hours

Tools you'll use

· Table saw

· Jig saw

· Router table with ¹/₂-in. flush-trimming bit, ¹/₂-in. straight bit, ³/₈-in. roundover bit

· Right-angle drilling guide

· Drill/driver

· Compass

· Clamps

· Drum sander

· Combination square

· Fine-tooth backsaw

Shopping list

☐ (1) ³/₄ in. × 4 × 8 ft. exterior plywood

☐ (1) ¹/₈ in. × 2 × 4 ft. bending plywood

☐ (4) ¹/₄ × 4-in. flathead brass machine screws, washers, nuts

☐ (12) ¹/₄ × 2-in. flathead brass machine screws

☐ (12) ¹/₄ × ¹/₂-in. threaded inserts

☐ #8 galvanized flathead wood screws (¹/₂-, 1¹/₄-in.)

☐ Two-part epoxy

☐ Moisture-resistant wood glue

☐ Exterior spar varnish

☐ Exterior latex primer, paint

Deck Chair

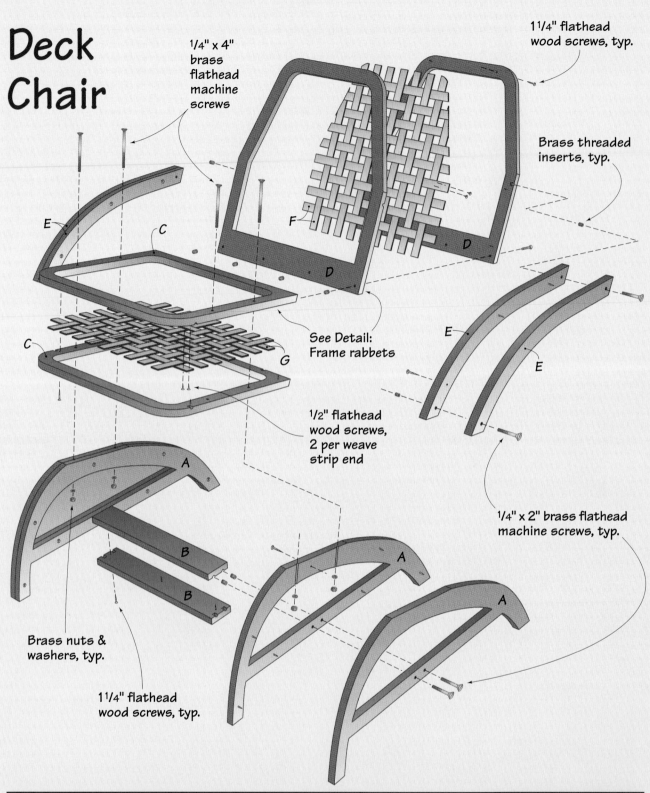

1/4" x 4" brass flathead machine screws

1 1/4" flathead wood screws, typ.

Brass threaded inserts, typ.

See Detail: Frame rabbets

1/2" flathead wood screws, 2 per weave strip end

1/4" x 2" brass flathead machine screws, typ.

Brass nuts & washers, typ.

1 1/4" flathead wood screws, typ.

E C F D E E

C G A B B A A

Woven Wood Deck Chair Cutting List

Part	No.	Size	Material	Part	No.	Size	Material
A. Legs	4	3/4 × 13 × 32 in.	Exterior ply	**E.** Arms	4	3/4 × 7 1/2 × 22 in.	Exterior ply
B. Leg stretchers	2	3/4 × 3 × 19 in.	"	**F.** Back weave	18	1/8 × 1 × 21 in.	Bending ply
C. Seat frames	2	3/4 × 22 × 18 1/4 in.	"	**G.** Seat weave	7	1/8 × 1 × 21 in.	"
D. Back frames	2	3/4 × 22 × 23 1/2 in.	"		9	1/8 × 1 × 17 1/4 in.	"

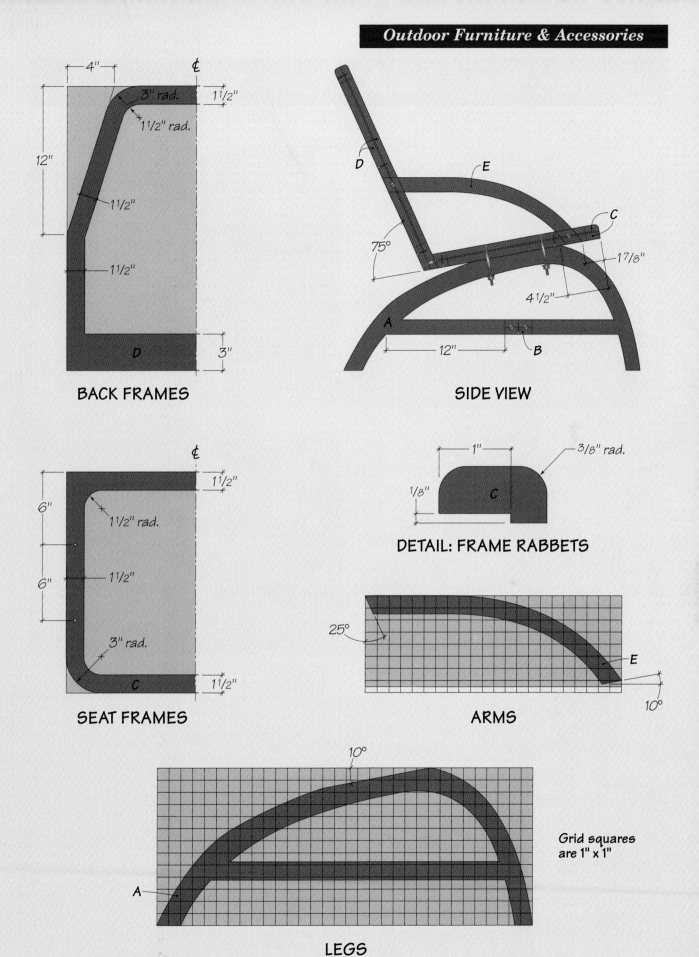

BACK FRAMES

SIDE VIEW

SEAT FRAMES

DETAIL: FRAME RABBETS

ARMS

Grid squares
are 1" x 1"

LEGS

MAKE THE LEGS

❶ Enlarge the leg pattern from the *Legs* drawing, page 417, to full size and use it to make a template from ¼-in. hardboard. Sand the cut edges smooth.

❷ Rough-out the leg shapes. Cut four rectangular leg blanks to size from exterior plywood. Using the leg template as a guide, trace about ¼ in. outside the template profiles onto each leg workpiece, and cut the legs to rough shape with a jig saw.

❸ Trim the legs to final shape. Screw the leg template temporarily to each of the legs with countersunk screws, and trim the legs to final shape with a piloted flush-trimming bit on the router table **(See Photo A)**.

❹ Fasten pairs of legs together with moisture-resistant wood glue and countersunk 1¼-in. flathead wood screws to make two double-thick legs.

❺ Cut the leg stretchers to size and shape, and laminate them together with glue and 1¼-in. screws to form one thick stretcher.

❻ Clamp the stretcher between the legs and drill for threaded inserts. See the *Side View* drawing, page 417, for stretcher placement. Drill two countersunk ¼-in.-dia. holes through each leg and about ⅝ in. deep into both ends of the stretcher **(See Photo B)**. Center the holes on the thickness of the stretcher, and lay them out so they are spaced 1½ in. apart. Unclamp the leg assembly and redrill the holes in the ends of the stretcher to the manufacturer's recommended diameter for fitting the threaded inserts.

❼ Twist the threaded inserts into the holes in the stretcher with a large screwdriver, using a dab of two-part epoxy to secure each insert in place **(See Photo C)**. Then assemble the legs and stretcher with 2-in. flathead brass machine screws.

BUILD THE SEAT & BACK

❽ Cut the seat frames and back frames to shape. Start by cutting pairs of seat and back blanks to size. Follow the dimensions given in the *Back Frames*

PHOTO A: Rough-out each leg with a jig saw, then screw a hardboard leg template to it and rout the leg flush to the template with a flush-trimming bit on the router table. Set the bit's depth so the bearing rides along the template as you rout the leg shapes.

PHOTO B: Clamp the stretcher in place between the two legs, and drill ¼-in. holes through the legs and into the stretcher for threaded inserts and machine screws. A right-angle drilling guide ensures straight holes.

and *Seat Frames* drawings, page 417, to lay out one back frame and one seat frame. Use a combination square to mark centerpoints for drawing the 1½- and 3-in.-radiused corners on these parts, and scribe the curves with a compass. Cut out the back frame and seat frame with a jig saw, and smooth the cut edges with a sander. Then use these two frame pieces as patterns to help you cut the other back and seat frame to match. Save the center cutouts; they can be used as material for the arms later.

❾ Rout the back and seat rabbets. The woven plywood seat and back supports will be captured

PHOTO C: After enlarging the stretcher holes to the proper diameter for the threaded inserts, screw in the inserts. A dab of two-part epoxy in each stretcher hole will lock the inserts in place.

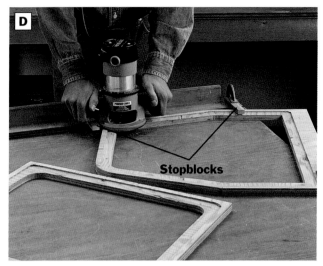

Stopblocks

PHOTO D: Rout 1-in.-wide, ⅛-in.-deep rabbets into the face of one seat and back frame. A shop-made jig insets the rabbet correctly from the edge of the frames, and stopblocks on the jig limit the router's path.

between the pairs of back and seat frames, which will fasten flush against one another. In order to do this, one member of each frame needs a shallow rabbet cut to accommodate the thickness of the plywood weave strips. However, the rabbet is too wide (1 in.) to rout with a piloted rabbet bit directly against the inside edges of the frames, so you'll need to build a jig from scrap ¾-in. wood to guide the cuts. *(See the tint box, below, for information on building the jig.)* Mark outlines for the rabbets onto one seat and back frame piece. Clamp the rabbeting jig at both ends along the edge of your bench. Butt one edge of a seat or back frame against the jig. Resting the router base on the jig and the frame, clamp scrap wood stopblocks onto the jig so they'll limit the path of the router to stay within your marked area. Plan to make the first round of rabbet cuts, machining one straight portion of the frames at a time. NOTE: *You'll have to reset the stopblocks to make each rabbet cut around the frame. Also, on the lower, straight edge of the*

Router rabbeting jig

Cut two wood strips 3 in. wide and 24 and 26 in. long. Screw them together to create an L-shaped bracket with the longer strip (it will be the jig's base) overhanging the shorter one (the fence) evenly at both ends. Install a ½-in. straight bit in your router. Measure the distance from the outside edge of the router base to the bit, and rip the jig's base down on the table saw so that when the router is placed against the jig's fence, the bit clears the jig base by ½ in.

back frame, insert a 2-in.-wide spacer strip between the jig's fence and the router base to offset the cut properly. Set the bit depth to ⅛ in., and make the first of two cuts around each frame. Then, move the router base away from the jig's back and make a second pass around the frames to remove the rest of the material, widening the rabbet to 1 in. **(See Photo D).** Round the radiused corners of the rabbets by carefully running the router along your rabbet layout lines by hand. Or, if you prefer, trim these curves with a sharp chisel.

🔟 Use a ⅜-in. roundover bit in the router to ease the inside and outside edges of the rabbeted seat and back frames as well as the outside edges of the other back frame. The straight, square edge of each frame where the seat and back meet does not get routed.

WEAVE THE SEAT & BACK FRAMES

⓫ Cut the seat weave and back weave strips to size. Cut up a few extra in case you break or miscut a few when weaving. Seal all surfaces of the strips with several coats of exterior spar varnish **(See Photo E).** Varnish the rabbeted areas on the frames as well.

⓬ Weave the seat. Begin by attaching the front-to-back (17¼-in.) strips. Place the middle strip in the rabbet and center it from side to side. Hold down one end with a spring clamp and fasten the other end with two countersunk ½-in. flathead screws. Attach the other weave strips working outward from the center strip, screwing one end of each

PHOTO E: Seal all surfaces of the seat and back weaving strips with two coats of spar varnish. Varnish the rabbets on the seat and back frames as well as the mating surfaces on the other seat and back frame.

PHOTO F: Fasten one end of the middle seat weave strip with screws while holding the other end with a spring clamp in the rabbet. Once the strip is fastened on one end, remove the clamp. Attach the remaining front-to-back strips in the same way, spacing them 1 in. apart.

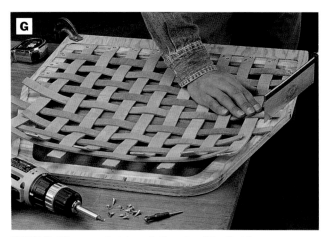

PHOTO G: After screwing down both ends of the first four cross strips on the back frame, continue weaving in the rest of the cross strips with their ends free. Then trim the weave to fit into the angled portions of the frame and screw the strips down one at a time.

strip to the frame 1 in. apart (**See Photo F**). Remove all the spring clamps so the ends of the strips are free. Then attach the side-to-side (21-in.) cross strips. Weave the first cross strip through the attached strips on the frame, starting down near their fixed ends, going over and under all the way across. Adjust the strip so there is an even 1⅛-in. gap between it and the inside edge of the frame, and fasten it into the rabbet at each end with two countersunk ½-in. flathead screws. Continue weaving cross strips up the seat, alternating which way you start weaving each strip to form a lattice. You should use seven strips. Space the strips 1 in. apart, with 1⅛-in. spaces between the outermost strips and the frame. Once the weave is complete, screw down the free ends of the front-to-back strips.

13 Weave the back frame. This time, attach the first set of strips (running vertically on the frame) at the lower end of the frame. As you work your way outward from the center, let the strips overhang the angled and corner sections of the frame. Weave the cross strips in, starting at the bottom of the frame. Make all the gaps a consistent 1 in. Attach the bottom four cross strips at both ends in the rabbet. Let the remaining cross strips overhang the angled portions of the frame, and continue weaving all the way up the frame with the strips loose. Then trim the overhanging strips to fit into the rabbet (**See Photo G**). Cut the vertical strips to fit into the rabbets as well, and screw them down to complete the back.

14 Assemble the back and seat frames. In the angled sections of the rabbeted back frame, the weaving strips overlap in some areas, doubling their thickness. In order to be able to screw the back frames together so they fit flush, you'll need to notch out these areas in the unrabbeted back frame. Set the back frame pieces together and mark spots on the unrabbeted frame that will need to be notched (**See Photo H**). Pare away ⅛ in. of material in these areas until the two frames fit snugly together. Assemble the back and seat frames with countersunk 1¼-in. screws.

ATTACH THE BACK FRAME TO THE SEAT FRAME
15 Cut a 15° bevel along the straight edge of the chair back and seat on the table saw (**See Photo I**). This will create the joint where the two frames meet.

16 Use a combination square to draw a line along the rear face of the back frame, ⅝ in. from the bottom (beveled) edge. Mark points along this line at 1 in. and 7 in. from each side of the frame. Clamp the back frame to the seat frame as shown in the *Side View* drawing, page 417, with the bottom edge of the back frame flush with the bottom of the seat frame. Drill countersunk ¼-in. machine screw holes perpendicular to the back frame at the marked points. Use a depth stop or a piece of tape wrapped around the bit to drill the holes 2 in. deep. Separate the frames and enlarge the holes in the seat frame to accept four threaded inserts. Use epoxy when you screw the inserts into the seat frame. Fasten the back frame to the seat frame with 2-in. flathead machine screws.

ASSEMBLE THE CHAIR

⓱ Make the arms. Follow the *Arms* grid drawing, page 417, to lay out and cut one arm to size. Use this workpiece as a template for cutting the other three arm pieces. Then laminate pairs of arms together with glue and 1¼-in. flathead wood screws to form two arms.

⓲ Attach the seat to the legs. Use a combination square to draw a line along the top face of each side of the seat frame, ¾ in. from the edges. Mark two points along these lines 6 in. and 12 in. from the back edge of the seat frame. Place the seat assembly on the leg assembly, and align them so the front edge of the seat overhangs the flat section of the legs by 4½ in. Clamp the seat to the legs with their sides flush. Drill ¼-in.-dia. countersunk holes all the way through the seat frame and legs at the four marked points. Fasten the seat to the legs with 4-in. brass machine screws, nuts and washers.

⓳ Install the arms. The front edge of each arm should be about 1⅞ in. from the front edge of the seat frame. Pivot the arms at this point until the back edges of the arms align with the back face of the chair back. Clamp the arms in place and drill a countersunk ¼-in.-dia. hole, 2 in. deep, where each arm intersects the back and seat frames. Remove the arms, drill and install threaded inserts and attach the arms to the seat and back frames with 2-in. brass machine screws (**See Photo J**).

FINISHING TOUCHES

⓴ Sand the unvarnished chair surfaces smooth and ease all sharp edges. Tape off and cover the varnished weaving with newspaper to protect it from paint. Prime all bare wood parts, and topcoat the chair with several coats of high-quality exterior latex paint.

PHOTO H: Mark the unrabbeted back frame in those areas that will need to fit around doubled-up weave strips. Remove this frame piece and notch out the marked areas with a sharp chisel.

PHOTO I: With the table saw blade tilted to 15°, cut a beveled edge on the seat and back frames where they will meet each other at an angle.

PHOTO J: Clamp the arm in position and connect it to the seat and back with 2-in. machine screws installed in threaded inserts.

Window Box

Brighten your view and add a touch more "curb appeal" to your home by outfitting your windows with these window boxes. We've kept the design simple so the style conforms to most any home style. Simplicity also means you can build several window boxes in one shop session. You'll find hanging these boxes is a snap, too, thanks to a pair of interlocking beveled cleats that hide behind the project when it's installed.

Window Box

Vital Statistics

TYPE: Window box

OVERALL SIZE: $36\frac{1}{2}$L by 8H by $11\frac{3}{4}$D

MATERIAL: Cedar

JOINERY: Butt joints reinforced with glue and screws or galvanized finish nails

CONSTRUCTION DETAILS:

- Decorative curved edges on front panel are cut with a jig saw
- Project installs with a pair of bevel-edged hanging cleats
- Exterior fasteners used throughout to resist corrosion
- Project designed to fit a standard planter insert measuring 30L by 6H by 8D

FINISH: Stain and/or wood preservative; could also be left unfinished

BUILDING TIME: 3-4 hours

Shopping List

- ☐ (1) 1 × 8 in. × 8 ft. cedar*
- ☐ (1) 1 × 6 in. × 4 ft. cedar*
- ☐ (2) 1 × 2 in. × 10 ft. cedar*
- ☐ 2-in. galvanized finish nails
- ☐ 1¼-in. deck screws
- ☐ Moisture-resistant wood glue
- ☐ Finishing materials (optional)

*We used cedar here, but other suitable woods for outdoor projects can be found on page 427.

Window Box: Step-by-step

BUILD THE BOX

❶ Crosscut the cedar boards for the front, back and two end pieces according to the dimensions given in the *Cutting List,* page 424.

❷ Refer to the *Front Layout* drawing, page 424, to draw the curved profiles on both ends of the front panel. Clamp the front panel to a worksurface and cut the curved profiles with a jig saw **(See Photo A).** Smooth the curves with sandpaper.

❸ Attach the sides to the front panel: Draw reference lines across the inside back face of the front panel, 1½ in. from

PHOTO A: Cut the curved profiles on the ends of the front panel with a jig saw.

Window Box

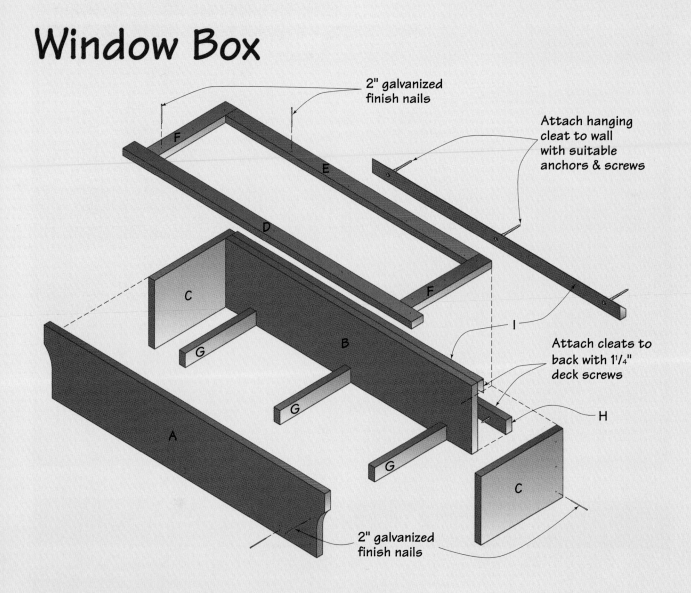

2" galvanized finish nails

Attach hanging cleat to wall with suitable anchors & screws

Attach cleats to back with 1¼" deck screws

2" galvanized finish nails

Part	No.	Size	Material
Window Box Cutting List			
A. Front	1	⅞ × 7¼ × 35½ in.	Cedar
B. Back	1	⅞ × 7¼ × 31 in.	"
C. Sides	2	⅞ × 7¼ × 10¼ in.	"
D. Front trim	1	⅞ × 1½ × 36½ in.	"
E. Back trim	1	⅞ × 1½ × 30½ in.	"
F. Side trim	2	⅞ × 1½ × 10 in.	"
G. Bottom supports	3	⅞ × 1½ × 9 in.	"
H. Blocking	1	⅞ × 1½ × 31 in.	"
I. Hanging cleats	2	⅞ × 1½ × 31 in.	"

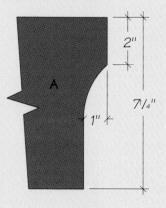

2"

7¼"

1"

FRONT LAYOUT

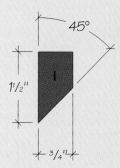

45°

1½"

¾"

HANGING CLEAT

either end. Spread glue on one end of each side piece and set the sides in place on the front panel so the outside faces of the sides align with the reference lines on the front panel. Attach the parts with 2-in. galvanized finish nails driven through the front and into the sides.

④ Install the back: Set the back in place between the sides, spaced 9 in. from the back face of the front panel. Mark this location and remove the back. Spread glue on the ends of the back, slip it into place between the sides and clamp the parts. Fasten the sides to the back with galvanized finish nails. Recess the nailheads with a nailset **(See Photo B).**

PHOTO B: Glue and clamp the box back in place between the sides, and fasten the parts with galvanized finish nails. Recess the nailheads with a nailset.

INSTALL THE BOTTOM SUPPORTS

⑤ Cross-cut three 9-in. bottom supports from cedar 1 × 2. Mark locations for the bottom supports inside the box on the front and back panels. Position one support so it will be centered on the length of the box. Locate the other two supports 2 in. in from the sides.

⑥ Test-fit the bottom supports in the window box, arranging the supports so the narrow edges are flush with the bottom edges of the box front and back. Then spread glue on the ends of the supports and clamp them in place inside the box. Fasten the supports with galvanized finish nails driven through pilot holes in the box front and back **(See Photo C).**

ADD THE TRIM

⑦ Cross-cut the trim front, back and two end pieces to length from cedar 1 × 2. Position the front trim piece on the top edge

PHOTO C: Glue and nail the three bottom supports in the box so the narrow edges are flush with the bottom edges of the box. Set the nailheads below the surface.

of the box front so it overhangs the ends and face of the box front by ½ in. Glue and nail the front trim piece.

⑧ Install the trim ends on the box ends so they butt against the back of the front trim piece and overhang the outside face of the box ends by ½ in. Glue and nail the trim ends in place.

⑨ Glue and nail the back trim

piece over the box back and between the trim ends. Align this trim piece so its outside edge is flush with the back ends of the trim end pieces.

⑩ Recess all of the nails holding the trim in place with a nailset **(See Photo D).**

INSTALL THE HANGING CLEATS & BLOCKING

The window box is designed with

PHOTO D: Install the four trim pieces around the top edges of the window box with moisture-resistant wood glue and nails. The front and end trim pieces should overhang the box by ½ in.

Edge guide

PHOTO E: Lay out the hanging cleats so you can cut the beveled edges in one pass. We cut the strips from a cedar 1 × 6 to provide adequate support for the saw base. We also screwed the cedar board near its edge to a strip of plywood to provide clearance below for the saw blade. An edge guide installed on the saw base makes these bevel-rip cuts easier to perform accurately.

a pair of bevel-edged hanging cleats to make mounting the box easy. One cleat fastens to the window box with the bevel edge facing down and toward the window box. The other cleat attaches to a windowsill or house siding with the bevel edge facing up and toward the house. In these alternating positions, the cleat bevels interlock when the window box is hung in place.

⑪ Lay out and cut the hanging cleats: You can cut bevels for both cleats in one saw pass if you lay out the cleats in the interlocked position along the edge of a 31-in. length of cedar 1 × 6. Cutting the cleats from a wide board also provides more support for your saw base. Set your circular saw or jig saw to cut a 45° bevel, and rip the first cleat from the board, cutting along the bevel-edge layout line (**See Photo E**). Reset the saw to 90° and rip-cut the second cleat from the board.

⑫ Install one hanging cleat on the window box: Mount the cleat beneath the back trim overhang so the beveled edge faces down and inward. Fasten the parts with 1¼-in. deck screws.

⑬ Cross-cut the blocking piece to length from cedar 1 × 2. Attach the blocking with screws so it is flush with the bottom back edge of the window box (**See Photo F**).

FINISH & MOUNT THE WINDOW BOX

⑭ Apply several coats of stain or clear outdoor wood preservative to the window box and remaining hanging cleat. You also can leave the wood bare, if you prefer, so it "weathers" naturally to a silvery gray color.

⑮ Choose a location for the window box that will be easy to access for planting and seasonal clean-out. Mount the remaining hanging cleat to the house so the beveled edge faces up and toward the house. When positioning the cleat on the house, keep in mind that the window box top edge will be 1½ in. higher than the top edge of the cleat. Fasten the cleat with long deck screws to a windowsill or directly to the house siding. Try to drive the screws so they'll hit wall framing members behind the house siding.

⑯ Hang the window box by interlocking the hanging cleats. If you want to mount the box permanently, drive additional screws through the box back and blocking into the house siding.

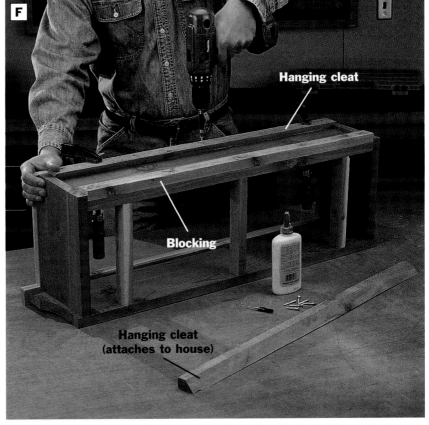

PHOTO F: Attach one hanging cleat and the blocking strip to the back of the window box with 1¼-in. deck screws and moisture-resistant wood glue. The other hanging cleat attaches to the house with deck screws.

Choosing woods for outdoor projects

Outdoor wood furniture can survive for many years in the elements, but you need to choose wood carefully. A number of wood species contain natural oils that make them more resistant to rotting, insect infestation and degradation from ultraviolet sunlight than other woods. We use Western red cedar for several projects in this book, but other excellent wood choices for outdoor projects include redwood, teak, cypress, white oak and Honduras mahogany. Some of these varieties are harder to find in many areas of the United States and can be quite expensive.

Treated lumber and exterior-grade plywood are also good options for outdoor projects, but you'll probably want to reserve these wood products for projects you plan to paint. Treated lumber is pressure-infused with chemicals that make it insect- and moisture-resistant. Exterior-grade plywood is made with waterproof glue, so it resists delaminating when it comes into contact with moisture.

Other less weather-durable woods, like red oak and pine, can be used for outdoor projects as well, but these

Naturally weather-resistant woods include, from left to right, redwood, cedar, white oak and teak.

woods must be topcoated thoroughly with primer and paint or other UV-protective sealers. It's a good idea to keep projects made from these woods in an area sheltered from moisture or direct ground contact and store them inside during seasons when they aren't in use.

Deluxe Tool Chest

Every woodworker dreams of owning a first-class, handmade tool chest for storing and exhibiting his most cherished tools. Made from white oak and white oak plywood, with walnut accents, this handsome chest is a challenging project that you'll display with pride for years to come.

Vital Statistics: Deluxe Tool Chest

TYPE: Tool chest

OVERALL SIZE: 22W by 15H by 12D

MATERIAL: White oak, white oak plywood, walnut

JOINERY: Tongue-and-groove frame-and-panels, butt joints reinforced with screws, finger joints, dado joints

CONSTRUCTION DETAILS:

· Strong, decorative finger joints on drawers

· Walnut handles with cove-shaped finger pulls

· Drawers mount on wooden slides

· Makes efficient use of materials

· Upper compartment and three drawers for large tool-storage capacity

FINISHING OPTIONS: Clear, protective topcoat

Building time

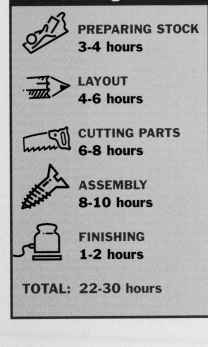

PREPARING STOCK
3-4 hours

LAYOUT
4-6 hours

CUTTING PARTS
6-8 hours

ASSEMBLY
8-10 hours

FINISHING
1-2 hours

TOTAL: 22-30 hours

Tools you'll use

· Jointer

· Table saw

· Planer

· Router table with $3/4$-in. core box bit, straight bits ($1/4$, $3/4$-in.), chamfer bit

· Bar or pipe clamps

· Jig saw

· Band saw

· Plug cutter

· Drill press

· Flush-cutting hand saw

· Compass

· Drill/driver

· Combination square

Shopping list

☐ (1) $1/4$ in. × 4 × 4 ft. white oak plywood

☐ (2) $3/4$ × 8 in. × 8 ft. white oak

☐ (1) $3/4$ × 4 in. × 2 ft. white oak

☐ Walnut (scrap)

☐ $20^3/8$-in. brass piano hinge

☐ (2) brass lid supports

☐ #8 brass flathead wood screws ($1^1/4$-, 2-in.)

☐ #6 × $1/2$-in. brass screws

☐ Wood glue

Deluxe Tool Chest

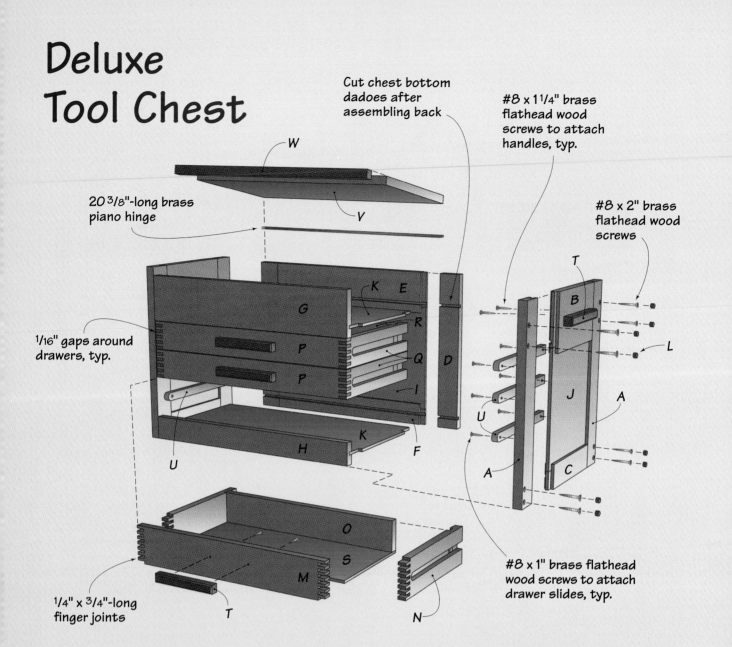

Cut chest bottom dadoes after assembling back

#8 x 1¼" brass flathead wood screws to attach handles, typ.

20 ³⁄₈"-long brass piano hinge

#8 x 2" brass flathead wood screws

¹⁄₁₆" gaps around drawers, typ.

#8 x 1" brass flathead wood screws to attach drawer slides, typ.

¼" x ³⁄₄"-long finger joints

Deluxe Tool Chest Cutting List

Part	No.	Size	Material	Part	No.	Size	Material
A. Side stiles	4	¾ × 2 × 15½ in.	Oak	**M.** Drawer front (lg)	1	¾ × 3½ × 20⅜ in.	Oak
B. Side rails (top)	2	¾ × 4¾ × 9 in.	"	**N.** Drawer sides (lg)	2	¾ × 3½ × 11¼ in.	"
C. Side rails (btm)	2	¾ × 2 × 9 in.	"	**O.** Drawer back (lg)	1	¾ × 3 × 19⅜ in.	"
D. Back stiles	2	¾ × 2 × 14⁹⁄₁₆ in.	"	**P.** Drawer fronts (sm)	2	¾ × 2½ × 20⅜ in.	"
E. Back rail (top)	1	¾ × 3¹³⁄₁₆ × 17½ in.	"	**Q.** Drawer sides (sm)	4	¾ × 2½ × 11¼ in.	"
F. Back rail (btm)	1	¾ × 2 × 17½ in.	"	**R.** Drawer backs (sm)	2	¾ × 2 × 19⅜ in.	"
G. Front rail (top)	1	¾ × 4 × 20½ in.	"	**S.** Drawer bottoms	3	¼ × 9¾ × 19⅜ in.	Plywood
H. Front rail (btm)	1	¾ × 2 × 20½ in.	"	**T.** Handles	5	¾ × ¾ × 6 in.	Walnut
I. Back panel	1	¼ × 17½ × 9¾ in.	Plywood	**U.** Drawer slides	6	½ × ¾ × 10¼ in.	Oak
J. Side panels	2	¼ × 9¾ × 9 in.	"	**V.** Lid	1	¾ × 11½ × 20⅜ in.	"
K. Chest bottoms	2	¼ × 11¼ × 21¼ in.	"	**W.** Lid handle	1	¾ × ¾ × 20⅜ in.	Walnut
L. Screw plugs	16	⅜ dia. × ¼ in.	Walnut				

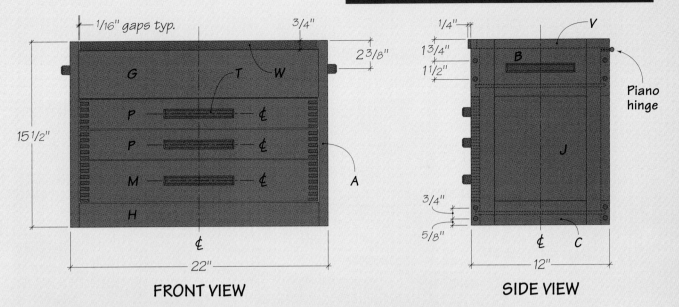

1/16" gaps typ.

3/4"

2 3/8"

G T W

P ¢

P ¢

M ¢

A

H

15 1/2"

¢

22"

FRONT VIEW

1/4"

1 3/4"

1 1/2"

V

B

Piano hinge

J

3/4"

5/8"

¢ C

12"

SIDE VIEW

M

P

M

P 2 1/2" 3 1/2"

DRAWER FRONTS (M & P)

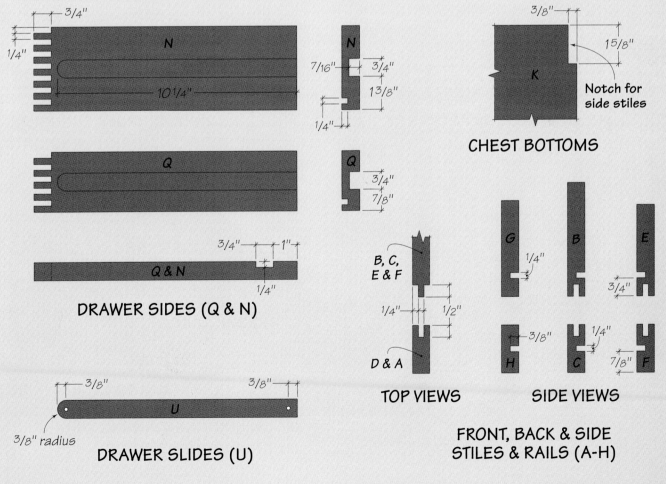

3/4"

1/4"

N

10 1/4"

N

7/16" 3/4"

1 3/8"

1/4"

3/8"

15/8"

K

Notch for side stiles

CHEST BOTTOMS

Q

Q

3/4"

7/8"

3/4" 1"

Q & N

1/4"

DRAWER SIDES (Q & N)

B, C, E & F

1/4" 1/2"

D & A

TOP VIEWS

G

1/4"

B

E

3/4"

H 3/8"

C 1/4"

F 7/8"

SIDE VIEWS

3/8" 3/8"

U

3/8" radius

DRAWER SLIDES (U)

FRONT, BACK & SIDE STILES & RAILS (A-H)

Deluxe Tool Chest **431**

Deluxe Tool Chest: Step-by-step

MAKE THE LID

❶ The tool chest lid is edge-glued from strips of narrower white oak stock. Joint and rip three strips of ¾-in. oak to 3⅞ in. wide. The board that will be in the center of the glue-up will need to be jointed on both edges; the other two each only need jointing on one edge. Cross-cut the chest lid strips to 20⅝ in. long.

❷ Edge-glue the three strips together to create the lid.

❸ When the glue has dried, scrape, plane and sand the lid panel flat and smooth. Joint one edge and rip it to 11½ in. wide. Cross-cut both ends so they're square, but only trim the lid to 20½ in. long for now. It will be cut to fit the cabinet later.

❹ Cut the lid handle from a piece of scrap walnut that's 20½ in. long. Rip-cut the handle to ¾ × ¾ in. (it will be cut to finished length later, along with the lid).

❺ Glue and clamp the lid handle to the front (jointed) edge of the lid. When the glue dries, sand the surfaces level and smooth.

BUILD THE SIDES & BACK

❻ Cut all the carcase parts to size. This includes the rails, stiles and insert panels for the frame-and-panel carcase sides, as well as the chest bottom panels that fit between the carcase sides, front and back.

❼ Cut ¼-in.-wide × ½-in.-deep grooves for the panel inserts in the edges of the side and back stiles

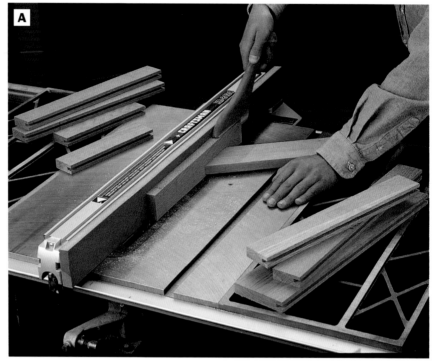

PHOTO A: Cut ¼ × ½-in. grooves in the edges of the side and back rails and stiles. The grooves should be sized so the plywood panels fit into them snugly. Using a featherboard and pushstick, cut the grooves by making multiple passes with the table saw blade.

PHOTO B: Cut tenons in the ends of the side and back rails. Use the miter gauge to push the stock and clamp a spacer block to the saw fence to keep the workpiece from binding. The tenons are cut by removing ¼ in. of material from each side.

and rails. We used a dado-blade set installed in the table saw to cut the grooves **(See Photo A)**.

❽ Cut ¼-in.-thick × ½-in.-long tenons on the ends of the side and back rails. We also used the dado-blade set for these cuts, trimming ¼ in. off each side of the ¾-in.-thick rails and stiles. Use the miter gauge to give a square cut. To keep the blades from causing the workpieces to bind, clamp a reference spacer block to the fence and use it to set up your cuts **(See Photo B)**.

❾ Cut ¼-in.-wide × ⅜-in.-deep grooves for the chest bottoms into the edges of the side rails and both front rails. The chest bottoms should fit snugly into the grooves, so rather than using a dado-blade set, make two passes with a standard table saw blade to custom-fit the grooves to the actual thickness of the plywood used to make the chest bottoms (plywood is usually undersized from its nominal size). The grooves in the upper rails should be ¾ in. from the lower edge of each board (See *Side Views,* page 431). All the lower rails are the same width (2 in.) and should have their grooves cut ⅞ in. from the bottom edges, centered on the inside faces of the boards **(See Photo C)**.

❿ Finish-sand the rails, stiles and panels before assembly.

⓫ Dry-assemble the sides and the back to test the fit. Trim a bit off the ends of the rail tenons if necessary so the joints come together tightly.

⓬ With the side and back panels inserted into the grooves (without glue), glue and clamp

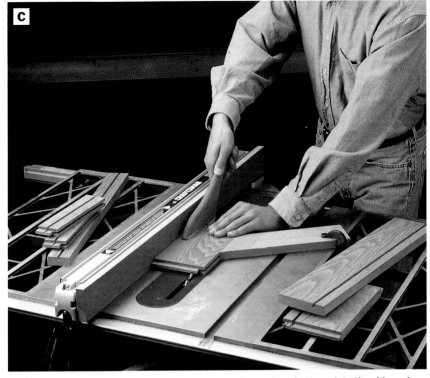

PHOTO C: Cut ¼ × ⅜-in. grooves for the upper and lower chest bottoms into the side and front rails. Use a featherboard and pushstick.

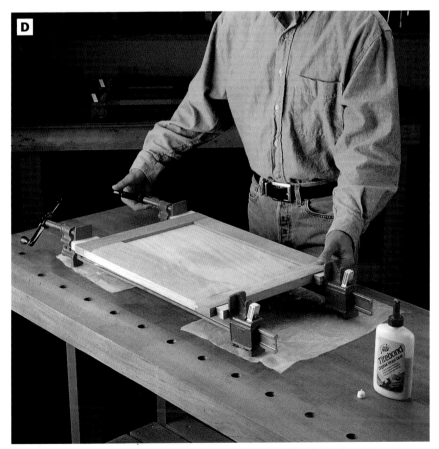

PHOTO D: Glue and clamp up the frame-and-panel assemblies for the back and the sides. Make sure the ends of the stiles are flush with the edges of the rails. Do not glue in the panels—they should "float" in the grooves.

PHOTO E: Using a jig saw, notch out the corners of the chest bottoms so they will fit around the ungrooved side stiles.

PHOTO F: Glue up the frame-and-panel assemblies and the chest bottoms to create the chest carcase. Reinforce the joints by driving screws through the side panels and into the ends of the front and back rails. Counterbore the pilot holes to accept 3⁄8-in.-dia. wood plugs.

together the mortise-and-tenon joints at the stiles and rails **(See Photo D).**

ASSEMBLE THE CARCASE

13 Cut 1⁄4-in.-deep × 3⁄8-in.-wide grooves for both the upper and lower chest bottoms in the assembled back frame. Cut all the way through, from end to end. Make the grooves the same distances from the bottom edge of the frame as those on the side frames, so they'll align when the carcase is assembled.

14 Cut 3⁄8-in.-wide × 15⁄8-in.-deep notches in the corners of the chest bottoms, as shown in the detail illustration on page 431. The notches allow the bottoms to fit around the side stiles. Use a jig saw to cut the notches **(See Photo E).**

15 To assemble the carcase, lay the sides on a piece of scrap plywood, inside-face-down. Lay out and drill counterbored pilot holes for #8 wood screws through the side stiles. Center the holes on the locations for the ends of the front and back rails, two holes per joint.

16 Finish-sand all carcase parts (sides, back, front rails, and carcase bottoms), and ease all sharp edges with 180-grit sandpaper.

17 Assemble the carcase with glue and #8 × 2-in. flathead wood screws **(See Photo F).** Attach the assembled sides to the front rails and the assembled back, with the chest bottoms glued into their grooves. Use padded clamps to hold the box together while you extend the pilot holes in the side stiles into the rail ends. The bottom edges of all the lower rails should be aligned.

The top edge of the front rail should be ¾ in. lower than the tops of the sides, and the top edge of the back should be 15⁄16 in. lower than the tops of the sides.

18 Cut the screw plugs from walnut scrap, using a plug cutter mounted in your drill press **(See Photo G).** After making at least 16 plug cuts, resaw the walnut on a band saw to release the screw plugs **(See Photo H).**

19 Apply glue to the ends of the plugs and insert them into the counterbored screw holes, tapping each plug home with a mallet. When the glue is dry, trim the plugs flush to the surrounding wood surface with a flush-cutting saw or dovetail saw **(See Photo I).** Sand the plugs smooth.

MAKE THE DRAWERS

The drawer fronts and sides are joined with finger joints (also called box joints). Use a jig to make accurate finger joints (you can purchase a finger joint jig at most woodworking stores, or you can build your own, as we did). Always test the jig setup first by cutting joints in scrap wood of the same dimensions as the actual parts. The joints should fit together snugly, without requiring any pounding to assemble.

20 Cut the oak drawer parts to size. Cut the drawer backs about ¼ in. wider than specified in the *Cutting List* (to about 2¼ and 3¼ in.).

21 We built a jig and used a table saw with a dado-blade set to cut the finger joints used to join the drawer parts. To make the jig, clamp an auxiliary plywood fence, roughly 6 × 16 in., to the miter gauge. Cut a ¼-in.-

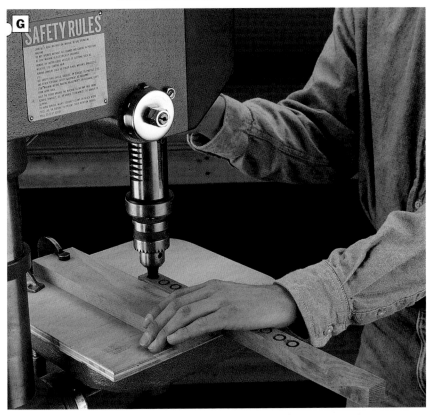

PHOTO G: Make walnut screw plugs on the drill press, using a ⅜-in. tapered plug cutter. Clamp a scrap piece to the drill press table to create a surface that helps keep the walnut stock stationary while you cut the plugs.

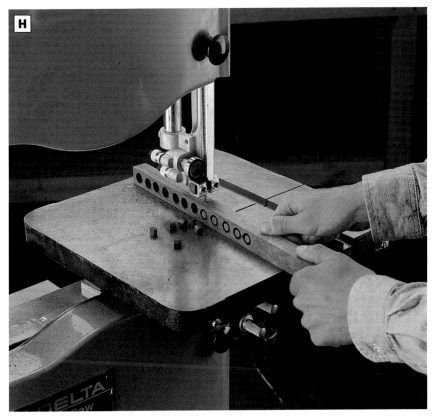

PHOTO H: Cut 16 to 20 plugs with the plug cutter, then resaw the walnut stock to about ⅜-in. thick to release the plugs.

PHOTO I: Use a flush-cutting saw or a dovetail saw to trim the walnut plugs flush. A flush-cutting saw has teeth without set so they won't damage the surrounding wood.

㉓ Reposition the workpiece so the slot you just cut fits down over the pin spacer, and make the next cut. Continue in this manner until all the joints in that end of the board are cut. Then flip it end-for-end and cut the fingers in the other end the same way. Make sure a pin is on the top.

㉔ Now, cut the mating joints in the front ends of the drawer sides. Since you started the joint with a pin on the first board, its mate must start with a slot (space). To do this, fit the first board you cut over the spacer strip, so the first pin will act as an offset spacer. Butt the mating board up against this board and cut a slot at the edge of the workpiece **(See Photo K).** Then remove the first board, move the mating piece over so the inside edge of the slot presses up against the spacer, and make the second cut. Continue to make cuts across the board, then cut the joint in the other drawer side by repeating the same procedure. Cut the finger joints for the other narrow drawer parts and then for the wider, lower drawer parts.

㉕ Rout ¼ × ¼-in. grooves for the drawer bottoms into the inside faces of the drawer sides and front, using a router with a ¼-in. straight bit (we used a router table, but you can use a router with a straightedge guide instead). The grooves should be stopped just before reaching the ends of the pins for the finger joints, but run all the way out the back ends of the drawer sides.

㉖ Trim the drawer backs to match the width of the other drawer parts, measured from the top edges down to the tops of the drawer bottom grooves.

㉗ The drawers will mount on wood glides attached to the inside faces of the chest sides. Grooves cut in the outer faces of the drawer sides fit over the glides. To cut the grooves in the drawer sides, install a ¾-in. straight bit in the router table and set the fence so the groove is the proper distance from the

wide × ¾-in.-deep slot about 6 in. from one end of the auxiliary fence by passing the fence over the dado-blade set. Cut a strip of hardwood to fit into the slot and serve as a pin spacer. Glue the spacer strip into the fence slot (you can see the spacer in place in **Photo J).** Now, reposition the auxiliary fence on the miter gauge so the inside face of the spacer is exactly ¼ in. (the thickness of one pin) from the saw blade.

㉒ Now you are ready to cut the finger joints. Start with the sides, front and backs for the narrower upper drawers. Stand the first workpiece (a drawer front) on end and butt its top edge up against the spacer strip and feed it over the blades **(See Photo J).** This will start the joint with a pin. When cutting, you can hold the board with your hand (hold it tightly, as the blades may tend to pull it) or clamp it to the fence for each cut. Shut off the saw and remove the workpiece after it clears the blades; don't drag it back through.

bottom edge of each board (this distance varies: See the *Drawer Sides* on page 431). Cut ¾-in.-wide × 7⁄16-in.-deep grooves in several passes, taking off no more than ⅛ in. of material at a time, and stopping the cut 1 in. from the front edges of the workpieces **(See Photo L).**

㉘ Since they're not visible, the drawer backs are attached to the sides with ordinary dado joints. Cut the ¾-in.-wide × ¼-in.-deep dadoes 1 in. from the back edge of each side (see page 431) with the dado-blade set in the table saw **(See Photo M),** or with a router and ¾-in. straight bit.

㉙ Finish-sand the insides of the drawer parts, taking care not to distort the mating faces of the finger joints or to reduce the thickness at the ends of the drawer back pieces.

㉚ Assemble the drawers. Apply glue to the mating surfaces of the fingers with a small brush or thin glue stick. Clamp the finger joints in both directions and tighten the clamps just until the joints are tight **(See Photo N).** To ensure that the inside faces are bottomed out against the slot shoulders, special attention must be paid to the clamping blocks: You can offset them from the joint altogether, as we did. Or, if you prefer direct pressure, you can cut notches in the clamping blocks so they only contact the side-grain fingers on each side of the joints. Clamp end-to-end across the backs, making sure the bottom edges of the back panels are flush with the tops of the drawer bottom grooves on the drawer sides (the drawer bottoms slip beneath the bottoms of the back panels and into the

PHOTO J: The jig we used consists of an auxiliary fence clamped to the miter gauge fence. A ¼-in.-wide × ¾-in.-deep slot in the auxiliary fence is filled with a pin spacer strip to use as a gauge for aligning the finger joint cuts. Make the first finger joint cut with the workpiece butted against the pin spacer strip.

PHOTO K: For boards that start with a slot, not a pin, use the mating board as a guide for cutting the initial slot. The end slot on the cut board fits over the pin spacer strip, with the outer pin on the workpiece fitting between the strip and the saw blade.

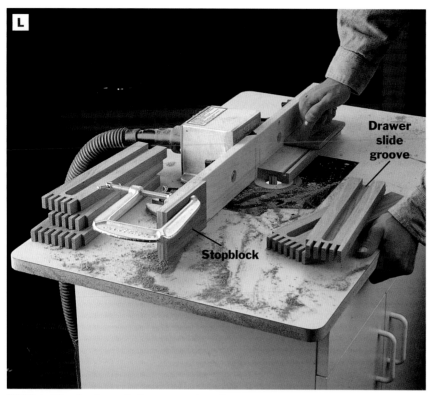

PHOTO L: After the drawer bottom grooves have been cut on the router table, rout grooves for the drawer slides. Both are stopped dadoes, cut in multiple passes.

PHOTO M: Cut the drawer back dadoes on the table saw with a dado blade, miter gauge, and rip fence. Push the stock across the blades carefully to avoid binding the workpiece between the blades and the rip fence. Remove the stock after it has cleared the blades.

grooves in the sides and fronts). Measure the diagonals across the corners of the drawer boxes and adjust the clamps as necessary to ensure the assemblies are square.

31 Cut the drawer bottoms to size from ¼-in. plywood, fitting them to the drawers. Make sure they are cut square.

32 Finish-sand the drawers and the bottoms, and ease all sharp edges with 180-grit sandpaper.

33 Slide one drawer bottom into its groove until it bottoms out in the drawer front and sits flush with the drawer back. It can be adjusted by tapping the bottom in at one end or the other, or by clamping lightly across the corners. Then lock it in position by screwing the bottom in. With the drawer upside down on a flat worksurface, drill evenly spaced, countersunk pilot holes through the bottom and into the drawer back and drive in three #8 × 1-in. screws (**See Photo O**). Do the same for the other two drawers.

MAKE & ATTACH THE HANDLES
34 Cut five ¾ × ¾ × 12-in. walnut strips for the handles. The finished length of the handles is 6 in., but the finger-pull coves are more easily and safely cut with the stock oversized.

35 Use a router table to rout the coves for the finger pulls on the undersides of the handles. Install a ¾-in.-dia. core box bit and adjust the cutter height and fence to cut the desired groove. Since the coves will be stopped at both ends, clamp startblocks and stopblocks to the fence to limit the cut. The cove should be 4½ in. long, leaving ¾ in. uncoved at each end of the final 6-in. length. To start the cut, push one end of a workpiece firmly against the startblock (on your right), keeping the other end on the table but away from the cutter. Holding the right end in the corner against the block, feed the other end into the cutter **(See Photo P)** until it rests against the fence. Then rout the cove by sliding the workpiece along the fence to the left until the other end strikes the stopblock **(See Photo Q).** Then, swing the trailing end away from the blade and remove the workpiece. Repeat the process with the other four handles.

36 Cut the handles to 6 in. long, making sure the coves are centered end-to-end.

37 Rout ¼-in. chamfers on all four outer edges of each handle Rout the long edges first. Then, rout the ends using a square scrap of ¾-in. plywood as a backup pushblock. Hold each handle tightly against the plywood and push the workpiece and the plywood block across the cutter together **(See Photo R).**

38 Finish-sand the handles, then attach them to the drawer fronts and the upper side rails, centered top-to-bottom and end-to-end. Use glue and two #8 × 1¼-in. wood screws per handle, driven through countersunk pilot holes and into the handles.

HANG THE DRAWERS

39 Make up the wooden drawer slides according to the dimensions given in the *Cutting List*. Trim the widths so they fit easily into the grooves of the drawer sides. The front end of each slide needs to be rounded to a ⅜-in. radius. First, find the center-

PHOTO N: Glue up the drawers, offsetting the cauls to allow the finger joints to close tightly. Clamp the finger joints from both directions, and measure the diagonals from corner to corner to check for squareness.

PHOTO O: Slide the drawer bottoms into the grooves in the drawer sides and front. Secure the drawer bottoms with three screws driven through the drawer bottom and into the bottom edge of the drawer back. Do not use glue.

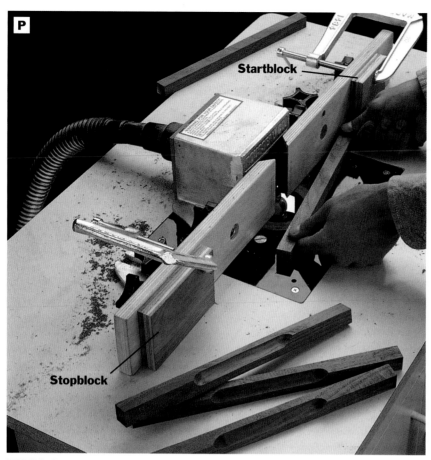

P

Startblock

Stopblock

PHOTO P: Rout cove-shaped finger pulls into the undersides of the handles using a router table fitted with a ¾-in. core box bit. Clamp a startblock and a stopblock to the table fence to guide your cuts.

point of the circle by using the 45° end of a combination square to draw diagonals from the square corners. The point where these lines meet is the center, and will also be where the screw holes will be located (do the same at the other end to locate the rear screw). Set a compass to ⅜-in. radius and swing an arc from this point around the end of the stock. Cut off the corners on a band saw and sand to the line with a stationary belt or disk sander, or cut to the line with a coping saw and file or sand smooth. Repeat this for all the drawer slides.

40 Mount the drawer slides, using spacers to align the heights. The bottom edges of the lower slides are 2⁵⁄₁₆ in. up from the chest bottom. The middle slides are 5⅜ in. up, and the upper slides are 7¹⁵⁄₁₆ in. up. Cut spacers from wood scrap and place them in between the

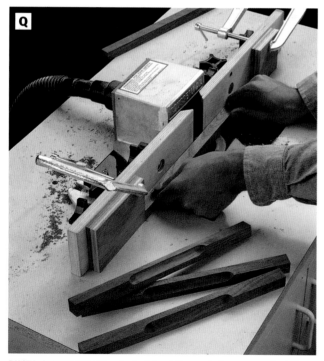

Q

PHOTO Q: With the bit spinning, feed the workpiece up against the fence, making sure it contacts the startblock. Then, feed it toward the stopblock until the cut is finished.

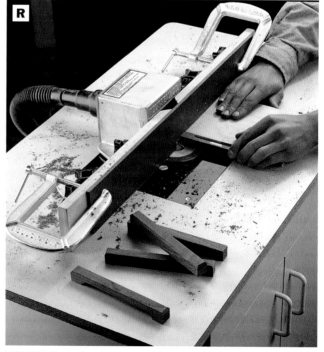

R

PHOTO R: Rout chamfers on the long edges of the handles first. Then use a backup pushblock to cut the chamfers into the ends of the handles (on the front faces of the handles only).

drawer slides on the insides of the chest. Drill countersunk pilot holes in the slides at the marked points on the ends and screw the slides to the side stiles. Remove the spacers **(See Photo S).** After you attach the slides, check the fit of the drawers. You may need to trim the thickness of the slides a bit. There should be an even ⅟16-in. gap around the drawers.

FINISHING TOUCHES

41 Mount the lid: Attach the piano hinge to the lid and back temporarily with one screw at each end and one near the middle. Check the fit of the lid. Trim it so there is an even ⅟16-in. gap on both sides and the front edge should have an even overhang. Once you're sure it's correct, mark the screw hole locations, remove the hinge and drive pilot holes for #6 × ½-in. brass wood screws. Drill pilot holes and drive screws along the length of the hinge **(See Photo T).**

42 Inspect the entire chest and smooth any roughness or sharp edges with sandpaper.

43 Prepare to apply the finish. Tape off the contact surfaces of the drawer slides and slide grooves to protect them from the finishing materials. Apply the finish (we used three coats of tung oil). When the finish has dried, remove the masking tape and wax the unfinished surfaces.

44 Attach the lid to the chest with the piano hinge.

45 Add brass lid supports on each side of the lid (optional).

PHOTO S: Mount the drawer slides using spacers to maintain even placement. After the slides are in place, remove the spacers.

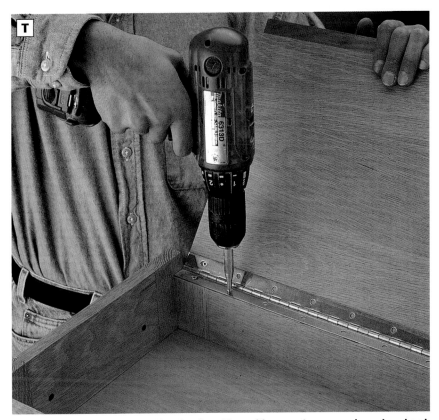

PHOTO T: Dry-fit the lid by attaching the piano hinge with one or two screws in each end and another in the middle. Remove the hinge, once you're satisfied that everything fits together, and reattach it after the finish is applied.

Index